Enlightenment Thought

An Anthology of Sources

Enlightenment Thought

An Anthology of Sources

Edited and translated, with an Introduction, by

MARGARET L. KING

Hackett Publishing Company, Inc.
Indianapolis/Cambridge

22 21 20 19   1 2 3 4 5 6 7

For further information, please address
   Hackett Publishing Company, Inc.
   P.O. Box 44937
   Indianapolis, Indiana 46244-0937

   www.hackettpublishing.com

Cover design by Rick Todhunter
Interior design by Laura Clark
Composition by Aptara, Inc.

Library in Congress Cataloging-in-Publication Data

Names: King, Margaret L., 1947– editor, translator.
Title: Enlightenment thought : an anthology of sources / edited and translated, with
   an introduction, by Margaret L. King.
Description: Indianapolis : Hackett Publishing Company, Inc., [2019] | Includes index.
Identifiers: LCCN 2018035094| ISBN 9781624667534 (pbk.) |
   ISBN 9781624667541 (cloth)
Subjects: LCSH: Enlightenment—Sources.
Classification: LCC B802 .E5456 2019 | DDC 190.9/032—dc23
LC record available at https://lccn.loc.gov/2018035094

For my grandson Henry—
may he live in an age of light

CONTENTS

CHRONOLOGY

DATE	CHAPTER	TEXTS	GENERAL EVENTS
1600			Giordano Bruno burned at the stake
1606			Dutch captain Willem Janszoon makes first documented landing in Australia
1620	1	Francis Bacon, *The New Instrument*	
1637	1	René Descartes, *Discourse on Method*	
1638	2	Anna Maria van Schurman, *Whether the Study of Letters Befits a Christian Woman*	
1648			Dutch independence following eighty-year revolt, 1566–1648
1648			Treaty of Westphalia; Thirty Years' War ends
1649			King Charles I of England executed
1650			Thomas Hobbes, *Leviathan*
1660			English monarchy restored
1666	2	Margaret Cavendish, *The Blazing World*	
1673	2	Bathsua Makin, *An Essay to Revive the Ancient Education of Gentlewomen*	
1677	1	Baruch Spinoza, *Ethics*	
1682			French royal court moved to Versailles
1685			Revocation of Edict of Nantes
1685	10	Anna Stanisławska, *Orphan Girl*	
1686, 1692	2	Mme. de Maintenon, *Letters on the Education of Girls*	
1687	1	Isaac Newton, *Mathematical Principles of Natural Philosophy*	

DATE	CHAPTER	TEXTS	GENERAL EVENTS
1688			First Quaker abolitionist declaration, Germantown, Pennsylvania, colony
1688	8	Aphra Behn, *Oroonoko*	
1689			Glorious Revolution in England
1689	3	John Locke, *Letter on Toleration*	
1689	3	John Locke, *Second Treatise on Civil Government*	
1689	3	John Locke, *Essay Concerning Human Understanding*	
1693	3	John Locke, *Some Thoughts Concerning Education*	
1695	3	John Locke, *The Reasonableness of Christianity*	
1696			John Toland, *Christianity Not Mysterious*
1697	1	Pierre Bayle, *Historical and Critical Dictionary*	
1700	10	Mary Astell, *Reflections on Marriage*	
1701–1713			War of the Spanish Succession
1709			Gottfried Leibniz, *Theodicy*
1716–1718	8	Mary Wortley Montagu, *Embassy Letters*	
1717			First Freemasons' lodge established, London
1725/ 1744	4	Giambattista Vico, *The New Science*	
1727			J. S. Bach's *St. Matthew's Passion*: first performance, Leipzig
1729			John Wesley founds the Methodist Society
1733	6	Voltaire, *Philosophical Letters*	
1734			Trial of John Peter Zenger in New York, a victory for freedom of the press
1735	4	Carl Linnaeus, *System of Nature*	

DATE	CHAPTER	TEXTS	GENERAL EVENTS
1737			Great Awakening begins, spreading in Protestant Europe and Anglo-American colonies, 1730s–1740s
1739–1748			Anglo-Spanish War of Jenkin's Ear (1739–1748); War of Austrian Succession (1740–1748)
1740	2	Émilie du Châtelet, *Fundamentals of Physics*	
1740	5	David Hume, *An Abstract of a Book Lately Published*	
1742			Handel, *Messiah*: first performance, Dublin
1747	5	Julien Offray de La Mettrie, *Man a Machine*	
1748	7	Montesquieu, *Spirit of the Laws*	
1750	4	Anne Robert Jacques Turgot, *The Successive Advancement of the Human Mind*	
1751	4	Jean le Rond d'Alembert, *Preliminary Discoursse*	
1754	9	Jean-Jacques Rousseau, *Discourse on the Origin and Foundations of Human Inequality*	
1755			Lisbon earthquake
1756	6	Voltaire, *The Culture and Spirit of Nations*	
1756–1763			Seven Years' War in America, Europe, and India
1758	5	Claude Adrien Helvétius, *On the Mind*	
1758	7	François Quesnay, *General Maxims*	
1759	6	Voltaire, *Candide*	
1761	9	Jean-Jacques Rousseau, *Julie, or the New Heloise*	
1762	9	Jean-Jacques Rousseau, *The Social Contract*	

DATE	CHAPTER	TEXTS	GENERAL EVENTS
1762	9	Jean-Jacques Rousseau, *Emile, or On Education*	
1763	6	Voltaire, *Treatise on Tolerance*	
1764	6	Voltaire, *Philosophical Dictionary*	
1764	7	Cesare Beccaria, *On Crimes and Punishments*	
1765			Stamp Act
1767	7	Adam Ferguson, *An Essay on the History of Civil Society*	
1767			British captain Samuel Wallis is first European to land on Tahiti
1770	8	Guillaume-Thomas Raynal, *Philosophical and Political History of European Colonies and Commerce in the Two Indies*	
1770	9	Jean-Jacques Rousseau, *Confessions*	
1771–1790	11	Benjamin Franklin, *Autobiography*	
1772	5	Paul-Henri Thiry, baron d'Holbach, *Common Sense*	
1772–1795			Partitions of Poland
1776	7	Adam Smith, *An Inquiry into the Nature and Causes of the Wealth of Nations*	
1776	11	Thomas Paine, *Common Sense*	
1776	11	Thomas Jefferson and others, *Declaration of Independence*	
1776–1783			American Revolution
1776–1789			Edward Gibbon, *Decline and Fall of the Roman Empire*
1777	8	James Cook, *A Voyage Towards the South Pole, and Round the World*	

DATE	CHAPTER	TEXTS	GENERAL EVENTS
1779	5	Gotthold Ephraim Lessing, *Nathan the Wise*	
1780	10	Denis Diderot, *The Nun*	
1782–1788	8	Johann Gottfried von Herder, *Ideas for a Philosophy of the History of Humankind*	
1784	4	Immanuel Kant, *What Is Enlightenment?*	
1786			Mozart, *Marriage of Figaro*: first performance, Vienna
1787	11	James Madison, *Federalist No. 10*	
1789			US Constitution
1789–1799			French Revolution
1790	12	Edmund Burke, *Reflections on the Revolution in France*	
1791	10	Olympe de Gouges, *Declaration of the Rights of Woman as Citizen*	
1791–1792	11	Thomas Paine, *The Rights of Man*	
1792	10	Mary Wollstonecraft, *Vindication of the Rights of Woman*	
1793–1794	12	Condorcet, *A Sketch of a Historical Portrait of the Progress of the Human Mind*	Reign of Terror
1794			Thermidor; fall of Robespierre
1799			Napoleon Bonaparte, First Consul of France

INTRODUCTION

What Is Enlightenment?

On August 3, 1914, the day before Britain declared war on Germany, British foreign secretary Sir Edward Grey remarked to journalist John Alfred Spender: "The lamps are going out all over Europe; we shall not see them lit again in our lifetime."[1] But who had turned them on?

Grey was referring, in a narrow sense, to the streetlamps that only in recent memory had been installed to illuminate European capitals: powered by gas from the first decades of the nineteenth century, and by electricity from the last two. But in a broader sense, he meant the forces of reason and civilization, soon to be eclipsed in the maelstrom of World War I, and perhaps irrecoverable. Those forces had coalesced in the European intellectual movement we call the Enlightenment: the era that saw the lights go on.

The thinkers who made the Enlightenment did not use that term, any more than the creators of the Renaissance knew that their age would one day be so named. The French intellectual elite referred to their era as the *Siècle des lumières*: literally, the "century of lights," or more loosely, the "age of clarification"; or they named the thinkers themselves the "lights" who illuminated the darkness. Employing the same metaphor, they referred to ideas that were *éclairés*: "clear," "illuminated," indeed "enlightened," that is to say, rational. Both the English and the French spoke often of "reason" and the excellence of whatever was "rational," or, for them the equivalent, "philosophical." The Spanish and Italians would use the term *Illuminismo* ("illumination"), and the Germans, *Aufklärung* ("clarification," "elucidation"). It is that German term, brilliantly expounded by the philosopher Immanuel Kant in his 1784 essay *Was ist Aufklärung?* (*What Is Enlightenment?*; for which see Chapter Four), that in the nineteenth century was translated into English as "Enlightenment."[2] The title of this Introduction borrows the title of his essay that more than any other single work encapsulates the significance of that era.

The Enlightenment was not the first intellectual movement in European history that valued reason—reason over instinct or emotion, reason over

---

1. For the quotation and its context, see https://blog.nationalarchives.gov.uk/blog/lamps-going-europe/.
2. The first use of the term "Enlightenment," capitalized, to denote a historical era, was in 1865, by J. H. Stirling; followed soon after, in 1893, by J. H. Tufts. *The Oxford English Dictionary*, ed. John Simpson and Edmund Weiner, 2nd ed. (Oxford: Clarendon Press, 1989), vol. 5, "Enlightenment"; online at http://www.oed.com.

ignorance, reason over superstition. It was the fourth. It followed upon, first, the scholasticism of the twelfth to fourteenth centuries in which European intellectuals disciplined Christian theology wielding the tool of Aristotelian philosophy; second, the humanism of the fourteenth to sixteenth, in which they recovered, edited, translated, commented on, and built upon the legacy of the "Ancients," the makers of the civilizations of Greece and Rome; and third, the Scientific Revolution, as it is often called, of the sixteenth and seventeenth, in which they deciphered the operations of the cosmos, aided by the telescope and mathematical calculations, and invented the disciplines of natural science. What was new was the scope of the Enlightenment, or this fourth age of reason: the number and variety of thinkers who were engaged in its explorations, who constituted, as they characterized themselves, a whole "Republic of Letters"; the size and distribution of its audience, who encompassed the whole of the European reading public; and especially, the target of its investigations. For the thinkers of the Enlightenment turned their gaze from the heavens to the earth, from cosmic to human matters: to human societies near and far in their historical evolution and contemporary reality; the human mind and the human body with which it was enmeshed; and the natural environment in which human beings acted and interacted, probed with the new tools of chemistry and biology.

As Enlightenment thinkers turned their eyes earthward, they repudiated assumptions that had long prevailed—repudiating, as Montesquieu put it, the instructions of their fathers and their teachers, accepting only the lessons acquired from experience of the world.[3] They rejected, above all, the authority of the "Ancients," who had dominated medieval and humanist culture, asserting instead the claims of the "Moderns," the experts of their own and recent generations. Refusing to bow to the hoary ghost of Aristotle and his ilk, the philosophers who had established the framework of logic and metaphysics within which Western thought had developed, they took that mission upon themselves and called themselves *philosophes*: the French term for "philosopher," but employed to describe a new kind of philosophy, that of the liberated and independent critic of inherited ideas.

The *philosophes* held their discussions not in university lecture halls, but in coffeehouses, reading groups, printshops, clubs, and salons—the last another French concept, denoting informal gatherings for witty conversation in the elegant homes of like-minded hosts and patrons. Escaping censors at home, they published their books abroad, especially in the Dutch Republic, which having emerged victorious from a century of revolutionary struggle was the most tolerant of European states and the main purveyor of forbidden books. They defied the repressions of the churches, especially

---

3. Montesquieu, *De l'esprit des lois* (*The Spirit of the Laws*), 1:4.4.

in Catholic regions, and while for the most part—there were exceptions—
steering clear of atheism, they questioned much of revealed Christianity and
argued strenuously for religious toleration. In large numbers, they joined the
Freemasons, a network of non-Christian, quasi-religious associations whose
rituals and creed paralleled, and almost parodied, those of the established
churches. They challenged the morality the churches proclaimed, affirming
instead moral principles grounded in reason, while supporting a counter-
culture of sexual libertinism. The age that celebrated reason also elevated
pornography.

The task of this volume is to answer the question posed at the head of
this Introduction by exploring the principal ideas and actors of the Enlightenment. It does so in twelve chapters, organized thematically and chronologically, comprising exemplary texts composed between 1620 and 1794: from
the origins of that movement in seventeenth-century metaphysics and cosmology to its culmination at the zenith of the French Revolution.

Chapter One, "Casting Out Idols: 1620–1697," looks at the revolutions
in thought accomplished by seventeenth-century philosophers and critics,
represented here by Francis Bacon, René Descartes, Baruch Spinoza, Isaac
Newton, and Pierre Bayle. The theme of "casting out idols," pinpoints a mission embraced by these authors that was fundamental to the Enlightenment:
to dispense with traditional authorities and to create new knowledge and a
new conceptual framework through the reasoning process. That mission is
signaled by Bacon's famous enumeration of idols to be toppled in his *Novum
organum* (*New Instrument*), following which appear selections from Descartes' *Discourse on Method*, exemplifying that author's prescription for rational thought; from Spinoza's *Ethics*, applying rational analysis to concepts of
God and substance; from Newton's *Principia*, presenting his laws of motion
and rules of reasoning; and from Bayle's *Dictionary*, providing as examples of
his skeptical outlook extracts from his entries on Pyrrho, Machiavelli, Luther,
Loyola, and Spinoza.

Chapter Two, "The Learned Maid: 1638–1740," explores the break-
through in the education of women achieved from the seventeenth to eighteenth century. This change was crucial to the Enlightenment project, in
which women participated as authors and thinkers, as salon hosts facilitat-
ing the informal discussion of ideas, and as subjects of learned discussion. It
opens with the pivotal work of Anna Maria van Schurman on *The Learned
Maid* (so titled in its first English translations), making the definitive case for
women's schooling. There follow selections from the works of Bathsua Makin
and Madame de Maintenon, who founded schools for girls in England and
France, respectively, and from Margaret Cavendish and Émilie Du Châtelet,
English and French authors exemplifying women's engagement in scientific
investigation.

Chapter Three, "A State of Perfect Freedom: 1689–1695," is the first of three chapters focused on a single author: here, John Locke, while Chapters Six and Nine focus in turn on Voltaire and Rousseau. In these three cases, the preeminence of an Enlightenment figure is recognized for the significance, scope, and impact of his achievement. Human freedom is the principal theme announced in Locke's works, central in his discussions of the state (the second treatise on *Civil Government*), the operations of the mind (*Essay Concerning Human Understanding*), religion (*Letter on Toleration* and *The Reasonableness of Christianity*), and education (*Some Thoughts Concerning Education*).

Chapter Four, "All Things Made New: 1725–1784," mirrors Chapter One. Whereas the first chapter considered the seventeenth-century envisioning of new universal systems enabled by the repudiation of traditional worldviews, the fourth observes the construction by Enlightenment thinkers of new systems describing not the cosmos but human—and animal—life in this world: biological, social, and intellectual. It opens with Giambattista Vico's discussion in *New Science* (as conventionally translated) of the evolution and cyclical destruction of all civilizations, past, present, and future, driven by the mechanisms of their unique cultural traits. Equally ambitious is the *System of Nature* propounded by Swedish naturalist Carl Linnaeus, which organizes all living and non-living things (animal, vegetable, mineral) by class, order, genus, and species in one comprehensive system. Along similar lines, the French thinker Jean d'Alembert proposes a comprehensive system of human knowledge in his *Preliminary Discourse* to the famous *Encyclopedia*—whose twenty-eight volumes by multiple authors would be published, as a landmark production of the Enlightenment, between 1751 and 1772. D'Alembert's contemporary, the economist Anne Robert Jacques Turgot describes in his 1750 discourse to the Sorbonne (University of Paris) the successive advance of the human condition. The German philosopher Immanuel Kant, likewise, in his essay "What Is Enlightenment?" discussed above, describes the emergence of the human mind from an immature state of dependence and naïveté to mature self-consciousness and rational capacity.

Chapter Five, "Mind, Soul, and God: 1740–1779," linking to Kant's "What Is Enlightenment?" in Chapter Four and Locke's *Human Understanding* in Chapter Three, turns to the problem of the human mind or soul and, by extension, God—for if the mind is a mere mortal organism, as some proposed, there is no immortal soul and no transcendent or "Supreme Being," as Enlightenment authors often termed the deity. Not all thinkers ventured so far in this inquiry, but some did, and the views of several pointed in that direction. The chapter opens with a selection from the Scots philosopher David Hume's *Abstract of a Book Lately Published*, his own commentary on his just-published *Treatise on Human Nature*, a skeptical account of the human mind understood to form ideas based only on sense impressions. Selections from two French works, Julien de la Mettrie's *Man a Machine* and Claude Helvétius' *On the Mind*, similarly link thought closely to perception and its biological substratum, diminishing the role of intuition or imagination in mental operations. Related to these, *Common Sense* by the German-born francophone writer d'Holbach (Paul-Henri Thiry, baron d'Holbach) under-scores the naturalistic view of the mind and explicitly rejects religion as a barrier to human progress. The German author Gotthold Ephraim Lessing, in contrast, remains an earnest believer in God, and vaguely a Christian God, while rejecting many theological and denominational truisms. The selection here from his drama *Nathan the Wise* depicts the equivalence of the three main theisms, Christian, Jewish, and Islamic.

Chapter Six, "Crush That Infamous Thing: 1733–1764," like Chapter Three, focuses on a single figure: in this case, Voltaire (François-Marie Arouet), whose fluid and forceful prose conveys a broad range of Enlighten-ment themes to a European-wide audience. The keystone of his thought is resistance to repressive institutions—the tyranny of kings, but even more that of the Catholic church, whose abuses were the specific target of his famous admonition to "Crush that infamous thing" (*écrasez l'infâme*). That attitude is observed in the selections given here, especially those from his *Letters Con-cerning the English Nation* and his *Treatise on Tolerance*. His *Essay on the Man-ner and Spirit of Nations* views the whole historical panoply as a record of savagery and crime, while his *Philosophical Dictionary*, consisting of 120 brief articles alphabetically arranged on a variety of topics, similarly condemns limitations on human freedom. Voltaire's novel *Candide* mocks the bland assurance expressed in grand theoretical terms by the German philosopher Leibniz that divine providence so ruled human life that even apparent evil was, in the end, all for the best.

Chapter Seven, "Toward the Greater Good: 1748–1776," building on both Locke's and Voltaire's statements, offers excerpts from the works of five advocates of political or economic liberty. The first and best known is the French nobleman Montesquieu (Charles de Secondat, baron de Montes-quieu), whose *Spirit of the Laws* argues for constitutional government featur-ing the separation of executive, legislative, and judicial powers, accommo-dated in each state to local conditions of geography, climate, and culture. The second is the French economist François Quesnay, who advocates in his *Gen-eral Maxims for the Economic Management of an Agricultural Kingdom* the least possible interference by the government in the unfettered workings of the economy: the policy known as *laissez-faire*. The third is the Italian statesman and jurist Cesare Beccaria, whose treatise *Of Crimes and Punishments* argues against excessive punishment, including by torture and execution, as not only barbarous but also ineffective. The Scots thinkers Adam Ferguson and Adam

Smith, finally, in their works, respectively, on *The History of Civil Society* and *The Wealth of Nations*, describe the workings of a just and productive civil society, while Smith, famously, stresses economic liberty as the prerequisite not only for justice but also for prosperity, the mysterious consequence of choices made on the basis of individual self-interest.

Chapter Eight, "Encountering Others: 1688–1785," observes authors of the Enlightenment era observing peoples of other cultures and conditions, beginning with two Englishwomen. Of these the first is Aphra Behn, whose novel depicting a noble African captured in his homeland and enslaved in Surinam (Dutch Guiana) is contemporaneous with, and echoes, the first Quaker critiques of slavery that would one day win the Western mind. The second is Lady Mary Wortley Montagu, who while accompanying her husband, then ambassador to the Ottoman court in Constantinople (Istanbul), reports empathetically on customs and mores of the Turks, especially Turkish women. There follow accounts of other places of European intervention and settlement around the globe by French author Guillaume-Thomas Raynal, in selections on Portuguese ventures in Asia and the African slave trade, and English explorer James Cook, in a selection reporting on his experience in Tahiti. The German philosopher Johann Herder explores, finally, in his *Ideas for a Philosophy of the History of Humankind*—as ample in its scope as Voltaire's *Universal History* or Montesquieu's *Spirit of the Laws*, but deeply informed by a knowledge of European imperialist ventures worldwide—the problem of cultural differentiation, anticipating the environmentalist and anthropological perspectives of the next century.

Chapter Nine, "Citizen of Geneva: 1755–1782," is the third devoted to a single figure, in this case the Swiss francophone author Jean-Jacques Rousseau. However important Locke and Voltaire were for the development of Western thought, neither matched Rousseau in impact on the contemporary audience. The public devoured his books; his novel *Julie, or the New Heloise* was the century's best seller. Born in Swiss Geneva, a Calvinist stronghold, rather than Catholic France, Rousseau seeks to free the individual not so much from absolute monarchy or official Catholicism, although he does not excuse these, as from a repressive moralism that imprisons the mind and stifles human potential. That theme is vividly expressed in works of which selections are given here: his *Discourse on Inequality*, his pedagogical treatise *Emile*, his novel *Julie*, and his autobiographical *Confessions*. His *Social Contract*, however, also represented here, a work perhaps more familiar to readers today than the others, is different. In it, clearly, he argues against political tyranny; but at the same time, curiously, in imagining a social compact of all the citizens of the state to possess an absolute and ineluctable power over the whole, he introduces a new form of domination: one exercised by the group over the individual.

Chapter Ten, "Vindications of Women: 1685–1792," looks at the role of women in the Enlightenment, continuing the discussion in Chapter Two that had observed the entrance of educated women into mainstream intellectual life. Here, though, the issue is women's resistance to limits on their social existence, which barred their further cultural advancement. The main obstacle was the European marriage system, in place for many long centuries. That system required women to marry the spouse approved by their fathers to suit the economic and social goals of the family. At that moment, they were to be assigned a dowry in satisfaction of any further claim on their natal family's wealth, which was to be inherited by the nearest male issue. Peculiar to Catholic Europe, the same end—securing family wealth and status—could be attained more cheaply by enrolling a daughter in a convent, where a smaller dowry secured lifetime maintenance. The selections given here from works of five authors angrily respond to this social mechanism that denied autonomy to daughters and freedom to wives and nuns. The English authors Mary Astell and Mary Wollstonecraft, writing respectively early and late in the Enlightenment era, squarely defy the legitimacy of this system they view as tyrannical, while the Frenchwoman Olympe de Gouges, writing in the early stages of the French Revolution, does so by employing the revolutionary rhetoric of her male contemporaries. To these polemical works are added the literary expressions of the Polish poet Anna Stanisławska, who in her autobiographical verse epic recounts the horrors of her forced marriage to a degenerate husband; and of the French author Denis Diderot, who in an impressive feat of imagination, though male, fully identifies with the protagonist of his novel, *The Nun*, to attack the companion system of forced conventualization.

Chapter Eleven, "American Reverberations: 1771–1792," crosses the Atlantic to observe the development of Enlightenment thought in a colonial setting. It opens with a selection from the *Autobiography* of Benjamin Franklin written late in life and published only in 1791, but depicting his early years in Boston and Philadelphia, when he first mastered the printing press and recognized its huge capacity to assist in the struggles that lay ahead. It then turns to two works of 1776, capturing the moment of the incipient American Revolution: excerpts from Tom Paine's *Common Sense* and from the Declaration of Independence, authored in large part by Thomas Jefferson, both works bespeaking their origins in the thought of John Locke. The third selection is from James Madison's *Federalist No. 10*, which draws on Montesquieu's *Spirit of the Laws* to argue that the balance of power between the states and the central executive is a bulwark against the destructive force of factions. The final selection is, again, by Tom Paine, whose *Rights of Man*, defending the French Revolution as he had the American, broadens Lockean rhetoric to fit expanded circumstances. Other than the three principal authors foregrounded in this volume—Locke, Voltaire, and Rousseau—Paine alone is represented by more than one work. That choice is deliberate, made so as to show how one figure bridged the two political revolutions that close the era of Enlightenment.

Chapter Twelve, "Enlightenment's End: 1790–1794," juxtaposes two writers of the Enlightenment's last phase to illustrate that closure. In his *Reflections on the Revolution in France*, Burke reiterates liberal principles while denying that Revolution's ability to create a viable new order better than the old, the product of the accretion of generations; and he expresses sympathy with the victims of Revolution—just how many there would be he did not yet know. In the tenth book ("epoch") of his *Sketch of a Historical Portrait of the Progress of the Human Mind*, as that Revolution rages around him, Condorcet writes a testament to the Enlightenment, reiterating and dilating upon the promises it offered: freedom, education, health, equality. Ironically, for history is the master of irony, as soon as he put down his pen, he died in his prison cell, cheating the guillotine by which he was to be executed the next day, by his own hand most likely, a suicide, or perhaps by the hand of a friend, the victim of compassionate murder.

The Enlightenment did not cause the French Revolution, but its time had come to a close at the point when that cataclysm erupted. It had promised freedom from the manacles of inherited ideas and oppressive institutions—the "infamous thing" Voltaire had wanted to crush; the chains that humankind, according to Rousseau, meekly accepted as the price of advanced civilization—which once cast off, would restore all to the "state of perfect freedom" that Locke had invoked.

It did not keep that promise. Questions persist. Would it have been possible to reshape society and culture in a self-generating, rational order, on the model of the cosmos that Newton and the metaphysicians had proposed? Once traditional systems of religion had been dismantled, would a secular system sustain as they had the moral values of individual conscience, free will, and the dignity of the individual? Was the aim prudent to remake according to a new design civilization that had evolved over long eons from deep roots, like trees in the forest, as Burke had queried, building on the insights of Vico and Herder? A forest that a wildfire could annihilate in a moment? That is to say, what the critical mind, so celebrated by Kant, could destroy, could it build anew?

Selection of texts

The twelve chapters of this book encompass fifty-seven texts by forty-four authors representing a wide range of participants in the Enlightenment phenomenon. Of necessity, the inclusion of some has meant the exclusion of others. The goal has been to choose authors and texts that illustrate major

Enlightenment themes and that represent a spectrum of regions, languages, genres, and perspectives. Looking at national origins, sixteen, or just over one-third, of the selected authors are French (including the German-born d'Holbach); eleven, or one-fourth, English; four Anglo-American (including the English-born Paine); three Scottish; three German; two Italian and two Dutch; and one each Swiss, Swedish, and Polish. In terms of genre, the fifty-seven texts include examples of, among others, treatise, essay, letter, speech, novel, drama, history, autobiography, pamphlet, travel account, and dictionary. They are composed in six languages: most in French (twenty-five) or English (twenty), amounting to nearly 80 percent of the total; and the rest in Latin (six), German (three), Italian (two), and Polish (one). The dominance of anglophone and francophone authors is unavoidable in any study of the Enlightenment, but it is moderated here by the substantial presence of authors of other origins and tongues. In terms of gender, finally, three-quarters of the authors (thirty-three) are male and one-quarter (eleven) female. For an era whose elites were overwhelmingly male, the proportion of women writers represented in the volume is substantial.

Editions and translations

The base texts for each of the fifty-seven titles appearing in this volume are cited in the Texts and Studies section that follows the twelve main chapters of this volume. Texts and Studies also supplies comments as needed on alternate versions or translations consulted, as well as selected recommendations for further reading. Thirty of the fifty-seven texts, or just over half, appear in my translation from the original languages, while seven appear in translations by other authors. The remaining twenty texts were originally written in English and have not required translation, but have been edited for easier legibility by nonspecialist readers. Modifications have been made in punctuation, capitalization, sentence length, and certain verb (e.g., "hast," "canst") and pronoun (e.g., "thou," "thee") forms. In addition, modern substitutes have been supplied silently for words that are not in current use or, if the original terms are retained for expressiveness, they are followed by a bracketed equivalent. The texts of both translated and original-English texts are annotated lightly as needed to explain obscure references.

Two matters that arise both in translating and editing these materials require comment. The first has to do with the modern ideal of gender neutrality, and the second with modern patterns of capitalization.

First, in the eighteenth century, "man" was frequently used to denote the universal condition of humanity, where moderns would speak of "human beings," or "persons," or "humankind." Wherever it was possible in translations that were mine to compose, I sought an alternate terminology. But in some cases it was not possible: the term "man" so evidently was used to denote the human condition it could not be altered without confusing the intended message; or, in the case of the *Declaration of Independence*, the use of the term "man" (as in "all men are created equal") is centrally important in a text that has an elevated importance in the American tradition, and could not be altered. In the seven cases where I have used translations by others, I have not challenged the translator's intent and have let the original terminology stand. In the case of La Mettrie's *Man a Machine*, for instance, the author's message would have been distorted had I changed what the translator retained. In the case of texts originally in English, I have altered "man," "men," and "mankind" where possible, but where that would have caused too great an intrusion on the original meaning or too seriously diminished the power of the rhetoric (as, for instance, in Paine's *Common Sense*), I have not done so. Throughout, I have avoided using "he/she" or switching to a plural verb to obtain gender neutrality, as these alterations would have been conspicuous and distracting.

Second, capitalization was frequently used in eighteenth-century prose, both in English and other languages, in mid-sentence and for common nouns, for expressive purposes. Nonetheless, it is distracting to the modern reader. In most cases, I have suppressed such capitalization. But in some cases I have allowed it where the rhetorical force of an argument would otherwise be lessened. Similarly, in many cases, I have allowed the capitalization of certain nouns that have more than ordinary weight as used in eighteenth-century writing: for instance, Law, Nature, Public, Man, Woman, as well as Creator and Supreme Being, locutions used instead of God to designate the deity.

Chapter One

Casting Out Idols: 1620–1697

Introduction

Just as the learned disciplines that we now have cannot help us learn new things, wrote the English philosopher Francis Bacon in his *Novum organum* (1620), or "New Instrument" for the discovery of truth, the method— Aristotelian logic—that we now employ "is useless for the generation of new knowledge." To extend the frontiers of knowledge, we must learn a new way to think. That was the task embraced by four leading seventeenth-century philosophers encountered in this chapter: Bacon himself (1561–1626); René Descartes (1596–1650); Baruch Spinoza (1632–1677); and Isaac Newton (1643–1727). These four are not themselves participants in the Enlightenment movement, but precursors. Their metaphysical and methodological work is the necessary platform for Enlightenment thought, which, even as its focus turned from metaphysics to other concerns, still employed the methods of critical analysis they had initiated.

Uniting these first four figures is their commitment to "casting out idols." This phrase, as well, derives from Bacon's *New Instrument*, excerpted here—the second part of his most ambitious work, the *Instauratio magna*, or *Great Restoration*, a momentous project, never finished, for a complete renewal of human knowledge. Bacon's *New Instrument* advocates a new method based on induction, the making of inferences from observed facts. Our pathway forward, he argues, is impeded by misconceptions: these are the "idols" that God had prohibited in the first of the Ten Commandments he delivered, as the Bible tells, to Moses, the leader of a redeemed Hebrew people. Immersed in the biblical rhetoric of England's long and tortuous Protestant Reformation, Bacon adroitly employs this analogy to lend weight to his argument. In the same way that the worship of idols distracts the worshiper from the one true God, the seeker for truth fails in his objective because of a stubborn reliance on misconceptions, false assumptions, and faulty inferences.

Wholly dissatisfied with the logic and metaphysics of Aristotle he had been taught at a Jesuit college, the Frenchman Descartes, like Bacon, sought a new way forward. In his most famous work, the *Discourse on Method* (1637), excerpted here, he proposes a novel strategy for ascertaining what is true depending entirely on abstract reasoning. By a process of systematic doubt,

1

he will reject all the concepts that are commonly accepted in order to arrive at those that are indisputably true. He finds that the non-existence of all else demonstrates irrefutably his own existence, as it is he who is doing the thinking. From that famous proposition, phrased epigrammatically as "I think, therefore I am," he further deduces the existence of God as the one greater being on whom his own existence depends. Clearly, Descartes does not proceed inductively, as Bacon proposes, from observed facts to more general conclusions. Rather, he does the opposite: discarding facts as unreliable, he discerns an axiomatic truth—his own existence—that does not require demonstration, and from that single and undeniable premise derives all further possible knowledge. Where Bacon inhabits a world of things the observation of which can yield understanding, Descartes discovers by his philosophical method that there are only two substances in the world: the thinking mind, occupying no space; and unthinking matter, extended throughout space.

Spinoza and Newton follow Bacon and Descartes in dismissing the methods and assumptions of the past and begin anew to construct a system of knowledge. Spinoza employs the geometric method, devised by the Greek mathematician Euclid, which builds on a scaffolding of self-evident axioms a series of propositions that are successively proved. In so doing, he elaborates a new philosophical, moral, and political vision. Where Descartes had identified two universal substances, mind and matter, Spinoza posits only one, which is Nature itself, identical with God: "God, or Nature," the phrase Spinoza uses systematically to name that principle. All other entities, whether mental or material, are appearances or modifications of that one universal substance. Notably, though Spinoza had been banished as a young man from his own religious community—he was a Jew born in Amsterdam to a family of Portuguese refugees—he did not, although others charged him with atheism, cease to believe in God. But the God he describes in his philosophical works, including the *Ethics* (1677), excerpted here, is not the personal God of Jewish or Christian scripture, but an impersonal substance. God is all of Nature, and he is perfect freedom; humans, as constituents of the Nature that is God, possess a limited freedom gained by self-awareness of themselves as parts of that universal substance.

Like Spinoza, the Englishman Newton takes all of nature as his subject, as he announces with a flourish at the opening of the third book of his *Philosophiae naturalis principia mathematica* (*Mathematical Principles of Natural Philosophy*, 1687), often referred to simply as the *Principia*: his aim is "to demonstrate . . . the structure of the system of the world." This he will do, announcing the laws that govern all the motions of objects in the universe, and employing them to explain the force of gravity that knits together all its component parts. Newton's universe is a self-governing machine, the forces holding it together generated by the other bodies making up the whole.

Newton's mechanical vision of the universe is the culmination of the work of earlier astronomers, including Nicolaus Copernicus, Johannes Kepler, and Galileo Galilei. But Newton ventures beyond these not only in scope but also in approach, for his mechanical vision implies a metaphysical one not unlike that delivered by Spinoza. He envisions an infinite universe wholly determined by its own laws, embracing all that is—not forgoing a personal God as Spinoza did, but reducing the impact of the deity's operations. Whereas Spinoza had imagined God to be part of and identified with Nature, for Newton, God is outside the system, and irrelevant to its functioning—even while, a faithful Christian, he reverences God as an eternal being who remains supreme.

Like Spinoza, Newton arranges his argument as a series of proofs. His proofs are mathematical, however, using numbers, and not verbal, as a geometrician's may be. What he accomplished is today called "physics," one of the "sciences"; but in Newton's day, "science" as we understand it was a part of philosophy, and specifically of "natural philosophy," while the word "science" then meant "knowledge" generally, and could equally describe the knowledge of literature as of mechanics. To Newton's contemporaries, he was a great philosopher who fully explained the great system of the cosmos.

With Pierre Bayle (1647–1706), we leave that prologue behind and come to the Enlightenment proper. Bayle is one of the first Enlightenment thinkers to embrace the new skeptical methods of Bacon, Descartes, Spinoza, and Newton, while shifting their gaze from the celestial to the terrestrial, and from the vastness of nature to the realm of human existence.

Born a Huguenot, as French Protestants were called, Bayle dallied briefly with Catholicism before returning to Protestantism. His apostasy having marked him for persecution as a relapsed heretic, causing grievous harm to his family, Bayle fled to the Netherlands, where he lived the rest of his life as a religious refugee. The experience of persecution fuels his skepticism as he assesses the individuals and ideas surveyed in his principal work, the *Historical and Critical Dictionary* (1697). Published just ten years after Newton's *Principia*, Bayle's *Dictionary* examines the whole record of human achievement, now reinterpreted for a new age.

An encyclopedia presaging the great Enlightenment *Encyclopedia* of 1751–1772 (for which see Chapter Four), this massive work contains more than five thousand headwords (titles of component articles) distributed over more than three thousand pages, bound in four volumes. It is a polyphonic work, communicating several interwoven messages at once. The main text, consisting of biographical and historical narratives, and sprawled across the breadth of each large folio-sized page, is accompanied by three different layers of notation, displayed across the surface in complex configurations. References to the principal narrative appear in the margins in small type keyed by a lowercase letter to the text. Larger excurses on the principal narrative, sometimes amounting to extensive meditations on related themes, appear in columns underneath the main text to which it is keyed by uppercase letters. References to these subsidiary excurses, finally, are given, again, in the margins in small type and keyed to the parent text by Arabic numerals. Bayle's object, it must be assumed, is not deliberately to confuse, but rather to illustrate the manifold relationships between ideas.

The narratives—considering now the main text spread across the tops of each page—display an enormous tonal range, from lofty philosophical discussions to conversational narrative to deft and cutting insinuation. The biographical profiles capture the personality of the subject, ancient or modern, reevaluating the achievements of iconic individuals, applauding some, critiquing others, the latter with some caution and indirection. Scattered among the many biographical entries are also thematic ones, such as those on the ancient Christian heresy of Manicheanism, which imagined there to be an eternal force for evil always opposed to a distinct one for good; or on the issue of obscenity, the presentation of images and ideas disruptive of prevailing morality. In all, Bayle morcellates and reconfigures the whole of human history, freeing his readers from the grip of its conventional representation.

From Bacon to Bayle, these seventeenth-century thinkers, and others like them—it has not been possible to include such other giants as the philosophers Blaise Pascal (1623–1662) and Gottfried Wilhelm Leibniz (1646–1716), or the political theorists Thomas Hobbes (1588–1679), Hugo Grotius (1583–1645), and Samuel von Pufendorf (1632–1694)—laid the foundations of the Enlightenment, launching the intellectual project that would characterize European thought in the next century, and linger to shape it until the present day.

Idols, or false notions

Francis Bacon, *The New Instrument* (1620)

Steeped in the scholastic philosophy of the late Renaissance universities, Francis Bacon proposes its abolition in his *Great Restoration*, his vast but unfinished guide to the renewal and increase of knowledge. The key to that renewal is the use of a "new instrument" (*novum organum*), as he titled the second part of the larger work: a different method of reasoning to replace the original *Organon* ("instrument"), the Aristotelian system of logic elaborated by European thinkers. Where they developed skeins of argumentation from sacrosanct first principles, Bacon urged those who sought to expand the domain of human understanding to immerse themselves in actual reality: in things, as they were observed, with all their connections and relations, in the natural world. To understand that reality, one must employ a new method—a tool, or instrument: that of induction, the drawing of inferences from the evidence of the senses.

Bacon makes these arguments in a set of nearly two hundred "aphorisms," or principles, "concerning the interpretation of nature and the realm of humankind," of which eighteen are given here, including those naming the four "idols" that hinder the mind in its pursuit of truth. These false premises and assumptions must be renounced, like the false idols and "graven images" that God forbids in the first of the Ten Commandments delivered by the hand of Moses: "You shall not bow down to them or worship them" (Exodus 20:4; NRSV).

Those four are the idols of the "tribe," of the "cave," of the "marketplace," and of the "theater." "Idols of the tribe" are those fallacious forms of thinking common to the whole human species, rooted in human physiology or psychology. "Idols of the cave" are those fallacies that arise within the isolated individual mind, as in a remote and desert cave. "Idols of the marketplace" are those fallacies that are conjured up in human communications with others, as information is distorted and misunderstood. "Idols of the theater" are those fallacies created by elites and experts, who impose their false knowledge on the defenseless common horde. The worship of these idols, which is to say the uncritical acceptance and purveyance of falsity, limits our ability to know the truth.

THE NEW INSTRUMENT

1. The human investigator,[1] who is both servant and interpreter of nature, can do and understand as much of the natural world, and only that much, as he has perceived by his eyes or grasped by his thought. There is nothing more that he may know or can do.

2. Neither the naked hand, nor the unaided mind, avails him. He has need of tools and aids to perform his task, which are as necessary for the mind as for the hand. And just as the tools wielded by the hand either cause motion or control it, so also the tools of the mind either spur the understanding or restrain it.

. . .

6. It would be absurd and senseless to assume that what has not yet been done can ever be done, except by methods never yet employed.

. . .

---

1. Bacon uses the term *homo*, or "man," an essentialization typical of his era; an attempt is made here to avoid it in most cases, but that has not been possible in all.

11. Just as the disciplines[2] we now have are useless for the discovery of new matters, so too the logic[3] that we now use is useless for the generation of new knowledge.

12. The logic that is now in use serves to fix and establish error (which is rooted in unexamined assumptions) rather than to seek out truth. Thus it does more harm than good.

. . .

19. Two pathways exist, and these are the only two possible, to the investigation and discovery of truth. One ignores the particulars of sense experience and flees to broadly general axioms,[4] from which principles, which are deemed to be final and inviolate, it extracts and establishes intermediate axioms. This is the approach currently in use. The other derives axioms from the particulars of sense experience, from which, proceeding gradually and steadily, it ascends at last to universal truths. This is the right way forward, but as yet untried.

. . .

31. In vain do we expect any great expansion of knowledge by superimposing what is new on what is old and ineffective. Rather, knowledge must be rebuilt from its deepest foundations. Otherwise, we spin forever in circles, making little or no progress.

. . .

36. There remains for us in fact only one simple mode of action: that we lead those who search for knowledge to the investigation of particular things in their orders and systems, so that they may in turn persuade themselves at last to give up their notions, and begin to immerse themselves in actual things.

. . .

38. Idols and false notions, which now occupy the human intellect and over-master it, not only so obstruct the minds of men that truth can scarcely enter, but even if access is granted, if men are not forewarned and as much as possible armed against them, they once again impede and disrupt the very process of pursuing knowledge.

---

2. Bacon uses the term *scientiae*, or "the sciences," the term used in this era to refer to the many disciplines by which truth might be known. Because this term is easily confused with the modern notion of "science," the term "disciplines" has been used instead.
3. Logic, as presented by the Greek philosopher Aristotle and developed in the European universities, was the standard method of inquiring into and extending knowledge.
4. Axioms are propositions that are self-evidently true, or more broadly, soundly established truths or principles.

39. There are four types of idols that oppress the human mind. To distinguish them, I have assigned names to each. I call the first type the idols of the tribe; the second, the idols of the cave; the third, the idols of the marketplace; the fourth, the idols of the theater.

40. The derivation of notions and axioms by true induction is surely the proper strategy for the isolation and elimination of idols; yet to define what these idols are is most useful. . . .

41. The idols of the tribe are rooted in human nature itself, and specifically in the tribe of men: that is, the human race. It is falsely asserted that ["man is the measure of all things," meaning that human perceptions correctly describe what is the case.][5] Rather on the contrary, all the perceptions whether of the senses or the mind convey information about the human condition, and not about the universe. And the human understanding is like a mirror that falsely reflects the rays[6] it receives, mixing its own nature with the nature of things, thus distorting and contaminating it.

42. The idols of the cave are the idols of the human individual. For each and every person . . . has his own particular cave or den, [a kind of psychological isolation] which distorts and corrupts the truth of nature—because of his own particular and peculiar character, or because of his education and relations with others, or because of the books he has read. . . . For surely the human spirit . . . is a fickle thing, always shifting, and almost random. . . .

43. The idols that arise from human interaction and society I call the idols of the marketplace, for it is there that humans congregate and carry on commerce. For humans associate with each other through words, but the words are invented by ignorant masses. Consequently, a clumsy and faulty use of words remarkably obstructs thought. . . . For plainly words overcome the intellect, wreak confusion, and ensnare people in countless silly controversies and falsehoods.

44. The idols, finally, that migrate into human minds from the many teachings of the philosophers, and from their perverse logical demonstrations, I call the idols of the theater, since so many philosophical notions have been

---

5. An expansion of Bacon's wording is interpolated here, for clarity. The notion that "man is the measure of all things" is an ancient statement of human preeminence, ascribed to the Greek philosopher Protagoras. Bacon modifies the meaning somewhat to say that what humans know through their senses is universally valid knowledge, a claim with which he disagrees.

6. The "rays" are the streams of light that radiate from the universe and impinge on the human senses, conveying images or information.

transmitted or invented, so many fables devised and farces concocted, that we find they have created fictitious and imaginary worlds. . . .

But more must be said both broadly and precisely about these different kinds of idols, so as to forewarn the human understanding.

I think, therefore I am

René Descartes, *Discourse on Method* (1637)

Like Bacon, searching for what is true, Descartes pursues his inquiry, unlike Bacon, not by examining things observed in nature, but by adopting a novel and unusual course of reasoning. First, he will doubt all truths, even the reality of the existence of the things around him, including his own body. In doing so, however, he apprehends a certain truth: that he, who is thinking about these matters, must exist. "I think, therefore I am," is the quintessentially famous statement that shouts out from the page. Not only does this proposition affirm the existence of Descartes, but it elevates the process of reasoning as a preeminent activity, one that is equivalent to and validates being.

Descartes goes further still, establishing as a corollary to the first proposition a second, the existence of God. He found that he could conceive of a being more perfect than himself—an idea that could only have been put into his mind by such a being, one possessing all the perfections that he, the thinking self, could imagine. This being "was, in a word, God."

His discovery is consequential: the existence of God validates the existence of all other things that exist. We shall forever doubt the reality of the things we imagine to exist unless the existence of God is presupposed. For "if we did not know that all that is real and true in us comes from a perfect and infinite Being, however clear and distinct our ideas might be, we would have no way of knowing that they had the perfection of being true."

DISCOURSE ON METHOD

I do not know if I should engage you in the first meditations that I undertook, as they are so metaphysical and abstruse that they will not be to everyone's taste. Nonetheless, so that others may judge whether the foundations I have laid are sufficiently solid, I rather feel it is necessary to speak of them. I have long been aware that out in the world one must sometimes assent to opinions that one knows are highly uncertain. . . . But since I wanted to devote myself wholly to the search for truth, I decided I must do otherwise, and reject as absolutely false everything about which I felt the slightest doubt. By so doing, I might then see if there remained anything at all of what I believed to be the case that was entirely certain. Accordingly, since our senses sometimes deceive us, I proceeded to suppose that there was nothing at all that was as we thought it to be. And since people sometimes err in reasoning, failing to solve even the simplest problems in geometry, and committing fallacies, I decided that I was likely to make mistakes as much as anyone else, and so rejected as false all the reasoning I had previously considered valid. And finally, considering that the very same thoughts that we have when awake can also come to us when we sleep, though none of them are real, I presumed that all the thoughts that had ever entered my mind were no more true than the phantasms of my dreams.

But then, even as I was thinking that everything was false, suddenly I realized that I, necessarily, who thought this, was something. And seeing that this truth—*I think, therefore I am*—was so solid and so sound that all the wildest speculations of the skeptics were not capable of toppling it, I decided I could without misgiving denote it as the first principle of the philosophy I was seeking.

Then, examining closely what I was, I noted that although I could imagine that I had no body, and that there was no world or any space that I inhabited, yet I could not imagine that I did not exist. On the contrary, my ability to doubt the existence of other things demonstrated firmly and certainly that I myself existed. On the other hand, if I only had ceased to think, while all the other things that I had previously doubted were real, I would have no reason to believe that I had ever existed. From this I realized that I was a substance whose entire essence, or nature, it was solely to think—and who, to exist, has no need to occupy space, nor requires any material thing. Consequently, this "I," that is to say the soul by which I am what I am, is entirely distinct from the body; and is indeed more knowable than the body; and if the body did not exist at all, moreover, it would in no way cease to be all that it is.

After that I explored as a general matter what is required for a proposition to be true and certain; for since I had just identified one that I knew to be such, I sought also to know in what its certitude consists. I noted that there is nothing whatever in this statement, "I think, therefore I am," that assures me it is true, except that, manifestly, in order to think, one must exist. I decided that I could take it as a general rule those things we conceive most clearly and most distinctly are all true—but that it is often difficult to determine which are those that we conceive distinctly.

Thereupon, I reflected on all the things I doubted, and realized, in consequence, the imperfection of my mind—for surely it is a greater perfection to know than to doubt. I set out to discover from what source I had learned to conceive of a thing more perfect than myself, and realized that, evidently, it must have been from some entity who was in fact more perfect. As for the concepts I had about many other things outside of myself—such as the sky, the earth, light, warmth, and a thousand others—I was not so concerned to know from where they had come, since I found nothing in them which might make them superior to me. If they were real, I concluded, they were emanations of my own nature, which possesses some kind of perfection; and if they were not, then I had created them out of nothing, that is to say that they were within me, who am in some way defective. But this explanation could not apply to the idea of a being more perfect than myself. For to have created it out of nothing would be an impossibility; and it would be equally impossible that the more perfect being should be an emanation or dependency of the less perfect, . . . [that is,] myself. There remained, accordingly, only the possibility that this idea had been put in me by a being who was truly more perfect than myself, who possessed all the perfections of which I could conceive—a being who was, that is to say, to put it in a word, God. . . .

. . .

Finally, if there are still those who are not sufficiently persuaded, by the reasons I have adduced, of the existence of God and of their own souls, I want them to recognize that all the other things they may believe are more real—such as, among others, their own bodies, and the stars, and the earth—are less certain. For though it is possible to have some faith in their existence, . . . [yet] since it is a question of a metaphysical[7] certainty, one cannot deny that there is insufficient basis for complete assuredness. . . . It is possible, surely, when asleep, to imagine that one has a different body, and sees other stars, and another earth, without any of these things being true. How is it we can know that the thoughts that come to us in dreams are less true than those [we have when awake]? Since often they are no less vivid and sharp? And let the finest minds examine this matter as much as they like: I do not believe that they can give any reason sufficient to dispel this doubt, unless they presuppose the existence of God . . . [Since] if we did not know that all that is real and true in us comes from a perfect and infinite Being, however clear and distinct our ideas might be, we would have no way of knowing that they had the perfection of being true.

---

7. That is, philosophical certainty, attained by disciplined reasoning.

God, or Nature

Baruch Spinoza, *Ethics* (1677)

Expelled by the Jewish community into which he had been born, Baruch Spinoza hewed a new philosophical path unencumbered by old loyalties. Like Bacon, he toppled idols, casting off the presuppositions that had limited all previous philosophy—although Bacon's empiricism did not appeal to him, albeit a lens-grinder and instrument-maker, who worked with his hands. Like Descartes, he sought a new metaphysics that trespassed and transcended the scholasticism that prevailed in European universities. But whereas Descartes envisioned a cosmos ordered as a binary system, consisting of the two antithetical substances of mind and matter, Spinoza envisioned a cosmos that was a single substance, one eternal, infinite, and omnipotent: "God," as he put it, "or Nature." For Spinoza, the two were one. Nature, created by God, was also God himself, the creator. God, understood as a substance whose essence was existence, was not a person as conventionally conceived: not the Yahweh of the Old Testament, who had spoken to Moses from the burning bush; and certainly not the crucified and risen Jesus of the New.

The previous seven or eight millennia of human culture with its polytheisms and monotheisms thus discarded, Spinoza constructs a wholly modern metaphysics. To do so, in his major work, the *Ethics* (1677), of which extracts are given here, he employs a new method: that of geometry, consisting of the propositions, proofs, and demonstrations invented by Euclid. Unbound from the mechanism of Aristotelian logic that had undergirded medieval philosophy, modern philosophical method would deliver the certainty and clarity of mathematics.

Spinoza's arguments are clearly stated, but the concepts are difficult. Some explanations in italics are inserted amid the passages that follow, which present examples from the first book of the *Ethics* of the definitions, axioms, and propositions on which Spinoza builds his concept of "God, or Nature." It is the fundamental concept of his philosophical system, and the platform for his belief in individual and political freedom.

Ethics, Part 1

Definitions

1. By that which is self-caused I mean that those whose essence involves existence; or that whose nature can be conceived only as existing.

2. A thing is said to be finite in its own kind [*in suo genere finita*] when it can be limited by another thing of the same nature. For example, a body is said to be finite because we can always conceive of another body greater than it. So, too, a thought is limited by another thought. But body is not limited by thought, nor thought by body.

3. By substance I mean that which is in itself and is conceived through itself; that is, that the conception of which does not require the conception of another thing from which it has to be formed.

4. By attribute I mean that which the intellect perceives of substance as constituting its essence.

5. By mode I mean the affections of substance; that is, that which is in something else and is conceived through something else.

6. By God I mean an absolutely infinite being; that is, substance consisting of infinite attributes, each of which expresses eternal and infinite essence. . . . [*explication omitted*]

7. That thing is said to be free [*liber*] which exists solely from the necessity of its own nature, and is determined to action by itself alone. A thing is said to be necessary [*necessarius*] or rather, constrained [*coactus*], if it is determined by another thing to exist and to act in a definite and determinate way.

8. By eternity I mean existence itself insofar as it is conceived as necessarily following solely from the definition of an eternal thing. . . . [*explication omitted*]

Axioms

1. All things that are, are either in themselves or in something else.

2. That which cannot be conceived through another thing must be conceived through itself.

3. From a given determinate cause there necessarily follows an effect; on the other hand, if there can be no determinate cause it is impossible an effect should follow.

4. The knowledge of an effect depends on, and involves, the knowing of the cause.

5. Things which have nothing in common with each other cannot be understood through each other; that is, the conception of the one does not involve the conception of the other.

6. A true idea must agree with that of which it is the idea [*ideatum*].

Propositions

Proofs, corollaries, and scholia following the propositions are omitted where bracketed. Spinoza's first eight propositions deal with the nature of substance, of which key points have already been laid out in his definitions. Substance precedes all other things, and there is nothing equal to itself. It is infinite, and it alone exists in the universe; its nature, or essence, is to exist.

1. Substance is by nature prior to its affections. [. . .]
2. Two substances having different attributes have nothing in common. [. . .]
3. When things have nothing in common, one cannot be the cause of the other. [. . .]

. . .

5. In the universe there cannot be two or more substances of the same nature or attribute. [. . .]
6. One substance cannot be produced by another substance. [. . .]
7. Existence belongs to the nature of substance. [. . .]
8. Every substance is necessarily infinite. [. . .]

. . .

This substance that Spinoza has now explicated is itself God, who is infinite and eternal, as are all of its parts and expressions (attributes and modes). God is the only substance that can exist in the universe, and everything that exists in the universe, or can be thought to exist, is within God.

11. God, or substance consisting of infinite attributes, each of which expresses eternal and infinite essence, necessarily exists. [. . .]

. . .

13. Absolutely infinite substance is indivisible. [. . .]
14. There can be, or be conceived, no other substance but God. [. . .]
15. Whatever is, is in God, and nothing can be or be conceived without God. [. . .]

. . .

God acts freely of his own nature, and causes all other things to be. Nor can those things act of themselves, but are wholly determined, or put into action, by God.

17. God acts solely from the laws of his own nature, constrained by none. [. . .]

. . .

19. God, that is, all the attributes of God, are eternal. [. . .]
20. God's existence and his essence are one and the same. [. . .]

. . .

25. God is the efficient cause not only of the existence of things but also of their essence. [. . .]

26. A thing which has been determined to act in a particular way has necessarily been so determined by God; and a thing which has not been determined by God cannot determine itself to act. [. . .]

27. A thing which has been determined by God to act in a particular way cannot render itself undetermined. [. . .]

. . .

29. Nothing in nature is contingent, but all things are from the necessity of the divine nature determined to exist and to act in a definite way. [. . .]

. . .

God's power creates all things in the only way they could have possibly been created.

33. Things could not have been produced by God in any other way or in any other order than is the case. [. . .]

34. God's power is his very essence. [. . .]

35. Whatever we conceive to be within God's power necessarily exists. [. . .]

The system of the world

Isaac Newton, *Mathematical Principles of Natural Philosophy* (1687)

In general appearance strikingly similar to Spinoza's *Ethics*, Newton's *Mathematical Principles* (commonly referred to as the *Principia*) abounds in axioms, rules, and propositions, accompanied by explications, comments, and demonstrations. And what it is these two thinkers seek to describe is the same: the entire universe. But where Spinoza, the metaphysician, attends to such matters as being itself, God, nature, substance, and freedom, Newton is concerned with objects in motion, large and small, as they are governed by universal laws and constitute the "system of the world." A sampling is given here of his methods and arguments.

The three axioms, or "laws of motion," are prefatory (following a set of definitions) to the three books of the *Principia*. These laws are for many people all that they know about Newton—and perhaps, for non-specialists, they are all that are really necessary, for they are fundamental to Newtonian physics and govern its operations. The first states, somewhat contrary to ordinary expectation, that a body in motion remains in motion unless it is stopped—no additional force is required to keep it in motion, but would, rather, alter its condition. Equally, a body at rest remains at rest unless it is moved by an external force. The second law explains how the velocity of a body in motion changes when such a force is applied to it. The third posits that every action of one body on another calls forth an action in response, equal in quantity and opposite in direction.

After examining in detail in the first two books (or parts) of the *Principia* the possible motions of bodies, Newton turns in the third book to consider the "system of the world," as he explains in his opening statement. He begins with four "rules of philosophizing," or "reasoning in philosophy," which are reminiscent of Francis Bacon's guidelines for inductive reasoning. Explanations given for events should be the simplest possible, as nature itself is simple. Conclusions are to be based on experiment and observation, and since only what is observed can be known, generalization is possible from the results of experiment and observation. Such conclusions are to be altered, moreover, as much as is necessary to accommodate newly discovered evidence, but not because countered by a contrary theory not grounded in evidence.

The propositions—here a sample of eight of thirty-three—apply what has been said earlier to explain the operations of the solar system. Of these eight, six belong to a series explicating the operation of the law of gravity within the solar system, positing how gravity acts to keep celestial bodies in their orbits, and exerts its force on all bodies, large and small, throughout the universe. The last two (propositions 10 and 11) speak more generally of a solar system managed by gravitational force, predicting the "exceedingly long" (in practical terms, eternal) motion of celestial bodies on the paths to which gravity compels them, and positing that the center of gravity of the solar system does not move.

PRINCIPIA: AXIOMS 1–3; BOOK 3 PREFACE; RULES 1–4, PROPOSITIONS 2–7, 10, 11

Axioms, or Laws of Motion

LAW ONE

Every body persists in a state of rest, or of uniform motion in a straight line, unless it is compelled to change its state by forces acting upon it.

LAW TWO

A change in the rate of motion is proportional to the motive force applied, and the change is effected in the same direction as that applied force.

LAW THREE

To any action there is an equal and opposite reaction; such that if two bodies exert a force on each other, that force is equal in magnitude for each, and opposite in direction.

Book 3: On The System of The World

In the preceding books [1 and 2], I have expounded the principles of philosophy; yet these are not so much philosophical as mathematical principles, by which it is possible to build philosophical arguments. These principles are the laws and conditions of motion and force, which are especially useful for philosophy. Lest they seem too forbidding, however, I have provided additional notes [scholia] as needed, expanding upon matters of general interest and fundamental for philosophy, such as the density and resistance of bodies, vacuums, and the transmission of light and sound. What remains to be done now is to demonstrate, using these same principles, the structure of the system of the world. . . .

Rules of Reasoning in Philosophy

RULE ONE

We should consider as causes of natural things only so many as are true and sufficient to explain the phenomena observed.

As the philosophers say, Nature does nothing in vain, and excess is vain when less will suffice. For Nature prefers simplicity, and does not enjoy a superfluity of causes.

RULE TWO

Therefore, as much as is possible, to natural occurrences of the same sort the same cause should be assigned.

Such that the same causes may be assigned to respiration in humans and animals; to falling stones in Europe and America; the light proceeding from the fire that cooks our dinner and from the sun; the reflection of light on the earth and on the other planets.

RULE THREE

The qualities of bodies . . . that are found to inhere in all those bodies that our experiments can examine may be considered to be the universal qualities of all bodies.

For since it is only by experiments that we can know the qualities of bodies, we must consider universal all those that are demonstrably true in all the experiments we can perform. . . .

RULE FOUR

In experimental philosophy, propositions developed by induction from observed phenomena may be considered perfectly or probably true, regardless of contradictory theories, until new evidence is adduced by which they may either be made more accurate or revised as needed.

This rule is necessary so that baseless theories may not injure conclusions drawn from evidence.

Propositions

. . .

PROPOSITION TWO

The forces by which the primary planets are constantly restrained from rectilinear motion and held in their orbits are directed to the sun, and are inversely as the square of the distance from those planets to the sun's center.

PROPOSITION THREE

The force by which the moon is held in its orbit directed to the earth, and is inversely as the square of the moon's distance from the earth's center.

PROPOSITION FOUR

The moon gravitates toward the earth, and by the force of gravity, it is constantly restrained from rectilinear motion and held in its orbit.

PROPOSITION FIVE

The satellites of the planet Jupiter gravitate toward Jupiter; those of Saturn, toward Saturn; and those of the sun, toward the sun. In all cases, they are constantly restrained from rectilinear motion and held in their curvilinear orbits by force of gravity.

PROPOSITION SIX

All bodies gravitate to their particular planets, and their weight in that particular planet, at an equal distance from the center of the planet, is proportional to the quantity of matter they contain.

PROPOSITION SEVEN

All bodies exert a force of gravity on other bodies, which is proportional to the quantity of matter they each contain.

. . .

PROPOSITION TEN

Celestial planetary motion can persist for an exceedingly long time.

PROPOSITION ELEVEN

The center of gravity of the earth, the sun, and all the planets, is immobile.

He searched for truth throughout his life

Pierre Bayle, *Historical and Critical Dictionary* (1697)

The critical eye that Bacon and Descartes brought to the problem of knowledge, and that Spinoza and Newton cast on the whole of the cosmos, Pierre Bayle directs to the history of humankind, and especially to the thinkers who were, for him, its principal actors. Of the more than five thousand articles included in the more than three thousand pages of the *Historical and Critical Dictionary*, a mere five, heavily abridged, are included here.

The first is the ancient philosopher Pyrrho, whose particular brand of skepticism, called Pyrhhonism, in its caution and reserve significantly resembles Bayle's own critical outlook. The next four, who flourished in the two centuries before Bayle's own lifetime, also speak in different ways to the author's own interests and attitudes. Bayle finds in the Renaissance political theorist Machiavelli a "republican spirit" that he admires, and indeed the terms he uses, in 1697, are premonitions of the rhetoric of 1789, the year of the outbreak of the French Revolution. A lifelong Protestant, at least nominally, Bayle also admires Luther, a "mere monk" who challenged, and nearly shattered, the religious monopoly of the Roman church. Bayle's oddly detailed and extended biography of Ignatius of Loyola, the founder of the Jesuit Order, contrasts strangely with his delicately phrased yet evident distrust of that enterprise—akin to the distrust that would result, in the next century, in the Order's expulsion from several European states. A similar disconnect is seen between Bayle's admiring sketch of Spinoza, the man—who had died barely a generation earlier having lived his whole life in the Netherlands, as Bayle still did, of all the regions of Europe the most free, and of Spinoza, the philosopher—whose views Bayle detested.

In just these few passages, Bayle reveals himself as an admirer of radical skepticism, of heroism in political and religious arenas, of republicanism, and of Protestantism—or, at least, as an opponent of Catholicism. And he shows himself more than ready to tangle with the most complex philosophical debates of his day.

HISTORICAL AND CRITICAL DICTIONARY

Pyrrho

A Greek philosopher born in Elis on the Peloponnesus, Pyrrho was a disciple of [the philosopher] Anaxarchus, whom he accompanied as far as India, doubtless in the train of Alexander the Great [326 BCE]—so identifying the era in which he flourished. He had been a painter before he turned to the study of Philosophy. His ideas differ only slightly from those of [the philosopher] Arcesilaus, for he taught, as the latter did, the incomprehensibility of all things. Wherever he looked he found both reason to affirm, and reason to deny the truth of the matter; and after he had thoroughly examined both sides of the question, he still withheld his judgment, concluding only that more investigation was needed. He searched for truth throughout his life, but always managed not to be satisfied with what he had discovered. Although he did not invent this method of philosophizing, it bears his name nonetheless: the method of disputing all things, without ever approving one side or the other but rather suspending judgment, is generally called Pyrrhonism. . . .

He really wasn't a madman as it sometimes seemed, and there is no doubt that he taught that the greatness and baseness of human actions, their justice and injustice, depended entirely on human laws and on custom. . . . His indifference was astounding: there was nothing that pleased him, and nothing made him angry. No one was ever more sure than he of the vanity of things. When he spoke, it mattered not to him whether anyone listened; and if his audience got up and left, he kept on speaking. . . .

Machiavelli

The Florentine Niccolò Machiavelli was a brilliant man who wielded an exquisite pen. He knew only a little Latin, but a learned man in whose service he worked introduced him to certain splendid passages from ancient authors, which he thereupon inserted in his works. . . .

He held the office of Secretary, and then of Historian of the Florentine Republic. The Medici[8] procured for him this last, well-remunerated post, in order to assuage the furor that had been aroused by what he had been made to suffer. He had been imprisoned under suspicion of involvement in the plots of the Soderini [family] against the house of Medici. He was strong enough to withstand the torture, and admitted nothing. The praise he heaped on Brutus and Cassius [assassins of Julius Caesar] in his *Discourses* and other books aroused the strong suspicion that he had been the instigator of an attempted coup. Nonetheless, he was not put to trial. But from this time forward he lived wretchedly, mocking everything, and renouncing all religion. In 1530, a medication he had been taking prophylactically caused his death. . . .

The most provocative of his books is a work on politics entitled *The Prince*. Many authors have refuted it. . . . Few authors have spoken of Machiavelli without damning his memory. Some excuse it, and try to defend him; and some even suggest that he was a zealous advocate of the public good, and that he only detailed the machinations of politics so as to awaken the detestation of Tyrants, and to inspire people everywhere to the preservation of Liberty. Even if one doubts that this was his true motive, one must at least recognize that by his behavior he showed himself to be fully imbued with the Republican Spirit. . . .

Luther

The story of Martin Luther, reformer of the church in the sixteenth century, is so well-known, and told in such a great number of books, . . . that I shall not indulge myself by repeating them. Instead, I take note of the lies that were circulated about him. Those who spread them paid no attention to their plausibility, or to the rules of the art of slander; and they possessed the audacity of those who are convinced that the public will blindly embrace all that they spew forth, however absurd it may be. They dared to claim that he was born from his mother's fornication with an incubus.[9] . . . They charged that, by his own admission, after struggling with his conscience for ten years, and ending by having none at all, he lapsed into atheism. . . . Shamelessly, they accused him of denying the immortality of the soul. They alleged that he harbored lewd and carnal notions of Paradise, and composed hymns in praise of drunkenness, a vice to which he had wholly succumbed. . . .

These slanders stemmed from inordinate zeal, or rather a driving obsession, which blinded them to the real flaws of this great man. It must be allowed that the impetuous ardor of his temperament elicited from him words that

---

8. The Medici were the ruling family of Florence prior to 1494 and after 1512.
9. An evil spirit thought to be a seducer of women.

merit condemnation, as when he professed his opinion of the Epistle of Saint James.[10] . . . Even his worst enemies had to admit that he had exceptional qualities. And History offers no more surprising accomplishment than that which he achieved: for that this mere Monk was able to strike so fierce a blow against Papistry,[11] such that another like it would bring the Roman Church to total ruination, this it is that one cannot sufficiently admire. . . .

Loyola

Founder of the Jesuits,[12] Ignatius of Loyola was born in 1491, . . . and as soon as he was old enough to bear arms, he looked for ways to distinguish himself. He gave proof of his great courage at the Siege of Pamplona, where he was wounded by a cannon ball which shattered his right leg.[13] While he recuperated from this wound, he formed the resolution to renounce earthly vanities, to go [on a pilgrimage] to Jerusalem, and to lead thereafter a most unusual sort of life. . . .

A detailed account follows of Loyola's studies, travels, and gathering of a group of companions who will form under his leadership the Society of Jesus, which won papal approval in 1540.

Made General of this new Order in 1541, Ignatius remained in Rome while his companions spread out over the face of Earth.[14] There he took up many projects, such as those for the conversion of the Jews, or for the rescue of prostitutes, or for the subvention of orphans. He found himself the target of the most vicious slanders, which in no way hindered his efforts to do all that could be done to promote the reputation and success of his Order. . . .

[*Ignatius was canonized and celebrated by later popes*], but despite all they did for him, there is nothing more surprising to be said on this subject than that his Order, in but a few years, has acquired prodigious power both in the Old World and the New, . . . [such that its] authority, which has risen so quickly to so high a zenith, seems daily to grow rather than diminish. . . .

But yet there are those who . . . maintain that several things have made this Society justly odious. Such great power is not acquired, they say, . . . without employing very artful political machinations. . . . Moreover, the

---

10. Luther had disparaged this book of the New Testament, as well as Hebrews, Jude, and Revelation.
11. A disparaging term, commonly used at this time by Protestants, for the Catholic church.
12. The Society of Jesus, commonly called the Jesuit Order or, as here, the Jesuits.
13. The fortress at Pamplona, Spain, stormed in 1521; Loyola was wounded in his right leg, while his left suffered multiple fractures.
14. The Jesuits founded educational institutions all over Europe, and missionized in the Americas, Asia, and Africa.

Jesuits have pursued most ardently and to the greatest extent . . . doctrines that . . . expose sovereigns to continual revolutions, Protestants to slaughter, and Christian morality to the worst degradation that can be imagined. . . .

Spinoza

A Jew by birth, and later a Jewish apostate, and in the end an Atheist, Benedict [Baruch] Spinoza came from Amsterdam. . . . He studied Latin under a physician who taught in Amsterdam, then applied himself at an early age to the study of Theology . . . after which he devoted himself entirely to the study of Philosophy. As he had a mathematical mind, wanting all things to be accounted for rationally, he soon realized that the doctrine of the Rabbis was not for him. It was clear that he disapproved of many principles of Judaism; for this was a man who resisted any constraint of conscience, and was a great enemy of dissimulation. . . . It is said that the Jews offered to tolerate his position, provided that he observed their rituals outwardly, and they even promised him an annual pension. But he could not bring himself to such hypocrisy. [*The conflict ends with Spinoza's excommunication from the Jewish community in Amsterdam.* . . .]

Once Spinoza had turned to philosophical studies, he . . . wanted to search for truth so much that, in a sense, he renounced the world in order better to pursue his goal. . . . Brilliant minds came to him from all regions. . . . He succumbed to a protracted illness of which he died in The Hague on February 21, 1677, at the age of a little more than forty-four years. . . . He died, it is said, a committed Atheist, and he took precautions that, should he lapse at the end, his inconstancy would not become known. . . .

Bayle now undertakes a discussion of Spinoza's philosophy, the flavor of which is detected in this brief passage.

This is not the right place to undertake a formal Disputation. It will be sufficient for me to present some general observations that attack Spinozism at its foundations, and to expose it as a System that rests on so strange a supposition that it annuls most of the common notions that generally govern Philosophical Discussions.

Chapter Two

The Learned Maid: 1638–1740

Introduction

The Enlightenment is the first intellectual movement—in Europe, or any-where else—where women play a significant role. They did so as authors, remarkably enough, but also as participants in the new realm of scientific investigation, and as the facilitators of learned conversation in the salons they hosted, which were one of the hallmarks of the age. Women's entry into learned society was made possible by the extended debate of the previous two centuries over women's moral and intellectual capacity and equal humanity to men, largely overturning, in the realm of theory at least, prevailing anti-woman assumptions. These matters resolved, the education of women, and their participation in intellectual discourse, might follow, as seen in the five cases presented in this chapter.

The chapter opens with the pivotal defense of the education of women first published in 1638 by the Dutch philosopher and Christian Pietist Anna Maria van Schurman (1607–1678). It then looks at England where, during an era of political revolution and reaction, the aristocrat Margaret Caven-dish (1623–1673) makes bold claims for women's admission to the highest ranks of intellectual culture, and the gentlewoman Bathsua Makin (c. 1600–c. 1675?), founder of a school for girls—at this time, a novelty—presents the argument for the education of women in the advanced studies previ-ously reserved for men. The French marquise and *salonnière* (salon hostess) Madame de Maintenon (1635–1719) also opens a school for girls, its more cautious, but still audacious vision documented in her letters and lectures. Discussion then jumps to the year 1740, when Gabrielle Émilie le Tonnelier de Breteuil, marquise Du Châtelet (1706–1749) publishes her *Fundamentals of Physics*, an introduction to physics based on Newton's *Principia* that she had read, and probed, in the original Latin. Over the course of a century, these five figures trace the emergence of women into the Republic of Letters.

Three years before the French author Marie de Gournay published, in 1641, her treatise on *The Equality of Men and Women*, which may be seen as the culminating statement on that matter, Anna Maria van Schurman had already published, in 1638, her Latin "dissertation," as she called it, *Whether the Study of Letters Befits a Christian Woman*. It was explosively popular, pub-lished in several editions between its first appearance in 1638 and 1749, and quickly translated into Dutch, French, and English. The English version of 1659, entitled *The Learned Maid: Or, Whether the Christian Woman May Be a Scholar*, was especially successful. That title preserves, as does the one given here, van Schurman's concern with "the study of letters" or of "the arts and sciences," rather than with "education," a term she does not use, entailing as it does modern concepts she did not intend.

Van Schurman's work deserved its fame: it is a quiet manifesto, written in a dry and technical Latin in tension with its audacious claim that women, because they were fully human and possessed of the same aspirations and capacities as men, should be admitted to the studies that were the portal to participation in intellectual life. Ironically—and it is inconceivable that the irony was not deliberate—it is structured as a formal logical exercise typical of the male academic discourse from which women had always been excluded. Its systematically defended propositions, conclusions, and refutations of adversarial arguments are strikingly at odds with its purpose: to make the case, with controlled and concealed passion, for women's right to learn.

Van Schurman's English contemporary Margaret Cavendish wrote often in support of women's education in her many works in prose and verse that she published in twelve separate volumes, five of which she issued in revised editions. *The Blazing World*, however, excerpted here, is not a work of advocacy but rather a mock-utopian epic/romance whose heroine is the paradigm of a learned woman. That unnamed Lady is not merely knowledgeable, curious, and energetic in her exploration of new ideas, but as Empress, is endowed with the wealth and power needed to support the individuals and institutions who will achieve the advancement of learning.

Cavendish herself had profited from such patronage, provided by her husband, thirty years older than she, a marquis (later raised to duke) and commander of royalist forces during the English Revolution, soon to culminate in the execution of King Charles I and the protectorate of Oliver Cromwell. Both were exiles in France when they married in 1645, and they remained in exile, mainly in the Netherlands, until the restoration of the English monarchy in 1660 permitted their return to England. Cavendish had begun her writing career abroad and continued it at home, astonishing London observers with her outlandish dress, composed by a pastiche of male and female accessories, her uncensored tongue, and her bold forays into male intellectual circles including that, famously, of the Royal Society, a gathering of leading scientific and philosophical thinkers, upon which she descended in 1667. The year before, she had published *The Blazing World* as a madcap companion piece, bound in the same volume, to the sober *Observations Upon Experimental Philosophy* that would be more to the taste of the gentlemen of the Royal Society. But it is *The Blazing World* that features a wholly new phenomenon, modeled upon its author: a female intellectual and potentate.

Bathsua Makin lived in the same world as Margaret Cavendish, and yet she did not. Her major work, *An Essay to Revive the Ancient Education of Gentlewomen* (1673), was published only six years after Cavendish's *Blazing World*, and like Cavendish, she traveled in literary circles linked to the Royal Society and to aristocratic and even royal households: in the 1640s, Makin had been tutor to Princess Elizabeth, daughter of King Charles I, and in 1673, she dedicated her *Essay* to Princess Mary (later Queen Mary II), daughter of James Stuart, Duke of York (later King James II). But Makin's origins were humbler: her father and her closest associates were schoolmasters or pedagogical theorists inspired by Johann Amos Comenius, the Czech advocate of universal education. She was a working woman whose financial situation was distressed. The school for gentlewoman at Tottenham High Cross that she advertised at the close of her *Essay* did not long survive; and it is not even certain whether, at the age of seventy-three, she ever assumed the title of headmistress that she boasts.

Nonetheless, Makin was a learned woman and professional educator at a time when both those conditions were rare, and her *Essay* is a pioneering defense of academic study beyond basic literacy and a curriculum of needlecraft and deportment. Her arguments are consistent with those of Cavendish, of whom she knew, and van Schurman, with whom she had corresponded. But her purpose diverges from theirs: where they had proposed the training at home of elite women, Makin proposes female schooling, a wholly different venture. The institutionalization of schooling would extend its availability to a broader public, if only to a middle-class audience able to pay the fee.

From England, attention shifts to France, where in 1686, Françoise d'Aubigné, marquise de Maintenon, a *salonnière* (salon hostess) during her first marriage but now secretly married to King Louis XIV, opened a school of the sort Makin had proposed: the Institution Royale de Saint-Louis (Royal Academy of Saint Louis) at Saint-Cyr, adjacent to the palace grounds at Versailles, the "premier European academy for women for over a century."[1] The women educated at Saint-Cyr, and subsequently in the pattern modeled there, went on to become nuns and wives, but also hostesses of the salons that were a principal cultural institution of the Enlightenment. Founded on a tradition of convent education that was well established in Catholic countries, although no longer available in contemporary England, instruction in "the virtues" was perhaps as prominent a goal as the study of the arts and sciences. Nonetheless, the impecunious aristocrats who were the chosen students at Saint-Cyr received the sound education that, as the school's founder believed, was the key to the cultural advancement of women.

---

1. The weighty judgment of John J. Conley, SJ, in the introduction to his edition and translation of Mme. de Maintenon's *Dialogues and Addresses*, 1. Cited in Texts and Studies.

In 1740, Émilie Du Châtelet published her *Institutions de physique* (*Fundamentals of Physics*), a work testifying to her mastery of Newton's *Principia*, no ordinary achievement. In this work written a little more than a century after van Schurman sanctioned the education of women, as in her translation of the *Principia* with appended commentary published posthumously in 1759, Du Châtelet abundantly demonstrates her considerable learning. Just as Cavendish in the 1650s and 1660s had claimed a place for women in the excitingly new but predominantly male world of natural science, Du Châtelet does so in the even more challenging post-Newtonian world of the 1730s and 1740s. With her work on Newton, acclaimed by her contemporaries as authoritative and still in use today, the membership of women in the Republic of Letters is definitively established.

In the work of these five learned women may be observed the establishment of the phenomenon of female education beyond the elementary level, access to many fields of knowledge previously barred to women, including those of philosophy and the new sciences, and the entry of women into the cultural mainstream as authors, as thinkers, and as participants in intellectual conversation. All these advances were seen to appertain to elite women only. Four of the five subjects of this chapter are themselves noblewomen—three of the grand aristocracy, the marquises Maintenon and Du Châtelet and the duchess Margaret Cavendish—who might be expected to ignore the prospects of girls of middling and poorer ranks; and even the bourgeois Makin, who had spent some part of her career interacting with members of the royal family, stipulated that some quantity of wealth was a prerequisite for schooling. Yet the ideals they represent would one day be expanded to include women of lesser social standing. When that opportunity emerged, this earlier phase of achievement will have been its necessary precondition.

A face raised toward heaven

Anna Maria van Schurman, *Whether the Study of Letters Befits a Christian Woman* (1638)

"Our thesis then stands," Anna Maria van Schurman triumphantly concludes her famous work asserting the fitness of women to pursue the study of letters, traditionally a male preserve. Written under the guidance of her mentor, the Dutch Calvinist professor Gisbertus Voetius (Gijsbert Voet), it is structured as a *dissertatio logica*, an academic exercise in formal logic—an unlikely vehicle for the expression of a passionate commitment to learning for women.

Van Schurman opens by stating the problem to be addressed, and proceeds to definitions and preliminary assumptions before restating that problem as a thesis to be proved. There follow fourteen arguments constituting the heart of her work, presented as syllogisms,[2] supported by brief ancillary discussions. Then with the refutation of five anticipated counter-arguments forthcoming from opponents, she declares that the thesis has been proved.

The excerpt that follows here focuses on the main lines of van Schurman's presentation, including eleven of the fourteen arguments, and omitting much of the logical scaffolding. Some explanations are interpolated, and some truncated statements expanded for greater legibility, and in a few cases, where the effect contributes to the power of her prose, non-standard capitalization is retained. Even with this simplification, the reader may find the format of logical statements at times off-putting. Yet amid this web of manipulated and sanitized reasoning, van Schurman's voice, a personal voice, is still heard, all the more intense because it is almost, but not quite suppressed. It is heard in her description of the ideal conditions in which a woman might pursue her studies, which is effectively a portrait of her own life circumstances as a young woman from a wealthy family, endowed with both freedom and leisure, and encouraged in her pursuits by her parents. Further, it is heard at a few points where the cool and sterile continuum of her prose is punctuated by moments of exaltation. In arguments three and four, for example, she posits that God created woman with "a face raised and lifted toward heaven," equipping her for "the contemplation and cognition of exalted and heavenly things"; and that woman "powerfully longs for a substantial and perpetual occupation," and as such is "ideally suited to the study of letters." Here van Schurman bursts forth from her chains, and urges other women to do the same.

Whether the Study of Letters Befits a Christian Woman

The Problem To Be Solved: Whether the Study of Letters Befits a Christian Woman.

We shall endeavor to prove the affirmative.

. . .

Preliminary presumptions:

First, regarding . . . the Christian woman, it is understood that she is gifted with at least average intelligence, and not incapable of learning.

---

2. The syllogism is a deductive argument containing three statements: a major premise, a minor premise, and a conclusion. It is a critical tool of Aristotelian logic, fundamental to medieval scholasticism, and is the form of argumentation commonly used in scholastic reasoning and disputation.

Second, it is understood that the necessary means of instruction are available, and that the circumstances of her household are not so straitened as to obstruct her progress. This presumption is introduced because there are few who are so fortunate as to have parents who are able or willing to educate their daughters themselves, and the employment of tutors in this region is an expensive option.

Third, it is understood that she is of that position and circumstance that she can sometimes be relieved of any general or specific responsibilities, such as, particularly, the requirements of religious devotion or household management. It follows clearly that, if she is young, she should be free of any burden of chores or duties; and that if she is older, she should either be unmarried, or if married, have the assistance of servants, who often relieve well-off matrons from most household tasks.

Fourth, the goal of her studies should not be to vaunt or preen herself or satisfy any kind of idle curiosity, but first and foremost, the glory of God, which is to say the salvation of her soul; and secondarily, that she may be made a better and finer person who, if such a duty is laid upon her, is able to instruct and guide her family, and also, to the greatest possible extent, to profit the whole of her Sex. . . .

This Then Is Our Thesis: The study of letters befits a Christian woman

For the proof of this thesis we offer the following arguments. . . .

1. Whoever is by nature endowed with the capacity, or the potential for the capacity to study all the arts and sciences, is suited to the study of all the arts and sciences. But women are endowed by nature with the capacity or the potential for the capacity to study all the arts and sciences.

    Therefore women are suited for the study of all the arts and sciences. . . .

2. Whoever by nature desires to know the arts and sciences is suited for the study of the arts and sciences. But Woman by nature desires to know the sciences and arts.

    Therefore women are suited for the study of all the arts and sciences. . . .

3. Whomever God has created with a face raised and lifted toward heaven is suited to the contemplation and cognition of exalted and heavenly things. But God created Woman with a face raised and lifted toward heaven.

    Therefore women are suited for the contemplation and cognition of exalted and heavenly things. . . .

4. Whoever powerfully longs for a substantial and perpetual occupation is ideally suited to the study of letters. But Woman powerfully longs for a substantial and perpetual occupation.

    Therefore women are suited for the study of letters. . . .

5. Whoever enjoys a tranquil and unfettered existence is suited to the study of Letters. But Women generally enjoy a tranquil and unfettered existence.

    Therefore women generally are suited for the study of Letters. . . .

    . . .

7. Whoever inclines to all virtue in general is also suited to the study of the arts and sciences. But Woman inclines to all virtue in general.

    Therefore Woman is suited to the study of the arts and sciences. . . .

8. Whatever perfects and adorns the human mind befits a Christian woman. But the arts and sciences perfect and adorn the human mind.

    Therefore the arts and sciences are fitting studies for the Christian woman. . . .

9. Whatever by its nature arouses in us a greater love and reverence for God befits a Christian woman. But the arts and sciences by their nature arouse in us a greater love and reverence for God.

    Therefore the arts and sciences are fitting studies for the Christian woman. . . .

    . . .

11. Whatever teaches prudence without any injury to reputation and modesty befits a Christian Woman. But the study of Letters teaches prudence without any injury to reputation and modesty.

    Therefore the study of Letters befits a Christian woman. . . .

12. Whatever fosters the true greatness of soul befits a Christian woman. But the Study of Letters contributes to true greatness of soul.

    Therefore the study of Letters befits a Christian woman. . . .

13. Whatever floods the human soul with pure and exquisite pleasure befits a Christan woman. But the study of Letters floods the soul with pure and exquisite pleasure.

    Therefore the study of Letters befits a Christian woman. . . .

Our Thesis Then Stands: The study of letters befits a Christian woman

Wherefore we conclude:

Sound and valid reasons, the testimony of the wise, and finally, the example of famous women, can and should encourage women to embrace this kind of life, assuming that they are equipped with the necessary leisure and the other aids and instruments for the study of Letters. And since it is best that the mind be imbued with the best studies from the very age of infancy, their parents, we believe, should be urged from the start to take this duty seriously.

The worlds I have made

Margaret Cavendish, *The Blazing World* (1666)

A ridiculous romance, a phantasmagoric epic, a witty utopia, *The Blazing World* is a feminist fantasy of indeterminate genre. In it an unnamed young Lady is abducted by a ship's captain and remains the only survivor when the ship founders in an ice storm. She finds her way to an unknown island, captivates its ruler, and is made Empress, in which role she engages in scientific and literary investigations. Rhetorically at the opposite pole from van Schurman's exercise in logic, Cavendish's work achieves the same end: the validation of women's learning, and with it, their emancipation and power. The passage given here begins with the Lady's reception by the Emperor of the new World, who vests her with absolute power. It is followed by highlights of her interviews with the Emperor's scientists and philosophers that recall Galileo's astronomical ventures and Bacon's critique of logical method. In closing, Cavendish prods her readers to engage in their own imaginative projects: if they do not like "the worlds I have made," she taunts, they may make worlds of their own and govern them.

THE BLAZING WORLD

No sooner was the Lady brought before the Emperor, but he conceived her to be some goddess, and offered to worship her; which she refused, telling him . . . that although she came out of another world, yet was she but a mortal. At which the Emperor, rejoicing, made her his wife, and gave her an absolute power to rule and govern all that World as she pleased. . . .

. . .

The rest of the inhabitants of that World were men of several different sorts, shapes, figures, dispositions, and humors . . . ; some were Bear-men, some Worm-men . . . ; some Bird-men, . . . some Spider-men, some Lice-men, . . . some Jackdaw-men, some Magpie-men, some Parrot-men, . . . and many more, which I cannot all remember . . . ; and . . . each followed such a profession as was most proper for the nature of their species, which the Empress encouraged them in, especially those that had applied themselves to the study of several arts and sciences; . . . and to that end she erected schools, and founded several societies. The Bear-men were to be her experimental philosophers, the Bird-men her astronomers, the . . . Worm- and Fish-men her natural philosophers, ... the Spider- and Lice-men her Mathematicians, the ... Magpie- and Parrot-men her Orators and Logicians, . . . etc. . . .

. . .

The Empress confers with these diverse groups of experts, whose disputes recall those among the author's contemporaries.

The Empress . . . caused a convocation first of the Bird-men, and commanded them to give her a true relation of the two celestial bodies, that is, the sun and moon, which they did with all the obedience and faithfulness befitting their duty.

The sun, as much as they could observe, they related to be a firm or solid stone, of a vast bigness; of color yellowish, and of an extraordinary splendor: But the moon, they said, was of a whitish color; and although she looked dim in the presence of the sun, yet had she her own light, and was a shining body of herself, as might be perceived by her vigorous appearance in moon-shiny-nights. . . . Concerning the heat of the sun, they were not of one opinion; some would have the sun hot in itself, [recalling] an old tradition, that it should at some time break asunder, and burn the heavens, and consume this world into hot embers. . . . Others again said, this opinion could not stand with reason; for fire being a destroyer of all things, the sun-stone after this manner would burn up all the near adjoining bodies. . . .

. . .

Wielding their telescopes, another group of experts evoke memories of Galileo's astronomical observations.

[Then] the Empress, . . . to avoid hereafter tedious disputes, and have the truth of the phenomena of celestial bodies more exactly known, commanded the Bear-men, which were her experimental philosophers, to observe them through such Instruments as are called telescopes, which they did according to her majesty's command; but these telescopes caused more differences and divisions amongst them, than ever they had before; for some said, they perceived that the sun stood still, and the earth did move about it; others were of opinion, that they both did move; and others said again, that the earth stood still, and sun did move; some counted more stars then others; some discovered new stars never seen before; . . . At last, the Empress commanded them to go with their telescopes to the very end of the pole that was joined to the world she came from, and try whether they could perceive any stars in it: which they did; and, being returned to her majesty, reported that they had seen three blazing-stars appear there, one after another in a short time, whereof two were bright, and one dim; but they could not agree neither in this observation. . . .

. . .

After they had thus argued, the Empress began to grow angry at their telescopes, that they could give no better intelligence; for, said she, now I do plainly perceive, that your glasses are false informers, and [which], instead of discovering the truth, delude your senses; wherefore I command you to break them, and let the Bird-men trust only to their natural eyes, and examine celestial objects by the motions of their own sense and reason. . . .

. . .

The Bear-men being exceedingly troubled at her majesty's displeasure concerning their telescopes, knelt down, and in the humblest manner petitioned, that they might not be broken; for, said they, we take more delight in artificial delusions, then in natural truths. Besides, we shall want employments for our senses, and subjects for arguments; for, were there nothing but truth, and no falsehood, there would be no occasion to dispute, and by this means we should want the aim and pleasure of our endeavors in confuting and contradicting each other; . . . wherefore we most humbly beseech your imperial majesty to spare our glasses, which are our only delight, and as dear to us as our lives. The Empress at last consented to their request, but upon condition, that their disputes and quarrels should remain within their schools, and cause no factions or disturbances in state, or government.

. . .

The Empress turns to the rhetoricians and logicians—and in a manner reminiscent of Francis Bacon, is not pleased with the confusion they sow.

After this, the Empress was resolved to hear the Magpie-, Parrot-, and Jack-daw-men, which were her professed orators and logicians; whereupon one of the Parrot-men rose with great formality, and endeavored to make an eloquent speech before her majesty; but before he had half ended, his arguments and divisions being so many, that they caused a great confusion in his brain, he could not go forward, but was forced to retire backward, with great disgrace both to himself, and the whole society. . . .

Lastly, her imperial majesty, being desirous to know what progress her logicians had made in the art of disputing, commanded them to argue upon several themes or subjects; which they did; and having made very nice discourse of logistical terms and propositions, entered into a dispute by way of syllogistical arguments, through all the figures and modes. . . .

. . .

Thus they argued, and intended to go on, but the Empress interrupted them: I have enough, said she, of your chopped logic, and will hear no more of your syllogisms; for it disorders my reason, and puts my brain on the rack; . . . and I'll have you to consider, that art does not make reason, but reason makes art; and therefore as much as reason is above art, so much is a natural rational discourse to be preferred before an artificial: for art is, for the most part irregular, and disorders men's understandings more than it rectifies them, and leads them into a labyrinth where they'll never get out, and makes them dull and unfit for useful employments; especially your art of logic, which consists only in contradicting each other, in making sophisms, and obscuring truth, instead of [clarifying] it. . . .

. . .

Cavendish closes with an "epilogue to the reader" in which she conflates the Lady's role as Empress and her own as author.

By this poetical description, you may perceive, that my ambition is not only to be Empress, but Authoress of a whole World; and that the Worlds I have made, . . . are framed and composed of the most pure, that is, the rational parts of matter, which are the parts of my mind. . . . And in the formation of those Worlds, I take more delight and glory, then ever Alexander or Caesar did in conquering this terrestrial world. . . . [A]nd if any should like the World I have made, and be willing to be my subjects, they may imagine themselves such, and they are such . . . ; but if they cannot endure to be subjects, they may create worlds of their own, and govern themselves as they please. . . .

A finer sort of cattle

Bathsua Makin, *An Essay to Revive the Ancient Education of Gentlewomen* (1673)

As advocates had done from the fourteenth century forward, in the opening sections of her *Essay to Revive the Ancient Education of Gentlewomen*, Makin presents the case for women's intellectual capacity. She draws on earlier catalogues of female achievement for familiar examples of notable figures, while also supplying some contemporary names, including Margaret Cavendish, duchess of Newcastle. Makin's approach is distinctive, however, in organizing this account according to disciplines, perhaps reflecting her pedagogical experience. Beginning with the general claim that women in past times had acquired learning, and even achieved eminence in the arts and sciences, she proceeds to detail those who had excelled in languages, oratory, logic, philosophy, mathematics, and poetry. She concludes this roundup by calling on contemporary women to pursue such learning, and offers the admonition with which the excerpt given here begins: "Care ought to be taken by us to educate Women in learning."

Makin recognizes that not all women will be educated: some do not have the natural aptitude, and others do not enjoy the comfortable circumstances required. But for girls of at least average ability and sufficient wealth, once skills necessary for their future roles as wives and mothers are taught (manners, bearing, and needlecraft), there will remain leisure better devoted to the arts, sciences, and languages than to the trivialities of fashion. Women so educated will be a benefit to themselves, their families, and their nation. Why did God give them rational minds, after all, if he intended them only to be "a finer sort of cattle," to be tyrannized over by men?

Finally, after refuting a series of objections that might be made to her project, Makin concludes on an entrepreneurial note: she advertises her own school for gentlewomen at Tottenham High Cross, then just outside of London, detailing the curriculum and stating her fee.

AN ESSAY TO REVIVE THE ANCIENT EDUCATION OF GENTLEWOMEN

In the first half of her Essay, Makin demonstrates that women have in the past excelled in all branches of knowledge of the arts and sciences. Now she proceeds to advocate for their education at the present day.

. . .

Care ought to be taken by us to educate Women in learning.

. . . I do not mean, that it is necessary to the . . . subsistence, or to the salvation of Women, to be thus educated. Those that are of humble rank in the world have not an opportunity for this education. Those that are of meager natural ability, though they have opportunity, cannot reach this. . . . My meaning is, persons whom God has blessed with the things of this world, that have adequate natural ability, ought to be educated in knowledge; that is, it is much better they should spend the time of their youth to be competently instructed in those things usually taught to gentlewoman at schools, and the surplus of their time to be spent in gaining arts, and languages, and useful knowledge, rather than to trifle away so many precious minutes merely to polish their hands and feet, to curl their locks, to dress and adorn their bodies; and in the meantime to neglect their souls, and not at all, or very little to endeavor to know God, Jesus Christ, themselves, and the things of nature, arts, and tongues that are subservient to these.

I do not deny but Women ought to be brought up to a comely and decent bearing, to needlecraft, to neatness, to understand all those things that do particularly belong to their sex. But when these things are competently cared for, and where there are endowments of nature and leisure, then higher things ought to be endeavored after. Merely to teach gentlewomen to frisk and dance, to paint their faces, to curl their hair, . . . is not truly to adorn, but to adulterate their bodies; yea, (what is worse) to defile their souls. . . .

Had God intended Women only as a finer sort of cattle, he would not have made them rational. Brutes, a few degrees higher than mandrills or monkeys, . . . might have better fitted some men's lust, pride, and pleasure; especially those that desire to keep them ignorant to be tyrannized over. . . .

. . .

In what disciplines, then, Makin asks, should women be instructed?

. . . The whole *Encyclopedia* of learning may be useful some way or other to them. . . . I would not deny them the knowledge of grammar and rhetoric, because they dispose to speak handsomely. Logic must be allowed, because it is the key to all sciences. . . . Languages ought to be studied, especially Greek and Hebrew, as these will enable to the better understanding of the Scriptures. Mathematics, more especially geography, will be useful. . . . Music, painting, poetry, etc., are a great ornament and pleasure. . . .

. . .

Makin now details the ways in which this kind of education will be useful to women.

1. The profit will be to themselves. Generally speaking, they will be able to understand, read, write, and speak their mother tongue, which they cannot well do without this. They will have something to exercise their

thoughts about, which are busy and active. Their social position ties them at home; if learning be their companion, delight and pleasure will be their attendants. . . . There is in all an innate desire of knowing, and the satisfying of this is the greatest pleasure. . . .

. . .

2. Women thus educated will be beneficial to their relations. . . . Many learned Men, having married wives of high ability, have themselves instructed them in all kinds of learning, the more to fit them for their conversation, and to endear them and their society to them, and to make them admired by others. The Woman is the glory of the Man; we rejoice in our children when eminent, and in our wives when excellent, either in body or mind.

. . .

3. Women thus instructed will be beneficial to the nation. Look into all history, those nations ever were, now are, and always shall be, the worst of nations, where Women are most undervalued; as in Russia, Ethiopia, and all the barbarous nations of the world. One great Reason why our neighbors the Dutch have thrived to admiration, is the great care they take in the education of their Women, from whence they are to be accounted more virtuous, and indeed more useful than any Women in the world. We cannot expect otherwise to prevail against the ignorance, atheism, profanity, superstition, idolatry, lust, that reigns in the nation, than by a prudent, sober, pious, virtuous education of our daughters. . . .

. . .

Makin pauses to restate her major claims before proceeding to refute anticipated objections.

Before I mention the objections, I shall state the propositions I have endeavored to prove. That which I intend is this, that persons of average ability, indifferently inclined and disposed to learning, whom God hath blessed with sufficient wealth that they are not cumbered in the world, but have liberty and opportunity in their childhood; and afterward, being competently instructed in all things now useful that concern them as Women, may and ought to be improved in more polite learning, in religion, arts, and the knowledge of things, in languages also as subservient to these, rather than to spend the leisure time of their youth, in . . . painting and dancing, in making flowers of colored straw, and building houses of stained paper, and such like vanities. . . .

. . .

Having answered anticipated objections, and outlined her teaching methods, Makin draws her argument to a close. She finishes on an entrepreneurial note, inviting those interested to attend her school.

I hope I shall by this discourse persuade some parents to be more careful for the future of the rearing of their daughters. You labor and care to get fat dowries for them, which sometimes occasions their ruin. Here is a sure dowry, an easy way to make them excellent. How many born to good fortunes, when their wealth has been wasted, have supported themselves and families, too, by their wisdom?

I hope some of these considerations will at least move some of this abused sex to set a right value upon themselves, according to the dignity of their creation, that they might . . . scorn to be bowed down and made to stoop to such follies and vanities, trifles and nothings, so far below them, and disproportionate to their noble souls, which are nothing inferior to those of Men, and equally precious to God in Christ, in whom there is neither male nor female. . . .

POSTSCRIPT

If any inquire where this education may be performed, such may be informed that a school is lately erected for gentlewomen at Tottenham-High-Cross, within four miles of London, . . . where Mrs. Makin is Governess, who was formerly tutoress to the Princess Elizabeth, daughter to King Charles the First; where, by the blessing of God, gentlewomen may be instructed in the principles of religion; and in all manner of sober and virtuous education: more particularly, in all things ordinarily taught in other schools, such as crafts of all sorts, dancing, music, singing, writing, keeping accounts, in which things half the time is to be spent; the other half to be employed in gaining the Latin and French tongues; and those that please, may learn Greek and Hebrew, Italian, and Spanish, in all which this gentlewoman has a competent knowledge. . . .

The basic rate certain shall be twenty pounds *per annum*: but if a competent improvement be made in languages, and the other things aforementioned, as shall be agreed upon, then something more will be expected. . . .

I warn you of the world

Madame de Maintenon, *Letter: On the Education of the* Demoiselles *of Saint-Cyr* (August 1, 1686), and *Instruction: On the World* (1707)

The granddaughter of Huguenot hero and poet Agrippa d'Aubigné, Madame de Maintenon, a Catholic convert, received a convent education—which she detested. Years later she founded her famous school at Saint-Cyr for the daughters of the impoverished nobility, described by the untranslatable term *demoiselles*, for whom Maintenon developed a structured curriculum, heavy on moral instruction, that would prepare them for the lives they most likely faced as nuns, caretakers of their aging relations, or wives of provincial noblemen. The shadow of the convent fell on Saint-Cyr, yet it was a secular institution renowned throughout Europe.

The brief excerpts given here are samples of two of the genres in which Maintenon wrote as director of Saint-Cyr. The first is a letter of August 1, 1686, written to the *dames de Saint-Louis* (the faculty of the school) about the education to be given to the *demoiselles*. Striking is the emphasis on reason: the goal, she writes, is not to stuff the girls' heads with facts but to form their ability to reason; and the youngest children should not be indulged with baby talk but spoken to "rationally": "since they can never be too rational, or rational too soon, it is essential to accustom children to the use of their reason as soon as they can talk and understand."

The second passage is from a *conseil* (instruction) to the older *demoiselles* (fourteen to twenty years old) "on the world": the privileged world, that is, of the high aristocracy. The recent visit in grand state by Marie Adélaide of Savoy, duchess of Burgundy, a former pupil of Saint-Cyr, had impressed and distracted the *demoiselles*, and Maintenon cautions them that her condition is not theirs. She urges her students to humble themselves and prepare for the meager careers they were likely to face on exiting the school. The message is harsh, but the tone is warm, and the warning is realistic: if you let a man take you to the opera, you will lose your reputation; as the wife of a provincial noblewoman, you may need to perform some manual labor. From the summit of absolute power, with memories of her own former powerlessness, Maintenon offers the impecunious young aristocrats of Saint-Cyr a fearsome, and not a blazing, world.

LETTER: ON THE EDUCATION OF THE *DEMOISELLES* OF SAINT-CYR

August 1, 1686

Since God has chosen me to assist with the institution the king has founded for the education of the poor *demoiselles* of his realm, I see it as my duty to communicate to those persons destined to rear them what my experience has taught me about how to give them a good education. Doing so is surely one of the greatest acts of austerity[3] that one can practice, because unlike all others it offers no respite, since the instruction of a child consumes all of one's life.

When the goal is only the memorization of facts, it is enough to teach them a few hours per day, and it would be highly imprudent to demand more of them; but when the goal is to form their mind, awaken their heart, lift up their spirit, destroy their evil inclinations—in a word, cause them to know and love virtue—we must always be at work, and seize every opportunity that presents itself. It is as necessary to be engaged in their amusements as in their lessons, and we must never leave them lest they suffer harm. . . .

We should be concerned not so much to furnish their minds as to form their ability to reason. In truth, by this method, the knowledge and ability of the teacher is less evident. A young girl who knows a thousand things by heart shines more in company and gratifies her relations more than one whose judgment it is that you have taken care to form, who knows how to hold her tongue, who is modest and restrained, and who never seems anxious to show off her wit. . . .

We must teach them all the delicacies of honor, integrity, discretion, generosity, and compassion, and portray virtue to be as beautiful and as lovable as indeed it is. A few little stories suitable for this purpose are properly and usefully employed both to instruct and amuse them. But it is essential that they understand that if virtue is not grounded in religion, it is not solid, and that God does not sustain it, but disapproves of those pagan and heroic virtues which are merely the effects of a dainty pride desirous of praise. . . .

We must enter into the amusements of children, but we should never converse with them in a childish language, or use childish ways. Rather, we must raise them to our level by always speaking to them rationally. In a word, since they can never be too rational, or rational too soon, it is essential to accustom children to the use of their reason as soon as they can talk and understand. . . .

The superficial accomplishments of knowing foreign languages and a thousand other attainments that are the proper adornments of the daughters of the grander nobility are not suitable for our students, as these matters take up time that could be more usefully employed. The *demoiselles* of the house of Saint-Louis should not be raised in this manner, even if one could: for as they lack wealth, it would be wrong to urge their hearts and souls to aspirations so little suited to their fortune and condition. . . .

---

3. An allusion to the monastic life, characterized by acts of self-denial and austerity.

INSTRUCTION TO THE *DEMOISELLES* OF THE TWO UPPER GRADES (AGES FOURTEEN TO TWENTY): *ON THE WORLD*

1707

Having neither sufficient strength nor health to instruct you as often as I would like, I have decided to speak to you here together all at once about a matter of which I want to warn you as soon as possible: that is, about the world. I fear, my children, that since you came here young, and with no knowledge of it, that you may have imagined the world to be wholly other than it really is. You may judge it only by external appearances which are, I admit, rather seductive for the young. . . .

Remember, my children, that we cannot love the world without displeasing our Lord Jesus Christ, and understand that when you leave here, you will have little because of the distressed situation of most of your families. Although a few of you may acquire what some call a fortune, you must nonetheless despise the world, and harbor thoughts, obey precepts, and conduct yourselves in a way quite opposed to it. The world that you imagine, its worldliness, is corrupt. There are, I acknowledge, some good Christians, and even saints, who live in that world, and I pray God with all my heart that those of you who must return to the world may be among that happy number. . . .

If you have no vocation for the convent, when you leave here, for the most part, you will go home to live with a father or a mother perhaps widowed, or sick, or demented. . . . You will spend most of your days knitting in your mother's room or your own, and you will surely not be thinking of buying a ticket to go to the theater—you will not even hear talk of it. Even less would you wish, if you are honorable, to be taken there by a man who, in paying for your seat, will ruin your reputation.

Others among you—and they will be the lucky ones—will find yourselves in the heart of the country and occupied with managing an estate, supervising the staff, seeing that they meet their responsibilities, that their work is well done, if they have cared for the livestock, for the chickens and the geese. In sum will need to give all their attention to the minutiae of housekeeping and even lend a hand with household tasks. If anyone, my children, has need of a store of virtue and devotion, it is surely such as these, who will likely experience a host of difficulties. These troubles must be offered willingly as a sacrifice to God who has ordained them to be so, . . . who in his great goodness accepts those sacrifices, and values them highly, when we have made them voluntarily.

Humble yourselves, my dear children. Why else has God allowed the great decline of the nobility if not to humble it, and perhaps to punish those of your ancestors who abused their authority and their wealth? Humble yourselves, therefore, and so consent to God's will. I do not mean thereby that you should lose heart; on the contrary, let it be proud and bold and determined never to do anything base. But I implore you to conceive an idea of the world that is more accurate and conformed to the truth and Christian piety.

The daybreak of your reason

Émilie Du Châtelet, *Fundamentals of Physics* (1740)

Aristocratic to the core, the mother of children, the lover of Voltaire, Émilie Du Châtelet devoted her leisure to the study of Newtonian physics, a study fundamental to the Enlightenment project: for Newton employed mathematical reasoning to explain the cosmic system as self-governing and self-regulating, thus dispensing with the need for metaphysics or theology. Du Châtelet was not alone in elevating Newtonianism as a mode of thinking. But she was exceptional in popularizing it—as others, she points out, popularized Descartes—so it would not remain the property of the learned few, but belong to the whole of the "thinking world."

Du Châtelet pursued the dissemination of Newtonian physics in two works: in her *Fundamentals of Physics*, published in 1740, dedicated to her son (but ironically, not her daughter); and in her translation of the *Principia*, with her own commentary appended, completed shortly before her death in 1740 and published posthumously in 1759. Excerpts from the preface to the first of these works are given here.

At thirteen, "at this daybreak of [his] reason," Du Châtelet's son was old enough to understand, she explains, the simplified explanation of physics she presents—all algebraic demonstrations omitted. He is young enough to learn quickly, but not so old as to be distracted by the "passions and pleasures" of the world. Descartes he will be able to read on his own with the assistance of commentaries already available. But she will introduce him to Newton so that he can take his place in the "thinking world" that was, in the age of Enlightenment, the world a young aristocrat must enter. Du Châtelet performs for her son the mission that she also performs for the Republic of Letters writ large: she delivers Newtonianism as a theoretical framework for the Enlightenment discussion of society and politics.

FUNDAMENTALS OF PHYSICS

1. The most sacred duty of humankind, I have always thought, is to give to children an education such that, when they become older, they do not regret having wasted their youth—for youth is the only age in which

one may truly acquire learning. You are now at that happy age, my dear son, when the mind begins to think, but the heart is not yet roiled by passions.

Now is perhaps the only time of your life when you can pursue the study of nature. Soon the passions and pleasures of your age will consume every moment; and when this storm of youth has passed, and you have paid to the madness of the world the tribute owed by your age and your rank, ambition will seize your soul. And even if at this more advanced though not necessarily more mature age, you wished to apply yourself to the study of the true sciences, your mind no longer having the quickness that is the property of youth, you will need to purchase with painful study what you could learn today with the greatest ease. And so I want you now to profit from this daybreak of your reason, and seek to defend you from an ignorance all too common among your peers, which always yields more loss, and less gain. . . .

2. The study of physics seems to be made for humankind. It concerns the things that are always around us, that supply our pleasures and our needs. I shall try in this book to put this science within your reach, detaching it from that admirable art, called algebra, which by separating facts from images dispenses with the senses and speaks directly to the understanding. You are not yet ready to understand this language—a language spoken by angels, it seems, rather than by humans; it is to be set aside for your study when you are older than you are now. But since what is true can be told in different ways, I shall try here to present it in a manner befitting your years, and to speak to you of things that can be understood with the aid only of simple geometry, which you have studied.

    Never cease to cultivate geometry, my son, which you learned in your earliest years. Without its aid little progress can be made in the study of nature, as it is the key to all discoveries; and if there are still many inexplicable matters in physics, it is only because no sufficient attempt has been made to solve them using geometry, and because, perhaps, its possibilities have not been sufficiently explored.

3. I am often astonished that, given that France possesses so many persons capable of doing so, no one has preceded me in this labor that I undertake today for you—for it must be admitted that, although we have several excellent books on physics in French, yet we do not have a complete presentation of the science. . . . For my part, though I deplore this lack I do not at all presume that I am capable of supplying it; rather, I propose in this book only to gather together for your review the discoveries scattered in many excellent Latin, Italian, and English books. Most of the truths they contain are known in France to few readers, and I want to

save you the task of unearthing them from sources whose difficulty may affright, and perhaps even repel you.

4. Although the work I undertake requires much time and labor, I shall not at all regret the trouble that it can cost me, and I shall believe it well expended if it can inspire in you love of the sciences, and the desire to cultivate your reason. What care and effort does one not expend every day in the uncertain hope of winning honors and increasing the fortune of one's children! Are the knowledge of truth and the habit of seeking and pursuing it goals not equally worth my efforts—especially in an age where the passion for physics pervades all of society, and begins to become part of the science of the world?

5. I shall not attempt to detail here the whole tally of the revolutions that physics has attempted to explain, as it would require a huge book to report them all. Rather, I plan to make available to you not so much what has been thought as what it is necessary to know. . . .

    We rise to knowledge of the truth like those gaints who scaled the heavens by each mounting on the shoulders of the one who came before.[4] Descartes and Galileo[5] paved the way for such as Huygens and Leibniz, those great men of whom you know only the names, to whose works I hope soon to introduce you; and it is by profiting from the laws of Kepler, and employing the theorems of Huygens, that Newton discovered that universal force [of gravity] operative in all of nature, which causes the planets to revolve around the sun, and exerts its weightiness on the earth.

6. The systems of Descartes and Newton share the attention today of the thinking world, on which account it is necessary that you be acquainted with both. But so many learned men have endeavored to explain and analyze Descartes' system that it will be easy for you to instruct yourself by their works. One of my aims in the first part of the present work is to acquaint you with the other part of this great process [of discovery], to introduce Newton's system to you, to show you how far it presses to make connections and determine probability, and how phenomena may be explained by the hypothesis of attraction. . . .

---

4. The metaphor of "standing on the shoulders of giants" was often repeated, most recently by Newton himself, but previously as early as the twelfth century.

5. Du Châtelet names in this passage, in addition to Descartes and Newton, already introduced, the scientists and philosophers Galileo Galilei (1564–1642); Christiaan Huygens (1629–1695); Gottfried Wilhelm Leibniz (1646–1716); and Johannes Kepler (1571–1630).

Chapter Three

A State of Perfect Freedom: 1689–1695

Introduction

If the primacy of reason was the guiding principle of the thinkers from Bacon to Bayle discussed in Chapter One, the guiding principle for John Locke (1632–1704), the subject of this chapter, is the primacy of freedom. His emphatic assertion of freedom from coercion both in outward action and in the inward being is a new note in the history of thought, and one of enormous consequence for modern times.

A philosopher, physician, Hellenist, and tutor, trained at Oxford, where he declined to become an Anglican priest to further his career, the protégé of scientist Robert Boyle and of politician Anthony Ashley Cooper, Lord Shaftesbury, John Locke published nothing before 1689, when he was already fifty-eight years old. During his incubation, Locke had witnessed the English Revolution, in which his father fought, Oliver Cromwell's Protectorate, and the royal Restoration; and with Shaftesbury soon after, he had helped craft English colonial policy for the Board of Trade by writing the *Fundamental Constitutions* for the Carolinas. Under suspicion of complicity in Shaftesbury's antiroyalist plots, he fled to the Netherlands in 1683; Shaftesbury had preceded him there, and had died in exile. In the vibrant intellectual world of the Netherlands, Locke engaged in learned conversations with natives and refugees, and prepared for publication of the works that would, on his return to England in 1689, finally see the light. He made that return journey on a royal yacht in the company of Mary, daughter of the dethroned king James II, en route to join her husband, William of Orange, with whom she would be crowned joint sovereign at the triumphal climax of the Glorious Revolution.

Five of Locke's works, all published in the six years between 1689 and 1695, are represented in this chapter. Their common theme is human freedom, central in his discussions of the state, in the *Second Treatise on Civil Government*; of the operations of the mind, in the *Essay Concerning Human Understanding*; of religion, in the *Letter on Toleration* and *The Reasonableness of Christianity*; and of education, in *Some Thoughts Concerning Education*.

Of these works only the first, Locke's *Letter on Toleration*, was written in Latin, the language of the university, but also, in the Dutch setting where he conceived it in his years of exile, a language generally known to European intellectuals of any origin. An extended letter (the first of four he would write on the topic) amounting to a brief treatise, it rested on Locke's long experience of religious conflict in England, and the new circumstances of his residence in the Netherlands. There he encountered the ebbing currents of the Dutch revolt against Spanish Catholic rule and subsequent establishment of a state that was pluralistic and multi-confessional (although predominantly Calvinist). And upon King Louis XIV's revocation in 1685 of the Edict of Nantes that had protected the right to worship of Huguenots (Calvinist Protestants) in France, he witnessed the flight of hundreds of thousands of those expelled, many to the Netherlands or England.

While these real-time circumstances condition the composition of his *Letter*, Locke was also aware of previous arguments for religious toleration, such as those by the Savoyard scholar Sebastian Castellio; the Dutch theologian Jacobus Arminius; the English founder of Rhode Island, Roger Williams; and, only three years before, the French thinker Pierre Bayle, a Huguenot exile himself (see Chapter One). In this context, it is no surprise that Locke would write that religious toleration was an essential principle of true Christianity or, as he put it most provocatively, the "true church"— a church of all believers that, as some advocates of the radical Reformation had proposed, had not yet been fully realized on the face of the earth. What was surprising, however, was the thunderous response to Locke's *Letter*, written not by a Christian sectarian embroiled in religious struggle but a pioneer of the Enlightenment. Published anonymously in the Netherlands in 1689 after Locke had already departed on his journey home, and immediately translated into English, Dutch, and French, it circulated widely and broadcast to a war-weary public a call for freedom of faith and conscience.

While still perched in the Netherlands, Locke tracked events across the English Channel where a second revolution gestated. He had at hand a draft of his *Two Treatises on Civil Government* composed even before he had sought asylum abroad to address both the present crisis and the broader issues of the origin and purpose of the state. The first of these refuted Sir Robert Filmer's *Patriarcha* (1680; posthumous) that had defended monarchy as the natural and inevitable form of human government. The second gathered earlier concepts inherited from ancient authorities and revised by Locke's seventeenth-century predecessors Hugo Grotius, Samuel von Pufendorf, and Thomas Hobbes to create arguably the most substantial and consequential political statement of the Enlightenment. He would publish both treatises in 1689, on his return to an England still engaged in the revolution that had been in progress nearly the whole of his lifetime.

The *Leviathan* of Thomas Hobbes, published in 1651 at the dark nadir of the English Revolution, sets the stage for Locke's *Second Treatise*. Hobbes claims that human society, given the essential sinfulness of human nature, descends inevitably to a chaotic and violent "state of war"—in which human existence, in his famous formulation, would be "solitary, poor, nasty, brutish, and short"—that could only be restrained by the coercive power of the state: the Leviathan, the name of a biblical sea monster.

To this scenario Locke responds with a sunnier vision. The "state of nature," the original condition of humankind, is a "state of perfect freedom," as well as of an abundance of goods supplied by God for the use of all. Competition among humans leads, briefly, to a "state of war" reminiscent of that posed by Hobbes, from which people rescue themselves by binding together in a political community—enacting a "social contract," to use a phrase recurrent in seventeenth- and eighteenth-century political thought—to restrain evildoers and protect both freedom and property. The will of the majority rules in this nascent civil government, but the laws made and power exercised are not permitted to exceed the bounds of justice—for in that case, those who freely submitted themselves to the authority of the state may by right dissolve it, and form a better one.

If Hobbes' *Leviathan* seems to allude to the disturbances of the first phase of the English Revolution, Locke's *Second Treatise* anticipates its resolution in the Glorious Revolution: for as though Locke had written the script, James II, an unacceptably Catholic king who exercised tyrannical power, as his enemies charged, was forced to abdicate; William and Mary were installed as joint monarchs; and the sovereignty of the English Parliament was enduringly established.

No less than in England, Locke's *Second Treatise* has struck many as prophetic of political events in the new United States of America. His concepts of essential human liberty, the civil goods of life, liberty, and the preservation of property (the third reconfigured as "the pursuit of happiness" in the American Declaration of Independence), and the right of citizens to dissolve an unjust government and construct one that would be responsive to the people are all fundamental themes of American political culture.

As momentous a work as the *Second Treatise*, Locke's *Essay Concerning Human Understanding* is a philosophical magnum opus, pursuing issues raised by Bacon and Descartes to pose a new epistemological and psychological model that resonates to this day. He had begun drafting it during the early years of his Dutch exile, ahead of its publication in 1689, the year that also saw the publication of the *Second Treatise* and the *Letter on Toleration*. It resembles those companion works in one essential regard: it asserts the absolute liberty of the human being, and in this case, necessarily, the complete non-determination of the human mind.

The mind is free because the mind is, by nature, empty: it is born with no innate ideas, as many thinkers, and most recently Descartes, had held. It is, instead, a "white paper" or "blank slate," or in the Latin, *tabula rasa*, a concept with a long pedigree, having descended from Plato and Aristotle to the humanist Erasmus and English theorists Sir John Fortescue and Thomas Starkey. Not being equipped with ideas, Locke contends, the mind acquires and assembles them, both from information gathered by the senses—a Baconian note—and by its own internal processes, which act upon and refine those ideas. This process of idea formation permits the elimination of the metaphysical structure that would be required if ideas were innate. Locke's understanding of the mind as a blank slate, limited by no inherent ideas, has largely dominated discussion from the Enlightenment forward, although in recent years it has been challenged by such thinkers as Noam Chomsky and Steven Pinker.

Just as he frees the mind, in his *Essay Concerning Human Understanding*, from the compulsion of innate ideas, Locke proposes, in *Some Thoughts Concerning Education*, to liberate the child from the coercion of teachers and parents. For child rearing and education had long been instruments of coercion—quite literal coercion; the humanist Desiderius Erasmus was haunted by memories of screaming children in the torture chambers, as he viewed them, of the schools. Such schooling, designed to discipline the child to the requirements of the adult world, was indifferent to the students' character, needs, or ambitions.

Humanist educators and Jesuit colleges had somewhat tempered the severity of that pedagogical system, but in 1693, when Locke published *Some Thoughts*, schooling was still a coercive regime. A former teacher himself—he had been tutor to Shaftesbury's grandson—and an ardent believer in personal liberty and the malleability of the human mind (malleable because it contains no innate ideas, but only those constructed by the individual's experience), Locke offers a new vision of education: one centered on the child. If schooling is to be a success, that success measured not so much by academic attainment as by the personal virtues, qualities, and competencies of the graduate, the child's nature and abilities must be central to the plan of instruction. Locke's views on the elementary education of children might be described today as "progressive," and many of his recommendations are operative in some of our finest schools.

Some Thoughts is a substantial work, twice as long as the *Letter on Toleration* and half the length of either the *Second Treatise* or *Human Understanding*. It follows the rearing of the child from infancy, when issues of health and nutrition are paramount, to early education and moral direction, to advanced instruction in languages, mathematics, history, and philosophy, topped off by music, fencing, and painting. The young child is the hero of this epic, completing Locke's view of the human person: a being endowed with absolute freedom, who generates his own ideas by the operations of his own mind, and who becomes what he will be not because of privileged birth or external constraint, but because he is guided "in the right way of knowing and improving himself"; and he will learn Latin "when he has a mind to do so."

In Locke's works considered up to this point, he is a revolutionary, opposing coercion in the realm of religion, identifying natural liberty as the necessary foundation of human political association, asserting the capacity of the human mind unaided by any other factor to generate and formulate ideas, and arguing for the education of the child respectful of his essential freedom and character. But in his *Reasonableness of Christianity*, while Locke avoids doctrinal disputation and denominational claims, which do not interest him, he turns to the Bible as the indispensable source of all truth—a truth that aligns well with contemporary Protestant theology. Any student of Locke's work will need to reconcile his evident orthodoxy, which he insists accords with reason, with his groundbreaking philosophy.

That orthodoxy was beginning to break down in other precincts of the Enlightenment. Scholasticism, the philosophical system established in the European universities from the twelfth century forward, rested on Aristotelian metaphysics and logic, and so achieved the marriage of Christian theology and reason. The cosmos, human society, and the articles of faith were all understood to be fundamentally rational. But with the dismantling of Aristotelianism, and with it scholasticism, by such thinkers as Bacon and Descartes, the gate was thrown open to skepticism and even atheism.

Overtly atheistic works had begun to circulate in the seventeenth century, among them the anonymous *Theophrastus redivivus*, which reappeared in the clandestine eighteenth-century tract *The Three Imposters*—those three being Moses, Muhammad, and Jesus, the principal figures of the three world theisms. John Toland's *Christianity Not Mysterious*, published in 1696, a year after Locke's *Reasonableness*, denied the divinity of Christ and outlined the essentials of deism, which dispensed with theological complexities while viewing God neutrally as Creator or Supreme Being. The metaphysics of Spinoza and implicit metaphysics of Newton had certainly pointed in that direction: by identifying God with nature, Spinoza reconfigured the deity as an impersonal, universal substance; and Newton, who remained a believer, in designing a self-generating and self-governing cosmos, effectively relegated the Christian God to the sidelines.

Amid these discussions, Locke asserts in his *Reasonableness of Christianity*, published in 1695, both the sovereignty of God and the identity of Jesus Christ as Messiah, or Savior. Lest anyone doubt his commitment to those assertions, argued at length in a treatise nearly as sprawling as *Some Thoughts Concerning Education*, he affirms it in two subsequent works: *A Vindication of the Reasonableness of Christianity* (1695), and *A Second Vindication of the Reasonableness of Christianity* (1697). To these may be added his four letters on toleration, of which the first has already been discussed, and his treatise on the epistles of Paul, completed shortly before his death in 1704. All these amount to an imposing body of largely orthodox religious thought by this avatar of

Enlightenment. Although many scholars prefer to ignore Locke's religious views, Locke is no deist and no atheist—however much he may have shared the antitrinitarian notions of his friend Isaac Newton, or wandered from the strict Puritanism of his youth or nominal Anglicanism of his maturity.

Locke's complex yet consistent vision of human personhood is composed from the different perspectives of politics, religion, philosophy, psychology, and pedagogy. That person, in sum, is a being who is absolutely free in mind, soul, body, and conscience, not to be deprived of that essential freedom by any external power—and a being who is assured of salvation by the death and resurrection of Jesus the Messiah.

The chief·criterion of the True Church

John Locke, *Letter on Toleration* (1689)

Locke's brief treatise on toleration, running ninety-three pages in its original 1689 Latin edition, presented in the form of a letter by an anonymous author to an unspecified addressee, was immediately translated into Dutch, French, and English, and won instant renown. Written at a time rife with religious wars, revolutions, expulsions, and persecutions, his message was welcome. The liberty of conscience he postulates in this, his first published work, will echo as well in his later works on civil government, the nature of the human mind, and education.

In the excerpts that follow from the opening pages of the *Letter*, Locke asserts in muscular prose the objections to coercion in matters of faith, and delineates the proper relations between state and church. The state, he argues, must tend to its own mission to guard the rights and property of its citizens, and may exert no coercive power over conscience. The freedom of the individual in matters of religion is absolute. All beliefs—with certain exceptions, among them Catholics (in the service, in effect, of a foreign government, that of the pope) and atheists (as the denial of the existence of God undermines human morality and community)—must be tolerated.

LETTER ON TOLERATION

Honored Sir,

Since you have asked what I thought about the mutual toleration by Christians of other Christians, I respond in brief that I hold such toleration to be the chief criterion of the True Church. However much some point to the ancient sacred places and lofty titles or liturgical splendor of their church, and others to the strict reformation of theirs, while all boast of the correct teachings of theirs (since all hold that their own beliefs are correct); these claims and others like them concern the human quest for power and struggle for dominion, and not the church of Christ. Those who lay claim to any of these yet lack charity, or mercy, or goodwill toward all humankind, even to those who are not Christian, are not really Christians themselves. . . . True religion exists for a different purpose: not for outward pomp, not for ecclesiastical domination, certainly not for the coercion of others, but so that we may lead lives of righteousness and piety. . . .

. . .

I call now upon the conscience of those who, pretending to act from kindly and friendly motives, under pretext of religion abuse, torment, despoil, and slaughter their victims. . . . For if, as they claim, it is from charity and concern for the souls of their victims that these persecutors expropriate their property, starve and torture them in loathsome prisons, and even rob them of life, in order to make them faithful Christians and win their salvation—why then do they permit whoring, fraud, malice, and other vices that they know were the shameless practices of the pagans, . . . to multiply unpunished in our midst?

   This behavior, and other such doings, are more opposed to the glory of God, the purity of the church, and the salvation of souls, than any kind of wayward but conscientious belief that is contrary to ecclesiastical norms, or any impropriety in the practice of worship, committed by a person of otherwise upright life. Why then, I ask, does this zeal for God, for the church, and for the salvation of souls—a zeal that burns as hot as the fire that consumes live victims at the stake—pass by those vices and crimes absolutely contrary to Christian principles and belief without correction or condemnation, while it eagerly exerts all its strength either to proliferate new ceremonies or to pronounce opinions, especially those of such great subtlety that they are impenetrable by ordinary people. . . .

. . .

The toleration of those who think differently in matters of religion accords both with reason and the Gospel to such an extent that, as though they had seen some apparition, those viewing its truth would be blinded by its bright light. . . . But lest any disguise their unchristian taste for persecution and cruelty as solicitude for the state and respect for its laws, or lest others, in the name of religion, seek impunity for their crimes and vices, . . . I urge first and foremost that a distinction be made between civil and religious matters, and the boundaries between church and state strictly defined. If this is not done, there will be no end of strife between those who genuinely cherish—or who pretend to cherish—either the salvation of souls or the well-being of the state.

As I see it, the state is a human association established solely for the preservation and promotion of civil goods, or rights. I designate those civil goods to be life, liberty, bodily soundness and safety, and the possession of external things, such as land, money, furnishings, and so on.

It is the duty of the civil magistrate, by laws fairly applied to all, to preserve intact the just possession of those things pertaining to this life belonging to all the people in general and each private person in particular. Those who attempt to violate what is just and right are to be restrained by fear of punishment, that punishment to consist in the deprivation or diminution of those civil goods that they would otherwise be entitled and able to enjoy. But since no one willingly surrenders any part of his property, let alone his liberty or his life, the magistrate, therefore, is armed with sufficient force, amounting to the total strength of the whole people, to inflict punishment on those who violate the rights of others.

Given, though, that these civil goods are the sole object of the magistrate's whole jurisdiction, and that the whole of civil power, its justice and authority, is limited and bound to the sole purpose of their protection and advancement, then civil power must not and cannot in any way be extended to the salvation of souls, as the following arguments seem to me to demonstrate.

First, the care of souls is not committed to the civil magistrate any more than to any other person. It is certainly not committed to him by God—because God never gave to any persons any authority of this sort over others, by which they might force others to embrace their own religion. Nor can such power in any way be granted by the people to the magistrate, because no one can so forfeit the care of his own eternal salvation to any other person, whether prince or subject, to prescribe what belief or mode of worship he must necessarily embrace—because no one can, even if he wished to do so, believe what has been prescribed by another, since the force and efficacy of true and salvific[1] religion consists only in faith. . . .

Second, the care of souls cannot be the province of the civil magistrate, because the whole of his power consists in coercion. But true and salvific religion consists in the faith that lives within the soul, without which faith nothing is acceptable to God. And such is the nature of the human mind, that no external force can coerce it to believe. Confiscation of property, imprisonment, or torture—these tools are used in vain if you seek by them to change what the mind holds to be true. . . .

Third, the care of souls can in no way be the province of the civil magistrate, because even if the authority of law and the threat of punishment were able to change people's minds, this in no way affects the salvation of souls. For if there be but one true religion, one way that leads us to heaven, what

---

1. Salvific: capable of bringing salvation.

hope is there that more people might reach that end if this condition were given to mortals: that they must set aside the dictate of their conscience and of reason and blindly embrace the teachings of their rulers, and worship God in the way that was set down by the laws of the land? Amid the multitude of princes and great diversity of religious views, the way that leads to heaven would become necessarily strait, and the gate narrow, and few would enter there,[2] and only in a single region! And—which is especially absurd and an insult to God—eternal felicity or damnation to hell would depend entirely on where one happened to have been born. . . .

. . .

Nobody, therefore—not individuals, nor churches, nor even states—can have any right to trespass upon the civil goods of any other person, or to expropriate any person's earthly goods, under pretext of religion. I ask those who think otherwise to consider what an infinity of provocations for war and strife they give thereby to humankind, what a huge incitement to rapine and slaughter and undying hatred. Nor can peace and security ever be established and maintained, nor any kind of human solidarity, if this view prevails: that God approves of domination, and that religion is to be spread by force of arms. . . .

Freedom from any superior power on earth

John Locke, *Second Treatise on Civil Government* (1689)

In his *Second Treatise on Civil Government,* Locke crafts a novel vision of the origins of a government responsible to the citizens who create it. The passages excerpted provide a skeletal account of his argument.

Each individual, in the "state of nature" (the original condition of human beings on the earth before societies and states took form), is entirely undetermined and free to live according to the "law of nature" (reason itself). Paramount among those freedoms is the ability to acquire property through one's own labor: that labor is "mixed" with the object upon which it is exerted, and so removes it from the "commons" (what is owned in common by all, as everything originally was in the state of nature) and "annexes" the product to the laborer. But humans, being what they are, seize as much property as

---

2. Cf. Matthew 7:14 (KJV): "Because strait is the gate, and narrow is the way, which leadeth unto life, and few there be that find it." All biblical citations in this section are from the Authorized (King James) Version.

possible, invading at will the property of others, and so fall into a "state of war," a chaotic and dangerous condition that makes it impossible for them to exercise, and perhaps to retain, their natural freedom.

In response, some number of them may surrender their natural liberty to join together in a society, or community, and thereby form civil government: a "body politic" or "commonwealth" (the English term used for "republic" or "state"). That commonwealth may have a governor, who must obey the laws enacted by the legislative power, which is the power exerted by the persons, or through their representatives, who had joined together as a political community. If the legislative power acts against the interests of the people, it may be dissolved; and if the governor abuses his power and disobeys the law, he is a tyrant, and may be deposed. These are the outlines Locke proposes of a properly instituted civil government that is responsible to the people as a whole, and assigned to protect the freedom that they retain even upon entering into society.

SECOND TREATISE OF CIVIL GOVERNMENT

CHAPTER 2: the state of nature

SECTION 4

To understand political power rightly, and derive it from its original, we must consider what state all people are naturally in; and that is, a state of perfect freedom to order their actions and dispose of their possessions and persons as they think fit, within the bounds of the law of nature, without asking permission or depending upon the will of any other person.

. . .

SECTION 6

But though this is a state of liberty, yet it is not a state of license. A person in the state of nature has an uncontrollable liberty to dispose of his person or possessions, yet he has not the liberty to destroy himself—or so much as any creature in his possession, unless some nobler use than its bare preservation calls for it. The state of nature has a law of nature to govern it, which obliges every one: and reason, which is that law, teaches all humankind, if they will only consult it, that in that all are equal and independent, no one ought to harm another in his life, health, liberty, or possessions. . . .

. . .

CHAPTER 3: the state of war

SECTION 16

The state of war is a state of enmity and destruction: and therefore declaring by word or action not a passionate and hasty, but a sedate settled design upon another person's life, puts him in a state of war with that person against whom he has declared such an intention, . . . for one may destroy someone who makes war upon him, . . . for the same reason that he may kill a wolf or a lion. . . .

. . .

SECTION 21

To avoid this state of war, . . . apt to break out upon every little difference, as there is no authority to decide between the contenders, is one great reason for people to put themselves into society, and quit the state of nature. For where there is an authority, a power on earth, from which relief can be had by appeal, there the continuance of the state of war is excluded, and the controversy is decided by that power. . . .

. . .

CHAPTER 4: of slavery

SECTION 22

The natural liberty of the human being is to be free from any superior power on earth, and not to be under the will or legislative authority of any person, but to have only the law of nature for his rule. The liberty of the human being in society is to be under no other legislative power but that established, by consent, in the commonwealth; nor under the dominion of any will, or restraint of any law, but what that legislative [power] shall enact. . . . Freedom then is . . . a liberty to follow my own will in all things, where no rule dictates otherwise; and not to be subject to the inconstant, uncertain, unknown, arbitrary will of another person. . . .

. . .

CHAPTER 5: of property

. . .

SECTION 27

Though the earth, and all inferior creatures, are common to all men, yet every individual has a property in his own person: this nobody has any right to but himself. The labor of his body and the work of his hands, . . . are properly his. Whatever he removes, then, out of the state that nature has provided and left it in, he has mixed his labor with it, and joined to it something that is his own, and thereby makes it his property. In that it is removed by this individual from the common state that nature has placed it in, by this individual's labor it has had something annexed to it that excludes the common right of other persons. . . .

. . .

SECTION 32

But the chief matter of property to be discussed now is not the fruits of the earth, and the beasts that subsist on it, but the earth itself. . . . I think it is plain that such property in land is acquired in the same way. As much land as a person tills, plants, improves, cultivates, and can use the product of, so much is his property. By his labor, as it were, he encloses it, or fences it off, from the common.[3] . . .

God, when he gave the world in common to all humankind, commanded each person also to labor . . . and subdue the earth, that is, improve it for the benefit of life; and to do so, he must expend something upon it that was his own—his labor. That person who, in obedience to this command of God, subdued, tilled, and sowed any part of it, thereby annexed to it something that was his property, which another had no title to, nor could take from him without causing injury.

. . .

CHAPTER 8: of the beginning of political societies

SECTION 95

Humans being, as has been said, by nature, all free, equal, and independent, no one can be put out of this condition, and subjected to the political power of another, without his own consent. The only way whereby any one person divests himself of his natural liberty and puts on the bonds of civil society is by agreeing with other people to join and unite into a community for their

---

3. In England, open lands that could be used by all members of a community for grazing livestock or gleaning were called "commons"; but from the late Middle Ages, landlords had increasingly "enclosed" parts of the common land, attaching them to their own estates. Locke here observes and does not condemn that process.

comfortable, safe, and peaceable living together, in a secure enjoyment of their properties, and a greater security against any who are not part of that community. This any number of persons may do, causing no injury to the freedom of the rest; they are left as they were, in the liberty of the state of nature. When any number of persons have so consented to make one community, or government, they are thereby consequently incorporated as one body politic, in which the majority have a right to act and bind the rest.

. . .

SECTION 97

And thus each person, by consenting with others to make one body politic under one government, puts himself under an obligation to every one of that society to submit to the determination of the majority, and to be bound by it. Otherwise, this original compact, whereby he incorporates with others into one society, would signify nothing—and would not be a compact at all, but he would be left free and under no other ties than he was in before in the state of nature. . . .

. . .

CHAPTER 9: of the ends of political society and government

SECTION 123

If a person in the state of nature is so free, as has been said; if he is absolute lord of his own person and possessions, equal to the greatest, and subject to nobody, why will he part with his freedom? Why will he give up this empire, and subject himself to the dominion and control of any other power? To which the answer is obvious: that though in the state of nature he has such a right, yet the enjoyment of it is very uncertain, and constantly exposed to the invasion of others. . . . That insecurity makes him willing to quit a condition which, however free, is full of fears and continual dangers: and it is not without reason that he seeks out, and is willing to join in society with others who are already united, or have a mind to unite, for the mutual preservation of their lives, liberties, and possessions, which I call by the general name, property.

. . .

SECTION 131

But though people, when they enter into society, give up the equality, liberty, and executive power they had in the state of nature, into the hands of the society, . . . the power of the society, or legislative [power] constituted by them, can never be supposed to extend farther than the common good. . . . And so whoever has the legislative or supreme power of any commonwealth is bound to govern by established standing laws, promulgated and known to the people . . . ; by impartial and upright judges, who are to decide controversies by those laws. . . . And all this is to be directed to no other end, but the peace, safety, and public good of the people.

. . .

CHAPTER 18: of tyranny

SECTION 199

As usurpation is the exercise of power that another has a right to, so tyranny is the exercise of power beyond right, which nobody can have a right to. And this is making use of the power anyone has in his hands not for the good of those who are under it, but for his own private separate advantage. When the governor, whatever his title, makes not the law, but his will the rule; and his commands and actions are not directed to the preservation of the properties of his people but to the satisfaction of his own ambition, revenge, covetousness, or any other irregular passion.

. . .

SECTION 202

Wherever law ends, tyranny begins . . . ; and whoever in authority exceeds the power given him by the law, and makes use of the force he has under his command to impose upon the subject what is not allowed by law, ceases on that account to be a magistrate; and . . . may be opposed as any other person would be who by force invades the right of another. . . .

. . .

CHAPTER 19: of the dissolution of government

. . .

SECTION 243

To conclude. The power that every individual gave the society, when he entered into it, can never revert to the individuals again as long as the society lasts, but will always remain in the community; . . . so also when the society has placed the legislative [power] in any assembly of persons, . . . the legislative [power] can never revert to the people while that government lasts. . . . But if they have . . . made this supreme power in any person, or assembly, only temporary; or else, when by the miscarriages of those in authority it is forfeited; upon the forfeiture, or at the determination of the time set, it reverts to the society, and the people have a right to act as supreme and continue the legislative [power] in themselves; or erect a new form; or under the old form place it in new hands, as they think good.

A white paper, with nothing written on it

John Locke, *Essay Concerning Human Understanding* (1689)

Locke establishes in the first book of the *Essay Concerning Human Understanding* that there are no innate ideas. In the second, from which are taken the excerpts given here, he explains how ideas arrive in the mind. The mind is only a "white paper," or "blank slate," on which ideas are written. The ideas arrive from external stimuli, either from the observation of external objects perceived by the senses, or by internal operations, in which the mind processes what information it has gathered and derives new ideas from that activity. The first process is sensation, from which simple ideas are formed; the other is reflection, by which simple ideas are assembled into complex ones. These two are the whole, complete, and only source of the ideas that exist in the mind. This model of the operation of the mind aggrandizes the individual, whose mental life belongs wholly to him, and undetermined by any other structure or force, may develop in complete freedom.

The section titles given here appear in the original as marginal tags.

Essay Concerning Human Understanding

Book 2

CHAPTER 1: OF IDEAS IN GENERAL, AND THEIR ORIGIN

Section 1: idea is the object of thinking

Each person is aware of his own thinking; and while he is thinking, that which his mind is intent on being the ideas contained within it, it is undoubtedly the case that people have in their minds several ideas, such as are those expressed by the words whiteness, hardness, sweetness, thinking, motion, man, elephant, army, drunkenness, and others. It is in the first place then to be inquired, how do they come by these ideas? It has long been assumed that people have innate ideas . . . stamped upon their minds from their very birth. This opinion I have, . . . examined already . . . in the previous book, and what I said there will be much more easily admitted, when I have shown from where the understanding may get all the ideas it has, and by what ways and degrees they may come into the mind, for which I shall appeal to each person's own observation and experience.

Section 2: all ideas come from sensation or reflection

Let us then suppose the mind to be, as we say, white paper,[4] with nothing written on it, without any ideas; how then are they supplied? How does the mind acquire that vast store of ideas which the busy and boundless human imagination has painted on it, with an almost endless variety? How does it acquire all the materials of reason and knowledge? To this I answer, in one word, from experience, on which all our knowledge is founded, and from which it ultimately derives all it knows. Our observation of external objects perceived by our senses, or of the internal operations of our minds perceived by our reflecting upon them, supplies our understandings with all the materials of thinking. These two kinds of observation are the fountains of knowledge from which spring all the ideas we have or can naturally have.

Section 3: the objects of sensation one source of ideas

By the first of these, our senses, applied to particular objects, convey into the mind several distinct perceptions of things, according to the various ways in which those objects affect them, and thus we come by those ideas we have of yellow, white, heat, cold, soft, hard, bitter, sweet, and all those which we call "sensible qualities." . . . This great source of most of the ideas we have, depending wholly upon our senses, and communicated by them to the understanding, I call SENSATION.

Section 4: the operations of our minds, the other source of them

Secondly, the other fountain from which experience supplies the understanding with ideas, is the perception of the operations of our own mind within us, as the mind processes the ideas it has acquired. These operations, when the soul reflects on and considers them, supply the understanding with another

---

4. The term "white paper" expresses in English the concept of the mind as a "blank slate," or *tabula rasa*, which originated with Plato and Aristotle and was used by scholastic philosophers.

set of ideas, which could not be had from external objects—among them perception, thinking, doubting, believing, reasoning, knowing, willing, and all the different actions of our own minds. When we become conscious of these and observe them operating in ourselves, we receive them into our understandings as distinct ideas, just as we form distinct ideas of external bodies affecting our senses.

This source of ideas everyone has wholly within himself; and though it is not sense, having nothing to do with external objects, yet it is very like it, and might properly enough be called "internal sense." But as I call the other source of ideas SENSATION, so I call this one REFLECTION, since the ideas it provides are those the mind obtains only by reflecting on its own operations within itself. By REFLECTION then . . . I mean that notice that the mind takes of its own operations, and how it performs them . . . , by which there come to be ideas of these operations in the understanding.

These two, I affirm—external material things, as the objects of SENSATION; and the operations of our own minds within us, as the objects of REFLECTION— are to me the only sources from which all our ideas take their beginnings. . . .

Section 5: all our ideas are of the one or of the other of these

The understanding seems to me not to have the least glimmering of any ideas that it does not receive from one of these two. External objects supply the mind with the ideas of sensible qualities, which are all those different perceptions they produce in us: and the mind supplies the understanding with ideas of its own operations.

Those, when we have taken a full survey of them and their several modes, combinations, and relations, we shall find to contain all our whole stock of ideas; and that we have nothing in our minds which did not come in one of these two ways. . . .

Let your rules be as few as possible

John Locke, *Some Thoughts Concerning Education* (1693)

Locke had been himself a teacher, the tutor to the grandson of his patron and close associate Lord Shaftesbury, and later offered advice to his friend Sir Edward Clarke of Chipley on the rearing of his children, addressing to him a prefatory letter to *Some Thoughts Concerning Education*. In that work, Locke's assumption of the essentially free condition of the human soul evokes a new pedagogy, while his vision of the human mind as a "blank slate," or "white paper" on which, at the outset, nothing is written, reinforces the importance of education. Since nothing is innate, education is everything; or, as he puts it, "the difference to be found in the manners and abilities of human beings is owing more to their education than to anything else."

Locke's program begins with infancy and continues through advanced studies and social skills. But the excerpts selected here deal with the early development of the child, and draw on discussions in Locke's broader philosophy. As each individual must develop his own abilities to withstand hardship and temptation, and develop a sound moral character, his essential nature and original freedom must be allowed to operate. The child will not learn by coercion, and certainly not by the prod of corporal punishment, a practice nearly universal in the schoolrooms of this era. Rules, as well, are useless; rather, a child should be guided to practice the right thing to do, and so by repetition come to make desirable behavior automatic, requiring no memorization of dictates and punishments. Learning to read, in contrast, which many see as the chief end of education, though it is important, should not be rushed. The child should be invited to find amusement in reading, which ideally will be "made a play and recreation" that he will be eager to pursue.

Some Thoughts Concerning Education

§ 32. . . . The difference to be found in the manners and abilities of human beings is owing more to their education than to anything else; thus great care is to be had of the forming children's minds, and giving them that preparation early which shall influence their lives ever afterwards. . . .

§ 33. As the strength of the body lies chiefly in being able to endure hardships, so also does that of the mind. And the great principle and foundation of all virtue and worth is placed in this, that a person is able to deny himself his own desires, cross his own inclinations, and purely follow what reason directs as best, though the appetite lean the other way.

. . .

§ 47. The usual lazy and quick form of chastisement, which is the rod,[5] the only instrument of government that tutors generally know or ever think of, is the most unfit of any to be used in education. . . .

§ 48. 1. This kind of punishment contributes not at all to the mastery of our natural propensity to indulge corporal and present pleasure, and to avoid

---

5. The "rod" stands for any of the number of instruments premodern schoolteachers used to discipline students, including also sticks and whips.

pain at any rate; but it rather encourages it; and thereby strengthens that in us which is the root from which all vicious actions spring. . . .

§ 50. 3. Such a sort of slavish discipline makes a slavish temper. The child submits, and dissembles obedience while the fear of the rod hangs over him; but when that is removed, and by being out of sight he can promise himself impunity, he unleashes his natural inclination; which by this way is not at all altered, but on the contrary heightened and increased in him; and after such restraint, breaks out usually with the more violence. Or,

§ 51. 4. If severity carried to the highest pitch does prevail, and works a cure upon the present unruly behavior, it often replaces that behavior with a worse and more dangerous disease, by breaking the mind; . . . and then, in the place of a disorderly young fellow, you have a low-spirited dejected creature . . . [who] . . . will be, all his life, a useless thing to himself and others.

§ 52. Beating then, and all other sorts of slavish and corporal punishments, are not the discipline fit to be used in the education of those who would raise wise, good, and [honorable] adults: and therefore very rarely to be applied, and that only on great occasions and cases of extremity. . . .

. . .

§ 64. And here permit me to take notice of one thing I think a fault in the ordinary method of education; and that is, the charging of children's memories, upon all occasions, with rules and precepts, which they often do not understand, and are constantly no sooner given than forgotten. . . .

§ 65. I have seen parents so heap rules on their children that it was impossible for the poor little ones to remember a tenth part of them, much less to observe them. . . . Let your rules, therefore, . . . be as few as is possible, and rather fewer than more than seem absolutely necessary. . . .

§ 66. But please remember, children are not to be taught by rules, which will be always slipping out of their memories. What you think necessary for them to do, implant in them by an indispensable practice, as often as the occasion returns; and, if it is possible, make occasions. This will create in them habits which, being once established, operate of themselves easily and naturally, without the assistance of the memory. . . .

. . .

§ 147. You will wonder, perhaps, that I put learning last, especially if I tell you I think it the least important part of education. This may seem strange in the mouth of a bookish man; and since this is usually the chief, if not the only bustle and stir about the rearing of children, this being almost the only thing that comes to mind when people talk about education, makes of my position the greater paradox. . . .

"What then, say you, would you not have him write and read?" . . . Not so, not so fast, I beseech you. Reading, and writing, and learning, I allow to be necessary, but yet not the chief business of education. . . .

§ 148. When the child can talk, it is time he should begin to learn to read. But as to this, permit me to emphasize here what is very apt to be forgotten, which is that great care is to be taken that reading never be made an obligation to him, nor that he look on it as a task. We naturally, as I said, even from our cradles, love liberty, and have therefore an aversion to many things, for no other reason, but because they are commanded. I have always wished that learning might be made a play and recreation to children, and that they might be brought to desire to be taught if it were proposed to them as a matter of honor, credit, delight, and recreation, or as a reward for doing something else, and if they were never scolded or corrected for neglecting it. . . .

§ 149. Thus children may be cajoled into learning the letters, and be taught to read without perceiving it to be anything but a sport, and so play themselves into doing that which others are whipped for. . . .

. . .

§ 195. This is, in short, what I have thought concerning a young gentleman's studies. . . . To conclude this part, . . . his tutor should remember that his business is not so much to teach him all that is knowable as to raise in him a love and esteem of knowledge; and to guide him in the right way of knowing and improving himself, when he has a mind to do so. . . .

From death, Jesus Christ restores all to life

John Locke, *The Reasonableness of Christianity, as Delivered in the Scriptures* (1695)

Oddly, as some might feel who construe the Enlightenment as tending to deism or atheism, Locke was a believing Christian, as he demonstrates amply in his own words. In *The Reasonableness of Christianity*, extracting proof texts from both Old and New Testament, he expounds such key Christian doctrines as the fall of man; original sin; justification by faith; the miracles, mission, and resurrection of Jesus; and the latter's identification as the

Messiah, or Savior. His arguments, fully consonant with contemporary Protestant theology, are deeply informed by his reading of the Bible, and heavily colored especially by the epistles of the apostle Paul—which are the subject of the last book he wrote, completed shortly before his death in 1704.

Italicized headnotes are inserted by the editor for easier legibility of Locke's exposition.

THE REASONABLENESS OF CHRISTIANITY

. . .

The fall from grace of Adam, the first man created by God, is the first step toward understanding the Christian doctrine of redemption.

It is obvious to anyone who reads the New Testament that the doctrine of redemption, and consequently of the Gospel, is founded upon the supposition of Adam's fall.[6] To understand, therefore, what we are restored to by Jesus Christ, we must consider what the scriptures show we lost by Adam. . . .

What Adam fell from was the state of perfect obedience, which is called justice, or righteousness, in the New Testament. . . . And by this fall, he lost paradise, a place offering tranquility and containing the tree of life; which is to say, he lost the state of bliss and the possibility of immortality. . . .

. . .

Adam being thus turned out of paradise, and all his posterity condemned to be born outside of it, the consequence was that all persons should die, and remain subject to death forever, and so be utterly lost.

From this condition of death, Jesus Christ restores all humankind to life; as the apostle Paul writes: "For as in Adam all die, even so in Christ shall all be made alive." How this comes to be, the same apostle tells us in the previous verse: "For since by man came death, by man came also the resurrection of the dead."[7] From which it appears that the life that Jesus Christ restores to all humankind is the same as that life that they receive again at the resurrection. Then they recover from death, which otherwise all humankind should have continued under, lost forever. . . .

. . .

For Christians, sin is the breaking of God's commandments, by which sin all are condemned to death, as Adam had been when expelled from Paradise.

---

6. Adam's fall from grace: his expulsion from the Garden of Eden for having disobeyed God's command, recounted in Genesis 3:17–21.

7. 1 Corinthians 15:22 and 21 (KJV).

But yet, "all have sinned, and come short of the glory of God," that is, the kingdom of God in heaven, . . . so that, "by the deeds of the law," no one could be justified, it follows, that no one could then have eternal life and bliss.[8]

Perhaps it will be demanded, "Why did God give so hard a law to mankind, that to the apostle's time no one of Adam's progeny had kept it? . . . Answer. It was such a law as the purity of God's nature required, and must be the law of such a creature as the human being. . . .

This then being the case, that whoever is guilty of any sin should certainly die and cease to be, the benefit of life, restored by Christ at the resurrection, would have been no great advantage—for as much as . . . death must have seized upon all humankind, because all have sinned, and the wages of sin is always death, after as well as before the resurrection—if God had not found out a way to justify some. That justification is granted to those who obey another law that God also gave, which in the New Testament is called "the law of faith," and is opposed to "the law of works."[9] . . .

. . .

The faith by which God justified Abraham, removing his sin and making him righteous, is offered to all; this is the Christian doctrine of justification by faith.

What was this faith, for which God justified Abraham? It was the believing in the promise God made in the covenant he made with Abraham. . . . By which it is clear, that the faith that God counted to Abraham as righteousness was nothing but a firm belief in what God declared to him, and a steadfast relying on him to accomplish what he had promised. . . .

The law of faith then, in short, is for everyone to believe what God requires him to believe, as a condition of the covenant he makes with him, and not to doubt that his promise will be fulfilled. . . . We must, therefore, examine and see what God requires us to believe now, as revealed in the Gospel. . . .

What then must Christians believe in order to be justified by faith? That Jesus is the son of God, and the Messiah, or Savior.

What we are now required to believe to obtain eternal life is plainly set down in the Gospel. The apostle John tells us that "he that believeth on the Son hath everlasting life: and he that believeth not the Son shall not see life."[10] . . .

---

8. Romans 3:23 and 20.
9. Cf. Romans 3:27.
10. John 3:36.

This statement makes plain that to believe in the Son, who is Jesus, is to believe that Jesus was the Messiah. . . . To convince people that he was the Messiah, Jesus did his miracles; and their acceptance of these, or their non-acceptance, made them to be, or not to be, of his church—believers, that is, or non-believers. . . . Plainly, then, the Gospel was written to convince people to believe this proposition, "That Jesus of Nazareth was the Messiah": which if they believed, they should have eternal life. . . .

And that he was the Messiah was the great truth of which he took pains to convince his disciples and apostles, appearing to them after his resurrection . . . [and commanding them] to teach all nations. . . .[11] We may observe that the preaching of the apostles everywhere, as reported in the book of Acts, tended to this one point: to prove that Jesus was the Messiah. Now indeed after his death, his resurrection was also commonly required to be believed as a necessary article, and sometimes solely insisted on: it being a mark and undoubted evidence of his being the Messiah. . . . And therefore those who believed him to be the Messiah, must believe that he was risen from the dead; and those who believed him to be risen from the dead, could not doubt of his being the Messiah. . . .

---

11. Matthew 28:19–20: "Therefore go and make disciples of all nations, baptizing them in the name of the Father and of the Son and of the Holy Spirit, and teaching them to obey everything I have commanded you."

Chapter Four

All Things Made New: 1725–1784

Introduction

The seventeenth-century metaphysicians and scientists refashioned the cosmos, detaching it from both the Aristotelian and the biblical frameworks in which it had long been situated. Now, as the Enlightenment unfolds, Europe's thinkers turn from the cosmos to the earth; from physical to biological nature; from metaphysical to human existence. In doing so, they construct new models to explain the human and terrestrial world that is now the object of their attentions.

In this chapter Giambattista Vico (1668–1744), professor of rhetoric at the University of Naples (Italy), envisions in his *New Science* the evolution and cyclical destruction of all civilizations, past, present, and future, driven by the mechanisms of their unique cultural traits. Offering in his *System of Nature* an equally vast depiction of the natural world, Swedish naturalist Carl Linnaeus (1707–1778)[1] organizes all living and non-living things (animal, vegetable, mineral) by class, order, genus, and species in one comprehensive system. The French economist Anne Robert Jacques Turgot (1727–1781), adopting Vico's vision of human progress from a nadir of original ignorance to a zenith of cultural achievement, but rejecting his pessimistic prediction of repeated civilizational failure, outlines in his 1750 discourse to the Sorbonne (University of Paris) the necessary successive advance of the human condition.

In his *Preliminary Discourse* to the famed *Encyclopedia*, of which more later, the French mathematician Jean le Rond d'Alembert (1717–1783), Turgot's contemporary and collaborator, proposes a comprehensive system of human knowledge as all-encompassing as the historical and biological paradigms offered by Vico and Linnaeus. In his essay *What Is Enlightenment?*, finally, the German philosopher Immanuel Kant (1724–1804) discerns a dramatic cleavage in human development, the point at which the modern age of Enlightenment departs radically from all prior ages. That cleavage occurs when an aware and literate public abandons its age-old dependence on the beliefs and reasoning of self-selected others to engage in rational inquiry and free discourse—and so ushers in the age of Enlightenment.

---

1. Latin Carolus; ennobled in 1761 with the name Carl von Linné.

Like Newton and Spinoza, Giambattista Vico, a man of modest origins and boundless intellectual ambitions, describes in *The New Science* (first published 1725; revised editions in 1730 and 1744) an entire universe: not that of the cosmos, but of human existence on Earth. Each human society, or Nation (adopting here and henceforth, for clarity, Vico's capitalization of significant nouns), cycles through a Course (*corso*) of three stages of development: the first, when emerging from the State of Nature (as envisioned by Hobbes, Locke, and other theorists), people live in awe of the gods; the second, when they are ruled by heroes, who claim a natural superiority to those who do their will; and the third, when humankind has become rational and constructs well-ordered political systems in which all are equal before the laws. But having reached this apex, the Nation becomes corrupt; individuals descend into selfishness and narcissism; the states totter and fall; and society collapses utterly in a Reversion (*ricorso*) to a primitive condition, from which an entirely new one will emerge. As each Nation matures, so too does its cultural, social, and political systems, which are all interrelated in a polyphonic system. The cycling of these societies is driven by human decisions freely made, not by chance or fate, and yet they inevitably follow the same pattern, as directed by divine Providence.

Vico's vision is remarkably original in its scope and in its complexity. His scope is limitless, as he subjects not just his own, but all civilizations to analysis—an approach he calls "philosophical." And the complexity of his historiographical approach, which he calls "philological," is entirely novel: whereas historians previously had celebrated great men or told the tales of war and conquest, Vico's new path is to track the social and ethnic variations among human communities and map the intersecting layers of human intellectual, cultural, and political activity.

Vico's influence during the Enlightenment was slight. His main impact came in the nineteenth century, when his work could be read in French and German translations, and his shadow fell on such thinkers as Hegel, Comte, and Marx. When Vico wrote early in the eighteenth century, the cultural dominance of Renaissance Italy had not yet entirely vanished, and many French, German, or English thinkers would have been able to access his work directly—were it not for the density, allusiveness, and, often, incoherence of his prose.[2] Nonetheless, it is clear that Herder knew his work, and there are echoes of his views in Montesquieu and Rousseau, among others. Surely, as well, Gibbon's colossal history of the *Decline and Fall of the Roman Empire*

---

2. I am not alone in this criticism: Vico's modern admirer Isaiah Berlin describes the rhetorician's style as "baroque, undisciplined, and obscure." *Vico and Herder: Two Studies in the History of Ideas* (New York: Viking, 1976), 3.

owed something to Vico's vision of a catastrophic *ricorso* that befalls even the most triumphant civilizations.

In 1687, Newton had announced that he would lay out the system of the world; and in 1725, Vico professed a similar ambition to explain the "new science" of all human existence on earth. Now the Swedish botanist Carl Linnaeus, proposed in his *System of Nature*, beginning in 1735 with the original edition of a mere ten printed pages, to explain the whole of God's creation, ordering the natural world in the three great kingdoms of mineral, vegetable, and animal, and in hundreds of subclassifications of Order, Genus, and Species. To each of these creatures, elaborating the binomial system of nomenclature still in use today, he affixed a pair of names: the first for Genus, the second for Species. Thus were born, as names, among thousands of others, *Hippopotamus amphibius* (the hippopotamus), *Canus familiaris* (the domesticated dog), and *Homo sapiens* (the human being). The last of these, the anatomically modern human, Linnaeus further subdivided into varieties, or racial categories, in a manner less acceptable to modern scientists, by superficial appearance and such psychological traits as "indolence" or "obstinacy." Such was the view from Enlightened Europe.

The small 1735 volume, consisting mostly of tightly printed taxonomic tables, is best known in its authoritative tenth (1758) and thirteenth (1789) editions, the latter reaching to three volumes and more than one thousand pages. Widely read, it made precise and comprehensive the earlier understanding of the order of created things, the "great chain of being" that reached from immobile masses of stone to the realm of the stars and God the Creator. It also paved the way for evolutionary theories that would soon appear, culminating in Charles Darwin's *Origin of Species* (1859) and *Descent of Man* (1871), which explained how all the creatures catalogued by Linnaeus came into being on earth.

Despite its success as a landmark of scientific thinking, Linnaeus' *System of Nature* has attracted recent criticism. In a post-evolutionary age in which the boundaries between peoples and sexes have become fluid, some critics lament the ruthless binaries of its classificatory method, and its built-in gender bias—apparent, for instance, in his identifying the class of mammals by the female breasts ("animals that suckle their young by means of lactiferous teats") and distinguishing the classes of plants by the number and type of their sexual organs. Such commentary would doubtless have struck Linnaeus as odd: as the pious descendant of Lutheran pastors in both paternal and maternal lines, his one aim was to celebrate the whole of God's creation.

By birth a member of the French Nobility of the Robe (a class that had acquired hereditary noble status through administrative service to the crown), Anne Robert Jacques Turgot, baron de l'Aulne, is best known as an economic liberal who had been mentored by proponents of *laissez-faire* principles. Both as a royal administrator and author, he opposed excessive regulation, advocated tax reform and deficit reduction, and sought wealth creation through free competition. But he also advanced original views on universal history, delivering in 1750, when he was a twenty-three-year-old student for the priesthood, an important speech on *The Successive Advancement of the Human Mind*. Given here almost in its entirety, it is considered to be the first major statement of the idea of progress that is a hallmark of the Enlightenment. Just as Vico's *New Science* and Linnaeus' *System of Nature* introduced entirely new conceptions of the human or natural world, Turgot here provides a new understanding of human history and possibility.

Like Vico, Turgot envisions all of history as "locked in a cycle of ever-recurrent events," such that everything perishes and is reborn only to perish again. But departing from the Vichian model, Turgot proposes that human beings, as exceptions in nature, rise above that system of inevitable cycles, and progress continuously if sometimes slowly in a broad range of endeavors: the arts and sciences, social relations, law, politics, and economics. Turgot's optimistic vision would come to characterize Enlightenment thought, and would culminate in Condorcet's masterwork, *A Sketch of a Historical Portrait of the Progress of the Human Mind* (1793–1794), discussed in Chapter Twelve.

Among Turgot's works were several contributions to the *Encyclopédie, ou dictionnaire raisonné des sciences, des arts et des métiers* (*Encyclopedia, Or Analytic Dictionary of the Sciences, Arts, and Trades*), the most ambitious intellectual product of the Enlightenment. Under the editorship of Denis Diderot (for whom see Chapter Ten) and, for the initial period 1752 to 1759, the joint editorship of Diderot with Jean le Rond d'Alembert, the *Encyclopedia* was published between 1751 and 1772. To the twenty-eight volumes that appeared by the latter date, more than one hundred authors had contributed a total of more than seventy thousand articles that circulated to thousands of subscribers in France and across Europe. Its goal was to present a new compendium, replacing those of the scholastic philosophers and baroque compilators, reflecting contemporary advances in knowledge not only in traditional fields, such as philosophy and rhetoric, but also of the natural sciences and practical and industrial arts.

In this effort, d'Alembert is a major participant, first as coeditor during its important first stage of publication; second as a contributor of some 1,400 articles; and finally, as the author (in consultation with collaborators) of its *Discours préliminaire* (*Preliminary Discourse*), or introduction, excerpted here. A sprawling discussion of more than fifty thousand words, the *Preliminary Discourse* outlines the new contours of knowledge for a secular age that had cast off not only the authority of the churches but even that of the once-revered Ancients, whose guiding principle was reason. In it, d'Alembert maps out all of human knowledge, grouped in the three classes of memory, reason, imagination, each further divided and subdivided to yield an entire tree of the contents of the human mind. His systematic scheme, summarized in a table occupying a single page of the *Encyclopedia*, resembles that of Linnaeus, who similarly employed tables to describe the complex "system of nature," with its interlocking gears of kingdoms, classes, orders, genera, and species.

The illegitimate son of a *salonnière* who refused to be burdened with an inconvenient child, d'Alembert was named after the church at whose door he was abandoned, later to be raised by a glassmaker's wife, at the expense of his absent father. Despite his obscure origins, he quickly distinguished himself as a mathematician and scientist, and was promoted by Parisian salon society to the position of prominence from which he could communicate the values of the Enlightenment that were embodied in the *Encyclopedia*, and prefigured in the *Preliminary Discourse*.

Enlightenment thinkers were often called, and called themselves, *philosophes* (French for "philosophers"), not because they all engaged in the usual pursuits of philosophy (metaphysics, ontology, epistemology, and so on), but because their method was "philosophical": empirical, that is, following Bacon; strictly reasoned, following Descartes; or demonstrated by "geometrical" proofs, following Spinoza and Newton. But Immanuel Kant, the fifth figure covered in this chapter, is to be considered a philosopher by the original definition of the term, and arguably the first and foremost of modern times. His principal theme of human autonomy is argued in, as elsewhere, his three monumental *Critiques*: the *Critique of Pure Reason* (1781, 1787), the *Critique of Practical Reason* (1788), and the *Critique of the Power of Judgment* (1790). The same message characterizes his essays, more informal in style, among them *Was ist Aufklärung?* (*What Is Enlightenment?*), published in 1784, and excerpted here.

Kant constructs in this essay no grand system of human history or knowledge, much less of all of nature, as had his predecessors Vico, d'Alembert, Turgot, and Linnaeus. But in seeking to understand the cultural shift that was then underway, he offers a new vision of human history, positing a great divide between the Enlightenment, an age of critical thought, and all that came before, an era of mental dormancy. As humankind advances from that earlier condition, it throws off its prior condition of dependency, in which others guided the thought and actions of all, to one of autonomy, where each person may think for himself. Far away from the tinkling salons of Paris inhabited by elites, Kant envisions the awakening—the *enlightening*—of a whole community, as each individual in turn is transformed and elevated to a new competence of mind and spirit. That advance can only occur in a context of political freedom, and requires the broad participation of a literate public. With this model, the first modern philosopher seems to prefigure the key features of modern Western civilization.

In the wilderness, they are reborn

Giambattista Vico, *The New Science* (1725/1730/1744)

The excerpts given here from book 4 and the conclusion of Vico's *New Science* illustrate his concept of the cycles through which all Nations run, from their origins to their dissolution. Those cycles traverse three stages: the first associated with the gods, when people see spirits at work everywhere; the second, with the heroes, rulers who consider themselves an "aristocracy," naturally superior to other humans; the third, the fully human, when people, having become rational, develop political systems responsive to law and equity. The chapters of book 4 describe these three stages in each of several categories of human culture, of which three are included here: "Nature" (meaning human nature, which for Vico varied over time), "Language," and "Government."

Following these exemplary sections is a paragraph from the conclusion presenting a description of the *ricorso* ("Reversion"), when an advanced Nation fails and its survivors seek refuge in the wilderness, returning to a primitive state from which the historical cycle may begin anew: "the survivors," Vico writes, "seeking to save themselves, flee to the wilderness; and there, like a phoenix, they are reborn." A final passage, which summarizes the whole historical cycle, argues that it is propelled not by chance or by fate, as other philosophers had proposed, but by human actions freely made within a divine providential system.

Given the complexity of Vico's prose, and the convolutions of his argument, some editorial interventions beyond the ordinary have been made. Transitional explanations are supplied in italics at the heads of sections. Capitalization of pivotal nouns (Course, Nation, Nature, Science, etc.) is preserved for clarity and expressiveness. Key terms such as "gentility" and "popular," which are retained as literal translations from the Italian in the standard 1948 English edition (see Texts and Studies), but have quite different resonances in modern English, are replaced with less distracting equivalents.

THE NEW SCIENCE

BOOK FOUR: The Course the Nations Run

The principles of this Science established . . . , and the divine and human origins of the Nations explained . . . , we shall now in this fourth book, illumined by this analysis both philosophical and philological, . . . outline the Course, or stages through which all Nations successively run, in all their variety and diversity, through the three ages . . . of gods, heroes, and humankind. . . .

THREE KINDS OF NATURE

By Nature, Vico means human nature or character, which evolved from an elementary stage when the imagination, rather than reason, predominated; to a "heroic" stage, whose leaders were convinced of their innate superiority and privilege to rule; to an "intelligent human" stage, which was rational and capable of moral action.

The first Nature was ruled by the imagination, which is strongest in those whose capacity for reasoning is weakest. It was a poetic nature, or rather creative, that could be called divine; for it attributed to physical bodies an essence animated by gods, assigning to each a different god expressive of its being. . . . This Nature was that of the theological poets, who in all the Nations were the first sages, as all the Nations were founded on the belief that each one had its own particular gods. It was, moreover, a fierce and cruel Nature; for led astray by their imagination, these early humans dreadfully feared the gods whom they themselves had created. . . .

The second was the heroic nature, the heroes believing themselves to be of divine origin . . . and possessing a natural nobility, seeing themselves . . . as the princes of the human race, and . . . vaunting themselves above the lesser, bestial, species of humankind. . . .

The third was intelligent human nature, on that account modest, benign and rational, guided by the laws of conscience, reason, and duty.

. . .

THREE KINDS OF GOVERNMENT

Paralleling the development of the Nature of human beings, the first types of government deferred to the authority of the gods, while the second was the government exercised by the "heroes," those who assumed a natural superiority over lesser, plebeian people in their midst. The third, in existence in Vico's day, is "properly human," and views all persons as equal under the law, whether the state in question is a city or a monarchy—for those were the two main state systems familiar to Vico in the European, and more particularly the Italian, domain.

The first kind of government was divine, or, as the Greeks would say, theocratic, based on the assumption that all authority came from the gods. . . .

The second kind of government was that of the heroes, an aristocratic government, or government by "the best," meaning in fact the strongest. . . . In this kind of government, because of their assumed natural nobility, . . . all civil functions were managed by the closed order of the heroes, and the plebeians, thought to be of bestial origin, were allowed only to live and indulge their natural instincts.

The third kind of government is properly human, in which, on account of the equality of that intelligent Nature that is the Nature particular to all humankind, all are equal under the laws, as all are born free in their cities . . . or in monarchies, where monarchs subject all equally to their laws. . . .

THREE KINDS OF LANGUAGES

In antiquity, Vico hypothesizes, there was no formal language, but only rites and ceremonies performed to enlist the benevolence of the gods. Among the heroes, equally, the actions of warriors were the main form of communication. But the language in use in Vico's time was a prose guided by reason, a fully developed "articulate speech."

. . .

The first of these was a divine mental language communicated by mute religious acts or ceremonies. . . . This language . . . was necessary in ancient times when humans did not yet have articulate speech.

The second language was that of heroic deeds, whereby military power acts as speech. . . .

The third language is that of articulate speech, which all the Nations use today.

. . .

CONCLUSION OF THIS WORK Concerning an Eternal Natural Republic, Achieving in Each Case the Highest State, Ordained by Divine Providence.

. . .

Vico describes the stages through which each society cycles—running its corso, *or Course—from a primitive bestiality to its highest political and cultural form; and then undergoes, as described here, a* ricorso, *or Reversion, an extreme remedy imposed by Providence when a society has become irreparably corrupted.*

But if these people fester in this final stage of civil disintegration, neither accepting one among their number as a ruler, nor succumbing to conquest by a stronger nation, then Providence imposes this ultimate remedy for their utter corruption: for . . . like wild animals, quarreling over nothing, they rage in fury, and . . . live like savage beasts in an utter solitude of mind and spirit . . . no two of them ever coming to agreement, but each following his own pleasure or whim. They then disperse into stubborn factions, and wage desperate civil wars that make forests of the cities, and wastelands of the forests. . . . And so these people . . . stunned and stupefied by this ultimate remedy imposed by Providence, no longer seek ease, delight, pleasure, and luxury, but only the basic necessities of life. Those few who survive . . . are restored to the primal simplicity of the earliest age of humankind, . . . and so to piety, faith, and truth, which are the natural foundations of justice, and are the blessings and splendors of God's eternal order.

. . .

It is not by chance, but by human actions freely chosen, as directed by divine Providence, that the cycle of nations unfolds.

Surely this plain and simple outline of the doings of all humankind . . . delineates the great city of Nations founded and governed by God. . . . While it is true that human beings themselves made this world of nations . . . , yet without a doubt it is the creation of a complex and paradoxical Mind ever superior to the particular purposes of human actions, whose small efforts it reshapes to serve the greater goal of preserving the human race upon this earth. For humans indulge their bestial lust, and abandon their offspring; in response, they institute chaste marriage, giving rise to the reign of families; of which the fathers, abusively exercising their power over their clients, cause the rise of cities; of which the ruling nobles, suppressing the plebeians, are compelled to obey the laws that are established to protect the liberty of the people; while the free people, chafing against the bridle of the laws they have made, are subjected to monarchs, who . . . cause them to be enslaved by stronger nations; whereupon the nations fail, and the survivors, seeking to save themselves, flee to the wilderness; and there, like a phoenix, they are reborn. What did all this was pure Mind, as it was done by human intelligence; it was not Fate, because it was done by free will; it was not Chance, because in perpetuity, from the same actions the same consequences result.

Without these Names, nothing can be known

Carl Linnaeus, *System of Nature* (1735)

The introduction that opens the expanded editions of Linnaeus' *System of Nature* begins with a rapturous hymn to God, the creator of all things, whose handiwork is evident in every natural body, animal, vegetable, or mineral.[3] There follows a series of definitions, from the greatest to the least, of the components of the natural world: the world, the stars, the four elements (as they were understood at the time) and their qualities, the earth, and all the bodies that inhabit its surface. Linnaeus then considers how nature can be known by human investigators. They apprehend objects, first, by their senses; and then they must name them, so as to distinguish each object or living thing from others that are similar. Without such naming, which is the whole purpose of Linnaeus' work, nothing can be known: "For if the Name of an object perishes, so also does all knowledge of it. These Names will be the alphabet without which no one may gain knowledge of Nature."

The author's use of capitalization, which is highly expressive, is retained.

THE SYSTEM OF NATURE

God everlasting, immense, omniscient, omnipotent—I awake, I see your presence and am astounded! I have seen your handiwork in all created things. . . . What wisdom! What imperishable perfection! I have seen the layering of Animals on Vegetables, and Vegetables on Minerals, and Minerals on the crust of the Earth . . . while Earth circles ceaselessly around the Sun, from which it takes its life; and the Sun spinning on its axis . . . , and the system of the Stars, indefinable in extent and number, held in motion and suspended in nothingness by an incomprehensible First Mover, the Being of all Beings, the Cause of all Causes, the keeper and guardian of the universe, the architect and master of the miracle of this world. . . .

The WORLD consists of all things . . . that can be known by our senses. It includes the Stars, the Elements, and the Earth itself. . . .

The STARS are remote, luminous bodies, that revolve in perpetual motion. They may be stars that radiate their own light, such as the Sun and the distant fixed stars; or planets, that reflect the light cast on them by the stars; of these the primary are Saturn, Jupiter, Mars, the Earth, Venus, and Mercury,[4] while the secondary ones revolve around them, such as the Moon around the Earth. . . .

---

3. Linnaeus' God-centered discussion of the purpose of his work is omitted, strikingly, from the standard seven-volume English edition of 1802–1806 (see Texts and Studies).

4. From the most distant to the nearest, the only planets known to Linnaeus.

The ELEMENTS are the simplest bodies, randomly dispersed in the atmosphere filling the spaces between the Stars, and have the following sets of qualities:

FIRE	Luminous	Resilient	Hot	Flaring	Vivifying
AIR	Transparent	Elastic	Dry	Encircling	Generating
WATER	Translucent	Fluid	Moist	Flowing	Conceiving
EARTH	Opaque	Fixed	Cold	Still	Sterile

Thus the whole World consists of qualities and their opposites, concord and discord.

The EARTH is a planetary sphere, rotating every twenty-four hours, and revolving around the sun once each year. It is enveloped in an atmosphere of Elements, and covered with a stupendous cortex of natural things, the understanding of which is the object of this study. . . .

NATURE is the immutable law of God, by which any thing is what it is, and does what it has been commanded to do. Nature, the builder of all things, by its own law, taught by no teacher, making no leaps, acting in silence, ensures that all is done properly, nothing done in vain, nothing in superfluity, giving each to each and all to all, seeking only order. . . .

NATURE consists of all the bodies on the Earth made by the hand of the Creator. . . .

- MINERALS are dense bodies, neither alive nor capable of sense.
- VEGETABLES are organic bodies, alive, but not capable of sense.
- ANIMALS are organic bodies, alive, capable of sense and of spontaneous movement. . . .

The three Kingdoms of Nature constituting the planet Earth, are accordingly these:

- The MINERAL, inhabiting the interior spaces of the Earth in formless masses, generated by particles randomly composed and configured.
- The VEGETABLE, clothing the Earth's surface in green, draw nourishment through thirsty roots, breathe the air with fluttering leaves, . . . and reproduce by dispersing their seed. . . .
- The ANIMALS, adorning the world, are sentient, breathe, and move freely, produce eggs by which they reproduce; they are motivated by hunger, pain, and the desire to mate; by preying on other animals and consuming vegetables, they control the populations of both.

TAXONOMIC TABLE of the Animal Kingdom (1735)

Linnaeus: Taxonomic Table of the Animal Kingdom (1735). Via Wikimedia.

HOMO SAPIENS,[5] the human being, the last, highest, and most perfect of created things that inhabit the surface of the Earth, protected by the stupendous signs of the Divine Majesty, by his intellect judging the handiwork of God's creation, and admiring its beauty, worships its Author. . . .

WISDOM, an attribute of the divine, is especially ascribed to Homo Sapiens, by which he rightly judges what his senses present to him. . . . The first step Wisdom takes is to know the thing itself, which is to apprehend its true Idea, which is distinguished from others by certain signs inscribed by the Creator. . . . So that this understanding may be communicated also to others, Wisdom assigns to each object a proper Name by which it will be distinguished from all others. For if the Name of an object perishes, so also does all knowledge of it. These Names will be the alphabet without which no one may gain knowledge of Nature.

METHOD, the soul of Knowledge, decrees that any natural body, at first sight, bespeaks its own distinctive Name, and this Name invokes all that has ever come to be known about it, such that, amid what seems to be a great confusion, the consummate order of Nature is discerned.

For the purpose of naming the things of Nature, this SYSTEM utilizes five divisions of natural things: they are Class, Order, Genus, Species, Variety. . . . The first action to be taken . . . by anyone seeking to gain knowledge of Nature is to inspect the object to be known, and according to its Genus, assign the name of its Species. The SCIENCE of Nature requires an exact knowledge of natural things and a corresponding systematic Nomenclature. . . .

. . .

All created things are the testimony of divine wisdom and power, and the foundation of human happiness. By their use the goodness of the Creator shines forth; from their beauty, the Wisdom of the Lord; from the governance of their preservation, number, and renewal, the power of his Majesty. Their investigation by ordinary persons is always estimable; by the truly wise and learned always honorable; by the crude and ignorant always regrettable.

. . .

❀ ❀ ❀

---

5. It appears that Linnaeus is the first to use this term (in the tenth edition of 1758) for the anatomically modern human being, utilizing the binomial (specifying genus and species) system of nomenclature of which he is inventor.

All the clouds at last are lifted

Anne Robert Jacques Turgot, *The Successive Advancement of the Human Mind* (1750)

At age twenty-three, while a student for the priesthood at the Sorbonne in Paris, on December 11, 1750, Turgot delivered a speech envisioning the unlimited progress of human civilization in the arts and sciences, law, politics, economics, and social relations. Unlike other species that are locked in the vise of cyclical recurrence, their fortunes systematically rising and falling, humans accumulate cultural achievements over the ages and so look to ever-increasing success. While much of his prose is rapturous and vague, Turgot specifies certain types of recent change that can be seen as harbingers of future accomplishment: the gradual maturation of political systems; the sudden and dramatic opportunities opened up by print technology; and the innovations of thinkers such as Galileo, Kepler, Bacon, Descartes, and Newton. Now that "all the clouds at last are lifted," even greater triumphs approach, for "the mutual dependence of all truths is discovered, which binds them all together so that each one illumines the other," and "though each day adds to the immensity of the sciences, each day renders them more comprehensible."

To assist the legibility of the text, transitional explanations are supplied in italics at the heads of paragraphs.

THE SUCCESSIVE ADVANCEMENT OF THE HUMAN MIND

Natural phenomena, obeying constant laws, are locked in a cycle of ever-recurrent events. All is reborn, all perishes; and in these successive generations, . . . time merely resuscitates, in each instant, the image of what it had caused to disappear.

The generations of humankind, in contrast, offer from age to age an always changing spectacle. Reason, the passions, freedom, unceasingly produce new occurrences. All ages are linked together by a sequence of causes and effects, which tie the present state of the world to all that came before. The manifold symbols of language and writing, allowing humans to preserve their ideas and communicate them to others, have made the knowledge that each separately acquires the common treasure of all, transmitted from one generation to the next as an inheritance ever enlarged by the discoveries of each new century. The human race, in consequence, to the eyes of a philosopher examining it from its origin, would seem one giant being, having itself, as does each single individual, its infancy and its development.

Societies are established, forming themselves into nations which in turn dominate others, or submit to them. Empires rise and fall; laws and governments follow upon each other; the arts and sciences are discovered and advanced, passing sometimes slowly, sometimes quickly, from place to place. Self-interest, ambition, the lust for glory constantly reshape of the world, flooding the earth with blood. Yet amid these ravages, manners improve; the human mind is enlightened; from their isolation, nations engage with each other; commerce and politics at last bring together all the regions of the globe; and the total mass of the human race, at times calmly, at others anxiously, in good times and in bad, marches ever forward, even if by small steps, to a greater perfection.

. . .

Turgot here reviews in general terms major political developments of the fifteenth to eighteenth centuries.

Different series of events unfold in the different countries of the world, and all tend finally, although by separate routes, toward the same goal: the restoration of the human spirit. For even in the dark night, one by one the stars appear. . . . At last, royal authority is seen to revive in France; the power of the people asserts itself in England; the Italian cities become republics in the likeness of ancient Greece; the small kingdoms of Spain, expelling the Moors, come together gradually as one. Soon the seas that had separated the nations, by the invention of the compass, now join them together. The Portuguese to the East, the Spanish to the West, discover new worlds. Finally, the universe is known. . . .

The printing press will bring enlightenment to all people and places.

What of that art born out of nowhere, seemingly to send flying off far and wide the writings and the glory of the great thinkers who are emerging? How slow in every way has progress been. For two thousand years, we have been able to read characters stamped on bronze medals—and only now, after so many centuries, some nobody has figured out that they can be stamped on paper! As soon as the treasures of antiquity, pulled from the dust, pass into every hand and reach into every corner, they will bring light to the intellects that have been lost in ignorance, and call forth genius from the depths of solitude. The time has come. Rise, Europe, from the night enshrouding you! . . .

A new age of intellectual exploration has begun, especially in the field of science. Turgot specifically notes the achievements of Galileo, Kepler, Bacon, Descartes, and Newton.[6]

---

6. Turgot also makes brief mention of the philosopher Leibniz, as Newton's rival; for whom, see the Introduction to Voltaire, Chapter 6.

Already the printing press has rescued from obscurity a multitude of facts, of experiences, of instruments, of ingenious methods that the practice of the arts has accumulated over the centuries. Already the products of two worlds that the immense power of commerce has laid out before our eyes have become the foundation of a science previously unknown, detached at last from alien speculations. Already, on all sides, intent eyes are fixed on nature. . . . The son of a Dutch artisan assembled for his amusement two convex lenses in a tube, so extending the range of what could be seen that in Italy, the eyes of Galileo discovered a new heaven. Already Kepler, searching among the stars for the numbers of Pythagoras, deduced two famous laws of planetary motion that would become one day, in the hands of Newton, the key to the universe. Already Bacon has traced for posterity the route it must follow.

What mortal dares to reject all past wisdom, and even those ideas that were believed to be most certain? Seeming to wish to extinguish the flame of knowledge so that he alone, by himself, might ignite it again as the pure fire of reason? . . . Great Descartes! If it was not possible for you always to reach the truth, at least you have destroyed the tyranny of error. . . .

. . .

All the clouds at last are lifted, and in every quarter, a bright light shines! What a crowd of great minds in every possible endeavor! What perfection of human reason! One man, Newton, has tamed infinity with the calculus; has revealed the properties of light which, while illuminating all, had hid itself; has put in his balance the stars, the earth, and all the forces of nature. . . . The several sciences previously concentrated in a small number of simple notions, known to all, now that they have become by their progress more extended and difficult, can only be envisioned separately. But even greater progress approaches, as the mutual dependence of all truths is discovered, which binds them all together so that each one illumines the other—because though each day adds to the immensity of the sciences, each day renders them more comprehensible; because the methods of knowing them multiply with each discovery; because the scaffolding rises alongside the edifice. . . .

A genealogical or encyclopedic tree of knowledge

Jean le Rond d'Alembert, *Preliminary Discourse* (1751)

The *Preliminary Discourse* to the *Encyclopedia*, prefacing the first of its twenty-eight volumes, offers a broad discussion of all the branches and byways of human understanding. In the sections excerpted here from its first part, d'Alembert introduces a taxonomy of that universe of knowledge, followed by a concise summary in tabular form. In the tradition of Bacon and Locke, d'Alembert holds that all knowledge comes from sense experience, either directly apprehended, or gathered and reflected upon. That knowledge falls, as Bacon proposed, into the three categories of History, Philosophy, and Poetry.[7] These areas of knowledge correspond to the three functions of the mind: respectively, Memory, Reason, and Imagination.

History, a field of knowledge requiring the exercise of Memory, includes sacred (the history of the church), human, and natural history. In the last category, d'Alembert includes not only the history of natural phenomena (such as meteors, plants and animals, and the elements), but also the "uses of nature," which encompasses all of the crafts and manufactures (such as goldsmith, glassmaking, ironmongery, and silk weaving) whose presence is an important and novel feature of the *Encyclopedia*.

Philosophy, a field requiring the exercise of Reason, includes the science of God (theology, here subordinated to philosophy, but heretofore considered superior to it), of human beings (including discussions of logic and ethics), and of nature (including mathematics, physics, chemistry, and the other sciences).

Poetry, a field requiring the exercise of the Imagination, embraces all forms of artistic creation: verbal, visual, and aural; and so, it includes literature (epic, drama, novel, etc.); the visual arts (painting, sculpture, architecture, etc.); and music (instrumental and vocal, theoretical and performative). All of these forms of artistic expression exist on a spectrum extending from the "profane" to the "sacred," as plays, for example, like paintings and chorales, can communicate sometimes religious, sometimes secular messages.

In sum, d'Alembert encompasses the whole range of human thought and creation in one analytical system, showing the relations of different mental endeavors to the three component functions of the mind and to each other. In doing so, he redefines and reevaluates the patterns and hierarchies of areas of knowledge that had existed from antiquity through the Renaissance.

---

7. The category of "poetry" includes all of what the author later refers to as the "Fine Arts," and so includes music and the visual arts as well as literature. The term "poetry" translates the Greek concept of *poesis*, the making of objects verbal or material.

Previously exalted fields, such as theology, while not eliminated, are subordinated; fields previously undifferentiated from a general concept of "philosophy"—such as meteorology or chemistry—are identified and affirmed; and fields not previously numbered among the liberal arts, but despised as mere "mechanical arts"—such as glassmaking or tanning—are promoted to a higher rank.

At the close of the *Preliminary Discourse*, d'Alembert presents his account of human knowledge in a complex table summarizing his taxonomy—a "visualized system" (*système figuré*) or map—of which a simplified schema is given after the narrative passages below.

PRELIMINARY DISCOURSE

The work whose first volume appears today has two aims. As an *Encyclopedia*, it intends to explain as possible the order and interrelations among the fields of human knowledge. As an *Analytic Dictionary of the Sciences, Arts, and Trades*, it intends to delineate for each Science, and each Art, whether liberal or mechanical,[8] the general principles that are its foundation, and the most important features of its nature and substance. . . .

With just a little reflection on the interconnections among ideas, it is easily seen that the Arts and Sciences support each other, seemingly linked together as though by a chain. But just as it is often difficult to reduce each Science or Art to a limited number of rules or general concepts, it is no less so to incorporate the infinitely varied branches of human knowledge into a unitary system. The first step we must take in this endeavor is to examine . . . the *genealogy* and the *filiation*[9] of the elements of what we know, how they came into being, and their distinctive characteristics—in a word, to delve deep into the origin and formation of our ideas. . . .

. . .

Having specified the different elements of our knowledge, and their distinguishing characteristics, it remains only for us to a design a genealogical, or

---

8. Literature, the visual arts, and music were considered "liberal" (later also called the "fine arts"), and such crafts and industrial trades as wool-weaving and ironmongery as "mechanical."

9. Both the terms "genealogy" and "filiation" describe the set of relationships that constitute a family, beginning with a single ancestor and branching out from generation to generation. D'Alembert is envisioning the relationship among different areas of knowledge as analogous to that among an extended family.

encyclopedic tree that gathers them into one system, showing the origin of each, and the relations among them.[10]

. . .

One could design this tree of knowledge according to several alternative divisions: between natural and revealed knowledge, . . . or speculative and practical knowledge, . . . and so on to infinity. We have chosen a principle of division best suited to demonstrate as much as possible both the encyclopedic order [i.e., horizontal] of what it is we know, and its genealogical order [i.e., vertical]. We owe this division to a famous author of whom we will speak later in this preface.[11]. . .

. . .

The objects that our mind engages are either spiritual or material; and our mind engages them either directly, or by reflection. Knowledge gained directly consists in the purely passive, in effect mechanical collection of information about objects that are observed, by the action of memory. Reflection is of two sorts . . . : either the mind thinks about the objects that have been directly observed, by the action of reason; or it imitates them, by the action of the imagination. The three ways, accordingly, that the mind engages the objects of its thinking are Memory, Reason, and Imagination. . . . These three faculties form the three fundamental divisions of our system of human knowledge, and its three general domains: History, related to Memory; Philosophy, to Reason; and Poetry, to Imagination.

. . .

These are the principal parts of our encyclopedic Tree, to be discussed in greater detail at the end of this *Preliminary Discourse*, where is found a kind of Map to which is joined a much more extended explanation than that appearing above. . . .

---

10. Here d'Alembert presents a "genealogical" tree as equivalent to an "encyclopedic"; later, he will present these terms as alternatives, not equivalents. His meaning seems to be that the tree is "genealogical" in that it shows vertical relationships between areas of knowledge, and "encyclopedic" in that it shows lateral or horizontal relationships among the three divisions of the intellectual realms of History/Philosophy/Poetry, corresponding to the mental functions of Memory/Reason/Imagination.

11. Here d'Alembert acknowledges his debt to Francis Bacon who, along with other giants of the previous century, he will celebrate later in the *Discourse*.

MAP of the System of Human Knowledge

The Understanding Analyzed

IMAGINATION — POETRY

Music
- Theory
- Practice
- Instrumental
- Vocal

Painting

Sculpture

Architecture

Engraving

Narrative
- Epic
- Madrigal
- Epigram
- Novel, etc.

Drama
- Tragedy
- Comedy
- Pastoral, etc.

Parable
- Allegory

REASON — PHILOSOPHY

General metaphysics / ontology

Science of God
- Natural theology
- Revealed theology
- Science of good and evil spirits

Science of man
- Pneumatology / science of the soul
- Logic
  ◦ Art of thinking
  ◦ Art of remembering
  ◦ Art of communicating
- Ethics
  ◦ General: good and evil; duties; virtue
  ◦ Particular: laws, jurisprudence

Science of nature
- Metaphysics of bodies / physics of extent
- Mathematics
  ◦ Pure: arithmetic, geometry
  ◦ Mixed: mechanics, geometric astronomy, optics, acoustics / pneumatics / art of conjecture
  ◦ Physicomathematics
- Particular physics
  ◦ Zoology: anatomy, physiology, etc.
  ◦ Physical astronomy: astrology
  ◦ Meteorology
  ◦ Cosmology
  ◦ Botany: agriculture, gardening
  ◦ Mineralogy
  ◦ Chemistry: chemistry, metallurgy, alchemy, natural magic

MEMORY — HISTORY

Sacred history

Ecclesiastical history

Civil: ancient and modern
- Civil history: memories, antiquities, complete histories
- Literary history

Natural history
- Uniformity of nature
  ◦ Celestial history
  ◦ History of: meteors; land and sea; minerals; plants; animals; elements
- Deviations of nature: celestial wonders; large meteors; wonders of land and sea; monstrous minerals, plants, animals; wonders of the elements
- Uses of nature: arts, crafts, and manufactures; work and uses of
  ◦ Gold and silver
  ◦ Precious stones
  ◦ Iron
  ◦ Glass
  ◦ Animal skin (leather)
  ◦ Stone, plaster, slate
  ◦ Silk
  ◦ Wool
  ◦ Etc.

D'Alembert: Map of the System of Human Knowledge. Simplified schema based on the translation of the French original included in the *Encyclopedia*.

SYSTÈME FIGURÉ des Connoissances Humaines[12]

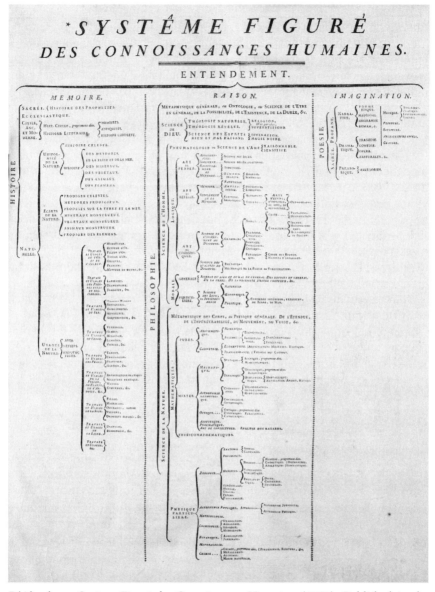

D'Alembert: *Système Figuré des Connoissances Humaines* (1751). Published in the *Encyclopédie*; available on Wikipedia.

---

12. Available at http://encyclopedie.uchicago.edu/content/système-figuré-des-connaissances-humaines-0.

Dare to know!

Immanuel Kant, *What Is Enlightenment?* (1784)

Answering the question posed in the popular magazine the *Berlinische Monatsschrift (Berlin Monthly)* of September 30, 1784, Kant defines Enlightenment as the process of casting off an old way of thinking, directed by bureaucrats, clergy, and experts, and adopting a new one: the independent thinking engaged in by autonomous individuals. That change requires a psychological shift, a repudiation of the self-imposed dependency on external authority that had prevailed in all eras before the present. This change, Kant argues, is now occurring, as the few individuals who break loose from the lazy and slothful mental habits of the past spur others to do the same, until the whole community—the Public at large—crosses a cultural frontier into a new historical era: that of Enlightenment. Such a change not just in individual behavior (indeed individuals, as employees or subordinates entrusted to execute particular missions, were not in that official setting free to think independently), but that of a group, requires the context of civil freedom, made possible by wise rulers such as the emperor, Frederick II, "the Great," the ruler of Prussia in whose university city of Königsberg (modern Kaliningrad, Russia) Kant was born, worked, and died.

A note on the translation: *Unmündigkeit*, the condition from which individuals must emerge to become enlightened, is generally translated as "immaturity," "minority," "nonage," or "tutelage." But the term used here is "dependency," which describes the condition of children and others subjected to guardianship, and usefully contrasts with the independence, and free exercise of mind and will, that Kant advocates.

WHAT IS ENLIGHTENMENT?

Enlightenment is the emergence of humankind from its self-imposed dependency, dependency being the inability of a person to think for himself without someone else's guidance. This dependency is self-imposed since its cause is not any failure of the mind, but the lack of courage and will to think undirected by another. *Sapere aude!*[13] Dare to know! Have the courage to think for yourself! This is the watchword of Enlightenment.

Laziness and cowardice are the reasons why so many people, though long past the age of childhood, still willingly remain in a state of childish dependency. . . . It is so easy to depend on others. I have a book that thinks for me; a pastor who acts as my conscience; a doctor who critiques my diet, . . . so I hardly need to bestir myself at all. There is no need for me to think, so

---

13. *Sapere aude*: the phrase of the Roman poet Horace, in his *Epistulae* 1.2.40.

long as I can pay—others will take over that bothersome task for me right away. . . .

So it is difficult for the individual to extract himself from this by now habitual dependency. He has become so fond of it that he is for the moment actually unable to exercise his own mind, since no one ever gave him the chance. Rules and regulations, those mechanisms for the sensible use, or rather misuse, of his natural gifts, are the shackles of his stubborn dependency. . . . Only a few have been able, therefore, by their own mental exertion, to unloose themselves from this dependency and take a bolder road forward.

But that a whole community, the Public, might achieve Enlightenment is highly possible—and indeed almost inevitable, if they are only left in freedom. For there will always be some who think for themselves, . . . who, once they have unburdened themselves from the yoke of dependency, will inspire others to form a rational estimation of their own worth and of each person's calling to think for himself. . . . For nothing but freedom is needed for enlightenment to take hold; and this kind of freedom is really the least fearsome there could be, that is, the freedom to make public use of one's reason in all matters.

But now I hear the cries from all sides: "Don't think," the officer says; "don't think, just march!" The tax-collector: "Don't think, just pay!" The pastor: "Don't think, just believe!" . . . All this amounts to the constriction of freedom. But what kind of limitation of freedom is the foe of enlightenment? And which is not, but rather promotes it?—My answer: the public use of reason must forever be free, and it alone can further the enlightenment of humankind; but its private use may actually be quite narrowly limited without in consequence greatly hindering the progress of enlightenment. By public use, I mean that which anyone might make of his own reason when presenting his thoughts to the whole reading Public. By private use, I mean that which a person might make of his reason in a particular civic post or office with which he has been entrusted. . . . In this case, clearly, he is not allowed to think; he must obey. . . .

It would be highly improper, accordingly, if an officer commanded to do something by his superior argued aloud, while on duty, about the appropriateness or usefulness of the order—he must only obey. But in fairness he cannot be forbidden, as a competent spokesperson, to present for the consideration of the Public observations about problems in military management. The citizen cannot refuse to pay the taxes demanded of him. . . . Yet the same citizen does not violate his civic duty if, as a competent speaker, he openly communicates his views on the inappropriateness or even the injustice of such exactions. In the same way, a pastor is bound, in teaching his catechism class and his congregation, to conform to the doctrines of the church he serves, since it was for that purpose that he was employed. But as a scholar he has complete freedom, and is even obliged, to inform the Public of all his carefully considered and well-meant thoughts on any deficiencies in those doctrines, and suggest possible improvements of religious and church management. . . .

If then it is asked: do we now live in an enlightened age? The answer is: no, but rather in an age of Enlightenment—that is to say, one that is becoming enlightened. As things now stand, we fall far short of the time when people in general are ready, or will soon be ready . . . to use their own minds assuredly and well, without the guidance of others. But there are already clear signs that the possibility will soon be open to them for their free exploration, and that the obstacles to universal enlightenment, and the emergence of humankind from its self-imposed dependency, become gradually fewer. In this sense, this age is an age of Enlightenment. . . .

Chapter Five

Mind, Soul, and God: 1740–1779

Introduction

Echoing Kant's call for a new birth of reason in his *What Is Enlightenment?* and Locke's rejection of innate ideas in his *Essay Concerning Human Understanding*, themes discussed in the previous two chapters, Chapter Five now turns to the problem of the human mind or soul and, by extension, God—for if the mind is a mere mortal organism, as some proposed, there is no immortal soul and no transcendent "Supreme Being," as Enlightenment authors often termed the deity. Not all thinkers ventured so far, but some did, and several veered in that direction.

The chapter opens with a selection from *Abstract of a Book Lately Published* by the Scots philosopher David Hume (1711–1776), the author's commentary on his own *Treatise on Human Nature*, the latter a skeptical account of the human mind understood to form ideas based only on sense impressions. Selections from two French works, *Man a Machine* by Julien Offray de La Mettrie (1709–1751) and *On the Mind* by Claude Adrien Helvétius (1715–1771), similarly link thought closely to perception and its biological substratum, diminishing the role of intuition or imagination in mental operations. Related to these, *Common Sense*, by the German-born francophone author Paul-Henri Thiry, baron d'Holbach (1723–1789), asserts a naturalistic view of the mind and vilifies religion as a barrier to human progress.

The German author Gotthold Ephraim Lessing (1729–1781), in contrast to these forerunners, believes in God, and vaguely a Christian God, while rejecting theological and denominational truisms. The selection here from his drama *Nathan the Wise* argues the equivalence of Christian, Jewish, and Islamic theisms. His call for tolerance, rather than unbelief, fittingly complements the arguments and assertions of the preceding authors.

Following Bacon and Locke, Hume argues that knowledge proceeds from sense experience, upon which the mind reflects, there being no other source—no innate knowledge, no Cartesian "clear and distinct" ideas arrived at by a deductive method. Yet he is more skeptical than his predecessors of what the mind can know, and thus of reason itself. Aiming in his principal works—the *Treatise on Human Nature* (1739–1740); *An Enquiry Concerning Human Understanding* (1748); and *An Inquiry Concerning the Principles of Morals* (1751)—to construct an empirically based "science of man" comparable to the science of the cosmos set forth in Newton's *Principia*, he examines the processes of the human mind, as though in a laboratory, to explain what forces other than reason guide its operations.

The excerpt given here is from Hume's own thirty-two-page summation, *An Abstract of a Book Lately Published* (1740), of his *Treatise on Human Nature* published over the previous two years—an unpopular work and a market failure in its time, but since regarded as a pivotal contribution to modern philosophy. In the *Abstract*, published anonymously but clearly by his hand, Hume outlines key principles of his philosophy that would be developed further in his later works. He demonstrates that it is not reason that guides the mind to such behaviors as to seek social solidarity, obey political authority, and believe in God, but rather feelings, imagination, intuition, fear, experience, and habit.

Like Hume, the French physician and philosopher La Mettrie doubts the rationality of the human mind, which he understands, instead, to be wholly material. Descartes had proposed that animal bodies were machines, operating without consciousness; and that even some unconscious operations of the human body were machinelike, though governed by mind. La Mettrie adopts Descartes' mechanical model, but dispenses with mind altogether. A human being is simply a machine, he announces in 1747 in his impishly provocative *Homme machine* (*Man a Machine*; or *Machine Man*), excerpted here.

The book was published anonymously in the Netherlands, to which refuge, following the publication of an earlier work that had unsettled the reading public, La Mettrie had fled in 1745. Here outrageous works might be published clandestinely; but his authorship was known, and in 1748, he fled once more, this time to Berlin and the court of the benevolent despot Emperor Frederick II of Prussia. There he died three years later, not yet forty-two years old, having feasted to excess, it is said, on truffled pheasant pâté.

Trained by the eminent Dutch physician Herman Boerhaave, La Mettrie was not an experimental scientist but a practicing physician whose observations led him to recognize the organic, or material, origins of mental states. If body is all matter, and matter functions as a machine that can think, there is no need to posit the existence of a soul, or of God. The first of three French materialists who appear in this chapter, La Mettrie posits a materialism that initiates a stream of thought influencing later theorists and culminating in Darwin.

Descended from a line of noted physicians, a prosperous government servant from the age of twenty-three, and the husband of a *salonnière*, Helvétius lived comfortably, retiring to the countryside in his last years to devote himself to study and philanthropy. His peaceable existence was interrupted by the publication in 1758 of his most important work *On the Mind*, of which an excerpt is given here. It shocked the public and elicited the condemnation of both the Parlement and the University of Paris. Cowed by this reception, the flexible Helvétius retracted his views three times. Nonetheless, the book was burned by the public hangman. Nonetheless, it was a resounding success all over Europe.

Like La Mettrie, Helvétius is a materialist who finds nothing transcendent in the mind, which he views as simply a device for the recording and reassemblage of physical sensations and memories of them. He presents this vision in the three component "discourses" of his book. In the first, he demonstrates that all human mental activity is reduced to sensation: even memory, which is the memory of sensation; and judgment, which is the discernment exercised about sensations previously received. In the second discourse, Helvétius considers the consequences of his theory for social existence. If this is the human mind—if there is within it nothing more elevated, or spiritual, or eternal—then there is no higher force that motivates good behavior; the organism seeks simply to maximize pleasure and avoid pain. Thus all choices seen externally as "moral" are actually decisions based on self-interest. Helvétius' view of human motivation would later impact Utilitarian theorists, including Jeremy Bentham and John Stuart Mill, and the Austrian psychoanalyst Sigmund Freud.

If this message is depressing, there is an upside, presented in the third discourse. Since all humans possess the same kind of mind, intellectual capacity does not significantly vary: all are equally capable of learning. Thus the differences between the intellectual attainments of individuals, and the cultural achievements of nations or civilizations, are due not to innate excellence but to chance and circumstance, of which the most important is education.

The German-born nobleman d'Holbach was the wealthy host of a Paris salon attended by the leading *philosophes* of the age—most of them atheists, he boasted. A frequent contributor to the *Encyclopedia* and a prolific author, d'Holbach is best known for his treatise *The System of Nature* (1770), of which the notorious *Bon sens* (*Common Sense*), excerpted here, is an abridged version published anonymously in Amsterdam in 1772. It opens with an inflammatory preface denouncing religion as a lie, priests as frauds, and God as the puffed-up hero of an improbable romance. These themes are elaborated in a sequel of 206 chapters. All that is needed to burst the bubble of deceit and fabrication is common sense, d'Holbach proposes. Enlightenment will come as the human being, escaping from "the labyrinth [of religious illusion] that engulfed his ancestors," begins to think.

The atheism implicit in Hume, La Mettrie, and Helvétius is explicit in d'Holbach. This atheistic tendency at the level of elite discourse sat atop a maelstrom of anti-church feeling in the broader population. The circulation of subversive texts such as the seventeenth-century *Theophrastus redivivus* and the eighteenth-century *Three Imposters*, along with John Toland's more mainstream *Christianity Not Mysterious*, has been noted in the introduction to Chapter Three. Accompanying these anti-faith diatribes was a torrent of sexually explicit and pornographic literature, circulated clandestinely in cheap print and fine bindings, including the lurid tales of the Marquis de Sade, John Cleland's fictional memoirs of Fanny Hill, and the exploits of Casanova. The international network of Freemasons, meanwhile, whose lodges and ceremonies mimicked the sacred places and rituals of the Catholic Church, and which attracted as members men of high rank and culture, was an institutional rebuke to that institution.

Yet Europe had not surrendered entirely to atheism. Most Europeans were adherents to one or another of the churches and sects, and even rural populations long resistant to conversion—like the *pagani* of ancient Rome—at last became fully Christianized during the Enlightenment. It was during this era that Pietism, an enthusiastic movement within Lutheranism, flourished in the German and neighboring lands, as did the related movements of Quakerism and Methodism in Britain, while revivalism took hold in Scotland and, across the Atlantic, the anglophone American colonies were swept by the evangelical Great Awakening of the 1730s to 1770s. At just this moment, as well, two of the greatest musical pronouncements of Christianity were performed for the first time: in 1727, in Leipzig, the *Saint Matthew Passion* of Johann Sebastian Bach; in 1742, in Dublin, the *Messiah* of George Frideric Handel.

In this context, rather than that of the Paris salons, Lessing, the son of a Lutheran pastor, wrote *Nathan der Weise* (*Nathan the Wise*), a drama about a truly moral man who happened to be a Jew. A poet, philosopher, and literary critic, Lessing is best known for his many plays—the first of which was written in 1748, when he was nineteen years old—and his *Laocoön, An Essay on the Limits of Painting and Poetry* (1767). *Nathan the Wise* was one of his last works, published two years before his death, and first performed posthumously in Berlin in 1783. Its hero Nathan is modeled on Lessing's close friend, the Jewish philosopher Moses Mendelssohn who led German Jewry into the cultural mainstream of the Enlightenment.

Set in exotic twelfth-century Jerusalem during the Third Crusade, described in iambic pentameter modeled after Shakespeare's, *Nathan the Wise* is a celebration of good people of all kinds: the Muslim ruler Saladin and his brothers and sisters, dead and living; a heroic knight Templar and a kindly friar; an adopted daughter and her loyal companion; and the generous, wise, and wealthy Jew Nathan. A momentary confusion entangling Christians, Jews, and Muslims is sorted out by the closing scene of the play, when all are united in a harmonious, familial whole. That is the ecumenical message of the play and of the famous scene at its center, when Nathan tells Saladin the story of the three rings, excerpted here. A story that had circulated for centuries before this retelling, and had been featured among the hundred stories in the famous *Decameron* of Renaissance author Giovanni Boccaccio, it argues for the mutual toleration of Christianity, Judaism, and Islam. These three theisms of the Western world, as Lessing sees it, though differing in some philosophical details, are equivalent faiths, indistinguishable from each other, the superior truth of any one of them never to be known.

The narrow limits of human understanding

David Hume, *An Abstract of a Book Lately Published* (1740)

In the excerpt given here from his summation of his own *Treatise on Human Nature*, Hume shows that it is experience, custom, or sentiment—not reason—that accounts for operations of the human mind. Reason alone is an insufficient basis for understanding the human condition.

Following Bacon and Locke, Hume posits that all knowledge comes from the perception of objects, which yields "impressions" of things sensed immediately, and "ideas" of things not immediately present to the senses. Having gathered these impressions and ideas, the mind seeks to find their relations, of which foremost is that of cause and effect. Hume offers the famous example of billiard balls in play to illustrate his point that what seems to be the effect of an action that caused it may not be that at all—we assume that one ball causes another to move, but have no rational basis for doing so. In fact, it is not by reason that the relation between cause and effect is established, but by experience. "We conclude that like causes, in like circumstances, will always produce like effects." What moves us to assume patterns of cause and effect, "a conclusion of such infinite consequence," is custom, not reason. Custom alone inclines us to assume that certain effects will always follow certain causes, that is, "to suppose the future conformable to the past"; "however easy this step may seem," . . . "reason alone would never, to all eternity, be able to make it."

This then is Hume's skepticism: "Almost all reasoning is . . . reduced to experience; and the belief, which attends experience, is explained to be nothing but a peculiar sentiment, or lively conception produced by habit."

An Abstract of a Book Lately Published

This book seems to be written upon the same plan with several other works that have had a great vogue of late years in England. The philosophical spirit, which has been so much improved all over Europe within these last fourscore [80] years, has been carried to as great a length in this kingdom as in any other. Our writers seem even to have started a new kind of philosophy, which promises more both to the entertainment and advantage of mankind, than any other with which the world has been yet acquainted. . . .

But it is at least worthwhile to try if the science of man will not admit of the same accuracy which several parts of natural philosophy are found susceptible of. . . . If, in examining several phenomena, we find that they resolve themselves into one common principle, and can trace this principle into another, we shall at last arrive at those few simple principles, on which all the rest depend. . . . This seems to have been the aim of our late philosophers, and, among the rest, of this author. He proposes to anatomize human nature in a regular manner, and promises to draw no conclusions but where he is authorized by experience. . . .

Our author [i.e., Hume] begins with some definitions. He calls a *perception* whatever can be present to the mind, whether we employ our senses, or are actuated with passion, or exercise our thought and reflection. He divides our perceptions into two kinds: that is, *impressions* and *ideas*. When we feel a passion or emotion of any kind, or have the images of external objects conveyed by our senses; the perception of the mind is what he calls an *impression*, which is a word that he employs in a new sense. When we reflect on a passion or an object which is not present, this perception is an *idea*. *Impressions*, therefore, are our lively and strong perceptions; *ideas* are fainter and weaker.

The first proposition this author advances is that all our ideas, or weak perceptions, are derived from our impressions, or strong perceptions, and that we can never think of anything which we have not seen without us, or felt in our own minds. . . .

. . .

It is evident, that all reasonings concerning *matter of fact* are founded on the relation of cause and effect. . . . In order therefore to understand these reasonings, we must be perfectly acquainted with the idea of a cause; and in order to do that, must look about us to find something that is the cause of another.

Here is a billiard-ball lying on the table, and another ball moving towards it with rapidity. They strike; and the ball, which was formerly at rest, now acquires a motion. This is as perfect an instance of the relation of cause and effect as any which we know, either by sensation or reflection. Let us therefore examine it. It is evident, that the two balls touched one another before the motion was communicated, and that there was no interval between the shock and the motion. . . .

This is the case when both the cause and effect are present to the senses. Let us now see upon what our inference is founded, when we conclude from the one that the other has existed or will exist. Suppose I see a ball moving in a straight line towards another, I immediately conclude, that they will shock, and that the second will be in motion. This is the inference from cause to effect; and of this nature are all our reasonings in the conduct of life: on this is founded all our belief in history: and from hence is derived all philosophy, excepting only geometry and arithmetic. If we can explain the inference from the shock of two balls, we shall be able to account for this operation of the mind in all instances.

Were a man, such as Adam,[1] created in the full vigor of understanding, without experience, he would never be able to infer motion in the second ball from the motion and impulse of the first. It is not anything that reason sees in the cause, which makes us infer the effect. . . .

It would have been necessary, therefore, for Adam . . . to have had *experience* of the effect, which followed upon the impulse of these two balls. He must have seen, in several instances, that when the one ball struck upon the other, the second always acquired motion. If he had seen a sufficient number of instances of this kind, whenever he saw the one ball moving towards the other, he would always conclude without hesitation, that the second would acquire motion. His understanding would anticipate his sight, and form a conclusion suitable to his past experience.

It follows, then, that all reasonings concerning cause and effect are founded on experience, and that all reasonings from experience are founded on the supposition that the course of nature will continue uniformly the same. We conclude that like causes, in like circumstances, will always produce like effects. It may now be worthwhile to consider what determines us to form a conclusion of such infinite consequence.

It is evident that Adam, with all his science, would never have been able to demonstrate that the course of nature must continue uniformly the same, and that the future must be conformable to the past. . . . But our experience in the past can be a proof of nothing for the future, but upon a supposition that there is a resemblance between them. This therefore is a point which can admit of no proof at all, and which we take for granted without any proof.

We are determined by custom alone to suppose the future conformable to the past. . . . It is not, therefore, reason, which is the guide of life, but custom. That alone determines the mind, in all instances, to suppose the future conformable to the past. However easy this step may seem, reason would never, to all eternity, be able to make it. . . .

. . .

---

1. The first man created by God, according to Genesis 2:4–17.

By all that has been said the reader will easily perceive, that the philosophy contained in this book is very skeptical, and tends to give us a notion of the imperfections and narrow limits of human understanding. Almost all reasoning is there reduced to experience; and the belief, which attends experience, is explained to be nothing but a peculiar sentiment, or lively conception produced by habit. Nor is this all. When we believe anything of external existence, or suppose an object to exist a moment after it is no longer perceived, this belief is nothing but a sentiment of the same kind.

The soul is but an empty word

Julien Offray de La Mettrie, *Man a Machine* (1747)

In brisk and biting prose, La Mettrie denies that the human mind—whose superior intelligence, in the Linnaean framework he otherwise adopts, should distinguish him from all others in the animal kingdom—is in any way transcendent. It belongs, rather, to matter: for in the "whole universe there is but a single Substance differently modified," as Spinoza had posited. It is a machine, composed of matter, embedded in the larger machine of the wholly material body. To understand the mind what is needed is not reflection, but dissection, the tool of the anatomist. Extract the brain from the body, and it is seen to be quite like that of the animals most similar to the human—"the monkey, the beaver, the elephant, the dog, the fox, the cat"— except that it is larger, more convoluted, and better supplied with blood because of its proximity to the heart.

The greater size of the human brain does not make it more competent, however, at least during the early stages of life. Place a human and an animal infant at the edge of a precipice overhanging deep waters: both will fall, but the human infant will drown, while the animal, gifted with instinct, swims safely away. What allows humans to exercise dominion over the rest of nature is education: the arts and sciences polish the "raw diamond" of the mind. Yet even that is but an advanced form of the training by which animals do our will. The geometer and the porter are trained for their positions no less than the circus monkey who brandishes his little hat to the applause of the crowd while riding his little dog.

In sum, the soul is "but an empty word," and the mind, like man himself, is a machine. La Mettrie throws down his gauntlet: "Dispute it now who will."

MAN A MACHINE

Man is so complicated a machine that it is impossible to get a clear idea of the machine beforehand, and hence impossible to define it. For this reason, all the investigations have been vain, which the greatest philosophers have made *a priori*. . . . Thus it is only *a posteriori* or by trying to disentangle the soul from the organs of the body, so to speak, that one can reach the highest probability concerning man's own nature, even though one cannot discover with certainty what his nature is. Let us then take in our hands the staff of experience, paying no heed to the accounts of all the idle theories of philosophers. . . .

. . .

How can human nature be known, if we may not derive any light from an exact comparison of the structure of man and of animals? In general, the form and the structure of the brains of quadrupeds are almost the same as those of the brain of man; the same shape, the same arrangement everywhere, with this essential difference, that of all the animals man is the one whose brain is largest, and, in proportion to its mass, more convoluted than the brain of any other animal; then come the monkey, the beaver, the elephant, the dog, the fox, the cat. These animals are most like man. . . .

. . .

The transition from animals to man is not violent, as true philosophers will admit. What was man before the invention of words and the knowledge of language? An animal of his own species with much less instinct than the others. In those days, he did not consider himself king over the other animals, nor was he distinguished from the ape, and from the rest, except as the ape itself differs from the other animals, i.e., by a more intelligent face. . . .

Words, languages, laws, sciences, and the fine arts have come, and by them finally the rough diamond of our mind has been polished. Man has been trained in the same way as animals. He has become an author, as they became beasts of burden. A geometrician has learned to perform the most difficult demonstrations and calculations, as a monkey has learned to take his little hat off and on, and to mount his tame dog. . . .

. . .

In spite of all these advantages of man over animals, it is doing him honor to place him in the same class. For, truly, up to a certain age, he is more of an animal than they, since at birth he has less instinct. What animal would die of hunger in the midst of a river of milk? Man alone. . . . Light a wax candle for the first time under a child's eyes, and he will mechanically put his fingers in the flame as if to find out what is the new thing that he sees. It is at his own cost that he will learn of the danger, but he will not be caught again. Or, put the child with an animal on a precipice, the child alone falls off; he drowns where the animal would save itself by swimming. . . .

Thus nature made us to be lower than animals or at least to exhibit all the more, because of that native inferiority, the wonderful efficacy of education which alone raises us from the level of the animals and lifts us above them. . . .

. . .

But since all the faculties of the soul depend to such a degree on the proper organization of the brain and of the whole body, that apparently they are but this organization itself, the soul is clearly an enlightened machine. For finally, even if man alone had received a share of natural law, would he be any less a machine for that? A few more wheels, a few more springs than in the most perfect animals, the brain proportionally nearer the heart and for this very reason receiving more blood—any one of a number of unknown causes might always produce this delicate conscience so easily wounded, this remorse which is no more foreign to matter than to thought, and in a word all the differences that are supposed to exist here. Could the organism then suffice for everything? Once more, yes; since thought visibly develops with our organs, why should not the matter of which they are composed be susceptible of remorse also, when once it has acquired, with time, the faculty of feeling?

The soul is therefore but an empty word, of which no one has any idea, and which an enlightened man should use only to signify the part in us that thinks. . . .

. . .

We are veritable moles in the field of nature; we achieve little more than the mole's journey and it is our pride which prescribes limits to the limitless. . . . We imagine, or rather we infer, a cause superior to that to which we owe all, and which truly has wrought all things in an inconceivable fashion. No; matter contains nothing base, . . . and Nature is no stupid workman. . . . Her power shines forth equally in creating the lowliest insect and in creating the most highly developed man; the animal kingdom costs her no more than the vegetable, and the most splendid genius no more than a blade of wheat. Let us then judge by what we see of that which is hidden from the curiosity of our eyes and of our investigations, and let us not imagine anything beyond. . . .

Break the chain of your prejudices, arm yourselves with the torch of experience, and you will render to nature the honor she deserves, instead of inferring anything to her disadvantage, from the ignorance in which she has left you. Only open wide your eyes, only disregard what you cannot understand, and you will see that the ploughman whose intelligence and ideas extend no further than the bounds of his furrow, does not differ essentially from the greatest genius—a truth which the dissection of Descartes' and of Newton's brains would have proved; you will be persuaded that the imbecile and the fool are animals with human faces, as the intelligent ape is a little man in another shape. . . .

. . .

Let us then conclude boldly that man is a machine, and that in the whole universe there is but a single Substance differently modified. . . . and I hereby challenge every prejudiced man who is neither anatomist, nor acquainted with the only philosophy which can here be considered, that of the human body. Against so strong and solid an oak, what could the weak reeds of theology, of metaphysics, and of the schools, avail. . . .

Such is my system, or rather the truth, unless I am much deceived. It is short and simple. Dispute it now who will.

All is reduced to sensation

Claude Adrien Helvétius, *On the Mind* (1758)

In the first chapter of the first of three "discourses" composing his treatise *On the Mind*, Helvétius establishes the fundamental principles that presuppose all that follows. The mind, for Helvétius, is not so much an organ, as it was for La Mettrie, as the process of thinking, which consists of two functions: sensation, the reception of information from external objects, called here "physical sensibility"; and memory, the continued presence, in weakened form, of that sensation. Memory, in fact, is really itself sensation, as nothing is remembered that was not originally perceived. And so, too, is judgment, the process by which the mind assesses the similarities and dissimilarities between objects and declares what it has discerned. What is being judged— the properties of objects—is also the product of sensation, as is judgment itself. In the end, there is no other mental activity than that of perceiving, relating, and defining objects presented to the senses. "All is reduced to sensation."

ON THE MIND

People endlessly debate about what must be called the "mind." They all pronounce the word; but no one attaches the same meaning to this word, and so they speak at cross-purposes. To arrive at a correct and precise understanding of this word "mind" and the various meanings it seems to convey, it is first necessary to consider the mind itself.

Either mind is considered to be the effect of the faculty of thinking (in which case the mind is nothing but the assemblage of a person's thoughts); or it is considered to be itself the faculty of thinking. In order to know what mind is according to this second definition, it is necessary to recognize what are the productive causes of our ideas.

We have within us two faculties, or if I may so put it, two passive powers whose existence is generally and clearly acknowledged. One is the faculty to receive the different impressions caused by external objects. This faculty is called *physical sensibility*. The second is the faculty of preserving the impression caused by these objects. This faculty is called *memory*, which is merely a sensation that is continued, but weakened. These faculties, . . . which we share with animals, I regard as the productive causes of our thoughts. . . .

. . .

Helvétius explains that these faculties would occasion very few ideas if they were not accompanied by physiological features and other circumstantial benefits that no animals, but only humans and advanced human societies possess. He further raises the question whether these faculties are spiritual or material in nature, a question often discussed by philosophers and one that has recently reemerged, but evades it as not being germane to the present discussion.

So to return to my subject, I say that physical sensibility and memory, or rather, to be more exact, that sensibility alone produces all our thoughts. In fact, memory is merely an organ of physical sensibility: the capacity in us that feels must also be necessarily the capacity that remembers; because to remember, as I am going to prove, is nothing other than to feel.

For when, by a sequence of my ideas or by the agitation caused by certain sounds within my ear, I recall the image of an oak tree, it is necessarily because my internal organs find themselves roughly in the same situation they were in when I had earlier perceived that oak. So this condition of those organs must incontestably produce a sensation. It is evident, accordingly, that to remember is to feel.

This principle established, I say further that it is within our capacity to perceive the resemblances or the differences, the consonance or dissonance that exist among diverse objects, in which consist all the operations of the mind. Now as this capacity is itself physical sensibility, everything, it follows, is reducible to sensation.

To assure ourselves of this truth, let us consider nature. Nature presents objects to us, which have relations with us and relations among themselves. The knowledge of these relations constitutes what is called the mind, which is more or less competent according to the degree that our knowledge of these relations is more or less complex. The human mind extends itself as far as its knowledge of these relations; but they form a boundary it will never pass beyond.

Accordingly, all the words that make up the various languages, which can be regarded as the aggregate of the signifiers of all the thoughts of humankind, recall for us either images, such as those summoned up by the words "oak," "ocean," "sun"; or they represent ideas, which is to say the different ways that objects relate to each other, and which are either simple, as with the words "greatness" or "smallness," or compound, such as "vice" or "virtue." Or, finally, they express the different relations that objects have with us, that is, our action upon them, as in the words "I break," "I dig," "I raise"; or else their action upon us, as in the expressions "I am wounded," "I am dazzled," "I am terrified."

. . .

The conclusion to what I have said to this point is this: if all the words of the various languages represented nothing but objects, or the relations of these objects to us and among themselves, the mind would in consequence consist entirely in the equivalation of our sensations and our ideas; that is to say, in discerning the resemblances and the differences, and the consonances and dissonances that exist between them. Now, since judgment is precisely this process of discernment, or at least the articulation of what is discerned, it follows that all the operations of the mind are reduced to judgment.

With the matter thus defined, I shall now consider whether "to judge" is not the same as "to feel." When I judge the magnitude or the color of the objects presented to me, it is evident that the judgment arrived at from the different impressions that these objects have made on my senses is simply, itself, a sensation. It could equally well be said in this way: that I judge or I feel that, of two objects, the one that I call a fathom[2] makes a different impression upon me than the other, which I call a foot; and that the color that I call "red" acts differently upon my eyes than the one that I call "yellow." From these examples I conclude that in any similar case, "to judge" is always the same as "to feel." . . .

. . .

From what has been said, the result is that the judgments arrived at by the means or methods that chance presents to us to reach a certain end are properly seen to be sensations. In sum, in humankind, all is reduced to sensation.

---

2. Fathom: a unit of length equal to six feet.

An endless web of fantasies and falsehoods

Paul-Henri Thiry, baron d'Holbach, *Common Sense* (1772)

In his no-holds-barred, intemperate, and often hilarious attack on theology, faith, and God himself, d'Holbach hurls charges that La Mettrie and Helvé-tius might have covertly approved, and even Hume might have entertained. Theology is an endless web of lies and ignorance, d'Holbach trumpets; God is a meaningless notion, the hero of an implausible romance that people revere because they are deceived. Far from promoting moral behavior, the priestly caste undermines it, promoting zealots and prompting cruel wars and persecutions. Reason, not faith, is the key to moral behavior and human well-being. As enlightenment proceeds, d'Holbach suggests, anticipating Kant, the prospect of a real Enlightenment emerges.

The excerpt is taken mainly from the author's preface, which states his key points. In the original, it is followed by 206 brief and aphoristic chapters, of which two samples, chapters 8 and 206, are given here.

COMMON SENSE

When we set aside our illusions to examine the opinions of humankind, we are surprised to learn that even in those matters that are considered most essential, nothing is more rare than common sense: that is to say, rarely does anyone exercise the minimum of thought necessary to grasp the simplest truths, reject the most blatant absurdities, or dismiss glaring contradictions. Take theology, for example, a science revered in all ages, in all nations, by the preponderance of mortals; a matter regarded as the most important, useful, and indispensable for the well-being of society. But in fact, if we exert our-selves just a tad to detect the principles on which this false science rests, we are forced to recognize that these principles long thought incontestable are nothing but imaginary suppositions, dreamed up by ignorance, propagated by fanaticism or fraud, cravenly adopted by the credulous, retained by un-thinking habit, and esteemed only because they cannot be understood. . . .

In a word, whoever will stoop to use common sense in matters concern-ing religion . . . will easily see that such beliefs have no firm foundation; that all of religion is a castle in the air; that theology is nothing more than the sys-tematized ignorance of natural causes, an endless web of fantasies and false-hoods. In every country and among all peoples, it is an impossible romance whose hero, God, is an assortment of ill-assorted qualities, whose name . . . is an empty word that people mouth constantly without being able to attach to it any ideas or attributes that cannot be exposed as lies. . . .

The idea of this meaningless being . . . would be a matter of indifference if it did not wreak infinite damage on this earth. Captivated by the notion that this phantom is a reality of great importance for them, rather than sensibly dismissing it as incomprehensible, people conclude instead that they must constantly dwell on it, ceaselessly meditate upon it, and never stop thinking about it. . . .

This is why so many nations have often been a home for the extravagances of mad visionaries, who by peddling their vapid speculations as eternal verities have aroused the enthusiasm of rulers and subjects and sent them off to war to fight for, as they insisted, the glory of God and the well-being of the state. A thousand times in every corner of the globe we have seen crazed fanatics slit each other's throats, burn each other at the stake, commit horrific crimes . . . , and spill streams of human blood. To what end? To validate, sustain, or propagate the impudent claims of some enthusiast, or to lend credence to the lies of some imposter, on behalf of a being who exists only in their imagination, and who only makes his presence known by the rancor, destruction, and folly he has visited upon the earth. . . .

Possessed by these terrifying phantoms, and guided by those determined to perpetuate its ignorance and fears, how has the human mind been able to progress? It is forced to vegetate in its primitive stupidity, looking for protection to invisible powers on which its well-being is supposed to depend. . . . And so the human being has been and remains always a child who knows nothing, a slave who dares nothing, a dunce who fears to think, and who cannot find his way out of the labyrinth that engulfed his ancestors. He believes he must submit to the yoke of his gods of whom he knows nothing but what is told in the fantastic stories of the priests, who having bound him by the chains of faith, remain his masters, if they do not abandon him defenseless to the absolute power of tyrants. . . .

Crushed by the double weight of spiritual and temporal power, people have been unable to instruct themselves and work for their betterment. As religion, politics, and morality became sanctuaries into which the profane might not enter, human beings had no other moral law than what their rulers and their priests plucked down from the unknowable regions of paradise. Entrapped by these theological notions, the human mind doubted itself, . . . feared truth, disdained reason, and dispatched it so as to blindly follow authority. . . .

Here is seen the real cause of the corruption of morals. . . . Ignorance and servitude have rendered humankind vicious and forlorn. Knowledge, reason, liberty alone can amend them and bring them happiness; but everything conspires to blind and mislead them. . . . To understand the true principles of morality, humans have no need of theology, nor of revelation, nor of gods. What they need is common sense. They need to enter into themselves, to reflect upon their own nature, to gauge their own pressing interests, and to pursue the best outcomes for society and of each of its members. They will easily recognize that virtue is to the advantage, and vice to the detriment of the human species. Let us tell all humans to be just, benevolent, moderate, sociable, not because their gods demand it, but to benefit humankind. Let us tell them to abstain from vice and from crime not because they will be punished in the other world, but because they will be punished here in this one. . . .

Human beings are miserable only because they are ignorant. They are ignorant only because everything conspires to prevent their enlightenment. They are vicious only because their reason is not yet sufficiently developed. . . .

. . .

8.

If God is an infinite being, there can be no proportion between God and humankind, neither in this world nor in any other—and so the idea of God can in no way enter the human mind. Even in an imagined afterlife . . . , the idea of the infinity of God would always remain equally remote from the human being's finite mind, so that he will no more be able to conceive of it when in heaven than he can here on earth. . . .

. . .

206.

For all of time, religion has done nothing but fill the human mind with darkness, imprisoning it in the ignorance of its real nature, its real duties, and its true interests. It is only by dispelling these clouds and phantoms that we discover the bases of truth, reason, and morality, and the real forces that must raise us to virtue. Religion is what obscures the causes of our misfortunes and the natural remedies that we could employ against them. Far from healing these ills, it inevitably exacerbates them, increases them, and makes them more long-lasting.

Let each believe that his own ring is real

Gotthold Ephraim Lessing, *Nathan the Wise* (1779)

In Act III Scene 7 of *Nathan the Wise*, midway through the play, there unfolds a gripping encounter between Nathan, the Jew, and the sultan Saladin, a Muslim. Saladin has inquired about the three religions of Judaism, Islam, and Christianity, and Nathan responds with a story of a ring with mystical powers passed over the generations from father to favorite son. In time, a father who loves his three sons equally has duplicates made, and gives one ring to each. The rings represent the three faiths; and just as the father's love for his children prevents him from valuing one over the others, so God, the tale implies, leaves unknown which of the three faiths is true.

Both Nathan and Saladin know the meaning of the allegory even as Nathan relates it—hence Saladin's discomfort, explicit in Lessing's stage directions. Saladin resists the truth that Nathan delivers—the truth of the equivalency of the three faiths, and the unknowability of God's will—as it would undermine his legitimacy. But he loves and respects Nathan, and knows that truth has been told.

The iambic pentameters of Lessing's text are rendered here as blank verse lines of irregular pulse. Stage directions, in italics, are in Lessing's original.

NATHAN THE WISE

NATHAN: Long ago in the East there lived a man
        To whom a loving hand had given a ring
        Of immeasurable worth. The stone was an opal,
        That flashed a hundred sparkling colors,
        And had the special power to make
        Whoever wore this ring in true faith
        Beloved of God and all humankind. No wonder
        That the man from the East never took that ring
        Off his finger, and was determined
        To keep it ever after within his house.[3]
        And so it was. He willed the ring at first
        To that one of his sons he loved the best,
        Instructing him in turn to leave the ring
        To the most beloved of his sons,
        And so again, setting birthright aside,
        The most beloved son might always be,
        By power of the ring, the foremost of his house.
        Sultan, do you understand what I am saying?

SALADIN: I understand you. Go on!

NATHAN: So this ring descended from son to son,
        To a father of three sons, in time,
        All three of whom were equally devoted
        To their father, who could not help but
        Love them all alike. At times the first,
        At times the second, or then the third,

---

3. "House" here and henceforth has the meaning of family, household, and lineage.

Seemed worthier of the ring—
And so each in turn tugged at his heart,
But he could not slight the others,
but giving in to pious weakness,
promised the ring to each of them.
And so it went—until the kindly father,
His death approaching, faced a dilemma.
It grieved him to deceive two of his sons
To whom he had made a promise—what could be done?
He sends in secret for a jeweler,
Instructing him to make two other rings
Just like the first, and to spare neither cost nor toil
To make sure each new ring he made
Was like—just like—the first. This the jeweler did.
He brought the two rings to the father,
Who could not tell them from the ring he had.
Relieved and joyful he called his sons to him,
One at a time, and gave them each his blessing,
And to each his ring—and died.
Do you hear this, Sultan?

SALADIN   *who turns away from him, distraught:*
          I hear you, I hear you! Get on with your story
          And bring it to a close, please!

NATHAN: It is concluded.
          What happened next, you know as well as I.
          As soon as the father died, each son showed up
          With his ring, and each one claimed to be master
          Of the house. They examined the rings—they quarreled—
          They complained. To no avail. It could not be discerned
          Which ring was real . . .

          [after a pause, Nathan awaiting the sultan's response . . .]
          No more can we determine
          Which faith is the true faith.

SALADIN: What? Is this the answer to my question?

NATHAN: Forgive me, I beg you—but how can I
          Make distinction between three rings
          Which the father took deliberate care to make
          In such a way they could not be distinguished?

SALADIN: The rings! Don't play games with me! I would have thought
          That the three religions that I named to you

             Could easily be distinguished—by vestments worn,
             By what may be eaten and what drunk!

NATHAN: But not at all by their fundamental truths.
             For are they not all rooted in their history,
             Inscribed on paper, or told by word of mouth?
             And history surely must be accepted wholly
             In good faith—must it not?
             Of whose good faith then are we least in doubt?
             Of our own kin? Of those whose blood we share?
             Of those who from our infancy gave proof of love?
             Of those who have never failed us? . . .
             How could I trust my forefathers less
             Than you do yours? Or to put it otherwise,
             Shall I ask you to declare your ancestors liars
             So as not to say the same of mine?
             Or those of Christians? Is it not so?

SALADIN   *[under his breath]*:
             By the living God! He is right! I must say nothing.

NATHAN: Now let us return to our rings.
             The three sons each complained to the Judge,
             Each swearing he had received the ring
             Directly from his father's hand—which was the truth!
             And with the ring the promise was received,
             To enjoy one day the primacy it bequeathed—
             As was no less the truth! The father, each swore,
             Could not have been false to him; and rather than
             Suspect so beloved a father, he would first—
             Although inclined to think the best of them—
             Charge his brothers with deception. . . .

SALADIN: And now, the Judge?—I must hear
             What you will have the Judge declare. Speak!

NATHAN: The Judge declares: if you do not now produce
             The father here before my judgment seat,
             I cannot rule. Do you think that I am here
             To work out riddles? Or do you expect
             The real ring to open its mouth and speak?
             But wait! I heard you say the real ring
             Has the miraculous power to render the wearer beloved
             Of God and men. This the false ring cannot do.
             The ring will decide! Now which one of you is loved

	The best by the other two? Go ahead, which?
	You have nothing to say? . . . Does each love only himself?
	Then all of you are frauds, and have been defrauded!
	Not one of your rings is real. . . .
SALADIN:	Splendid! Splendid!
NATHAN:	And so, the Judge continued, though not my judgment,
	I offer my advice: Do this—
	Let things stand as they are. Each of you
	Has his ring, given to him by his father.
	Let each believe that his own ring is real.
	Perhaps the father wished to bear no longer
	The tyranny of a single ring.
	And surely he loved all three of you,
	And loved you all alike, so did not wish
	To disadvantage two of you
	To privilege just one. So on with it!
	Let each rejoice in his father's love . . .
	Let each one strive to prove
	His ring's stone's great power. . . .
	And if the stone still works its power
	For the children of your children's children,
	Then come again in a thousand thousand years
	Before this judgment seat,
	When a greater One than I will sit and speak.
	Now go! Said the prudent Judge.
SALADIN:	God! God!
NATHAN:	Saladin,
	Do you feel yourself to be this great, awaited One?
SALADIN	*hurling himself upon Nathan, grabbing his hand, which he does not release for the remainder of the scene:*
	Am I dust? Am I nothing? God!
NATHAN:	What is it, Sultan?
SALADIN:	Nathan, dear Nathan!
	The thousand thousand years of your Judge
	Have not yet come. His judgment seat is not mine.
	Go! Go! But be my friend.
NATHAN:	Has Saladin nothing more to say to me?
SALADIN:	Nothing.

Chapter Six

Crush That Infamous Thing: 1733–1764

Introduction

Voltaire (born François-Marie Arouet; 1694–1778) stands at the midpoint of the Enlightenment era—and is, arguably, its voice. It is his message that sums up all the rest: impatience with unjust authority, superstition, and triviality; a strike for freedom of thought, speech, and worship; a reevaluation of the past and new orientation toward the future; and a hatred, above all, of the institutions that burden and torment the human spirit, especially the Catholic Church, but a few others as well. Ranging over every inch of the cultural universe in seven-league boots, he is not deep or difficult (he is a *philosophe*, not a philosopher), but quick, ruthless, and entertaining. "*Ecrasez l'infâme!*" ("Crush that infamous thing!") is his famous watchword.

This chapter offers samples from across the spectrum of Voltaire's thought, and from, of the many genres in which he wrote, omitting poetry and drama, those of history, the letter, the novel, the treatise, and the encyclopedia.

Chased out of France for a peccadillo that turned dangerous, Voltaire spent the years 1726 to 1728 in England, the so-called nation of shopkeepers that would soon best his native France and seize European, and with it world, primacy. The twenty-five *Lettres philosophiques* (*Philosophical Letters*, 1733) that he wrote not as letters in the ordinary sense, but as a series of anecdotal, but investigatory, reports on the English nation and people, implicitly address the question, Why was England so free? Because of its fluid, multifarious society and culture, Voltaire replies, a contrast to the social and cultural gridlock at home. Not only aristocrats, but also inventers and entrepreneurs mattered there; not just a king, but also a Parliament; not just one church, though only one was "established," but several belief systems, including those of Quakers, Presbyterians, and even Arians, purportedly extinct. It is telling that of his twenty-five letters "on the English," seven concern religion, as opposed to five about philosophers and two about politics. Still more striking, the first four profile Quakers, who were not merely Protestants, but a dissident minority resistant to the prevailing Calvinist and Lutheran orthodoxies and politically disadvantaged by British law. Voltaire especially admires the common sense of these proud outcasts, their refusal to be intimidated, and their unwillingness to defer to authority. He himself will be no Quaker, but he lionizes their bold, yet quiet resolve.

England won Voltaire's affection, but most other nations of the world won his strident disapproval. In his universal history, *Essai sur les moeurs et l'esprit des nations* (*The Culture and Spirit of Nations*, 1756), a work of more than two thousand pages in 197 chapters, Voltaire sweeps up the whole of the past, and declares it "disfigured" by cruelty, tyranny, and lies. *The Spirit of Nations* was his most ambitious history, for it embraced everything that had ever happened anywhere, including in those realms of the globe—eastward to China and Japan, westward to the Americas—where Europeans had recently entered and asserted their dominion; his more modest endeavors included histories of the Holy Roman Empire and the reign of King Louis XIV. As Voltaire narrates this ocean of past time, he seems to aim to obliterate it: certainly, its wars, persecutions, and hypocrisy. If so, his destructive historiography is emblematic of the Enlightenment rejection of the past, in favor of venturing forward into new domains of justice, civility, and creativity. Historical events are deemed worthy, it seems evident in the book's last summary chapter excerpted here, only if they anticipate the values of the Enlightenment.

Turning from a critique of the world's nations to that of a flawed philosophy, as he saw it, Voltaire undertook in his 1759 novel *Candide* the destruction of the *Theodicy* (literally, "God's justice") of German philosopher Gottfried Wilhelm Leibniz (1646–1716). *Candide* bears the subtitle "or *Optimism*," for that is what it is about: the absurdity of an optimistic outlook in a world gone so horribly wrong, and the absurdity, specifically, of Leibniz's optimistic defense, in the face of conspicuous evil, of God's benevolence—an argument Voltaire sums up devastatingly in the recurrent pronouncement that all is for the best in this "best of all possible worlds." This is the message taught the young hero Candide by his tutor and mentor Dr. Pangloss, a man learned in "all tongues," as his name declares, and all branches of philosophy. In his many adventures the novel relates, Candide finds out how wrong Pangloss is: he is wounded in the Seven Years' War (1756–1763); nearly drowned in the tsunami raised by the catastrophic Lisbon earthquake of 1755, as told in the excerpt given here; tortured by the Inquisition; nearly killed many times on his journeys through South America and Europe and on to the Ottoman Empire. All the while Candide searches for his first love Cunégonde, now hideously deformed, whom he rescues more than once and settles with at last, together with Pangloss and his other companions. Exhausted by all they have suffered, they are now intent only on the cultivation of the little farm that is their last refuge—"We must cultivate our garden," Candide famously concludes.

Had he still lived, Leibniz would not have recognized his *Theodicy* in Voltaire's brutal satire. The only full-length book Leibniz published in his lifetime, *Theodicy* explains how God can both be just and the creator of a world in which evil exists and people suffer. His general argument is plausible: if God is, as Christians and others believed, both omniscient (all-knowing) and omnipotent (all-powerful), nothing happens that is not within his purview; therefore all that occurs must be part of a divine providential plan. Many theologians would have agreed with this view, and many still do. But Voltaire rips, ravages, and morcellates it; earthquakes, war, and human malevolence, in ceaseless occurrence, are his proofs—forces that debase, destroy, and devour. Human existence is marked by hideous evil, leaving survivors no option but to do whatever they can do, and "cultivate" their "gardens."

In an event that could have been added to Voltaire's tale of horrors, on January 8, 2015, at the office in Paris of the satirical magazine *Charlie Hebdo*, terrorists slaughtered twelve staffers in the name of Allah, the Arabic word for God, whose name they evoked amid the carnage. They then dispersed through the city to murder five more. The massacre roused an outpouring of rage and sorrow from French people. Voltaire's *Traité sur la tolérance* (*Treatise on Tolerance*, 1763), more than 250 years after its first publication, became a best seller.[1]

Tolerance had been originally written in response to a specific incident, as its subtitle announces: "on the occasion of the death of Jean Calas." Executed wrongfully in 1762 for the murder of his son, as Voltaire explains in the first chapter of the work, Calas was a Huguenot, the minority of French Protestants who had been officially expelled by King Louis XIV in 1685, reversing the Edict of Nantes of 1598 granting freedom of worship. A Huguenot exodus from France transpired, enriching the productive populations of the Netherlands and England. In France, those who remained were vulnerable to persecution, as occurred in this case when a ferocious mob demanded the death of an innocent man because of his Huguenot faith.

Two hundred years after Sebastian Castellio first argued against the persecution of heretics, more than one hundred after Jacobus Arminius and Roger Williams had added their voices, and some seven decades since Enlightenment pioneers Pierre Bayle and John Locke published the first modern pleas for religious toleration, Voltaire responds to a horrific, if isolated incident of unjust persecution in the south of France—a region where heresy, and its suppression, had long thrived. This episode, both terrifying and senseless, encapsulates Voltaire's relentless battle against superstition and repression, summed up in his plea to "crush that infamous thing."

Where *Tolerance* addressed a single episode of brutality and fanaticism, Voltaire addresses in the year that followed the full panoply of malfeasance in his reprise of Bayle's *Critical Dictionary* (see Chapter 1): the *Dictionnaire philosophique* (*Philosophical Dictionary*, 1764), which subjects a broad array of theoretical concepts and historical figures to critical destruction. It possesses a different scope and organization—Voltaire's *Dictionary* comes to not quite

---

1. See contemporary articles cited in Texts and Studies, under Chapter Six, *Traité sur la tolérance*.

six hundred entries, Bayle's more than five thousand—but is similar in critical spirit. The effect of several decades of Enlightenment discussion is evident in Voltaire's choice of topics, which include not only such figures as "Moses" and "Zoroaster," but also "Newton" and "Locke"; and not only concepts such as "Hell" and "Purgatory," but also "Freedom of Thought" and "Litterati" (*gens de lettres*). In these brief essays that range over every conceivable field of knowledge, Voltaire's hatred of repression and celebration of human invention and intellect shine brightly.

When the *Philosophical Dictionary* was published, Voltaire was old, sick, and facing his last years. An exile on his extensive Swiss estate, he tended his cabbages and his rabbits—cultivating his garden, like his hero Candide—and managed from afar his stupendous self-made fortune and the clandestine publication of his works. An illegitimate son who had changed his name and crafted his own identity, the admirer of Quakers, the critic of Leibniz, the avenger of the persecuted, he wielded his pen prodigiously to "crush that infamous thing."

This is the country of sects

Voltaire, *Philosophical Letters* (1733)

Of Voltaire's twenty-five *Philosophical Letters*, seven concern religion: "This is the country of sects," he writes, pointing to the variety of beliefs that flourish in a country that is free because it permits the free exercise of religion. Though he does not neglect the Anglican Church, he deprecates it as a machine of the established elite—one that attracts converts seeking to get ahead and duly rewards those who rise to places of honor with wealth and security. The group he seems most to admire is not this established one but the Quakers, to whom he devotes four letters: noncomformists who scorn to wear the dress, swear the oaths, or fight the wars of the dominant majority.

The letters excerpted here, the first, fifth, sixth, and seventh, profile Quaker and antitrinitarian noncomformists, Scottish Presbyterians, and the Anglican faithful.

PHILOSOPHICAL LETTERS

First Letter: On the Quakers

It seemed to me that the doctrine and the history of so extraordinary a group deserved investigation by some thoughtful person to learn about them, I sought out one of the most famous Quakers in England, who, after thirty years in trade, knew how to set limits on his fortune and his desires, and had withdrawn to the countryside near London. I went to find him in his retreat; it was a small, well-built house, clean and without decorations. The Quaker was a fresh-looking old man who had never been ill because he had never known either passion or intemperance: I have never in my life seen a more noble or a more engaging countenance than his. He was dressed like all others of his religion, in a coat unpleated at the sides, and without buttons on the pockets or sleeves; and he carried a large flat-brimmed hat like those of our clergymen. He received me with his hat on his head, and came toward me without the slightest bow. . . .

. . .

After a healthy and frugal meal, which began and ended with a prayer to God, I set about to question my man. I began with the question that good Catholics frequently ask Huguenots:

"Dear Sir," said I to him, "have you been baptized?"

"No," answered the Quaker, "and neither are my brethren." "What the deuce!" I replied, "then are you not Christians?"

"My son," he replied gently, "do not swear. We are indeed Christians, and we try to be good Christians, but we do not believe that Christianity depends on throwing cold water and a bit of salt on the head."

. . .

"With regard to communion," I asked, "what do you do?" "We do not celebrate this." "What? No communion?" "None, except for the communion of hearts." And again he cited Scripture. He preached a fine sermon against communion, and spoke in inspired tones to prove that the sacraments were simply human inventions, and that the word *sacrament* appears nowhere in the Gospels.

. . .

"We dress somewhat differently from other men, so that we are always warned not to resemble them. Others wear their badges of honor; we wear our Christian humility; we flee idle pleasure, theaters, games; we would be much pitied if these trifles filled the hearts in which God dwells; we never take an oath, not even in a court of law; we believe that the name of the Almighty should not be prostituted in a miserable human controversy. When we must appear before magistrates for some business that involves others (for we never ourselves go to law) we affirm the truth by a *yes* or a *no* and the judges believe what we have said while so many Christians perjure themselves on the Bible. We do not go to war; it is not because we fear death—on the contrary, we bless the moment that unites us with the

Supreme Being—but because we are neither wolves, nor tigers, nor hounds, but men, but Christians."

Fifth Letter: On the Anglican religion

This is the country of sects. An Englishman, being a free man, goes to Heaven by whatever path he chooses.

However, although each one here may serve God as he wishes, the real religion, the one by which one makes one's fortune, is the Episcopal sect called the Anglican Church, or simply the Church. One can hold no post, either in England or in Ireland, unless one is a faithful Anglican; this fact, which provides convincing proof, has converted so many nonconformists[2] that today not more than a twentieth part of the population remains outside the dominant Church.

The Anglican clergy has retained many of the Catholic ceremonies, especially that of receiving tithes[3] in a meticulous fashion. They also piously intend to dominate.

In addition, they encourage in their flocks as best they can a holy zeal against the noncomformists. . . .

. . .

As far as morals are concerned, the Anglican clergy are better behaved than are the French. Here is the reason: All churchmen are educated in the Universities of Oxford or of Cambridge, far from the corruption of the capital; they are called to the honors of the Church only after many years, at the age when men's chief passion is avarice, and their ambition has nothing to feed upon. . . .

Sixth Letter: On the Presbyterians

Only in England and Ireland is the Anglican religion established. Presbyterianism is the dominant religion in Scotland. This Presbyterianism is simply pure Calvinism as it used to exist in France and continues in Geneva.[4] Since the priests of this sect receive but scant wages from their churches, and since, therefore, they cannot live in the luxury enjoyed by the bishops, they have naturally undertaken to preach against the honors that they cannot obtain. . . .

. . .

---

2. Nonconformists: non-Catholic dissenters from the Anglican church, barred from public office and other privileges.
3. Tithes: taxes that go the church, traditionally one-tenth.
4. The French Huguenots, expelled in 1685, were Calvinists, as were the citizens of Geneva, where Calvin had ministered, and of several other Swiss cities.

Were there only one religion in England, despotism would be a threat; were there two, they would be at each other's throats; but there are thirty, and they live happily and at peace with one another.

Seventh Letter: On the Socinians, or Arians, or Antitrinitarians

There is here a small sect of very learned ecclesiastics and laymen, who do not call themselves Arian or Socinian, but who do not share the opinion of Saint Athanasius on the question of the Trinity, and who will tell you bluntly that the Father is greater than the Son. . . .[5]

. . .

You see that revolutions occur in opinions as they do in empires. The Arian doctrine, after three hundred years of triumph and twelve centuries of neglect, was born again of its ashes; but it has returned inopportunely, at a time when the world has a surfeit of sectarian disputes. This sect is still too small to be permitted public meetings. It will obtain permission, no doubt, if it becomes larger, but everyone is so lukewarm about these matters that a new or revived religion can scarcely succeed. Is it not amusing that Luther, Calvin, Zwingli, all those unreadable writers, should have founded sects that together cover all of Europe?[6] That ignorant Mahomet [Muhammad] should have given a religion to Asia and Africa, and that Newton, Clarke, Locke, Le Clerc, etc., the greatest philosophers and the best writers of their time, have scarcely managed to assemble a tiny flock, one that is indeed shrinking daily?[7]

This is what it means to arrive in the world at the right moment. . . . If Cromwell were reborn, he who cut off the head of his king and made himself the sovereign, he would be a simple London merchant.

---

5. Arians were members of an ancient heresy that did not consider Christ coequal to God the Father. Socinians were a Reformation-era antitrinitarian sect. Both resemble the Antitrinitarians, later Unitarians, who could be found in England and the anglophone American colonies.
6. Voltaire names the three most prominent Reformers, Martin Luther, John Calvin, and Ulrich Zwingli; and Muhammad, founder of Islam.
7. For Isaac Newton and John Locke, see in this volume, respectively, Chapters 1 and 3. Voltaire further names the English scholar Samuel Clarke and Swiss biblical critic Jean Le Clerc, both contemporaries.

Disfigured by myth, until enlightenment comes

Voltaire, *The Culture and Spirit of Nations* (1756)

Voltaire's summation of the 2,150[8] pages of his universal history appears in the last, 197th, chapter, excerpted here. Distinguishing between the *moeurs* (translated here as "character"; see note below) and the *faits* ("deeds" or "events") observed in the historical record, he attempts to see their inter-relations: that is to say, he does not offer a mere chronology of events, but a discussion of their meaning related to the diverse peoples performing and affected by those happenings. His judgment, overall, is grim: the greater part of history, all over the globe, but particularly in Europe, is "disfigured by myth," and will remain so "until philosophy comes at last to enlighten humankind"—the transformation in progress in his own era. Singling out the conspicuous misbehavior of the popes and clergy of the Catholic Church, and the horrors of religious wars fought over minutiae of doctrine, he concludes that all of history is "a jumble of crimes, lunacy, and misery." And yet, noting Europe's splendid cities, rich agricultural resources, indus-triousness, and creativity, Voltaire offers hope: "Once a nation cultivates the arts, . . . it rises easily from its ruins, and is restored once more."

A note on the translation: translated literally from the French, the title of this work would include the words "manners" or "customs and spirit of nations." For our generation, however, both "manners" and "customs" seem precious or trivial; while for Voltaire's generation, "manners" and "customs" meant what we mean by culture: the whole assemblage of atti-tudes and assumptions of a people, displayed in their language, arts, and laws.

THE CULTURE AND SPIRIT OF NATIONS

Chapter 197: Summation of this whole history up to the beginning of the great century of Louis XIV

I have now traversed this vast spectacle of transformations from Charlemagne . . . to the time of Louis XIV.[9] What will be the outcome of this labor? What profit does one derive from history? We have observed the deeds and the culture of peoples. Let us see what benefit we reap from the knowledge of either one or the other. . . .

History is everywhere disfigured by myth, until philosophy comes at last to enlighten humankind. And when it comes finally amid this darkness, it finds minds so blinded by centuries of error that it can scarcely undeceive

---

8. In the 1829 edition utilized; cited in Texts and Studies.

9. Charlemagne (Charles the Great; 742–814), king of the Franks from 768, emperor of the Romans 800–814; Louis XIV (1638–1715), king of France, 1643–1715.

them. It finds ceremonies, monuments, events, established to celebrate illusions. . . .

It is clearly evident how much culture has changed almost everywhere on earth since the time of the barbarian invasions until our day. The arts, which both soften and elevate minds, began a bit to be reborn from the twelfth century. But the most depraved and absurd superstitions, smothering this seedling, brutalized nearly all minds. These superstitions spread among all the savage and ignorant peoples of Europe, melding everywhere the ludicrous to the barbarous. . . .

For several centuries, popes were elected only with their weapons in their hands . . . and these gods on earth, by turns assassins and assassinated, poisoners and poisoned, enriching their bastards while issuing decrees against fornication, anathematizing, banning tournaments while waging war, excommunicating and deposing kings while selling to the people remission of their sins, were at the one and same time the scandal and the horror of Catholic Europe, and its sovereign divinity.

You have seen, in the twelfth and thirteenth centuries, monks become princes, as did bishops—these monks and bishops everywhere at the summit of feudal government. They established ridiculous customs, as outlandish as their morals, such as the exclusive right to enter a church with hunting hawk in hand. . . . You have seen among these barbarous absurdities the bloody barbarism of the wars of religion. . . . The blood flowed on the battlefield and on the scaffold, over theological disputes, here in this country and there in another, over five hundred years, almost without interruption. And this plague lasted as long as it did because morality was ever neglected in favor of dogma.

And so it must be acknowledged once again that, in the sum, all of this history is a jumble of crimes, lunacy, and misery, amid which we have seen a few great deeds, and a few good times, as one discovers a village scattered here and there in a barren desert. . . .

Amid these ravages and devastations that we observe across nine hundred years, we see a love for order that secretly moves the human species, and that has prevented its total ruination. It is one of those forces of nature which always recovers its strength. It is this that has created the codes of law, so that the law and its ministers are revered in Tonkin [Vietnam] and Formosa [Taiwan], as in the Roman Empire. . . .

It appears from this panorama that everything that is rooted in human nature is the same from one end of the universe to the other; but that everything that depends on culture is variable, and that any resemblance is merely accidental. The empire of culture is far vaster than that of nature, extending to the limits of all customs and values, propagating variation on the face of the universe. Nature, in contrast, diffuses unity, establishing everywhere a tiny number of invariable principles. Thus the foundation, which is nature, is the same everywhere, but culture produces diverse outcomes. . . .

From the tableau we have made of Europe since the time of Charlemagne until our own, it is apparent that this part of the world is incomparably more populous, more civilized, more wealthy, more enlightened, than what it once was, and is even far superior to the condition of the former Roman Empire, excepting Italy. . . .

If one considers the prodigious number of splendid cities, from St. Petersburg [Russia] to Madrid [Spain], built in places that were deserts six hundred years ago; or recalls the immense forests that once covered the earth from the banks of the Danube to the Baltic Sea and as far as the center of France, it is starkly evident that as land has been brought into cultivation, the population has flourished. Agriculture . . . and commerce have been valued far more than they were in former times. . . .

How flourishing then would have been Europe's condition without the turmoil of constant wars over trivial matters, and often for mere caprices! What degree of perfection would the cultivation of the land not have reached, and how even more greatly the arts which manufacture its products have conferred security and prosperity in civil life, if that astonishing number of men and women had not been uselessly interred in cloisters! . . .

For a very long time, civil wars have desolated Germany, England, France; but these misfortunes have been quickly repaired, and the flourishing state of these countries proves that human industry has brought them much further than previously had their savagery. . . . Once a nation cultivates the arts,[10] when it is no longer subjugated or enslaved by a foreign power, it rises easily from its ruins, and is restored once more.

The best of all possible worlds

Voltaire, *Candide* (1759)

The whole of *Candide* responds to Leibniz's *Theodicy*, but this episode of the Lisbon earthquake of November 1, 1755, which took some thirty thousand lives and left the city in ruins, does so most pointedly. Voltaire saw

---

10. By "arts," Voltaire means the whole range of human artistic and industrial activity.

the Lisbon earthquake as the very embodiment of inexplicable evil and testimony to the failure of divine providence, and mimics the Leibnizian argument for the justice of God in the outlandish pronouncements of Dr. Pangloss, tutor and companion to the innocent Candide. In chapter 5, given here in full, Candide and Pangloss are on a ship in Lisbon harbor when the earth shakes, their ship sinks, and the next stage of their adventures begins. Arrived in Lisbon, Pangloss discourses amid the wreckage on sufficient causes and universal reason in the hearing of an agent of the Inquisition, who tests the philosopher's views on free will—a doctrine of the church that seems to contradict the Leibnizian argument for the divine determination of all events. Pangloss replies cheerfully, doubling down on his explanations. But he has said too much, and at the close of the chapter, both he and Candide, though they live in the best of all possible worlds, are about to be arrested by the Inquisition.

This text appears in the translation by David Wootton (cited in Texts and Studies). The annotations are mine.

CANDIDE

. . .

Half of those on board, struck down, dying of those inconceivable agonies that the rolling of a vessel conveys to the nerves and to all the fluids of a body when it is shaken in opposing directions, didn't even have the strength to worry about the danger they faced. The other half cried out and prayed aloud; the sails were torn, the masts broken, the vessel took on water. Those who could work did what they could; but they were all at cross purposes, and no one took command. The Anabaptist[11] lent a hand; he was on the prow; a furious sailor hit him hard and laid him out on the deck; but the blow he gave him was so hard that he lost his balance and fell overboard head first. . . .

Candide ran to the side, and caught sight of his benefactor, who came up to the surface for a moment before being swallowed forever. He wanted to throw himself into the sea after him, but the philosopher Pangloss prevented him, proving to him that the Bay of Lisbon had been especially made so that the Anabaptist could drown in it. While he was proving this by logical deduction, the vessel foundered and everyone died, with the exception of Pangloss, of Candide, and of the brutal sailor who had drowned the virtuous Anabaptist; the wretch swam successfully to the shore, while Pangloss and Candide were carried ashore clinging to a plank.

---

11. The Anabaptist Jacques had assisted Candide earlier in the narrative, and is referred to as the latter's "benefactor."

When they had recovered a little they set out on foot for Lisbon; they had some money in their pockets with which they hoped to save themselves from starvation now that they had escaped drowning.

No sooner had they passed through the gates of the town, weeping over the death of their benefactor, than they felt the earth tremble under their feet; the sea in the port began to boil, and the ships at anchor were smashed to pieces. Gusts of wind showered sparks and glowing cinders over the streets and squares of the city; the houses collapsed, the roofs leveled with their foundations, and their foundations shattered; thirty thousand inhabitants, randomly selected without regard to age or sex, were crushed in the ruins. The sailor said to himself, with a whistle and a swear word, "There'll be good pickings here!" "What can be the sufficient reason[12] of this phenomenon?" asked Pangloss. "This is the end of the world!" cried Candide. The sailor at once ran into the middle of the ruins, risked death looking for money, found some, took it, got drunk, and having slept it off, bought the favors of the first willing woman that he met among the ruins of the shattered houses, surrounded by the dying and the dead. Pangloss, however, caught hold of his sleeve: "My friend," he said to him, "that's no good, you're falling short of the standard set by universal reason, you're not spending your time as you should." "Christ!" said the sailor. "I'm a sailor and I was born in the colonies. I've made four voyages to Japan, and four times I walked on the crucifix.[13] I'm just the man to talk to about universal reason!"

Some falling rocks had wounded Candide, who was stretched out in the street and covered in debris. He said to Pangloss, "Alas! Get me a little wine and some oil; I'm dying." "This earthquake isn't something new," replied Pangloss. "The city of Lima in South America felt the same shocks last year. The same causes, the same effects. There must be a fissure of sulfur underground that stretches from Lima to Lisbon."[14] "There is no better explanation," said Candide. "But for God's sake, get me a little oil and some wine." "What do you mean there *is* no better explanation!" replied the philosopher. "I maintain that my answer is proven and there *could* be no better explanation." Candide fainted and Pangloss brought him a little water from a nearby fountain.

Next day, having found some bits and pieces to eat while picking their way between the ruins, they recovered some of their strength. Then they worked alongside everyone else to give what help they could to their companions who had escaped death. A few residents, whom they had helped, gave

---

12. Sufficient reason: a philosophical principle that posits everything must have a reason, cause, or basis.

13. Trampling on the crucifix was a demonstration of the repudiation of Christianity required at this time of all Europeans entering Japan.

14. As a philosopher, Pangloss is happy, even in the absence of material evidence, to supply explanations for natural events as much as for metaphysical ones.

them as good a lunch as one could hope for after such a disaster. It is true that the meal was mournful; the guests mingled tears with their food, but Pangloss consoled them, assuring them that things could not be otherwise. "For," said he "all this is the best there could be; for if there is a volcano under Lisbon, then it couldn't be anywhere else. For it is impossible that things could be placed anywhere except where they are. For all is well."

A little dark man, an agent of the Inquisition, who was sitting beside him, politely joined in the conversation, and said: "I gather, sir, that you do not believe in original sin; for if all is as good as could be, then there has not been a fall, nor are we punished for it."[15]

"I very humbly beg pardon of Your Excellency," replied Pangloss even more politely, "for the fall of mankind and their punishment were necessary events in the best of all possible worlds."[16] "Good sir, then you don't believe in free will?" asked the agent. "Your Excellency will excuse me," said Pangloss, "but free will is compatible with inflexible necessity; for it was necessary that we should be free; since after all the will is determined . . ." Pangloss was in the middle of his phrase when the agent gave a nod of his head to his guard, who poured him a glass of Port to drink.

Are we not all children of the same God?

Voltaire, *Treatise on Tolerance* (1763)

Voltaire's extended plea for religious toleration revolves around a recent incident in southern France narrated in chapter 1 of his treatise. The young Huguenot Marc-Antoine Calas was found hanged, likely a suicide, in the house where lived his father, Jean Calas, mother, brother Pierre, and a maid-servant, joined that night by a young friend, Lavaisse, recently arrived from out of town. The townspeople, believing that Marc-Antoine had been on the verge of repudiating his Protestant faith and becoming Catholic, imme-diately suspect the members of the Calas household of having murdered the young man to avert his apostasy. The would-be convert is celebrated as

---

15. "Original sin" is the sin borne by all humans for the acts of Adam and Eve in the Garden of Eden that contravened God's commands. As a result of those acts, committed freely, for God had given both man and woman free will, both were expelled from the Garden, that expulsion constituting the fall of humankind.

16. In this conversation, Pangloss is explicating, and at the same time parodying, Leibniz's explanation that the necessary determination of all things is compatible with the exercise of free will—and indeed, that position is maintained today by many Christian theologians.

a martyr by the Catholic mob, while his friend and family are charged with murder, and his elderly father duly executed for that imaginary crime.

The twenty chapters of Voltaire's treatise that follow this narrative are a disquisition on toleration. It concludes with chapter 22, "On universal tolerance," from which some closing statements are given here.

TREATISE ON TOLERANCE

Chapter 1: A brief history of the death of Jean Calas

The murder of Calas, committed by the sword of justice in Toulouse[17] on March 9, 1762, is a most extraordinary event meriting the attention of our age and of posterity. . . .

. . .

Religion, suicide, parricide come together in this strange affair. It prompts us to ask whether a father and a mother strangled their son in order to please God; if a brother strangled his brother, or if a friend strangled his friend; and if the judges should reproach themselves for having executed an innocent father on the wheel,[18] or for having set free a guilty mother, brother, and friend. . . .

. . .

Some fanatic in the mob cried out that Jean Calas had hanged his own son Marc-Antoine. This accusation was repeated, and in no time it was unanimous. Others added that the deceased was to have made his abjuration [of his Protestant faith] the next day, and that his family and young Lavaisse [who were Protestant], had strangled him out of hatred for the Catholic religion. A moment later, no one doubted this claim; the whole village believed that this was an article of faith for Protestants, that his own parents must assassinate a son who had decided to convert.

Once people's minds are aroused, they do not stop. They imagined that the Protestants of Languedoc had assembled the night before; that they had chosen by the vote of a plurality one of their own as executioner; that the young Lavaisse had been chosen; that this young man had within twenty-four hours received the news of his election and come from Bordeaux to assist Jean

---

17. A city in southern France, the capital of the former province of Languedoc, a region that had long been prone to religious turmoil.
18. "To break on the wheel": a traditional and painful form of capital punishment by which the bones of the condemned person were bludgeoned as he was turned on a rotating wheel.

Calas, his wife, and their son Pierre, to strangle him who was their friend, son, and brother.

David, the captain of Toulouse, excited by these reports and wanting to look good by arranging a prompt execution, acting against established rules and ordinances, had the members of the Calas family thrown in prison, along with their Catholic maidservant, and Lavaisse.

Zealous Catholics bizarrely honor the corpse of the deceased Calas, who had been on the verge of returning to their church before, they claimed, he had been murdered by his Protestant kin.

An official statement was then published, no less vicious than this imprisonment. It went further: Marc-Antoine Calas had died a Calvinist,[19] and as such, and if he had taken his own life, his body, as was the practice, would have been dragged on a hurdle.[20] Instead, he was buried with lavish ceremony in the church of St. Etienne, ignoring the priest who protested this profanation. . . .

Marc-Antoine was buried with the solemn service accorded to martyrs. Never has any church celebrated a veritable martyr with greater ceremony; but this ceremony was ghastly. On a bier beneath a magnificent canopy, they positioned a skeleton so as to represent Marc-Antoine Calas, the palm [of martyrdom] in one hand and in the other the pen with which he was to sign his abjuration of heresy—signing thereby, in effect, his father's death warrant.

Now nothing remained to be done to this poor wretch, an attempted suicide, but canonization.[21] All regarded him as a saint; some called on his name, some prayed at his tomb; some asked for a miracle, while others told the stories of miracles he had performed. . . . From this moment, the death of Jean Calas seemed inevitable.

That fate seemed even more certain given that the year in which these events occurred, 1762, was the two hundredth anniversary of the massacre of four thousand Huguenots at Wassy in 1562 that marked the beginning of the French religious wars. The Calas incident coincided with the celebration of that event.

The village was adorned with the trappings of this solemnity, which further enflamed the heated imagination of the inhabitants. The scaffold on which the Calas family were to be executed, it was publicly said, would be the finest ornament of the celebration; divine providence itself would deliver these

---

19. The French Protestants, known as Huguenots, were followers of Calvin's reform principles.
20. A defamatory postmortem punishment for suicides, duelists, and some other offenders. The hurdle is a wooden panel or fence section.
21. In the Catholic religion, martyrs are often subsequently canonized, or recognized as saints of the church, if they had performed miracles in life, or their relics did so after death.

victims to be sacrificed for our holy religion. . . . And this in the present age! At a time when philosophy has made such progress! . . .

. . .

Jean Calas was broken on the wheel, the others discharged, but destroyed. There follows an extended discussion of toleration and persecution, culminating in the passages given here from chapter 22, after which the work closes with a final prayer and several postscripts.

Chapter 22: On universal tolerance

No great skill, no refined eloquence is required to prove that Christians should tolerate each other. I persist: I declare to you that we must accept all human beings as our brothers. What! My brother the Turk?[22] . . . The Jew? . . . Yes, without a doubt. Are we not all the children of the same Father, and creatures of the same God?

. . .

It is true that such absurd horrors [as that of the Calas persecution] do not every day defile the face of the earth; but they have been frequent, and they would compose a volume much larger than the Gospels, by which they are condemned. Not only is it cruel to persecute, in this short life that we live, those who do not think like us, but I find it excessively bold to assign them to eternal damnation. . . .

. . .

O worshipers of a merciful God! . . . If in adoring him whose whole law consists in these words, "Love God and your neighbor,"[23] you have overburdened this pure and holy law with sophistries and incomprehensible arguments; . . . if you have assigned to other peoples the penalty of eternal punishment for the omission of a few words or a few ceremonies that they could not have known, I would say to you, as I weep for humankind:

"Transport yourself with me to the day when all will be judged, and when God will deal with each according to his deeds. I see all the dead of ages past and of our own appearing in his presence. Are you sure that our Father and

---

22. The Ottoman Turks, who were Muslims, invaded Christian Europe in the fourteenth century, initiating a conflict that continued through the seventeenth century, after which distrust lingered between adherents of the two religions. Jews had long been permitted residence in Europe, and were officially protected from persecution, but outbreaks of hostility against the Jewish minority by the Christian majority were recurrent. Voltaire's assertion of the kinship between the three theisms here anticipates Lessing's (see Chapter Five).
23. Cf. Matthew 22:36–40, among similar Gospel passages.

Creator will say to the wise and virtuous Confucius, to the lawmaker Solon, to Pythagoras, . . . to Socrates, to Plato,[24] . . . to so many others who were paradigms of humanity: Go, you monsters, to suffer punishment infinite in intensity and duration, so that your suffering may be eternal as I am eternal! And you, my beloved Jean Châtel, [François] Ravaillac, [Robert-François] Damiens, [Louis-Dominique] Cartouche,[25] and others who died according to the correct formulas, sit with me at my right hand and share forever my empire and my delight."

You recoil in horror at these words; and now that they have escaped my lips, I have nothing more to say.

If a book displeases you, refute it!

Voltaire, *Philosophical Dictionary* (1764)

The topics of the nearly six hundred articles appearing in Voltaire's *Philosophical Dictionary* range from religion to philosophy to politics to daily life. The five selected here are chosen to illustrate Voltaire's views about issues not yet addressed in this chapter: "equality"; "slaves"; "woman"; "man"; "freedom of the press." They are given in the order in which they appear in the original work, alphabetically according to their spelling in French.

In the first, second, and last of these articles, Voltaire expresses views consistent with the emerging liberal consensus that has endured into the twenty-first century, although it is now challenged. Voltaire assumes the essential equality of all human beings, but doubts that social equality is an attainable ideal. He is deeply opposed to slavery. And he supports freedom of the press, arguing that printed words are not dangerous—as individuals, armies, states, or churches surely are; they should be refuted if they are wrong, but not suppressed.

In the third and fourth articles, in striking contrast, profiling the generic "Woman" and generic "Man," Voltaire offers traditional stereotypes of male and female body types that he sees as mirroring psychological and intellectual capacities, the male outpacing the female—this, though he circulated in Parisian salons led by women conversationalists, and though for more than a

---

24. Voltaire names a series of sages and philosophers from ancient China (Confucius) and ancient Greece (Solon, Pythagoras, Socrates, Plato).

25. Voltaire names here a series of four persons believed to have been assassins inspired by religious zealotry—a series in contrast to the sages and philosophers named in the previous sentence.

decade he had been the lover and colleague of the brilliant scientist Émilie Du Châtelet. Not even Voltaire, whose voice was virtually the voice of the Enlightenment, escaped the prejudices of his age.

PHILOSOPHICAL DICTIONARY

Égalité [Equality]

Clearly, all men[26] in possession of their natural faculties are equal. They are equal in their performance of animal functions, and equal when they exercise their understanding. . . .

. . .

If this world were what it ought to be, if man found everywhere an easy and assured subsistence and a climate suited to his nature, then clearly, it would have been impossible that any man reduce another to his service. . . . In this natural state . . . domination would have been a fancy, an absurdity that no one ever considered: Why search for servants when you require no sort of service? . . .

. . .

But in our unhappy world, society is necessarily divided into two classes: the one, that of the rich who command; the other, that of the poor who serve. And these two are further subdivided into a thousand ranks, and these thousand are still further subdivided. . . .

. . .

The human species is such that it cannot exist without there being an infinitude of productive men who possess nothing at all. . . . Equality is thus at once the most natural condition, and the most illusory. . . .

Esclaves [Slaves]

. . .

Slavery is as ancient as war, and war as ancient as human nature. . . . No legislator in ancient times attempted to abolish slavery. On the contrary, the peoples who most valued liberty—the Athenians, the Spartans, the Romans, the Carthaginians—were those whose laws dealt most harshly with their slaves. . . .

---

26. In this case, the translation does not reach for the more inclusive terms "human being" or "humankind," since Voltaire's use of the term "men" is clearly restrictive.

The Gospels do not report that Jesus Christ said a single word recalling humankind to that original liberty for which they were clearly born. Nothing is said in the New Testament about this state of degradation and suffering to which half of the human species was condemned. . . .

. . .

Voltaire addresses the question raised by some whether it is not better to be a slave, assured of subsistence, than a servant.

It is for the men in that condition about which they dispute to decide which they prefer. Ask the filthiest laborer, dressed in rags, fed on black bread, sleeping on straw in an unroofed hovel—ask him if he would rather be a slave, better fed, better dressed, better housed. Not only will he respond by recoiling in horror, but will be horrified that you dared to make the proposal.

Then ask a slave if he would like to be free, and you will see how he responds. Thus the issue is summarily decided.

Femme [Woman]

Woman in general is weaker than Man, smaller in frame, less capable of hard work. Her blood is more watery, . . . her members more rounded, her arms less muscular, her mouth smaller, . . . her belly larger. These features distinguish women around the globe, among all races, from Lapland to the Guinea coast, in America as in China. . . .

. . .

Being weaker of body than men are, women have more skillful fingers. . . . Unable to sustain the heavy labor of masonry, carpentry, metallurgy, or the plow, they are inevitably assigned the lesser and easier tasks within the house, and especially with the care of children. Leading a more sedentary life, their nature is gentler than that of the race of men. . . .

. . .

Some women have been deeply learned, just as some have been warriors. But no woman has ever been an inventor. . . . In no republic have they ever played the smallest role in government. . . .

Homme [Man]

. . .

Reason, industrious hands, a brain capable of forming general concepts, a language supple enough to express them: these are the great benefits that the Supreme Being has accorded to Man, to the exclusion of all other animals.

The male, in general, lives a shorter life than the female. He is always larger, relatively speaking. . . . His strength is almost always superior. . . . All the arts were invented by him, and not by Woman. . . .

The human species is the only one that knows it must die—and this it knows only by experience. A child raised in isolation on a desert island would have no more awareness of death than a plant or a cat. . . .

. . .

What would Man be in the state we call "pure nature"? . . . Man, abandoned to pure nature, would have as language only a few grunted sounds. The species would shrink to nothingness because of the scarcity of food and lack of shelter, especially in our harsh climates. He would have no more knowledge of God and the soul than of mathematics. His ideas would atrophy, stifled by the overriding need to find nourishment. It would be better to be a beaver than a Man.

Liberté d'imprimer [Freedom of the press]

What harm can be done to Russia by Rousseau's prediction [that other nations would soon destroy it]? None. . . . The nations that will destroy the Russians are literature and mathematics, and the social niceties and manners that degrade man and pervert his nature.

Between five and six thousand pamphlets were published in Holland against [French king] Louis XIV. Not one of them caused his defeat at the battles of Blenheim, Turin, and Ramillies.

In general, we have as much a natural right to make use of our pen as of our tongue, suffering its perils, risks, and misfortunes. . . .

. . .

Consider, please, what state has been destroyed by a book? The most dangerous, the most pernicious of all is that of Spinoza. Not only, as a Jew, does he attack the New Testament, but as a scholar, he destroys the Old. His atheistic system is better constructed and better reasoned, a thousand times over, than those of [the Greek philosophers] Strato [of Lampsacus] and Epicurus. It would take the most profound sagacity to respond to the arguments by which he demonstrates that one substance cannot form another.

Like you, I detest this book, which I understand perhaps better than you, and to which you have made a deficient response. But can you claim that this book has changed the course of history? . . .

. . .

If a book displeases you, refute it! If it bores you, do not read it!

But oh! You tell me, the books of Luther and Calvin have destroyed the Roman church in half of Europe. Why don't you also tell me that the books of the patriarch Photius[27] destroyed the same Roman church in Asia, Africa, Greece, and Russia? . . .

. . .

No, Rome was not vanquished by books. It was vanquished because it disgusted Europe with its rapacity; with its hawking of indulgences; by insulting men, seeking to govern them like cattle; by abusing its power so excessively that the astonishing thing is that it retains the loyalty of even one village. . . .

---

27. Photius: the ninth-century patriarch of Constantinople was the able systematizer of Greek orthodox Christianity that would soon split irreparably with Latin Catholicism.

Chapter Seven

Toward the Greater Good: 1748–1776

Introduction

In 1776, Jeremy Bentham (1748–1832) formulated the moral theory of Utilitarianism with these words: "it is the greatest happiness of the greatest number that is the measure of right and wrong."[1] Although Utilitarianism would have a major impact on public policy in the approaching industrial age, it emerged from Enlightenment discussions in the middle of the eighteenth century. As thoughts shifted from the cosmos to earth, and from God to humankind, the question arose, How can human society best be ordered for the maximum benefit of its inhabitants? The five thinkers presented in this chapter, writing in the not quite thirty-year period from 1748 to 1776, address this question.

Charles de Secondat, baron de Montesquieu (1689–1755), the first of these five authors, was the principal political theorist of the Enlightenment,[2] who examined how constitutional structures might discourage tyranny and promote the interests of the people. The second, also French, François Quesnay (1694–1774), founded the physiocratic movement that advocated complete economic freedom: the principle of *laissez-faire*. The third, the Italian nobleman and statesman Cesare Beccaria (1738–1794), inquired whether the administration of criminal justice by the state sufficiently considered the rights and interests of the citizens. The fourth and fifth, both Scots, were leading figures of the Scottish Enlightenment that was conspicuous, as much as the French, for its intellectual and scientific culture. Adam Ferguson (1723–1816), a pioneer of historical sociology, examined the historical record to understand the origins and advancement of civil society. Adam Smith (1723–1790) developed arguments for free trade and strategies for economic growth that might promote the general welfare.

---

1. As quoted by J. H. Burns, "Happiness and Utility: Jeremy Bentham's Equation," *Utilitas*, 17, no. 1 (2005), 46. Burns proposes that Bentham coined the phrase after reading Beccaria's *On Crimes and Punishments*, discussed in the present chapter.
2. Other contenders are Jean-Jacques Rousseau and Edmund Burke. Rousseau, who wrote famously on politics in his *Social Contract*, and will be discussed in Chapter Nine, was not primarily a political thinker, and his *Social Contract*, however fertile and imaginative, is not a systematic political work. Burke, author of *Reflections on the Revolution in France*, is a powerful political thinker who will be discussed below in Chapter Twelve.

A probing analyst of political systems and an advocate of political liberty, Montesquieu would exert enormous influence on later theorists, among them Herder (see Chapter Eight), the writers of the American Constitution, and such nineteenth-century thinkers as Alexis de Tocqueville. Likewise, he drew upon the whole heritage of Western political thought, utilizing the ancients Aristotle and Cicero; the medieval scholastics Thomas Aquinas and Marsilius of Padua; the more recent Dutch and German internationalists Grotius and von Pufendorf; the Italian philosopher Vico; and the English political theorists Hobbes and Locke. He stands at the crossroads of these traditions, past and future, equipped with a thorough training in Roman and modern law, and maps out a framework of different possible constitutional models.

In his earlier works, the *Persian Letters* (1721), Montesquieu had critiqued modern French civilization from the perspective of imaginary travelers from Persia (modern Iran); and in the *Considerations on the Causes of the Greatness of the Romans and Their Decline* (1734), following Machiavelli and anticipating Gibbon, he had attempted to explain the trajectory of that empire. But in *The Spirit of the Laws* (1748, revised posthumous edition 1757), his last major work and his culminating lifework, he broadened his range. As the scientific observer of constitutional systems worldwide, he identifies three such systems: republics (which can be either democratic or aristocratic), monarchies, and despotisms. In the same work, he relates these types of government, as they have appeared historically, to sets of social, cultural, and material conditions—among the latter, notably, is climate, which almost monocausally directs the political choices that are made in each global setting. But in this work as well, most consequently for later European and American readers of Montesquieu, he defines as the best constitutional system one whose three main powers—legislative, executive, judicial—so check each other as to prevent the eruption of tyranny, and to secure the political liberty of the whole population.

Montesquieu was an aristocrat whose family could be traced back more than three centuries—and thereby a member of a dominant social caste whose ascendance was tied to the monarchy and invested in the appropriation of peasant labor. And yet, he detested tyranny, denounced slavery, and proposed ways in which government could be so structured as to admit maximum participation of the people and deter the concentration of despotic power.

Not a nobleman, but merely the son of a peasant landowner, Quesnay was apprenticed to a surgeon, eventually rising to become personal physician to King Louis XV, who ennobled him and brought him to the Palace of Versailles. There he devoted himself to economic studies, leading a coterie of economic theorists known as physiocrats, best remembered for their motto: *laissez-faire, laissez-passer* (roughly, "let it happen, let it go").

Quesnay's views are concisely expressed in his thirty *Maximes générales de gouvernement economique d'un royaume agricole* (*General Maxims for the Economic Management of an Agricultural Kingdom*, 1758), excerpts of fifteen of which are given in this chapter. In these, Quesnay presents his fundamental thesis that the diligent cultivation of the land alone produces a surplus, which when reinvested produces a greater surplus still, which if allowed to circulate freely will result in an overall increase of wealth benefiting all the inhabitants of a nation. His identification of land as the only source of wealth was already obsolete at a time when industrial development—which Quesnay considered "sterile"—was well underway in England. But the principle would long prevail that free, unregulated trade more greatly promoted the wealth of the nation than do the fees and regulations that burdened commerce in the mercantilist strategies then employed by the European states. This fundamental principle of modern economic liberalism would be developed further by Adam Smith, of whom more shortly.

Unlike the baron de Montesquieu or the royal physician Quesnay, Beccaria, the son of a Lombard patrician, lived in obscurity, his one main accomplishment a remarkable, explosively successful book: *On Crimes and Punishments* (1764). A two-hundred-year legacy of arguments for toleration, replete with protests against judicial cruelty in matters of belief, permitted Beccaria to broaden the arena to deplore judicial cruelty against actual criminals. The aim in the prosecution of crime, he argued, should not be to extract vengeance, but merely to put an end to the malfeasance—and so to leave the state innocent of the blood of the malefactor.

Conceived and developed in discussions among a circle of Italian Enlightenment thinkers in Milan, the work was crafted by Beccaria and guided through several editions. It journeyed to France and England—where Bentham read it, extracting from it the notion of the "greatest good for the greatest number" as noted earlier; and from England across the Atlantic, where the writers of the Bill of Rights (first ten amendments) of the American Constitution included among other prohibitions, following Beccaria, those against "cruel and unusual punishments" and coerced self-incrimination. In Italy, as well, Beccaria's work produced results. On November 30, 1786, the death penalty was abolished for the first time anywhere in Europe, in the Grand Duchy of Tuscany under its Habsburg ruler, the future Holy Roman Emperor Leopold II.[3]

---

3. A similar attempt was unsuccessful in Lombardy, although it was considered. See "The Opinion of the Undersigned Members of the Committee Charged with the Reform of the Criminal System in Austrian Lombardy for Matters Pertaining to Capital Punishment (1792)," in the collection of sources on the reception of Beccaria's work *On Crimes and Punishments and Other Writings* (cited in Texts and Studies), 153–60.

From Italy, where the latest ideas reached only small coteries in a few major cities, attention turns to Scotland, a small country equally remote from Paris and its glittering salons, the hub of Enlightenment civilization. France had a population of some twenty-five million in the middle of the eighteenth century. In contrast, by its first census in 1755, Scotland had a population that was one-twentieth of that number, just one and one-quarter million. Its largest city, Edinburgh, numbered 57,000 inhabitants, about one-tenth the size of Paris. And yet Scotland was arguably the second most important Enlightenment center, the intellectual flowering of its middle-class elite coincident with the nation's union with England. Scottish universities, academies, printing houses, and reading societies fostered a network of discussion of industrial development, scientific investigation, philosophy, and literature that nurtured some of the most important thinkers of the Enlightenment. Among these were David Hume, considered in Chapter Five, and Adam Ferguson and Adam Smith, considered in the present chapter, all three of whom, for at least part of their careers, held university posts at Edinburgh or Glasgow. A primary concern for the theorists of the Scottish Enlightenment was the betterment of the human condition, believed by many to depend on the advancement of civil society: the web of cultural and social activity engaging citizens outside of the official institutions of the state.

In his *Essay on the History of Civil Society* (1767), Adam Ferguson addresses just this issue. Like Vico, Voltaire, and Montesquieu, he finds that the laboratory of history yields principles to guide the present and to foster those institutions and behaviors that lead to a greater public good. After an exploration of essential human nature, the *Essay* examines the societies of early human communities, or "rude nations"; the history of political societies, including the effects of climate and population and the possibility of civic liberty; the role of commerce; and the causes of civilizational decline.

Ferguson's contemporary and compatriot Adam Smith, as well, is concerned with the moral dimensions of civil society, and envisions an existence where people will enjoy maximum freedom and well-being. His early work, *The Theory of Moral Sentiments* (1759), like Ferguson's, explores the networks of sentiment and obligation that hold human societies together. But the work for which he is renowned worldwide is *The Wealth of Nations* (1776). In it he critiques the prevailing mercantilist policies that had previously been targeted by the physiocrats, by which nations in competition seek to accumulate the greatest wealth by regulating and managing national economies. Instead, he advocates maximum economic freedom, which will correlate with political liberty and a higher level of human well-being. With

Smith, the quest for a more free and humane society culminates in a new science, that of political economy, a leading field of inquiry in the century soon to dawn.

When people today look back at the Enlightenment, they see it through the filter of the violence and bloodshed of the intervening French Revolution, with which the story of the Enlightenment ends. But Enlightenment thinkers writing in the pre-revolutionary era were concerned not with revolution, but with the evolution of human societies toward greater compassion, civility, abundance, and freedom. In sketching what a society might look like whose institutions and energies aimed for a common good, the thinkers presented in this chapter anticipate not the violent political cataclysm that, in France, brought this era to a close, but rather Utilitarianism, a movement that advanced in the post-revolutionary period, aiming to secure, in Bentham's classic phrase, "the greatest happiness of the greatest number."

Things must be so ordered that power checks power

Charles de Secondat, baron de Montesquieu, *The Spirit of the Laws* (1748)

The excerpts given here are taken from chapters 4 and 6 of book 11 of *The Spirit of the Laws*, entitled "Laws That Comprise Political Liberty: Their Relation to the Constitution." Political liberty depends, Montesquieu explains, on the separation of powers, and specifically those three powers that together make up the constitution, or system of laws: the executive, the legislative, and the judicial. These powers interact in delicate balance, each checking the other. The legislative checks the executive by making laws, but does not otherwise interfere with executive action. The executive, which directs the state, checks the legislative power by withholding consent, or vetoing, its laws. The judicial power, whose main function is to punish crime, also exists to resolve disputes, and thus must remain strictly separate from either legislative or executive agencies lest it become itself dictatorial. The result is a stable yet dynamic system of checks and balances, with each branch active in its own right, and coordinating with the others. The country that most nearly achieved this ideal in his own day, Montesquieu argues, was England. Hence much of this discussion is placed under the rubric "The English Constitution," at the head of chapter 6.

Chapter 4: What liberty is [continuation]

Neither democracy nor aristocracy is free by nature. Political liberty exists only in those governments where power is moderated . . . [and] only when there is no abuse of power. But all experience proves that every man with power is led to abuse it. . . . To prevent the abuse of power, things must be so ordered that power checks power. . . .

. . .

Chapter 6: The English constitution

In every government, there are three sorts of powers: the legislative; the executive, in regard to those matters determined by the laws of nations; and the judicial, in regard to those matters determined by the civil law.

By virtue of the first, the ruler or magistrate makes laws, either temporarily, or for all time, as well as correcting or abrogating those already in existence. By virtue of the second, he makes war or peace, sends or receives ambassadors, ensures security, and makes provision against invasion. By virtue of the third power, he punishes crimes, or passes judgment upon disputes arising among individuals. This is called the judicial power; the second, simply the executive power of the state.

For a citizen, political liberty is that tranquility of mind which derives from his sense of security. Liberty of this kind presupposes a government so ordered that no citizen need fear another.

When both the legislative and executive powers are united in the same person or body of magistrates, there is no liberty. For then it may be feared that the same monarch or senate has made tyrannical laws in order to execute them in a tyrannical way.

Again, there is no liberty, if the power to judge is not separated from the legislative and executive powers. Were the judicial power joined to the legislative, the life and liberty of the citizens would be subject to arbitrary power. For the judge would then be the legislator. Were the judicial power joined to the executive, the judge could acquire enough strength to become an oppressor.

All would be lost if the same man, or the same body, whether composed of notables, nobles, or the people, were to exercise these three powers: that of making laws, that of executing public decisions, and that of judging crimes or disputes arising among individuals. . . .

. . .

In a free state, every man who is considered a free citizen ought to be governed by himself. Hence the people as an estate [group] . . . ought to have the legislative power. However, since that is impossible in large states and subject to many disadvantages in small ones, the people must do by its representatives everything it cannot itself do.

Everyone knows much better the needs of his city than those of other cities; he is a better judge of his neighbors' capacities than those possessed by their other compatriots. Members of the legislative body should not be drawn, therefore, from the nation in general. What is more appropriate is that the inhabitants of every place of importance elect a representative.

The great advantage of representatives is their capacity to discuss public business. For this the people [as a body] are quite unfitted, and this is among the greatest disadvantages of democracy. . . .

. . .

The executive power ought to be in the hands of a monarch, because this part of government, which almost always requires rapid action, is better administered by one person than by many. On the other hand, whatever is determined by the legislative power is often better decided . . . by many than by one.

If there were no monarch, if the executive power were entrusted to a number of persons taken from the legislative body, there would no longer be any liberty. For the two powers would be united, the same persons would sometimes in fact share, and always have the power to share, in both.

If the legislative power were to go without meeting for a considerable time, there would no longer be any liberty. For one of two things would occur: either there would no longer be any legislative decisions, and the state would fall into anarchy; or else decisions would be taken by the executive power, which would thus become absolute.

It would serve no purpose to have the legislative body always in session. Not only would this be inconvenient for the representatives, it would also preoccupy the executive power, which would think, not of doing what it is meant to do, but rather of defending its prerogatives, and its right to execute [legislation].

Furthermore, were the legislative body continually in session, it might happen that new representatives would be chosen only to replace those who had died. In that case, if the legislative body were ever corrupted, there would be no remedy. When different legislative bodies succeed each other, the people, if it has a bad opinion of the one in power, may place its hopes upon the one that will succeed it. But if the legislative body always remained the same, then in the event that it were corrupted, the people with nothing further to hope from legislation, would either be overcome by fury, or fall into indolence.

The legislative body ought not to meet at its own initiative. For a body is not considered to possess a will until it is in session. If the decision to meet were not unanimous, then it would be impossible to determine which in fact is the legislative body, that part in session, or that part which is absent. Were it to have the power to adjourn itself, it might happen that it would never adjourn, and this would be dangerous in the event that it attempted to encroach upon the executive power. Besides, there are better and worse times for convening the legislative body. Thus it ought to be the executive power, which on the basis of what it knows about the circumstances, sets the time and duration of legislative meetings.

If the executive does not have the power to check the designs of the legislative, this body would become despotic. For it if could arrogate to itself all the power it wished, then it would annihilate all other powers.

But it does not follow that as a matter of reciprocity, the legislative ought to have the power to check the executive. For there are limits to what the executive power can do, and these derive from its very nature. It is unnecessary to set further bounds. . . .

But if in a free state, the legislative power ought not to have the power to check the executive, it has the right and ought to have the means to investigate how the laws it has passed have been carried out. . . .

. . .

As has been said, the executive power ought to take part in legislation through its power to veto, without which it would soon be stripped of its prerogatives. But if the legislative power participates in executing what it has enacted, then the executive power will be just as much undone.

If the monarch were to participate in legislation by his power to make laws, there would no longer be any liberty. Nevertheless, if he is to defend himself, he must take part in legislation, and this by his power to refuse consent. . . .

Here, then is the fundamental constitution of the government being discussed. . . . These three powers ought to produce repose, or inaction. But since the nature of things requires movement, all three powers are obliged to act, and to act together.

Complete freedom of trade must be ensured

François Quesnay, *General Maxims for the Economic Management of an Agricultural Kingdom* (1758)

Quesnay's thirty "general maxims," or "guiding principles," of which fifteen are excerpted here, are a concise summary of the physiocratic economic program. They offer direction, to continue with the wording of his title, "for the economic management of an agricultural kingdom": implicit here are the notions that the economy will be primarily agricultural, as was that of the kingdom of France (of whose king Quesnay was a personal dependent), and that it will be actively managed by a monarch concerned to advance the prosperity of the nation.[4]

Modern readers may be surprised that Quesnay advocates both monarchical rule, as stated in maxim 1, and economic freedom, as seen in maxims 3–5, 13, 18, and 25. They will recognize the discussion of such matters as taxation, infrastructure, demographic pressure, and regulation; see maxims 3, 5, 17–20, and 26. Above all, Quesnay argues that land, not industry, is the sole source of wealth; see especially maxims 1, 3, and 12–15.

GENERAL MAXIMS

1. *There must be one sovereign authority superior to all the individual members of the society and to all the wrongful interventions of particular interests*: for the object of domination on the one hand, and obedience on the other, is the security and lawful interests of all. The system of countervailing forces in a government[5] is a disastrous notion that can only lead to discord among the elite and the oppression of the humble. The division of societies into different ranks of citizens, such that some exercise sovereign authority over the others, detracts from the general interest of the nation and promotes dissension among the competing interests of different groups of citizens. Such division would disrupt the administration of an agricultural kingdom which must unite all interests in the service of one overriding objective—that is, to the prosperity of the agricultural sector, which is the source of all the wealth of the nation and that of all its citizens.

. . .

---

4. It is not only France that Quesnay has in mind here but also China, whose benevolent and all-powerful emperor, as Quesnay viewed it, surrounded by an advisory council of scholars, not nobles, took direct interest in the productivity of the land and of the labor force. Quesnay would celebrate his model of China some years later in his *Despotisme de la Chine* (1767; *The Despotism of China*), cited in Texts and Studies.

5. Without naming Montesquieu, Quesnay rejects the latter's prescription made a decade earlier for the separation and counterbalancing of the powers of government.

3. *The sovereign and the nation must never forget that the land is the one and only source of wealth, and that it is agriculture that multiplies it.* For as wealth increases, so does population. Population and wealth together cause agriculture to prosper, invigorate trade, and animate industry, thus augmenting and perpetuating wealth. On this abundancy depends the success of all aspects of the administration of the kingdom.

4. *The possession of property both immovable, i.e., land, and movable must be guaranteed to those who are the legitimate owners;* because the security of property is the essential foundation of the economic order of a society. Without this security of ownership, the land would remain uncultivated. No proprietors or farmers would be willing to invest the sums necessary to cultivate the land and increase its value if the ownership of the land and its products were not guaranteed them. It is the assurance of permanent possession that inspires the willingness to labor and to employ wealth for the improvement of agriculture as well as commercial and industrial enterprises. . . .

5. *Taxation must not be destructive, or out of proportion to the total value of the national revenue.* It should only increase if revenue increases. It should be based directly on the net product of the land and not on income or the price of goods, or it will boost the cost of collection, interfere with trade, and erode year by year the wealth of the nation. Nor should it be levied on the property of landed farmers, because the nation's agricultural wealth must be seen as an endowment to be protected carefully in order to sustain the public fisc [treasury], national revenue, and the subsistence of all classes of citizens. Otherwise taxation degenerates into robbery and causes a deterioration that will quickly ruin the state.

. . .

12. *The children of wealthy farmers must remain resident in the countryside in order to perpetuate the labor force.* For if anything prompts them to abandon the countryside and attracts them to the cities, they take with them the wealth of their fathers that had been employed in agriculture. . . .

13. *Each individual must be free to cultivate on his own land whatever products his interests, his abilities, or the nature of the soil suggest to him will produce the most profitable harvest.* Monopoly should not be promoted in agriculture, because it reduces the general revenue of the nation. . . .

14. *The raising of livestock should be encouraged.* For it is the manure of these beasts that enrich the land so that it yields rich harvests.

15. *The land devoted to the cultivation of grain should be concentrated wherever possible into large holdings managed by the wealthier farmers.* For the costs of maintenance and repair of outbuildings are less, and in general there

is less expense and more net profit in large than in small agricultural enterprises. . . .

. . .

17. *The networks for transporting the products of agriculture and manufacturing should be facilitated* by making needed repairs of the roads and for the navigation of canals, rivers, and the ocean. For the more the costs of trade are reduced, the more the nation's revenue is increased.

18. *The price of foodstuffs and merchandise within the nation should not be artificially lowered,* as such intervention will disadvantage the nation in commercial exchange with foreign countries. As the market value goes, so goes the profit. To have abundance with low prices is not wealth; to have scarcity with high prices is poverty; but to have abundance and high prices is opulence.

19. *Do not believe that the low price of foodstuffs is beneficial for the common people.* For the low price of foodstuffs lowers their wages, lowers their standard of living, makes it harder for them to find employment in agricultural labor or more lucrative occupations, and destroys the national revenue.

20. *Do not lower the standard of living of the poorest citizens.* For in that case they will not be able to contribute sufficiently to the consumption of those commodities that must be consumed only within the country, which would retard the creation of wealth and diminish the national review.

. . .

25. *Complete freedom of trade must be ensured.* For the policy for domestic and foreign trade that is surest, best, and most profitable for the nation, is that of complete freedom of exchange.

26. *Pay less attention to the increase of population than to the increase of revenue.* For it is far better to have greater affluence, which produces greater revenues, than to sustain the pressing needs for subsistence, exceeding revenues, that a large population occasions; and there are more resources available for the needs of the state when the population is well off, and also greater capacity for the promotion of agriculture.

27. *The government should be less concerned with reducing costs than with promoting the prosperity of the nation.* For very great expenditures cease to be excessive if they result in the augmentation of wealth.

The nation's war against the citizen

Cesare Beccaria, *On Crimes and Punishments* (1764)

The flavor of Beccaria's elegantly reasoned critique of the prevailing system of crimes and punishments is detected in these four brief excerpts. He argues in chapter 6 that crimes are more or less severe to the extent that they injure the "public good" (*ben pubblico*) to a greater or lesser degree, and that punishments must be proportional to the severity of the crime. He continues in chapter 7 to assert "that the only true measurement of crimes is the harm done to the nation": not, that is, to the evildoer's intention, which is irrelevant and likely unknowable; and not to some absolute notion of the sinfulness of the crime, a consideration that pertains only to God, and not to humans.

In chapter 16, condemning torture, an ancient procedure used for many purposes, Beccaria points to the absurdity that to torture someone not yet convicted of a crime means, as has happened innumerable times in many nations, that an innocent person is punished for a crime he did not commit. A further injustice results, moreover, if he is not strong enough to withstand torture and incriminates himself, while a guilty person who is strong enough to endure the pain is acquitted: "This is a sure way to acquit robust scoundrels and to condemn weak but innocent people."

Finally, in chapter 28, Beccaria addresses the ultimate punishment, the death penalty, arguing that the state and the law have no authority to put a person to death, for their authority comes from the "general will" (*volontà generale*) of the people, which is the "aggregate of private wills"—and which person has granted to the state the right to take his life? The death penalty is not a "right" of the state, therefore, but rather the "war of the nation against a citizen," and as such proper only if that citizen, so long as he is alive, has the capacity to endanger the state—if he is a threat, as it might be said today, to national security. The other possible argument for capital punishment, that it deters other wrongdoers, Beccaria disputes and disproves. In all, capital punishment is wrong because it is an "example of cruelty." How can a nation condemn homicide, when it is itself willing to commit that very deed?

On Crimes and Punishments

6. Proportion between crimes and punishments

Not merely is it in the common interest that crimes not be committed, but that they be more infrequent in proportion to the harm they cause society. Therefore, the obstacles that restrain men from committing crimes should be stronger according to the degree that such misdeeds are contrary to the public good and according to the motives which lead people to crimes. Thus, there must be a proportion between crimes and punishments.

. . .

If an equal punishment is meted out to two crimes that offend society unequally, then men find no stronger obstacle standing in the way of committing the more serious crime if it holds a greater advantage for them.

7. Errors in the measurement of punishments

The preceding reflections give me the right to assert that the only true measurement of crimes is the harm done to the nation, and hence those who believe that the intention of the perpetrator is the true measurement of crimes are in error. Intention depends on the actual impression objects make on the mind and on the mind's prior dispositions; these vary in each and every man with the extremely rapid succession of ideas, emotions, and circumstances. Thus, it would be necessary to frame not only a separate law code for each new citizen, but a new law for each crime. Sometimes men with the best intention inflict the worst evil on society, and, at other times, they do the greatest good for it with the most wicked will.

. . .

Finally, some think that the gravity of sin should play a part in the measurement of crimes. The fallacy of this opinion will be immediately apparent to anyone who impartially examines the correct relationships between men and men and between men and God. . . . The seriousness of sin depends upon the unfathomable malice of the human heart, and finite beings cannot know this without revelation. How, then, can a standard for punishing crimes be drawn from this? In such a case, men might punish when God forgives and forgive when God punishes. If men can be in conflict with the Almighty by offending Him, they can also be so by punishing.

. . .

16. Torture

The torture of the accused while his trial is still in progress is a cruel practice sanctioned by the usage of most nations. Its purpose is either to make the accused confess his crime, or to resolve the contradictions into which he has fallen, or to discover his accomplices, or to urge him of infamy for some metaphysical and incomprehensible reason or other, or, finally, to find out other crimes of which he may be guilty, but of which he is not accused.

A man cannot be called "guilty" before the judge has passed sentence, and society cannot withdraw its protection except when it has been determined that he has violated the contracts on the basis of which that protection was granted to him. What right, then, other than the right of force, gives a judge the power to inflict punishment on a citizen while the question of his guilt or innocence is still in doubt? . . . But I add, moreover, that one confuses all natural relationships in requiring a man to be the accuser and the accused at the same time and in making pain the crucible of truth, as though the criterion of truth lay in the muscles and fibers of a poor wretch. This is a sure way to acquit robust scoundrels and to condemn weak but innocent people. . . .

. . .

The outcome of torture, then, is a matter of temperament and calculation that varies with each man in proportion to his hardiness and his sensitivity, so that, by means of this method, a mathematician could solve the following problem better than a judge could: given the strength of an innocent person's muscles and the sensitivity of his fibers, find the degree of pain that will make him confess himself guilty of a given crime.

. . .

28. The death penalty

This vain profusion of punishments, which has never made men better, has moved me to inquire whether capital punishment is truly useful and just in a well-organized state. By what alleged right can men slaughter their fellows? Certainly not by the authority from which sovereignty and law derive. That authority is nothing but the sum of tiny portions of the individual liberty of each person; it represents the general will, which is the aggregate of private wills. Who on earth has ever willed that other men should have the liberty to kill him? . . .

The death penalty, then, is not a *right*—for I have shown that it cannot be so—but rather a war of the nation against a citizen, a campaign waged on the ground that the nation has judged the destruction of his being to be useful or necessary. If I can demonstrate that capital punishment is neither useful nor necessary, however, I shall have vindicated the cause of humanity.

The death of a citizen cannot be deemed necessary except for two reasons. First, if he still has sufficient connections and such power that he can threaten the security of the nation even though he be deprived of his liberty, if his mere existence can produce a revolution dangerous to the established form of government, then his death is required. The death of a such a citizen becomes necessary, then, when the nation is losing or recovering its liberty, or in times of anarchy, when disorder itself takes the place of law. Under the calm rule of law, however, and under a regime that has the full support of the nation, that is well armed against external and internal enemies with force and with public opinion . . . , I see no necessity whatever for destroying a citizen. The sole exception would be if his death were the one and only deterrent to dissuade others from committing crimes. This is the second reason for believing that capital punishment could be just and necessary.

. . .

Beccaria disproves the argument for deterrence, concluding:

Capital punishment is not useful because of the example of cruelty which it gives to men. If the passions or the necessity of war have taught people to shed human blood, the laws that moderate men's conduct ought not to augment the cruel example, which is all the more pernicious because judicial execution is carried out methodically and formally. It appears absurd to me that the laws, which are the expression of the public will and which detest and punish homicide, commit murder themselves, and, in order to dissuade citizens from assassination, command public assassination.

There is no peace in the absence of justice

Adam Ferguson, *An Essay on the History of Civil Society* (1767)

Like Vico, Voltaire, and Montesquieu, Ferguson seeks to find in the historical record models of how human societies are structured, how they change, and how they may best serve the needs of their members. In these excerpts from his *Essay* (section 6, "Of Civil Liberty," from part 3, "On the History of Policy and Arts"), he addresses the role of law in promoting a harmonious society; the limits that might be placed on private property; the relative merits of a popular assembly and an assembly of representatives; and the success of England in achieving to a great degree a just and fair civil society.

Italicized subheads are supplied by the editor for greater legibility.

An Essay on the History of Civil Society

Law and justice as conditions of a harmonious society

There is no peace in the absence of justice. It may subsist with divisions, disputes, and contrary opinions; but not with the commission of wrongs. The injurious, and the injured, are, as implied in the very meaning of the terms, in a state of hostility.

Where men enjoy peace, they owe it either to their mutual regards and affections, or to the restraints of law. Those are the happiest states which procure peace to their members by the first of these methods: But it is sufficiently uncommon to procure it even by the second. . . .

Law is the treaty to which members of the same community have agreed, and under which the magistrate and the subject continue to enjoy their rights, and to maintain the peace of society. The desire of lucre is the great motive to injuries: law therefore has a principal reference to property. It would ascertain the different methods by which [261] property may be acquired, as by prescription, conveyance, and succession; and it makes the necessary provisions for rendering the possession of property secure. . . .

Where the citizen is supposed to have rights of property and of station, and is protected in the exercise of them, he is said to be free; and the very restraints by which he is hindered from the commission of crimes, are a part of his liberty. No person is free, where any person is suffered to do wrong with impunity. Even the despotic prince [262] on his throne, is not an exception to this general rule. . . .

. . .

An unequal distribution of wealth has consequences for the functioning of society.

It has been proposed to prevent the excessive accumulation of wealth in particular hands, by limiting the increase of private fortunes, by prohibiting entails,[6] and by withholding the right of primogeniture in the succession of heirs. It has been proposed to prevent the ruin of moderate estates, and to restrain the use, and consequently the desire of great ones, by sumptuary laws. These different methods are more or less consistent with the interests of commerce, and may be adopted, in different degrees, by a people whose national object is wealth: and they have their degree of effect, by inspiring moderation, or a sense of equality, and by stifling the passions by which mankind are prompted to mutual wrongs. . . .

This end is never perfectly attained in any state where the unequal division of property is admitted, and where fortune is allowed to bestow distinction and rank. It is indeed difficult, by any methods whatever, to shut up this source of corruption. Of all the nations whose history is known with

---

6. Entail: a legal mechanism by which inheritance of property is limited to a subset or to all of the owner's lineal descendants.

certainty, the design itself, and the manner of executing it, appear to have been understood in Sparta alone. . . .

A protracted discussion of the Spartan constitution follows.

. . .

Government led by a sovereign collective body, whether a popular assembly or an assembly of representatives, is favorable to the rights of the citizen.

Where the sovereign power is reserved by the collective body, it appears unnecessary to think of additional establishments for securing the rights of the citizen. But it is difficult, if not impossible, for the collective body to exercise this power in a manner that supersedes the necessity of every other political caution.

If popular assemblies assume every function of government; and if, in the same tumultuous manner in which they can, with great propriety, express their feelings, the sense of their rights, and their animosity to foreign or domestic enemies, they pretend to deliberate on points of national conduct, or to decide questions of equity and justice; the public is exposed to manifold inconveniences; and popular governments would, of all others, be the most subject to errors in administration, and to weakness in the execution of public measures.

To avoid these disadvantages, the people are always contented to delegate part of their power. They establish a senate to debate, and to prepare, if not to determine, questions that are brought to the collective body for a final resolution. They commit the executive power to some council of this sort, or to a magistrate who presides in their meetings. . . .

. . .

England's success in achieving a just and fair civil society

Rome and England, under their mixed governments, the one inclining to democracy, and the other to monarchy, have proved the great legislators among nations. The first has left the foundation, and great part of the superstructure of its civil code, to the continent of Europe. The other, in its island, has carried the authority and government of law to a point of perfection, which they never before attained in the history of mankind.

Under such favorable establishments, known customs, the practice and decisions of courts, as well as positive statutes, acquire the authority of laws; and every proceeding is conducted by some fixed and determinate rule. . . . The people in both reserved in a manner the office of judgment to themselves, and brought the decision of civil rights, or of criminal questions, to the tribunal of peers, who, in judging of their fellow-citizens, prescribed a condition of life for themselves. . . .

. . .

The history of England, and of every free country, abounds with the example of statutes enacted when the people or their representatives assembled, but never executed when the crown or the executive was left to itself. The most equitable laws on paper are consistent with the utmost despotism in administration. Even the form of trial by juries in England had its authority in law, while the proceedings of courts were arbitrary and oppressive.

We must admire, as the keystone of civil liberty, the statute which forces the secrets of every prison to be revealed, the cause of every commitment to be declared, and the person of the accused to be produced, that he may claim his enlargement [release], or his trial, within a limited time. No wiser form was ever opposed to the abuses of power. But it requires a fabric no less than the whole political constitution of Great Britain, a spirit no less than the refractory and turbulent zeal of this fortunate people, to secure its effects.

Led by an invisible hand

Adam Smith, *An Inquiry into the Nature and Causes of the Wealth of Nations* (1776)

The passages excerpted here introduce some of the principal themes of Smith's momentous work. It is the wealth of the nation, he argues, that secures the welfare of its citizens. The whole wealth of a nation depends on what it produces, and that productivity, in turn, setting aside such factors as its "soil, climate, or extent of territory," on its labor force: "the annual labor of every nation is the fund which originally supplies it with all the necessaries and conveniences of life which it annually consumes." How well the labor force functions, therefore, is a critical question. Smith suggests that more is produced when there is a "division of labor": when the tasks of production are analyzed and distributed among different groups of workers so that each is performed better and faster.

By this rational mechanism, developed by individuals seeking to enhance profit in their own enterprises rather than by any kind of government regulation or management, productivity, and thus wealth, is increased. Government regulation also deters, and does not encourage, the generation of new wealth from an initial store of *capital*, or monies available for investment after necessities have been purchased. The wealth of the nation, instead, is increased when each individual engages his own capital as he prefers for his own benefit: "It is his own advantage, indeed, and not that of the society, which he has in view." Yet in so doing, that person contributes to the enrichment of the nation: it is as though he is "led by an invisible hand to promote an end which was no part of his intention."

AN INQUIRY INTO THE NATURE AND CAUSES
OF THE WEALTH OF NATIONS

Introduction and Plan of the Work

The annual labor of every nation is the fund which originally supplies it with all the necessaries and conveniences of life which it annually consumes, and which consist always either in the immediate produce of that labor, or in what is purchased with that produce from other nations.

According therefore, as this produce, or what is purchased with it, bears a greater or smaller proportion to the number of those who are to consume it, the nation will be better or worse supplied with all the necessaries and conveniences for which it has occasion.

But this proportion must in every nation be regulated by two different circumstances; first by the skill, dexterity, and judgment with which its labor is generally applied; and, secondly, by the proportion between the number of those who are employed in useful labor, and that of those who are not so employed. Whatever be the soil, climate, or extent of territory of any particular nation, the abundance or scantiness of its annual supply must, in that particular situation, depend upon those two circumstances. . . .

The plan for the four divisions, or books, of the work follows.

. . .

Book 1, Chapter 1: Of the Division of Labor

The greatest improvement in the productive powers of labor, and the greater part of the skill, dexterity, and judgment with which it is anywhere directed, or applied, seem to have been the effects of the division of labor. . . .

Smith supplies here his famous example of a pin factory, where several workers, each laboring on a different component task of pin-making, are seen to be far more productive than workers who each assemble the whole manufactured pins, one at a time.

. . .

This great increase of the quantity of work which, in consequence of the division of labor, the same number of people are capable of performing, is owing to three different circumstances: first to the increase of dexterity in every particular workman; secondly, to the saving of the time which is commonly lost in passing from one species of work to another; and lastly, to the invention of a great number of machines which facilitate and abridge labor, and enable one man to do the work of many. . . .

. . .

Book 1, Chapter 2: Of the Principle which gives Occasion to the Division of Labor

This division of labor, from which so many advantages are derived, is not originally the effect of any human wisdom, which foresees and intends that general opulence to which it gives occasion. It is the necessary, though very slow and gradual, consequence of a certain propensity in human nature which has in view no such extensive utility; the propensity to truck, barter, and exchange one thing for another.

Whether this propensity be one of those original principles in human nature, of which no further account can be given; or whether, as seems more probable, it be the necessary consequence of the faculties of reason and speech, it belongs not to our present subject to enquire. It is common to all men, and to be found in no other race of animals, which seem to know neither this nor any other species of contracts. . . . Nobody ever saw a dog make a fair and deliberate exchange of one bone for another with another dog. Nobody ever saw one animal by its gestures and natural cries signify to another, this is mine, that yours; I am willing to give this for that. . . .

In civilized society [man] stands at all times in need of the cooperation and assistance of great multitudes, while his whole life is scarce sufficient to gain the friendship of a few persons. In almost every other race of animals each individual, when it is grown up to maturity, is entirely independent, and in its natural state has occasion for the assistance of no other living creature. But man has almost constant occasion for the help of his brethren, and it is in vain for him to expect it from their benevolence only. He will be more likely to prevail if he can interest their self-love in his favor, and show them that it is for their own advantage to do for him what he requires of them. Whoever offers to another a bargain of any kind, proposes to do this. Give me that which I want, and you shall have this which you want, is the meaning of every such offer; and it is in this manner that we obtain from one another the far greater part of those good offices which we stand in need of. It is not from the benevolence of the butcher, the brewer, or the baker, that we expect our dinner, but from their regard to their own interest. We address ourselves, not to their humanity but to their self-love, and never talk to them of our own necessities but of their advantages. . . .

And thus the certainty of being able to exchange all that surplus part of the produce of his own labor, which is over and above his own consumption, for such parts of the produce of other men's labor as he may have occasion for, encourages every man to apply himself to a particular occupation, and to cultivate and bring to perfection whatever talent or genius he may possess for that particular species of business. . . .

. . .

Book 4, Chapter 2: Of Restraints upon the Importation from Foreign Countries of such Goods as can be Produced at Home

After a discussion of protective tariffs, a tool of mercantilist policy that he opposes, Smith discusses how capital is best employed in the production of goods.

. . .

The general industry of the society never can exceed what the capital of the society can employ. . . . No regulation of commerce can increase the quantity of industry in any society beyond what its capital can maintain. It can only divert a part of it into a direction into which it might not otherwise have gone; and it is by no means certain that this artificial direction is likely to be more advantageous to the society than that into which it would have gone of its own accord.

Every individual is continually exerting himself to find out the most advantageous employment for whatever capital he can command. It is his own advantage, indeed, and not that of the society, which he has in view. But the study of his own advantage naturally, or rather necessarily, leads him to prefer that employment which is most advantageous to the society. . . .

. . .

It is only for the sake of profit that any man employs a capital in the support of industry; and he will always, therefore, endeavor to employ it in the support of that industry of which the produce is likely to be of the greatest value, or to exchange for the greatest quantity either of money or of other goods. . . .

But the annual revenue of every society is always precisely equal to the exchangeable value of the whole annual produce of its industry, or rather is precisely the same thing with that exchangeable value. As every individual, therefore, endeavors as much as he can both to employ his capital in the support of domestic industry, and so to direct that industry that its produce may be of the greatest value, every individual necessarily labors to render the annual revenue of the society as great as he can. He generally, indeed, neither intends to promote the public interest, nor knows how much he is promoting it. By preferring the support of domestic to that of foreign industry, he intends only his own security; and by directing that industry in such a manner as its produce may be of the greatest value, he intends only his own gain, and he is in this, as in many other cases, led by an invisible hand to promote an end which was no part of his intention. Nor is it always the worse for the society that it was no part of it. By pursuing his own interest he frequently promotes that of the society more effectually than when he really intends to promote it.

Chapter Eight

Encountering Others: 1688–1785

Introduction

From the eleventh century forward, Europeans ventured into other regions of the world as merchants, crusaders, and explorers. But beginning around 1500, inspired by the ideology of Christian mission and aroused by the lure of wealth, they ventured further, reaching the Americas and the farthest reaches of the Eastern Hemisphere. Shifting from exchange and observation to conquest and dominion, they acquired territories, expropriated wealth, compelled and persuaded conversion, subordinated nations, and enslaved peoples.

The full consequences of this imperialist and colonialist thrust would not be recognized for some time, but the first implications were already apparent to Enlightenment authors. Vico, Voltaire, and Montesquieu, as seen in Chapters Four, Six, and Seven, examined the variety of customs, beliefs, and political structures of civilizations, ancient and modern, beyond the borders of contemporary Europe. The five authors included in this chapter press that inquiry further, the first four[1] actually journeying to distant realms, while the fifth, who never ventured abroad, crafts an understanding of civilizational identity to accommodate the reality unveiled by the recent explorations of others.

The English playwright and novelist Aphra Behn (1640–1689), an early observer of the colonialist venture, offers a critique of its most loathsome component: the enslavement of African laborers for American plantations. Also English, the poet and letter-writer Lady Mary Wortley Montagu (1689–1762), during her husband's term as ambassador to the Ottoman Empire, an Islamic state on Europe's southeastern border, casts a keen eye on life in that realm and especially on its women, whose lives were both more restricted and less fettered than those of their European counterparts. The French priest Guillaume-Thomas Raynal (1713–1796), assisted by a team of collaborators, provides a history of European ventures in his *Histoire philosophique et politique . . . des . . . deux Indes* (*Philosophical and Political History of . . . the Two Indies*), that is, the eastward Middle Eastern and Asian and westward

---

1. Or perhaps only three; Aphra Behn's early residence in South American Surinam has not been definitively established.

American zones of expansion. While Raynal's history is punctuated by reflections and tirades, including an indictment of slavery, the English naval commander James Cook (1728–1779) delivers a more even-tempered eyewitness report from journeys around the world on which he embarked three times. Lastly, the German philosopher Johann Gottfried von Herder (1744–1803) supplies a cultural explanation for the diversity of civilizations, determined both by natural constraints ("climate") and the creative ("organic") power of the human imagination.

One of the first professional women writers in English, Aphra Behn published in 1688 one of the first English novels: *Oroonoko: or, The Royal Slave* (1688). Told by an unidentified female narrator, it is the story of the noble African Oroonoko—whose name provocatively echoes that of the South American river Orinoco that runs not far from Surinam, an English colony from 1650 to 1667, and the setting of the second part of the work. The grandson of a king, Oroonoko is in love with the beautiful maiden Imoinda; and so is his grandfather. An ugly rivalry ensues, and Imoinda is snatched from Oroonoko and sold into slavery. Oroonoko suffers the same fate some time later. The lovers are reunited in Surinam, and with the names assigned them of Caesar and Clemene, serve their new masters. Clemene is now pregnant, and to win their freedom and that of his fellow slaves, Caesar leads a rebellion that is brutally suppressed. To save his beloved from recapture and rape, and with her enthusiastic assent, Caesar kills Clemene. Caesar is captured and dismembered alive as he stoically smokes a pipe, courageous to the end, indomitable in death.

Intersecting here are several imponderable themes. Paramount is that of slavery, seen as brutal and inhuman. In contrast to its savagery is the essential and radiant nobility of the hero Oroonoko, an African of royal blood— suggesting the intrinsic value of royal status even in the context of an implicit critique of slavery, slave masters, and the hierarchical societies from which they come. Complicating these interactions is the vivid voice of the female narrator: as a member of the slaveholding class, she is a superior; as an admirer of male heroism, a subordinate; as a helpless observer of the royal slave's murder, a disenfranchised woman in a male-dominated colonial society. Embracing all these tensions is a global perspective, evoking a triangle of England–Africa–America—echoed in the racial triangle of white, black, and Indian—that is not only the superstructure of the novel but maps the history of the Atlantic world in the early modern era.

Oroonoko was published in 1688, the year of the Glorious Revolution in England, which would unseat a king and establish the authority of Parliament. In that same year, strikingly, four Quakers in Germantown, Pennsylvania, issued a statement against slavery that inaugurated the first abolitionist movement in the history of the world.

Born the year Behn died, Montagu was the daughter of an aristocratic Member of Parliament that had just triumphed in England's Glorious Revolution; from 1712, she was the wife of another, from whom she eventually separated to lead a defiantly unconventional existence, much of it abroad. A self-taught classicist who devoured the works of the Latin poet Ovid and translated those of the Greek philosopher Epictetus, she was an advocate for women's education, if not more broadly for women's social equality. She was a prolific author of poems and letters, her correspondence from 1709 to 1762 filling three volumes in its 1837 edition. That correspondence includes her famous "embassy letters" of 1716–1718, often published separately, written when as a young wife and mother she accompanied her husband on a diplomatic mission to Constantinople, the capital of the Ottoman Empire. Her letters vividly describe the social customs of the Muslim Turks, with a special focus on the lives of women. It is notable that, just as Aphra Behn as a woman and outsider was one of the first to explore the issue of slavery in its African and American settings, Montagu as a woman and outsider offered to Europeans an early eyewitness account of Turkish society and culture.

Taking in "the Two Indies" (*les deux Indes*)—the two domains, that is, East and West, of the past three centuries of European expansion—the Jesuit-trained priest Raynal offers an analytical history, replete with critical assessments, celebrations, and condemnations. Extremely popular, it was published in tens of editions in France and abroad in various multivolumed formats: the editions of 1770, 1774, and 1781, for instance, containing its nineteen books in, respectively, six, seven, and ten volumes. Raynal was not the sole author, but incorporated contributions from various unnamed authors (most have now been identified by modern scholars), with Diderot playing a major role from the second edition forward.

The work opens with European expansion eastward, beginning with the Portuguese explorations and settlements around Africa, the Arabian Sea, and the Indian Ocean, followed by the ventures of the British, French, Dutch, and Spanish in India, the East Indies (modern Indonesia), and the Philippines, and on to Indochina, China, and Japan. It then turns to westward expansion, following the same European powers across the Atlantic to the West Indies and North and South America. The excerpts given here offer a glimpse of Raynal's discussion of the Portuguese advance in the Arabian zone, and of the beginning of African slavery in the Americas.

While Raynal and his coterie surveyed Europe's global ventures from their armchairs in Paris, Captain James Cook, the self-made and scantily educated son of a farm laborer, joined the navy as an ordinary seaman in 1755. He rose to be a skilled navigator and surveyor who, accompanied by astronomers, botanists, and artists, led three global expeditions, all documented in multivolumed works written in plain but compelling prose. On these voyages, he explored and charted barely known regions of both the Pacific and Atlantic Oceans, including Tahiti and Hawaii (which he discovered, and where he was killed in 1779), New Zealand and Australia. The excerpt here is from his famous account of the island of Tahiti, appearing in the report of his second voyage: *Voyage towards the South Pole, and Round the World* (1777).

When the seasoned explorer Cook set off to follow the ice edge of Antarctica, the youthful Herder had just published his provocative *Yet Another Philosophy for the History of the Formation of Humankind*[2] (1774): an implicit critique of the Enlightenment's faith in progress and its assumption of a substratum of a constant human nature. By then, navigators, adventurers, merchants, missionaries, and conquistadors had visited every corner of the globe and introduced Europe's reading public, avid for tales of novelty and savagery, to the many peoples and civilizations—which they called "races" or "nations"—that inhabited the planet. The tale was largely one of the derring-do of Europeans and the backwardness of everyone else (except the widely admired Chinese), but a few voices were raised in favor of the Others who lived far away. Rousseau, as will be seen in the next chapter, celebrated the natural innocence and potentiality of the human being in a state of nature, popularized as the "noble savage"; and the four authors already introduced in this chapter, in different settings, empathized with the non-European peoples they encountered.

Herder, however, our fifth speaker, theorizes that empathy. For him, all human communities, which he calls "nations," are equally worthy, as all are formed of peoples experiencing a particular set of material constraints, summed up as "climate," and sharing a unified set of beliefs, customs, and memories (here evoking Vico; see Chapter Four), all rooted in language. Accused by some later historians of the sin of "nationalism" that culminated in twentieth-century atrocities, especially those of Nazism, Herder explicitly rejected ruthless militarism and imperialist ventures, along with the oppression by states of their own citizens, while honoring the indigenous and spontaneous creativity of human beings deployed across the globe in their disparate sodalities.

In the excerpts given here from his masterwork *Ideas for a Philosophy of the History of Humankind*[3] (published in four parts, containing twenty books in all, respectively in 1784, 1785, 1787, and 1791), Herder expands the vision set forth earlier in *Yet Another Philosophy of History*. He proposes

---

2. One of several ways of translating Herder's impregnable German; also encountered are "Another Philosophy," and "This Too a Philosophy . . ."; "humankind" is given for *Menschheit*, more often rendered as "mankind."

3. Another stab at rendering the title of a work by Herder; also encountered are "Sketch," or "Outline" or "Reflections" on, of, or for a philosophy, etc.; *Menschheit* is again rendered here as "humankind," found elsewhere as "mankind" or "humanity."

the environmental foundation of human culture, which is created by the vital force of imagination, communicated in the language invented by poets and transmitted within the family from generation to generation. Denying prevailing Enlightenment assumptions of racial division, the potency of reason, and the inevitability of progress toward an ideal future, Herder echoes Vico in identifying culture as the key element in human history, while granting no single culture priority over others—a notable stance in an age of imperialist expansion.

Thus died this great man

Aphra Behn, *Oroonoko: or The Royal Slave* (1688)

The excerpts from *Oroonoko* given here are glimpses taken from a work of extraordinary range and complexity. They include the narrator's opening with its offer of plain truth; the hero's capture and shipment to South America; the tragic murder of Imoinda/Clemene by the hand of her lover Oroonoko/Caesar; and the gruesome execution of the latter, an African and a slave, the culmination and central claim of the narrative delivered in five stark monosyllables: "Thus died this great man."

The italicized subheads are supplied by the editor to clarify the narrative sequence.

OROONOKO

I do not pretend, in giving you the history of this Royal Slave, to entertain my reader with adventures of a feigned hero, . . . nor in relating the truth, design to adorn it with any accidents but such as arrived in earnest to him: and it shall come simply into the world, recommended by its own proper merits and natural intrigues; there being enough of reality to support it, and to render it diverting, without the addition of invention.

I was myself an eyewitness to a great part of what you will find here set down; and what I could not be witness of, I received from the mouth of the chief actor in this history, the hero himself, who gave us the whole transactions of his youth. . . .

Following the story of Oroonoko and Imoinda in Africa, he is captured and transshipped to Surinam.

. . .

Possessed with a thousand thoughts of past joys with this fair young person, and a thousand griefs for her eternal loss, [Oroonoko] endured a tedious voyage, and at last arrived at the mouth of the river of Surinam, a colony belonging to the King of England, and where they were to deliver some part of their slaves. . . .

Oroonoko was first seized on, and sold to our overseer. . . . When he saw this, he found what they meant; for, as I said, he understood English pretty well; and being wholly unarmed and defenseless, so as it was in vain to make any resistance, he only beheld the captain with a look all fierce and disdainful. . . . So he nimbly leaped into the boat, and showing no more concern, suffered himself to be rowed up the river, with his seventeen companions.

Oroonoko's life as slave Caesar, reunion with Imoinda:

It was thus for some time we diverted him; but now Imoinda began to show she was with child, and did nothing but sigh and weep for the captivity of her lord, herself, and the infant yet unborn; and believed, if it were so hard to gain the liberty of two, it would be more difficult to get that for three. Her griefs were so many darts in the great heart of Caesar, and taking his opportunity, one Sunday, when all the whites were overtaken in drink . . . , he . . . [gathered] about an hundred and fifty were able to bear arms, such as they had, which were sufficient to do execution with spirits accordingly: for the English had none but rusty swords. . . .

Caesar, having singled out these men from the women and children, made an harangue to them, of the miseries and ignominies of slavery; counting up all their toils and sufferings, under such loads, burdens, and drudgeries as were fitter for beasts than men; senseless brutes, than human souls. . . . "And why," said he, "my dear friends and fellow-sufferers, should we be slaves to an unknown people? Have they vanquished us nobly in fight? Have they won us in honorable battle? And are we by the chance of war become their slaves? . . . [N]o, but we are bought and sold like apes or monkeys, to be the sport of women, fools, and cowards; . . . . And shall we render obedience to such a degenerate race . . . ? Will you, I say, suffer the lash from such hands?" They all replied with one accord, "No, no, no; Caesar has spoken like a great captain, like a great king."

. . .

To this Caesar replied that honor was the first principle in Nature, that was to be obeyed; . . . . To which they all agreed—and bowed. After this, he spoke of the impassable woods and rivers; and convinced them, the more danger the more glory. . . .

He said they would travel towards the sea, plant a new colony, and defend it by their valor; and . . . at least they should be made free in his kingdom, and be esteemed as his fellow-sufferers, and men that had the courage and the bravery to attempt, at least, for liberty; and if they died in the attempt, it would be more brave than to live in perpetual slavery.

They bowed and kissed his feet at this resolution, and with one accord vowed to follow him to death; and that night was appointed to begin their march. . . .

. . .

Failure of the slave rebellion; Caesar makes a deal with Tuscan, but both are captured.

But they were no sooner arrived at the place where all the slaves receive their punishments of whipping but they laid hands on Caesar and Tuscan, faint with heat and toil; and surprising them, bound them to two several stakes, and whipped them in a most deplorable and inhuman manner, rending the very flesh from their bones, especially Caesar, who was not perceived to make any moan, or to alter his face, only to roll his eyes on the faithless Governor, and those he believed guilty, with fierceness and indignation; and to complete his rage, he saw every one of those slaves, who but a few days before adored him as something more than mortal, now had a whip to give him some lashes, while he strove not to break his fetters; though if he had, it were impossible: but he pronounced a woe and revenge from his eyes, that darted fire, which was at once both awful and terrible to behold.

When they thought they were sufficiently revenged on him, they untied him, almost fainting with loss of blood, from a thousand wounds all over his body; . . . and led him bleeding and naked as he was, and loaded him all over with irons, and then rubbed his wounds, to complete their cruelty, with Indian pepper, which had like to have made him raving mad. . . . They spared Imoinda, and did not let her see this barbarity committed towards her lord, but . . . shut her up; which was not in kindness to her, but for fear she should die with the sight, or miscarry, and then they should lose a young slave, and perhaps the mother.

. . .

Caesar, still alive, plots his end.

Being able to walk, and, as he believed, fit for the execution of his great de-sign, he begged Trefry to trust him into the air, . . . which was granted him: and taking Imoinda with him . . . , he led her up into a wood, where . . . he told her his design, first of killing her, and then his enemies, and next himself, and the impossibility of escaping, and therefore he told her the necessity of dying. He found the heroic wife faster pleading for death than he was to propose it, when she found his fixed resolution; and, on her knees, besought him not to leave her a prey to his enemies. He . . . took her up, and embracing of her with all the passion and languishment of a dying lover, drew his knife to kill this treasure of his soul. . . .

All that love could say in such cases being ended, . . . the lovely, young, and adored victim lays herself down before the sacrificer; while he, with a hand resolved, and a heart breaking within, gave the fatal stroke, first cutting her throat, and then severing her yet smiling face from that delicate body. . . . As soon as he had done, he laid the body decently on leaves and flowers . . . but when he found she was dead, and past all retrieve, . . . his grief swelled up to rage; he tore, he raved, he roared like some monster of the wood, calling on the loved name of Imoinda. A thousand times he turned the fatal knife that did the deed toward his own heart, with a resolution to go immediately after her; but dire revenge, which was now a thousand times more fierce in his soul than before, prevents him: and he would cry out, "No, since I have sacrificed Imoinda to my revenge, shall I lose that glory which I have purchased so dear, as the price of the fairest, dearest, softest creature that ever Nature made? No, no!" . . .

He remained in this deplorable condition for two days, and never rose from the ground where he had made her sad sacrifice; at last rousing from her side, . . . he resolved now to finish the great work; but . . . found his strength so decayed that he swayed to and fro, like boughs assailed by contrary winds; so that he was forced to lie down again. . . .

. . .

Caesar is captured.

. . . Caesar heard he was approached: and though he had, during the space of these eight days, endeavored to rise, but found he wanted strength, yet looking up, and seeing his pursuers, he rose, and reeled to a neighboring tree, against which he fixed his back; and being within a dozen yards of those that advanced and saw him, he called out to them, and bid them approach no nearer, if they would be safe. . . . So that they stood still, and . . . asked him what he had done with his wife . . . He, pointing to the dead body, sighing, cried, "Behold her there." . . .

. . .

The death of Caesar:

And turning to the men that had bound him, he said, "My friends, am I to die, or to be whipped?" And they cried, "Whipped! no, you shall not escape so well." And then he replied, smiling, "A blessing on thee"; and assured them they need not tie him, for he would stand fixed like a rock, and endure death. . . .

He had learned to take tobacco; and when he was assured he should die, he desired they would give him a pipe in his mouth, ready lighted; which they did. And the executioner came, and first cut off his members, and threw them into the fire; after that, with an ill-favored knife, they cut off his ears and his nose and burned them; he still smoked on, as if nothing had touched him; then they hacked off one of his arms, and still he bore up, and held his pipe; but at the cutting off the other arm, his head sunk, and his pipe dropped, and he gave up the ghost, without a groan or a reproach. . . .

Thus died this great man, worthy of a better fate, and a more sublime wit than mine to write his praise: yet, I hope, the reputation of my pen is considerable enough to make his glorious name to survive all the ages, with that of the brave, the beautiful, and the constant Imoinda.

Not one sins the less for not being Christian

Lady Mary Wortley Montagu, *Embassy Letters* (1716–1718)

In the excerpts that follow from three letters all written on April 1, 1717, Montagu introduces her female correspondents in England to her impressions of life in the Ottoman Empire, describing an all-female bathhouse; the freedom afforded Ottoman ladies by their concealing dress; and the Turkish practice of vaccination against smallpox, that she would bring back to England. Notable are her openness to Turkish customs, especially those regarding women, that are wholly foreign to her experience as an English aristocrat. "The Turkish ladies don't commit one sin the less for not being Christian," Montagu writes slyly with a tangle of negatives about women engulfed in robes designed to ensure their modesty, but which instead, by ensuring anonymity, permit their illicit sexual ventures.

Embassy Letters

To the Lady ————

Adrianople, April 1, 1717

I am now got into a new world, where everything I see appears to me a change of scene. . . . I won't trouble you with a relation of our tedious journey; but I must not omit what I saw remarkable at Sophia, one of the most beautiful towns in the Turkish empire, and famous for its hot baths, that are resorted to both for diversion and health. I stopped here one day on purpose to see them. . . . I went to the *bagnio* [bath house] about ten o'clock. It was already full of women. It is built of stone, in the shape of a dome, with no windows but in the roof, which gives light enough. There were five of these domes joined together, the outermost being less than the rest, and serving only as a hall, where the porteress stood at the door. . . .

The next room is a very large one paved with marble, and all round it, raised, two sofas of marble, one above another. There were four fountains of cold water in this room, falling first into marble basins, and then running on the floor in little channels made for that purpose, which carried the streams into the next room, . . . with the same sort of marble sofas, but so hot with steams of Sulphur proceeding from the baths adjoining it, it was impossible to stay there with one's clothes on. The two other domes were the hot baths, one of which had cocks [pipes controlled by valves] of cold water turning into it, to temper it to what degree of warmth the bathers have a mind to.

I was in my traveling habit, which is a riding dress, and certainly appeared very extraordinary to them. Yet there was not one of them that showed the least surprise or impertinent curiosity, but received me with all the obliging civility possible. I know no European court where the ladies would have behaved themselves in so polite a manner to a stranger. I believe in all there were two hundred women. . . .

The first sofas were covered with cushions and rich carpets, on which sat the ladies; and on the second, their slaves behind them, but without any distinction of rank by their dress, all being in the state of nature, that is, in plain English, stark naked, without any beauty or defect concealed. Yet there was not the least wanton smile or immodest gesture among them. . . . There were many amongst them as exactly proportioned as any goddess . . . and most of their skins shiningly white, only adorned by their beautiful hair divided into many tresses, hanging on their shoulders. . . .

. . .

They generally take this diversion once a week, and stay there at least four or five hours. . . . The lady that seemed the most considerable among them entreated me to sit by her, and was ready to undress me for the bath. I excused myself with some difficulty. They being all so earnest in persuading me, I was at last forced to open my shirt, and show them my stays [corset]; which satisfied them very well for, I saw, they believed I was so locked up in that machine, that it was not in my own power to open it, which contrivance they attributed to my husband. . . .

Adieu, madam: I am sure I have now entertained you with an account of such a sight as you never saw in your life, and what no book of travels could inform you of. It is no less than death for a man to be found in one of these places.

To the Countess of ———

Adrianople, April 1, 1717

I wish to God, dear sister, that you were as regular in letting me have the pleasure of knowing what passes on your side of the globe, as I am careful in endeavoring to amuse you . . . by giving you a full and true relation of the novelties of this place, none of which would surprise you more than a sight of my person, as I am now in my Turkish habit, though I believe you would be of my opinion, that it is admirably becoming. . . .

The first piece of my dress is a pair of drawers, very full, that reach to my shoes, and conceal the legs more modestly than your petticoats. . . . Over this hangs my smock of a fine white silk gauze, edged with embroidery. . . . My *caftan*, of the same stuff [fabric] with my drawers, is a robe exactly fitted to my shape, and reaching to my feet, with very long strait falling sleeves. . . . The headdress is composed of a cap . . . which is in winter of fine velvet embroidered with pearls or diamonds, and in summer of a light shining silver stuff. . . .

As to their morality or good conduct, I can say . . . the Turkish ladies don't commit one sin the less for not being Christian. . . . It is very easy to see they have more liberty than we have. No woman, of whatever rank, is permitted to go into the street without two muslins: one that covers her face all but her eyes, and another that hides the whole dress of her head, and halfway down her back; and their shapes are wholly concealed by a think they call a *ferigee*, which no woman of any sort appears without. . . . You may guess how effectually this disguises them, so that there is no distinguishing the great lady from her slave. . . . This perpetual masquerade gives them entire liberty of following their inclinations without danger of discovery. . . .

To Miss Sarah Chiswell

Adrianople, April 1, 1717

   In my opinion, dear Sarah, I ought rather to quarrel with you for not answering my . . . letter of August till December, than to excuse my not writing again till now. I am sure there is on my side a very good excuse for silence. . . .

. . .

A propos of [regarding] distempers [illnesses], I am going to tell you a thing that I am sure will make you wish yourself here. The smallpox, so fatal, and so general amongst us, is here entirely harmless by the invention of *engrafting*, which is the term they give it. There is a set of old women who make it their business to perform the operation every autumn . . . when the great heat is abated. People . . . make parties for this purpose, and when they are met . . . the old woman comes with a nutshell full of the matter of the best sort of smallpox, and asks what veins you please to have opened. She immediately rips open that you offer to her with a large needle (which gives you no more pain than a common scratch), and puts into the vein as much venom as can lie upon the head of her needle, and after binds up the little wound with a hollow bit of shell; and in this manner opens four or five veins. . . .

   The children or young patients play together all the rest of the day, and are in perfect health to the eighth. Then the fever begins to seize them, and they keep their beds two days, very seldom three. They have very rarely above twenty or thirty in their faces, which never mark; and in eight days' time they are as well as before their illness. . . . Every year thousands undergo this operation; and the French ambassador says pleasantly, that they take the smallpox here by way of diversion, as they take the waters in other countries. There is no example of any one that has died in it; and you may believe I am very well satisfied of the safety of the experiment, since I intend to try it on my dear little son.

Do you not restore to them their liberty?

Guillaume-Thomas Raynal, *Philosophical and Political History of European Colonies and Commerce in the Two Indies* (1770)

The excerpts given here offer glimpses of the European project in both East and West, taken from the first and sixth volumes of the third edition published in Geneva in 1781. In the first episode, Raynal focuses on the threat to European commerce and autonomy from the Ottoman takeover of the Mediterranean region, countered successfully by Portuguese exploration and ultimately domination of the sea lanes from the east coast of Africa, past the Arabian waterways, and on to India. His negative portrayals of the Muslim Turks, and of the Islamic Arab states they had conquered, contrast with his celebration of the captains Vasco da Gama and Afonso de Albuquerque, who had secured for Portugal the sea route to the riches of Asia. Turning westward, Raynal describes the devastation of the native peoples, the failure to impress the survivors as a labor force, and the consequent introduction of African slavery to the Americas. The section closes with an account of the capture of African slaves in the Guinean hinterland, and an eloquent denunciation—perhaps by Diderot?—of the institution of slavery.

PHILOSOPHICAL AND POLITICAL HISTORY

Book 1, Chapter 13: *The Portuguese sea route to Asia*

Europe had barely begun to breathe at last and to cast off the yoke of servitude that had debased its inhabitants since the Roman conquests and the establishment of feudal law. Tyrants without number, the oppressors of multitudes of slaves [i.e., serfs], had been ruined by the lunacy of the crusades. To sustain these extravagant expeditions, they had been obliged to sell their lands and their castles, and to grant to their vassals, for a payment in silver, certain privileges that allowed them to reach at last the status of human beings. From that moment the right of property ownership began to be introduced among ordinary people, giving them that kind of independence without which property itself is only an illusion. And so the first glimmerings of freedom that have illumined Europe were the unintended product of the crusades; and for once the madness of conquest contributed to the well-being of humankind.

If Vasco da Gama had not made his discovery [of a route to India around the Cape of Good Hope], the flame of liberty would have been extinguished once again, and perhaps for all time. The Turks were poised to drive out those savage nations that had come from the farthest corners of the earth to drive out the Romans;[4] they would soon become, like their predecessors, the scourge of humankind, ready to impose on us, already oppressed by our own masters, an even greater oppression. This would inevitably have happened, if

---

4. Raynal refers to the seventh-century conquest of the eastern and southern regions of the Roman Empire by Arab Muslims.

the fierce conquerors of Egypt[5] had not been repelled by the Portuguese in their several expeditions to India. The wealth of Asia would have opened to them the wealth of Europe. Commanders of all the world's commerce, they would surely have assembled the most formidable navy the world has ever known. How could we have blocked the invasion of our continent by this people, whose religion and politics both spur them to conquest? . . .

. . .

And so the Turks, whose practice it is regularly to strangle their sultan,[6] have never considered changing their government. Such an idea was inconceivable to minds as enervated and corrupt as theirs. Thus freedom would have died in all the world; all would have been lost, if that one [Portugal] of all Christian nations that was most superstitious and, it might be said, debased, had not halted the progress of Islamic fanaticism, and arrested the impetuous surge of their conquests by cutting off the lifeline of their wealth. Albuquerque went still further. Having choked off the sea route from Arabian waters to the Indian Ocean, he next sought to acquire dominion in the Persian Gulf. . . .

Book 11, Chapter 1: *Native peoples and African slaves in the Americas*

We have seen vast territories invaded and devastated, their innocent and placid inhabitants either massacred or locked in chains. A frightful solitude sits on the ruins of a once thriving population. Vicious usurpers butcher each other, their corpses heaped upon the corpses of their victims. What will be the outcome of such crimes? More of the same, and the same again, but followed by another perhaps less bloody, but more revolting: the trade in human beings, bought and sold by human beings. . . .

. . .

Some speculators . . . reasoned that a soil and climate so different from ours could furnish crops that we either lacked, or for which we had to pay too high a price; and so they proposed to grow them. Certain obstacles, seemingly invincible, stood in the way of the realization of this plan. The original inhabitants of the land no longer existed; and those who had not been exterminated, because of their lassitude, their indolence, their insurmountable aversion to work, were unlikely instruments to serve the greed of their oppressors. Born in a mild climate, these natives could not sustain the heavy labor of tillage

---

5. From its 1453 conquest of Constantinople, the Ottoman Empire had expanded throughout the Mediterranean region, conquering Egypt by 1517.
6. Potential heirs to the throne were candidates for strangulation when a new sultan, the Turkish sovereign, was raised to power from among their midst.

under a scorching and insalubrious sun. Self-interest, fertile in expedients, prompted these speculators to seek laborers in Africa, where the vile and inhuman traffic in its inhabitants is an age-old custom. . . .

. . .

Book 11, Chapter 17: *Slave-hunting in West Africa*

In the West African kingdoms of Guinea, the ownership of some persons by others is of ancient origin, and widely practiced. . . . Slaves are procured through warfare, occasioning the multiplication of conflicts. . . . In addition, slavery is assigned as a punishment, not only for murder or theft, but even for debt and adultery. . . . Inland, tribal chiefs may seize from surrounding villages everyone they can find. Children are thrown into sacks, men and women muzzled to silence their cries. . . .

. . .

Just as gold is the currency of Europe's trade with the New World, slaves are the currency of the trade Europeans carry on in Africa. Their bodies are the treasure of the Guinea kingdoms, and each day their number is reduced, leaving to the inhabitants no wealth but the commodities they consume. . . . Thus the European commerce in slaves, over time, has nearly exhausted the commercial wealth of this region. . . .

. . .

Groups of slave merchants form a kind of caravan conducting . . . several files of thirty or forty slaves, carrying the food and water needed to sustain them in the arid deserts they traverse. The manner of securing them, without delaying their progress, is ingeniously designed. A wooden fork some eight or nine feet long is put around the neck of each slave. . . . So that these merchants may sleep quietly at night, they tie the arms of each slave to the tail of the fork he carries. So bound, he cannot flee, nor even attempt to gain his liberty. . . .

    In reading this horrific tale, reader, is not your soul aroused to the same indignation that I feel in writing it? Do you not, in your mind, furiously assail these despicable traders? Do you not shatter the forks that entrap these miserable wretches? And do you not restore to them their liberty?

Some things which are rather interesting

Captain James Cook, *Voyage towards the South Pole, and Round the World* (1777)

On his second world voyage (1772–1775), Cook stopped, as he had before, at Tahiti (then called Otaheite) and its neighboring islands in the South Pacific. Today part of French Polynesia, Tahiti had first been reached by English navigator Samuel Wallis in 1767. In this account of his visit in September 1773, Cook considers the presence of syphilis on the island and the possibility that it had been brought by Europeans; describes a condition of food scarcity; investigates whether the islanders practiced human sacrifice; and skeptically assesses the reputation for sexual immorality possessed by Tahitian women. Although he betrays prejudices typical of a European of his era—a disdain for the lower classes, a higher standard for female sexual morality than for male—Cook is open as an observer to the views and the customs of the native peoples, finding among them "some things which are rather interesting."

Italicized subheads are supplied by the editor to identify the sections of the narrative.

VOYAGE TOWARDS THE SOUTH POLE

Book 1, Chapter 14: September 1773

I shall now give some farther account of these islands; for although I have been pretty minute in relating the daily transactions, some things which are rather interesting have been omitted. . . .

Did Europeans bring syphilis to Tahiti?

Soon after our arrival at Tahiti, we were informed that a ship . . . had been in at Owhiaiurua harbor near the southeast end of the island, where she remained about three weeks, and had been gone about three months before we arrived. . . . At this time, we conjectured this was a French ship; but on our arrival at the Cape of Good Hope, we learned she was a Spaniard, which had been sent out from America. The Tahitians complained of a disease communicated to them by the people in this ship, which they said affected the head, throat, and stomach, and at length killed them. They seemed to dread it much, and were continually inquiring if we had it. . . .

Were it not for this assertion of the natives [that it had been first brought to the island by French navigator Louis-Antoine de Bougainville in 1767], . . . I should have concluded that long before these islanders were visited by Europeans, this or some disease which is near akin to it, had existed amongst them. For I have heard them speak of people dying of a disorder, which we interpreted to be the pox [i.e., smallpox], before that period. But be this as it will it is now far less common amongst them than it was in the year 1769, when I first visited these isles. For notwithstanding most of my people made pretty free with the women, very few of them were afterwards affected with the disorder, and those who were had it in so slight a manner that it was easily removed. But amongst the natives, whenever it turns to a pox, they tell us it is incurable. . . .

Scarcity on the island of Tahiti:

The island of Tahiti which, in the years 1767 and 1768, . . . swarmed with hogs and fowls, was now so ill-supplied with these animals that hardly anything could induce the owners to part with them. The few they had . . . among them seemed to be at the disposal of the kings. . . . During the seventeen days we were at this island, we got but twenty-four hogs; the half of which came from the two kings themselves; and I believe the other half were sold us by their permission or order. We were, however, abundantly supplied with all the fruits the island produces, except breadfruit, which was not in season either at this or the other isles. Coconuts and plantains were what we got the most of; the latter, together with a few yams and other roots, were to us a succedaneum [substitute] for bread. . . .

The practice of human sacrifice:

As I had some reason to believe that amongst their religious customs, human sacrifices were sometimes considered as necessary, I went one day to a *Marai* [sacred space] in Matavai, in company with [his colleague] Captain Furneaux; having with us, as I had upon all other occasions, one of my men who spoke their language tolerably well, and several of the natives, one of whom appeared to be an intelligent, sensible man. In the *Marai* was a *Tupapow* [a table], on which lay a corpse and some viands; so that everything promised success to my inquiries. I began with asking questions relating to the several objects before me: if the plantains, etc. were for the *Eatua* [a deity or spirit]? If they sacrificed to the *Eatua* hogs, dogs, fowls, etc.? To all of which he answered in the affirmative. I then asked, if they sacrificed men to the *Eatua*? He answered, *Taata eno*; that is, bad men they did, first *Tiparrahy*, or beating them till they were dead. I then asked him if good men were put to death in this manner? His answer was no, only *Taata eno*. . . .

I asked him several more questions, and all his answers seemed to tend to this one point, that men for certain crimes were condemned to be sacrificed to the gods, provided they had not wherewithal to redeem themselves. This, I think, implies that on some occasions, human sacrifices are considered as necessary, particularly when they take such men as have, by the laws of their country, forfeited their lives, and have nothing to redeem them; and such will generally be found among the lower class of people. . . .

The treatment of women:

Great injustice has been done the women of Tahiti . . . by those who have represented them, without exception, as ready to grant the last favor [i.e., sexual intercourse] to any man who will come up to their price. But this is by no means the case; the favors of married women, and also the unmarried of the better sort, are as difficult to be obtained here as in any other country whatever. Neither can the charge be understood indiscriminately of the un-married of the lower class, for many of these admit of no such familiarities. That there are prostitutes here, as well as in other countries, is very true, perhaps more in proportion, and such were those who came on board the ships to our people, and frequented the post we had on shore. By seeing these mix indiscriminately with those of a different turn, even of the first rank, one is at first inclined to think that they are all disposed the same way, and that the only difference is in the price. But the truth is, the woman who becomes a prostitute does not seem, in their opinion, to have committed a crime of so deep a dye [sort] as to exclude her from the esteem and society of the community in general. On the whole, a stranger who visits England might, with equal justice, draw the characters of the women there from those which he might meet with on board the ships in one of the naval ports, or in the purlieus of Covent Garden and Drury Lane [two London venues often frequented by prostitutes]. I must, however, allow that they are all completely versed in the art of coquetry, and that very few of them fix any bounds to their conversation. It is, therefore, no wonder that they have obtained the character of libertines.

The inner genius of my being

Johann Gottfried von Herder, *Ideas for a Philosophy of the History of Humankind* (1785)

The selections given here from the second part of Herder's *Ideas for a Phi-losophy* touch on some of his key arguments. First, Herder argues that the human species is physically and mentally one: there are no racial divi-sions among humankind, but only cultural ones. Second, he attaches those cultural differences to "climate," in a broad sense: to the whole set of material circumstances which confronts any particular human community in the place it inhabits, including its topography, soil, flora and fauna, and, more narrowly, what we would call climate. Third, he sketches how human lives are formed by climate, and how also, by art and policy, they change it. Fourth, he introduces the vital principle, or organic power, that is the source—the "genesis"—of all living things and their creative capacities: "the cause of my natural powers, the inner genius of my being." Finally, the human imagination, the engine of cultural formation, powered by this vital principle and shaped by climate, is biologically grounded but inherited linguistically: transmitted by the words that mothers murmur to their infants.

Italicized subheads are supplied by the editor for greater legibility.

IDEAS FOR A PHILOSOPHY OF THE HISTORY OF HUMANKIND, SECOND PART (1785)

Book 7, Chapter 1

Individual human beings differ in mind and appearance, but the human species is everywhere the same.

In nature, no two leaves on a single tree are quite alike; and still less are any two human faces or forms. . . . So each human being is in fact a world, outwardly similar to others, but inwardly a unique and incomparable creature.

Equally, no human being is an autonomous substance, but is bound up with all the elements of nature, . . . contributing to the alterations of the universe, and by them also altered. . . . He is an endless harmony, a living self, constructed by the harmony of all the powers encircling him. . . .

But since the human mind seeks unity in all this multiplicity, and since the divine mind, its prototype, has welded into one the immeasurable diversity of all earthly things, so also we here turn away from the boundless empire of alteration to this elemental fact: The human species on this Earth is everywhere one and the same. . . .

Some . . . have proposed naming as "races" four or five divisions of humankind based on region of origin or skin color; but I see no basis for this terminology. . . . Colors melt into each other . . . and are in the end merely the varied hues of one great painting that extends through space and time over all the Earth. . . .

Book 7, Chapter 2

One single human species has established itself in every region of the earth,
where it is conditioned by the local environment, or "climate."

Look at those locusts of the Earth, the Kalmucks and Mongols:[7] they could
inhabit no other zone than their steppes and their mountains. . . . The Arab
in the desert belongs to that wasteland, along with his noble steed, and his
patient, long-suffering camel. . . . His simple clothing, his way of life, his customs, and his character are suited to his environment, and after the passage
of thousands of years, his tent still embodies the wisdom of his ancestors. . . .

It is clear why all sentient people, who have been conformed to their
environments, so love the very land and are inseparable from it. From infancy
it has conditioned their bodily constitution and their way of life, their joys
and their occupations: their whole spiritual horizon is climatic [i.e., formed
by their environment]. Take them away from the land, and you have taken
all they have. . . .

The whole vocabulary of human feeling is insufficient to express the desperate grief with which a purchased or captured African slave leaves the shores
of his ancestral land, never to see it again in his lifetime. . . . And by what
right did you even approach the land of these unfortunates, you brutes, let
alone rip them from it by theft, craft, and cruelty? . . .

[A similar case is] the enduring hatred that American natives feel toward
Europeans . . . , the irrepressible feeling that "This land is ours! You do not
belong here!" . . . The instant their inborn love of the land is aroused, its
flame erupts and rages furiously. . . . To us this seems abominable, as it no
doubt is. Yet it was the Europeans who provoked this rage: For why did they
come to this land? Why did they come as bellicose, brutal, and overbearing
despots? . . .

Book 7, Chapter 3

Climate: what it is, and what effect it has on the human body and mind:

. . .

[Although climate generally is determined by position on the earth], the
proximity of the sea in one case, the direction of the winds in another, or the
height or depth of the land, or the effects of mountains, rain, and mist, cause

---

7. The Mongols are a pastoral people who originated in Mongolia and whose empire in the
thirteenth and the fourteenth centuries reached into Europe, China, and the Middle East; the
Kalmucks are Buddhist Mongols now established in Russia near the Caspian Sea.

local modifications to the general rule, such that regions adjacent to each other may have quite different climates. . . .

. . .

A region's elevation or depression, its topography and products, the food and drink enjoyed there, the way of life, the employments of its people, even their clothing and customs, arts and amusements . . . all paint in their sum a portrait of climatic power. . . .

. . .

Though climate is the assemblage of forces and influences acting upon it, to which both plants and animals contribute . . . , clearly the human being is placed in its midst as master of the Earth to change it according to his design. . . . Europe was once a damp, dark forest . . . that now sees the sun, and with the alteration of its climate, the inhabitants themselves have been changed. . . . We can view the human species, therefore, as a swarm of bold but tiny trolls who have over the ages swept down from the mountains to subdue the Earth and alter their habitat with their little fists. . . .

Book 7, Chapter 4

Genesis: the life force, organic power, creates all forms on earth:

How awestruck must that person have been who first saw the miracle of the creation of a living being! Globules caught in shooting streams of fluid coalesce into a living core, and from this core a creature of the Earth is born. . . . What would he call this miraculous thing, he who first beheld it? This, he would say, is *living, organic power.* I do not know from where it comes, nor what it is in its innermost essence; but that it exists, that it lives, that by its operations it calls forth organic components from the chaos of homogeneous matter—that I see, that is undeniable.

. . .

This life force we all have in us; it is with us in sickness and health, . . . tiring eventually in old age, but living still in some ways even after death. . . . It is not the rational faculty of our soul, for reason in no way created our body, which it does not recognize, and wields only as the alien and unwelcome tool of its ratiocination. Yet the faculty of reason is bound up with this life force, as all the powers of nature are interconnected. . . . So just as I know that I think, yet do not know what is my reasoning faculty, so also I feel and see that I live, yet do not know, in the same way, what the life force itself may be. This force is innate, organic, genetic; it is the cause of my natural powers, the inner genius of my being. . . .

Book 8, Chapter 2

The human imagination is both organic (powered, that is, by the life force) and climatic (formed, that is, by its natural environment); but it is inherited and transmitted across generations.

We have no idea of those things that lie outside the circle of our experience. . . . The ideas, likewise, of every people native to a region are bounded by its limits. . . .

Compare the mythologies of Greenland, India, Lapland, Japan, Peru, and Africa—a complete geography of the poetic soul. . . . Each nation is so deeply imprinted with its own system of representation because it is theirs, interlocked with its heaven and its earth, sprung from its way of life, conveyed from fathers and forefathers. . . .

Why is this? Has each one of these several different human tribes invented its own mythology, which it then loves as its own creation? Not at all; they have not invented it; they have inherited it. . . .

Here, I believe, is the crux of the matter. . . . Our mythologies are largely learned with our ears, through the telling of tales. The unknowing child greedily drinks in these tales that, like his mother's milk, like the festal wine of his ancestral lineage, flow into his soul and feeds it. They seem to him to explain what he sees; they convey to the young the way of life of their people and the glory of their ancestors; they implant in those fully grown a lifelong and ineradicable commitment to nation and group. . . .

. . .

The imagination, it could be said, remains the least understood, and possibly the least understandable of all the powers of the human soul. In that it is intertwined with the whole framework of the body, especially with the brain and nerves . . . , it seems to be not only the foundation or ligament of all the soul's highest powers, but also the knot that binds body and soul together. . . . As such, necessarily, it is that which is first transmitted from parents to children. . . .

The existence of innate ideas has long been disputed, and as the term was understood, the clear answer is that they do not. But to probe the matter further, considering the mind's capacity to interconnect and combine certain ideas and images, it seems that nothing opposes, but everything supports the possibility that it—that capacity— is indeed innate. If a child can inherit six fingers, . . . or the shape of head and face, it would be no wonder if the fabric of the brain, down even to its most complex organic convolutions, were also hereditary.

. . .

Great World Spirit, how you must view all the shadows and phantasms that flit about on our earthly globe! For we ourselves are shadows, and our imagination dreams only shadowy visions. . . . And yet our species is formed in this labyrinth of the imagination. The human mind inclines to pictures because they sketch the likeness of things; it seeks and finds in the thickest clouds the rays of truth. . . . So we wander over the Earth wrapped in a web of human fantasies—but where the midpoint of this web may be to which all our wandering leads, as its scattered rays lead back to the sun, that is the question.

Chapter Nine

Citizen of Geneva: 1755–1782

Introduction

If Voltaire is the voice of the Enlightenment (see Chapter Six), Jean-Jacques Rousseau (1712–1778) is arguably its heart. Rousseau views the passions, formerly censured by Christian theologians as prompts to sin, as the genuine expressions of the inner heart—and it is the heart, for Rousseau, rather than reason, that demarcates the nature of the human being.

The works of which samples appear in this chapter span the narrow band of Rousseau's most productive years from 1754 to 1770. The *Discourse on the Origin and Foundations of Human Inequality* (1754) views the journey of the human being from the state of nature to the existing social and political order as a downward trajectory from freedom to corruption, dependency, and slavery. The *Social Contract* (1762) envisions a genuinely democratic civil government, in which every member participates and guides the whole by a collective, general will—a concept that harbors within it, arguably, regardless of Rousseau's intent, also the seeds of despotism. The prior year, Rousseau published the epistolary novel *Julie* (1761), recording the quest of two lovers for a life together that was not to be, as their passions were thwarted by the expectations and conventions of society. The next year, the same that saw the publication of *The Social Contract*, Rousseau's *Emile* (1762) outlined a mode of education that would protect the natural innocence of the child from the "false opinions" of the whole phalanx of social controllers. His *Confessions*, completed in 1770 although not published until 1782–1789, the first major work of that name since the *Confessions* of the fourth-century Saint Augustine, is a product of Rousseau's later career. Unashamedly, it profiles the career of a man unsuccessful in the ordinary sense who never ceased to value the whole and authentic human self to be found in his mythical "state of nature."

Throughout his works, Rousseau takes up the same themes—even in that book professedly devoted only to himself, the *Confessions*. His hero is the human being "in all the truth of nature." His almost inevitable fate is to be captured and corrupted by society and its "false opinions." But means can be found—by creating a new kind of state, by falling in love, by choosing different methods of child rearing and education—to evade that dreaded end.

In his political works, Rousseau sets the essential human being—alone, unaware, and unconcerned—against society and the state: the one corrupts, the other oppresses. As human beings move from their original state into society, learning new skills, building complex relationships, and acquiring property, natural inequality, previously of little importance, explodes into social inequality, causing the subservience of some and the domination of others. The "state of war" that results, envisioned earlier by Hobbes and Locke, where the poor steal or suffer, and the rich exploit and dominate, precedes a political settlement, and the birth of civil government. But who governs? Will sovereign power be exercised by the tyranny of a few, or the general will of the whole populace? These are the issues that, in different tonalities, come to the fore in two of Rousseau's most important political statements: the *Discourse on the Origin and Foundations of Human Inequality* and *The Social Contract*.

Written with fervor and conviction, the *Discourse on Inequality* is a hymn to the freedom and innocence of the human being in his natural state—a condition characterized, as well, by ignorance and solitude. Here, all are equal. As humans develop new skills and acquire social attachments, though, inequality emerges, and with it greed and ambition. A few possessed by these passions set off in pursuit of property and power, reducing the unwitting many who have not seized those advantages to poverty and dependency. The dispossessed turn violently on their new masters, who respond in kind, triggering a state of war. To settle it, the rich trick the multitude into accepting the rule of law, promising security and justice for all. The poor "raced to meet their chains," the rich having succeeded in their scheme to subject "the whole human race to perpetual labor, servitude, and wretchedness."

The Social Contract begins where the *Discourse on Inequality* ends: the great majority of humankind is in chains, subjected to a small group of the wealthy and powerful, the "strongest," who rule by might. Rousseau proposes a solution: the acceptance of a "social contract" by the people at large, calling for the formation of a new type of government, a "social compact," in which all will surrender their individual freedom to the collective authority, the "general will," in order to regain their freedom in association with their peers. The general will, the summation of all their individual wills, will be sovereign and inalienable. But in serving the general will, the individual person is, in effect, serving his own interests, and is thus ruler as well as ruled.

Rousseau's understanding of the social compact is a recipe for direct democracy that could only exist at the level of the city, as distinct from the legislative bodies envisioned by Locke and Montesquieu that act as a check on executive power. But the concentration of power in the hands of the multitude that Rousseau depicts arouses some uneasiness: is this a new kind of despotism, even totalitarianism? Clearly, Rousseau intended a social compact that would free the majority from oppression by the few and preserve the innate dignity of each human individual. But there always lurks the danger that once a body is created that dispenses with all masters by making the generality of humankind itself the master, it may become, there being nothing outside the system to challenge it, the most intolerable master, and tyrant, of all.

The *Discourse on Inequality* and *The Social Contract* are of great interest today to scholars of political thought and the trajectory of revolutions. But in the eighteenth century, the two works that put Rousseau's name on everyone's lips were his sensational novel *Julie, ou la nouvelle Héloïse* (*Julie, or the New Heloise*) and his treatise *Émile, ou de l'éducation* (*Emile, or On Education*).

The year *The Social Contract* appeared, with its appeal to personal sacrifice for the common good, Rousseau published the novel *Julie, or the New Heloise* that gripped the soul of Europe, featuring two lovers from "a small town at the foot of the Alps" who sacrificed themselves to their passion. Consisting of 163 letters, ranging from around 1,500 to 15,000 words, irregularly divided in six parts, *Julie* tells the story of the illicit romance between Julie and St. Preux, her tutor, later the tutor of her sons; and their relations with Julie's husband, Wolmar, and her cousin Claire. It is remarkable, and unprecedented, for the direct expression of powerful feelings by persons of lofty character: embodiments, in sum, of the virtue that Rousseau celebrates in all his works.

Julie recalls, as Rousseau intended—he deliberately inserted the modifier "or the new Heloise" not as mere subtitle but part of the title of the work—the love affair between the twelfth-century philosopher Abelard and his student Heloise, who gave birth to his child, and spent the rest of her life in the convent where he deposited her, as he finished his in a monastery. Abelard and Heloise, like Julie and St. Preux, felt all their lives the consequences of their love for each other. But the medieval lovers accepted the greater authority of divine law over human passion, while Rousseau's Swiss couple, inhabitants of a small town not far from the author's native Geneva, identified with Calvinism's stern moralism, did not. Julie redeems them both by the sacrificial death with which the novel culminates: she had leapt into an Alpine lake to rescue her cousin's drowning child. It is her atonement for their adulterous passion.

An international success, *Julie* saw more than one hundred French editions in the years after its first publication, and many others in translation. In it, Rousseau combats triumphantly what was for him, though not for Voltaire, *l'infâme*, "that infamous thing." As much as Rousseau detested the tyranny of kings and popes, he detested more the censorious moral code that would deny the validity and dignity of human passion.

Julie was not just about love; it was also about education, a theme that runs throughout the novel. Not only is St. Preux Julie's tutor, but in parts 4

and 5, describing Julie's life as mother and wife, Rousseau's views on education and child rearing emerge in letters exchanged between the lovers, as
well as in conversations between Julie, Wolmar, and St. Preux, who has been
summoned to tutor Julie's children. These discussions anticipate the themes
expounded in full in *Emile*, a treatise that resembles a novel, just as the novel
Julie, in this regard, resembles a treatise.

 Emile, or On Education follows the education of the child of that name
from infancy through adolescence, urging the loosening of constraints on
the very young child, and for the older one, advocating learning grounded
in experience and not instilled by rote. Famously, he condemned swaddling
infants, then the universal custom, and praised maternal breast-feeding. As
well, he deplored contemporary methods of teaching children to read and
write, not introducing Emile to those technologies until the age of twelve,
and giving him at that juncture a very particular first book: Defoe's *Robinson
Crusoe*, about a solitary man living in the state of nature who must rely for his
survival on his experience and skills.

 Strikingly, but fittingly for a pedagogical theorist who defied all the
norms, Rousseau wrote *Emile* at the request of a woman, a mother who
had asked him for advice: "This miscellany of reflections and observations,"
Rousseau opens his book, "disordered and largely disconnected, was begun
to please a good mother who knows how to think." Rousseau's address to
a mother contrasts with prior pedagogical works that had been written for
fathers: those, for instance, of Plutarch, Quintilian, Elyot, and most recently
Locke. His recommendations address the maternal concern for the welfare of
the child more than the paternal concern for the child's progress and success.
And women, and mothers, enthusiastically read Rousseau, abandoning swaddling as he instructed them, and taking up the practice of breast-feeding the
children to whom they had given birth.

 The themes of *Emile* dovetail with those Rousseau raises elsewhere. As
in the *Discourse*, Rousseau looks at the human being in a natural state—the
infant and young child, as yet unshaped by society—hoping to establish a
pattern of education that will preserve the natural freedom of the child and
avoid corruption and constraint as society takes hold. As in *Julie*, where passions raged against the bridles imposed by moral codes, Rousseau condemns
methods of rearing that limit and censor natural feeling.

 Natural feelings run high in Rousseau's *Confessions*, his colossal medita-
tion on himself that does not blush to examine the inner springs of his being:
a project with "no precedent" that will find "no imitator," he writes, but will
reveal "a man in all the truth of nature—and this man will be myself." And
so it does, relating "confessions" of behavior that do the author little credit:
of unhappy sexual adventures, of conscienceless lying and stealing, of chronic
unsociability, of the abandonment—a shocking irony for an author who had

advocated the humane treatment of children—of all five children born to him by his female companion and housekeeper, a former laundress. The *Confessions* describes the events of Rousseau's life through 1765, the peak of the author's career, and is for its earlier stages still the principal source on which biographers rely. Completed in 1770, it was published only posthumously, in two parts, in 1782 and 1789.

Like *Julie* and *Emile*, the *Confessions*, too, is about education: Rousseau's own; and specifically, his education in the passions, begun in his seventh year when he, with his father, pored over the books left to them by his mother— for she had died giving him birth, as Rousseau announces at the outset of the work. Born to a family of higher social status than his father, she had left to her husband and child the libraries of her father and uncle. In the excerpts given here, Rousseau provides a striking account of his intellectual awakening, as father and child together, bound in a tight spiritual embrace, consume her legacy. The scene recalls Herder's argument that the origin of culture is found in the tales told, the words murmured by mother to child. This enculturation by his mother was prophylactic: it warded off all the artificialities and excrescences of the world, and left Rousseau a natural man, as he wished to be: a man in the state of nature.

A rootless and unsettled wanderer, Rousseau regularly identified himself as a "citizen of Geneva," and aptly so. That Swiss city, the capital of international Calvinism, was his natural and intellectual birthplace, and although he renounced his citizenship twice, and was certainly no pious Protestant, its thoughts and values colored his outlook. The son of an artisan, not an aristocrat, he had his roots here, and was forever a stranger to the cool and crackling wit of the Paris salons that nourished French Enlightenment culture. His enemies were neither monarchy nor the Catholic Church, but rather the tyranny exercised by social convention. His concerns with natural innocence, the cultivation of virtue, and the corruption of both by the driving forces of greed and ambition, are Genevan.

The most cunning project ever to enter the human mind

Jean-Jacques Rousseau, *Discourse on the Origin and Foundations of Human Inequality* (1754)

Social inequality is not a natural human condition, according to Rousseau, but emerges in historical time. In the immense span of early history, when, as he sees it, there was scarcely any development of human society or

culture, the human being lived alone, unknowing, and unattached, not recognizing even his own children, existing simply to fulfill his simple needs.
Inequality begins to emerge in that state of nature with the invention of the
arts, especially, of metallurgy and agriculture. At this point, the ownership
of property begins as well, and with it, inevitably, human inequality. The
possessors and the dispossessed devolve into the nightmarish state of war
that Hobbes and Locke had imagined. At last, the rich, seeking to secure
their wealth, undertake "the most cunning project ever to enter the human
mind": they convince the desperate and predatory multitude to agree to
the establishment of a state that, governed by just laws, as the rich deceit-
fully promise, would protect all equally. The gullible masses accept the bait,
"rac[ing] to meet their chains," their liberty irretrievably lost, their perpetual
enslavement ensured.

Highlights of this story Rousseau tells are given in the excerpts that follow. The italicized heads are supplied by the editor to clarify the sequence
of argument.

Discourse on the Origin and Foundations of Human Inequality

Introduction

I conceive of two kinds of inequality in the human species: one that I call
natural or physical, because it is established by nature, and consists in the difference of age, health, the strength of the body, and qualities of mind or soul;
the other that may be called moral or political inequality, because it depends
on some sort of convention . . . that other people have authorized. This consists in the different privileges that some may enjoy more than others, such
as being wealthier, more respected, or more powerful, so compelling others
to obedience. . . .

What then is the purpose of this *Discourse?* To mark that moment in the
progress of things when, law putting an end to violence, nature was subjected
to law; and to explain by what amazing chain of events the strong agreed
to serve the weak, and people bought an imaginary peace at the cost of real
contentment. . . .

My friend, from whatever country you come, whatever you may think,
listen. . . . I shall speak to you of a time long gone. How much you have
changed from what you were!

Part One

*Rousseau depicts the life of human beings in a state of nature, a wilderness in
which only the simplest wants are satisfied, and the instinct for self-preserva-
tion is moderated by a natural compassion for others.*

And so we see the human being in a state of nature, wandering through the forests, without tools, without speech, without a home, without war, and without ties, . . . subject to few passions and sufficient to himself, . . . sensing only his true needs, noting only what he cared to see. . . . If he chanced to make some discovery, he could not communicate it, as he did not know even his own children. Art perished with its inventor, there being no transmission of knowledge nor progress, as generations uselessly rolled on. . . . The species had already grown old, while the human being was still an infant. . . .

In this unchanging state of nature, there was little inequality among humans.

It now remains for me to reveal the origin of inequality, and its progress in the successive developments of the human mind . . . , [considering] the accidental changes that, while they advanced human reason, debased the species, achieving, in adapting him to society, the corruption of the human being, and so bring both the world and humankind from that time long ago to the point where we see them now.

Part Two

The first person who, having enclosed a plot of land, had a mind to say, "This is mine," and found people simple enough to believe him, was the true founder of civil society. How many crimes, wars, and murders, how much misery and horror would he have spared humankind who, tearing down the fence or filling the ditch, had cried to his companions: "Do not listen to this imposter! You are lost if you forget that the fruits of the earth belong to all, but the earth to no one!" But it seems certain that things had already come to that point where they could not continue as before: for the idea of property depends on many earlier notions that could only have emerged over time, and was not formed all at once in the human mind. . . .

Rousseau traces the development of a more complex society within the state of nature.

So long as people were content with their rustic huts, so long as they were satisfied with clothes made from animal skins sewn with thorns or fishbones, . . . their lives were free, healthy, good, and happy as could be for as long as they lived. . . . But as soon as one person needed the help of another, or realized that it was beneficial for one person to have provisions for two, equality disappeared, property was instituted, labor became necessary, and the vast forests were transformed into pleasant fields watered by human sweat, in which slavery and misery could soon be seen to take root and sprout alongside the harvest. . . .

The arts of metallurgy and agriculture flourish, and with them the ownership of property.

Things in this state could have remained equal, if talents had been equal, and if, for example, a perfect balance was always reached between need for iron and the consumption of foodstuffs; but nothing sustained that balance, and it failed. The strongest did most of the work; the more skilled accomplished more by theirs; the cleverest found ways to lighten his load; the farmer had more need of iron or the blacksmith more of wheat, so that by the same labor, one prospered while the other barely survived. Thus natural inequality advances imperceptibly . . . and the effects of human differences become more visible and durable. . . . Matters having come to this point, it is easy to imagine the rest. . . .

With the further development of skills and knowledge, given innate differences between people and other circumstantial factors, property accumulation continues, wealth is used and abused, and human inequality increases.

Before the signs that represent wealth were invented, it could only be measured in land and livestock, the only real possessions that humans possessed. But now when inheritances had grown in number and extent to the point where they covered the whole of the earth . . . , no one could acquire more except by taking it from others. Those who due to their weakness or laziness had been unable to acquire any now became poor, although they had lost nothing, everything around them changing while they changed not at all; they were obliged either to accept their subsistence from the hands of the rich, or to seize it, thus giving birth to . . . either domination and servitude, or violence and robbery. The rich for their part . . . had no plan but to subjugate and enslave their neighbors. . . .

It is not possible that people had not at last reflection on so miserable a situation, and on the calamities that had overcome them. The rich especially must soon have felt how disadvantageous to them was a perpetual war in which they bore all the cost. . . . Besides, . . . they knew that their [usurpations] rested on only a precarious and improper foundation, and that having acquired them only by force, force could remove them. . . . Even those who had become wealthy by their own industry could scarcely claim a better basis for their ownership. They could boast, "It is I who built this wall; I earned this land by my own labor." To which their critics could respond: "Who gave you its boundaries? And by what right do you demand payment from us for labor we never imposed on you? Do you not know that a multitude of your brothers perish, or suffer from need of what you have in excess, and that you should have sought the explicit and unanimous consent of humankind to appropriate for yourself from the bounty belonging to all anything that exceeded your share?"

Lacking valid reasons to justify himself and sufficient strength to defend himself, . . . the rich man . . . conceived at length the most cunning project ever to enter the human mind: he would use in his own behalf the very weapons of those who attacked him, making allies of his adversaries, filling their heads with alien ideas, and giving them different institutions that were as favorable to him as the law of nature was unfavorable.

With this intention, having explained to his neighbors the horror of a situation that armed each of them against all others and rendered their possessions as onerous as their wants, . . . he freely invented specious reasons to lead them to his goal. "Let us unite," he said to them, "to guard the weak from oppression, restrain the ambitious, and assure to each the possession of what belongs to him. Let us institute rules of justice and peace that all without exception would be obliged to obey, and which will in some way repair the blows of fortune by subjecting equally the weak and the strong to mutual responsibilities. In a word, instead of turning our forces against ourselves, let us gather them into one supreme power that may govern us by wise laws, protect and defend all the members of the group, repulse common enemies, and maintain us in eternal concord."

Much less than a discourse of this sort was sufficient to deceive ordinary people, easily seduced, . . . who were in any case . . . too greedy and ambitious to manage for long without masters. All raced to meet their chains believing they had secured their liberty; for having sufficient sense to recognize the advantages of a political settlement, they did not have enough experience to foresee its dangers. . . .

Such was, or must have been, the origin of society and of laws, which gave new shackles to the weak and new strength to the rich, irretrievably destroyed natural liberty, established forever the law of property and inequality, changed a clever usurpation into an irrevocable right, and for the profit of a few ambitious individuals subjected the whole human race to perpetual labor, servitude, and wretchedness.

The supreme direction of the General Will

Jean-Jacques Rousseau, *The Social Contract* (1762)

"The human being is born free, and everywhere he is in chains," reads the famous opening of the first chapter of the first book of *The Social Contract*. The rule of the strongest, prevailing everywhere, strangles the essential, innate liberty of the human being. Rousseau proposes a different kind of government headed not by the strongest, but by the totality of the people, each person surrendering his individual powers to the assembly of the whole, so as to be at once subject and sovereign, the ruler and the ruled. The social compact thus formed gives expression to the "General Will" of the whole of its members, or associates. The General Will is sovereign, but its sovereignty does not oppress. While they have surrendered their individual freedom, the members gain a collective freedom, become their own masters, and are unchained. Some highlights of Rousseau's argument are given in the excerpts provided here.

SOCIAL CONTRACT

BOOK ONE

1. Subject of this first book

The human being is born free, and everywhere he is in chains. He who believes himself to be the master of others does not escape being more of a slave than they. How did this change come about? I do not know the answer. How can it be rectified? This question I believe I can resolve. . . .

. . .

6. On the social compact

I suppose that people have reached the point where the obstacles that hinder their remaining in the state of nature overcome the efforts each person can make to remain in that state. That primitive state, then, can subsist no longer, and the human race would perish if it did not alter its mode of existence.

The human species, therefore, . . . has no other means of saving itself than by uniting to form a sum of forces that can . . . act in concert. . . . This sum of forces can only be born from the cooperation of many; but the force and freedom of each person being the first instruments of his conservation, how can he engage with others . . . without neglecting his own needs? This . . . is the fundamental problem for which the social contract provides a solution. . . .

. . .

The clauses of this contract, . . . properly understood, all come down to a single principle: the total surrender of each member, with all of his rights, to the whole community. . . . In the end, while giving himself to all, each member gives himself to no one; and since there is no member over whom he does not acquire the same right that he cedes on faith, he gains the equivalent of all he loses, and greater strength to conserve what he has.

So if one strips the nonessentials from the social compact, one will find it comes down to the following: each of us in common places his person and all his power under the supreme direction of the General Will; and we as a body receive each member as an indivisible part of the whole.

In an instant, in place of the private personhood of each contracting member, this act of association produces a moral and collective body composed of as many members as there are voices present, which receives by this one act its unity, its common self, its life, and its will. . . .

. . .

7. On the sovereign

As soon as this multitude is thus united in a body, one cannot harm any one of the members without attacking the whole body. . . . So that the social compact, therefore, does not become just an empty formulation, it tacitly affirms this commitment that alone can give force to the others: that whoever may refuse to obey the General Will be constrained to do so by the body as a whole; which signifies simply this: he will be forced to be free. . . .

8. On the civil state

This passage from the state of nature to the civil state produces a quite remarkable change in the participant, substituting in his behavior justice for instinct, and giving to his actions the moral quality that they previously lacked. It is only now, when the voice of duty replaces that of physical impulse and right replaces appetite, that the person who had always thought only of himself finds himself forced to act on other principles, and to consult his reason before responding to his desires. . . . [Accordingly], his faculties are stretched and developed, his ideas extended, his sentiments ennobled, his soul wholly uplifted to such a point that . . . he should bless always the happy moment that he left [his old ways] behind forever, and transformed him from a dumb and bounded animal to an intelligent and truly human being.

. . .

BOOK TWO

1. That Sovereignty is inalienable

The first and most important consequence of the principles established above is that only the General Will can direct the forces of the state according to the end for which it was instituted, which is the common good; for if the conflict between the interests of individuals made the establishment of society necessary, it is the reconciliation of these same interests that made it possible. It is what these different interests have in common that forms the social bond, and if there had not been some point at which all those interests came together, no society could exist. Accordingly, it is exactly on the basis of this common interest that society should be governed.

I say therefore that Sovereignty being nothing other than the exercise of the General Will, it can never be alienated, and that the Sovereign, which is the collective being, cannot be represented except by itself. Power can be delegated, but not the will. . . .

. . .

4. On the limits of Sovereign power

If the State or the City is only a moral person whose life consists in the union of its members, and if the most important of its concerns is its own conservation, it requires a universal and compulsive power to move and arrange each part in the manner most suitable to the whole. Just as nature gives to each human being an absolute power over all his members, the social compact gives to the body politic an absolute power over all its members, and it is this same power that, directed by the General Will, as I have said, bears the name of Sovereignty.

❀ ❀ ❀

Two lovers from a small town at the foot of the Alps

Jean-Jacques Rousseau, *Julie, or The New Heloise* (1761)

The excerpts given here are taken from the first and sixth parts of the six-part epistolary novel: letters 1 (to Julie) and 4 (from Julie) from part one, and letter 12 from part six, Julie's last to St. Preux. The beginnings of the relationship are viewed in the first two letters, when Julie is a young girl approaching marriageable age and St. Preux is her tutor. Its painful end, just as the two lovers had planned to escape together, is revealed in the third.

Delivered as an enclosure to the mammoth letter 11 written by her husband and describing her death, letter 12 was written by Julie as she lay dying. Now the wife of another man and the mother of his sons, she promises St. Preux her everlasting love.

JULIE

PART ONE

LETTER 1, TO JULIE

I must flee from you, Mademoiselle, I see that clearly. I shouldn't have waited this long; or rather, I should never have laid eyes on you. But now what am I to do? What course should I take? You promised me friendship—you see my perplexity, advise me.

You know that I entered your house only on the invitation of Madame your mother. Knowing that I had acquired some few talents, she believed that they could be employed, in a place without teachers, for the education of a daughter whom she loved. Delighted, for my part, to adorn with the flower of learning one so promising by nature, I dared to take on the dangerous task, without foreseeing the peril, or at least without fearing it. I shall not reveal to you that I begin to pay the price of my boldness. . . .

. . .

I see only one way, Mademoiselle, to escape from this predicament: it is that the hand that threw me into it must pull me out. As you caused me to sin, so you must assign the penalty, and so at the least, out of pity for me, deign to forbid me your presence. Show my letter to your parents, refuse me entry to your house, send me away in whatever manner you please. I can endure anything you do to me, but by myself, I cannot leave you.

You, send me away! I, leave you! And why? How is it a crime to recognize your merit, and to love what demands esteem? . . . I allow that one could imagine you even more beautiful than you are, but more lovable and more worthy of a decent man's heart—no, Julie, that is not possible. . . .

. . .

Very well, I promise, I swear, for my part, to do all I can to recover my reason, or to suppress the turmoil that I feel surging in the depths of my soul. But then, for pity's sake, do not look at me with those soft eyes that pierce me within. Hide from mine your face, your gaze, your arms, your hands, your golden hair, your gestures. Avoid my urgent and imprudent glances. Silence that voice that stirs the emotions of whoever hears it. Be someone, alas! other than you are, so that I can recover my heart. . . .

. . .

In a word, whatever fate you ordain for me, at least I shall not need to reproach myself for having hoped too much. And if you have read this letter, you have done all that I could dare to ask of you, even if there were no refusal for me to fear.

. . .

LETTER 4, FROM JULIE

I must admit it at last, this fatal secret, so poorly hidden! How often have I sworn it would not escape my heart as long as I lived! That you are in danger wrests it from me; it bursts forth, and honor is lost. Alas! I have kept my word too well. Is there a death more cruel than to outlive honor?

. . .

So awful is my situation that I can no longer turn to anyone but to him who has reduced me to this state, so that, to save me from disgrace, you must be my sole defender against yourself. I could, I realize, delay this confession of my despair; I could for some time longer disguise my shame, and only slowly admit it to myself. . . .

. . .

I believe, I hope, that the heart to which I felt I could give all of mine will not deny the generosity I expect from it. I hope as well, if he is base enough to take advantage of my weakness and the avowal he has wrested from me, that my scorn, my indignation, would restore to me the reason I have lost; and that I would not myself be so base as to fear a lover of whom I would have to be ashamed. You shall be virtuous, or despised; I will be respected, or cured. This last hope remains for me before I hope for death.

PART SIX

LETTER 12, FROM JULIE

We must abandon our plans. All has changed, my good friend. Let us endure this change without a murmur; it comes from a wisdom greater than ours. We dreamed of being together; what we dreamed was not good. It is a blessing that heaven has prevented it, and so, no doubt, prevented much misfortune.

I have long lived in illusion [that my love for you had ended]. This illusion was salutary for me; it vanishes at the moment when I have no more need of it. You believed that I had been cured, and I believed that to be so. . . . Yes, I wanted enormously to stifle that passion that enlivened me, that gathered deep within my heart. There it awakens the moment when it need be feared no more; it sustains me when my strength languishes; it revives me as I lie dying. My friend, I make this confession without shame. This feeling that persisted in spite of myself was involuntary. In no way did it injure my innocence: . . . if my heart . . . was yours, that was my torment and not my crime. I did all it was my duty to do. My virtue remains unstained, and my love remains without remorse.

I dare to celebrate my past; but what would I have had to say about the future? One day more, perhaps, and I would have acquired guilt. . . . My friend, I leave at an opportune moment, content with you and with myself. I depart in joy, and my departure is in no way cruel. After so much sacrifice, I count as nothing what remains to me to do: it is only to die one more time.

. . .

I have only a word more to say to you, about my children. . . . [My husband] Monsieur de Wolmar will convey to you the observations I have made on your memoir, and on the character of my two sons. I have only begun to write this document. I give it to you not as a rule to be followed, but submit it to your judgment. Don't make scholars of them; make of them kind and just men. Speak to them from time to time of their mother. . . . You know how dear they were to her. . . . I grow tired. This letter must come to a close. In leaving my children in your care, I separate from them with less pain; I feel that I remain with them.

Farewell, farewell, my sweet friend. . . . It is no longer I who speaks; I am already in the arms of death. When you see this letter, worms will be eating the face you loved, and her heart where you no longer dwell. But can my soul exist without you? Without you, what happiness can I know? No, I do not leave you, I go to await you. . . . I die in this sweet expectation: filled with joy to have purchased at the cost of my life the right to love you always without guilt, and to tell you so once again!

Build a fence around your child's soul

Jean-Jacques Rousseau, *Emile, or On Education* (1762)

The selections from *Emile* given here are from the preface and books 1 and 2 (of 5), dealing respectively with the first two and the next ten years of a child's life. In the first book, Rousseau finds in the child the universal human being in his natural state of innocence, but assailed by the limits placed on him—especially the tight swaddling clothes that were the custom in pre-modern times—and denied the proper love and nourishment that mothers should provide, but too often withhold. In the second, he argues that real learning proceeds from experience, and not from the study of books, which are alien to the child's nature and beyond his comprehension. A wise and loving mother can best rear her child—a boy; Rousseau's expectations of a girl's education are quite different—not by doing something, but rather nothing; or rather, she should "build a fence around [her] child's soul" to protect him from the malignancy of the world and its false values.

EMILE

Preface

Nothing is known about infancy. The more we pursue our false notions about it, the more confused we become. The learned concern themselves with what children need to know, not considering what children may be ready to learn. They are always searching for the grown person in the child, without thinking about who the child is now, before he is grown. . . . Begin, therefore, by getting to know your children better—for most assuredly, you do not know them at all. . . .

Book 1: Infancy

All is good as it issues forth from the hand of God; all degenerates in the hands of humankind . . . [which] will have nothing as it was made by nature, not even the human being, who must perform tricks like a show horse, and be conformed to a pattern, like an ornamental tree in the garden. . . .

It is you whom I address, wise and tender mother, who has known not to take the common path, but to protect this young tree from the assault of false opinions. Care for it, water this seedling lest it die. One day its fruits will delight you. Now is the time to build a fence around your child's soul. Let someone else trace its circuit, but you must erect the wall.

. . .

To form this unique individual, what is it we must do? We have much to do, without a doubt: we must prevent anything from being done. . . .

In society, where each place is labeled, each person must be reared to fill the one meant for him, and if he does not fill it, he is fit for nothing else. Education is useful only to the extent that it coincides with parental wishes; otherwise, it is harmful to the student, if only because it has imbued him with prejudices. . . .

In the natural state, all people being equal, their common vocation is to be human, and whoever has been well trained for that profession cannot badly perform any other. It matters not whether a student is destined for the sword, the church, or the law, nature summons him first not to the calling chosen by his parents, but to life. Life is the trade I want to teach him. On leaving my hands, he will be, I grant, neither a magistrate, nor a soldier, nor a priest: he will be, first and foremost, a human being. . . .

If each person's future were so firmly fixed that it could never change, then the current method of education might have some value. . . . But given the variability of human existence, given the restless and unsettled spirit of this age which overturns everything in each generation, can a more senseless program be conceived than to rear a child as though he will never have to leave his bedchamber, and will always be attended by his servants? . . .

Rousseau turns to the care of infants, a prelude to their education, and condemns the practice of swaddling.

The newborn infant needs to stretch and move his limbs, to revive them from the torpor resulting from so long a time spent rolled up in a ball. Their limbs are stretched, it is true, but they are not allowed to move. Even the head is subjected to a cap. It is as though we fear the infant might seem to be alive. . . . He was less cramped, less pinched, less constrained in the womb than in his swaddling clothes. What has he gained by being born? . . .

The first sensation infants feel is one of pain and woe. They find only obstacles to all the movements they need to make; more wretched than a criminal in irons, they struggle vainly, they are frustrated, they cry. . . . As only the voice is free, why should they not use it to complain? They cry because you are hurting them. If you were strangled as they are, your cries would be louder than theirs.

What is the origin of this mindless custom? . . . Because mothers, scorning their first duty, not wanting to nurse their children, sent them off to wet nurses. . . . These loving mothers who, unburdened by their infants, are free to enjoy the amusements of the town, do they know how their baby in his swaddling clothes is treated in the village? At his first whimper, he is hung from a nail like a bundle of rags, and while the nurse, unconcerned, goes about her business, the unhappy child hangs there, crucified. . . .

Having ceased to nurse their infants, women no longer care to have them. The condition of being a mother having become onerous, the natural consequence is that a way is found to escape it entirely. . . . But when mothers deign to nurse their infants, . . . natural feeling will be revived in every heart. . . . Correcting this one abuse will soon bring about a general reformation, and nature will reclaim its rights. . . .

Book 2: Ages two to twelve

Rousseau argues that the teaching of reading is oppressive and should be postponed until the child is ready to learn.

In sparing children their lessons, I spare them the instruments of their greatest misery—books. Reading is the scourge of childhood, and nearly the only activity that we offer it. At age twelve, Emile will barely know what a book is. But surely, you say, he must learn how to read! I agree: he must learn to read when reading becomes useful for him; until then, its only use would be to bore him. . . .

How has it happened that this skill, so useful and so agreeable, torments children? Because they are forced to labor at it unwillingly, and for purposes that they comprehend not at all. A child is not eager to value the instrument by which he is tormented. But make that instrument serve his pleasures, and in no time he will master it without your help.

People make a great fuss in seeking out the best methods of teaching reading. They invent special desks and cards; the child's room is turned into a printing shop. . . . A tool more certain than all of these, one that is always overlooked, is the desire to learn. Give the child this desire, and you may put aside your desks and your dice. Any method will work.

The need of the present moment—that is the great motivator, the only one that leads surely to the goal. Sometimes Emile receives written invitations from his father, mother, relations, or friends, for a dinner, or a walk, or a boating party, or to attend some public festival. These notes are short, clear, concise, and well-written. He must find someone to read them to him, and this someone cannot be found at that moment. . . . The moment passes, and so does the event. Eventually the note is read to him, but it is too late. Oh! If only he had known how to read it by himself! . . .

Shall I now turn to the teaching of writing? No, I shall not waste my time on such a trifle; this is a treatise on education.

This man will be myself

Jean-Jacques Rousseau, *Confessions* (1770)

In the opening pages of the *Confessions*, Rousseau describes his birth to loving parents, his mother's death, and his spiritual awakening occasioned by the reading at age seven, together with his inconsolable father, of her collection of romantic novels. His acquisition of literacy and the sensitization of his passions that are the constant fuel of his creative work occurred spontaneously and at once. His narrative of this first experience conditions all that follows in a life marked by intense feelings and the powerful convictions they engendered.

CONFESSIONS

Book 1: 1712–1719

I undertake a project for which there is no precedent, that when achieved will have no imitator. I want to show to my fellow beings a man in all the truth of nature—and this man will be myself.

. . .

Rousseau was born following his father's return from abroad and reunion with his wife, the author's mother.

I was the melancholy fruit of this return. Ten months later, I was born, sickly and weak. I cost my mother her life, and my birth was the first of my misfortunes.

I did not then know how my father bore this loss, but I know that he never recovered. In his mind, he saw her again in me, never able to forget that it was I who had taken her from him. Whenever he embraced me I heard in his sighs, and felt in his convulsive grasp, bitter regret mixed with his caresses, all the more tender on that account. When he said to me, "Jean-Jacques, let us speak of your mother," I said to him, "Very well, father, but then we shall cry," that mere word already calling forth his tears. "Ah!" he said with a groan, "restore her to me, console me for her, fill the emptiness she has left in my soul. Could I love you so much, if you were only my son?" Forty years after losing her, he died in the arms of a second wife, but the name of the first was on his lips, and her image implanted in his heart.

These were the authors of my days. Of all the gifts that heaven bestowed on them, a heart that feels is the only one that they passed on to me. That feeling heart was the cause of their happiness, and of all my misfortunes. . . .

I know nothing of my first five or six years. I do not know how I learned to read. I only remember the first books I read and their effect on me. It is from this moment that I date my awareness of myself, never since interrupted. My mother had left us her novels, and we picked them up to read after supper, my father and I. At first the aim was only for me to practice my reading with the aid of entertaining books; but soon our interest became so intense that we read them to each other, without pause, and passed our nights in this occupation. Never did we stop before the end of the volume. Sometimes my father, hearing the swallow's song at morning, said sheepishly: "Let us go to bed; I am more a child than you are."

By this dangerous method I quickly acquired not only extreme facility in reading and comprehension, but a knowledge of the passions rare for my age. I already understood the sentiments associated with actions of which I had no concept. I had no thoughts, but only feelings. This confusion of emotions, which rained on me like blows, had no effect on my reasoning power, for that had not as yet developed. But they formed in me an outlook of a different stamp, and gave me bizarre and romantic notions of human existence that subsequent experience and reflection have never been able wholly to erase.

The novel-reading sessions ended [when I was seven years old] in the summer of 1719. The following winter, I moved on to other things. My mother's library had been exhausted, so we turned to that portion of her father's that had been left to us. Happily, here were good books; and it could scarcely have been otherwise, as this library had been collected by a minister, one who truly deserved that title, and indeed a learned man in the mode that then prevailed, and one of taste and discernment. [Jean] Le Sueur's *History of the Church and the Empire*, [Jacques-Bénigne] Bossuet's *Discourse on Universal History*, Plutarch's *Lives* [*of the Noble Greeks and Romans*], [Giovan Battista] Nani's *History of Venice*, Ovid's *Metamorphoses*, [Jean de La] Bruyère's *Characters*, [Bernard Le Bovier de] Fontenelle's [*Plurality of*] *Worlds* and *Dialogues of the Dead*, and a few volumes of Moliere, were moved into my father's workshop, and there I read them to him every day while he worked.

My enthusiasm for these books was unusual and perhaps unprecedented for one of my age. Plutarch became my special favorite. The pleasure I took in reading his *Lives* over and over rather cured me of novels, and soon I was rating Agesilaus, Brutus, and Aristides, ahead of Orondates, Artemenes, and

Juba. This fascinating reading, and the conversations between my father and me that it occasioned, aroused in me that free and republican spirit, that proud and indomitable character, resistant to the yoke and to servitude, that have tormented me throughout my life, finding myself often in those situations least suitable for their expression. Thinking constantly of Rome and Athens, as though living with their great men, having been myself born the citizen of a republic, and the son of a father whose love for his country was his strongest passion, I was inflamed by their example, I fancied myself a Greek or Roman, I became the character whose life I read; engaged by the tales of their qualities of constancy and intrepidity, my eyes flashed and my voice boomed. One day at table when I related the adventure of [the Roman hero] Scaevola, [who had demonstrated his bravery by burning his hand over a fire,] those present were frightened to see me stretch my hand out over a chafing dish in illustration of his deed.

Chapter Ten

Vindications of Women: 1685–1792

Introduction

Chapter Two of this volume, "The Learned Maid," told the story of women's claim for education, sampling works that argue women's capacity for higher learning, describing the founding of women's schools, and documenting the achievements of highly educated women. Women's advancement, however, accomplished not until modern times (and perhaps not yet accomplished), required not only education, but also the disruption of the ancient and enduring marriage system that, among the propertied classes, required the accommodation, and sometimes the sacrifice, of daughters to the economic and social interests of families. Arguments against this marriage system are heard from the seventeenth century forward, as in the excerpts given here from selected works by five English, Polish, and French authors, of whom four are female, and one male: Mary Astell (1666–1731); Anna Stanisławska (1651–1701); Denis Diderot (1713–1784); Mary Wollstonecraft (1759–1797); and Olympe de Gouges (1748–1793).

The never-married English philosopher Mary Astell, the first of these authors, was born to a prosperous family of middling rank, but lived, having received no dowry upon her father's premature death, by her pen and her wits. Following up on her radical proposal for a "Protestant nunnery" in which women, prior to marriage, might improve their minds (*A Serious Proposal to the Ladies*, 1694/1697), she published in 1700 her equally bold *Reflections on Marriage*. A rambling work driven by anger and impatience, it portrays traditional marriage as a malignant institution that sacrifices women to men, often their intellectual and moral inferiors, and to the family. While marriage is a necessary institution for the rearing of children, Astell concedes, it affords little scope to women's desires or abilities. In marriage, men seek wealth (for a main object in marrying was to secure access to the wealth a woman conveys from her natal family); power over their wives, often treated as an "upper servant"; and entertainment, beauty, and comfort. What women may seek is not a matter of interest.

Astell eviscerates the marriage institution, and mocks the men who profit by it. Yet the criticism of that institution as it was practiced in premodern Europe is more devastatingly expressed in literary works that exercise the power of words to arouse emotions and spur action. Included here are portions of two such works. The first is by the Polish aristocrat Anna Stanisławska, who would be married three times, twice happily and by choice. But in the "Aesop episode" of her autobiographical verse epic, composed in fifteen years before the publication of Astell's *Reflections*, she describes her first marriage to a bumbling monster who aspired to kill her. It is a unique account in a woman's vivid voice of a marriage to which she had been compelled by her parents for the economic and social benefit of the family.

"The days of my bondage begin," Anna Stanisławska observes as, the marriage rite completed, the wedding guests sit down "and brace themselves for the speeches" (Threnody 6, Stanza 43). She tells the story of her coerced marriage and eventual triumphant liberation in twenty-nine verse "threnodies," or lamentations, modeled on the threnodies composed a century earlier by the Polish Renaissance humanist and poet Jan Kochanowski for the death of his young daughter. Her imitation was appropriate in that she, too, lamented the death of a daughter: herself, the daughter of the father who for selfish and mercenary motives conveyed her into the arms of an impossible husband, but who in the end, from the grave, through his surrogates, achieved the dissolution of that unjust contract.

The novel *La religieuse* (*The Nun*, composed around 1760, published 1780/1796) by Denis Diderot is the second literary work considered in this chapter. In it, speaking in the female voice of the narrator, he describes the forced conventualization (enclosure in a female monastery) of a young girl. Her parents, who detested her, coerced her to take vows that would bind her for life, while they employed their wealth to procure advantageous marriages for the two daughters they preferred. In the convent, she is systematically deceived, imprisoned, and physically and sexually abused, an experience from which she eventually escapes to face a life of solitude and hopelessness. Diderot exposes the fraudulence of a marriage system that sacrificed women to a corrupt religious establishment, sustained by a patriarchal system that subordinated the welfare of daughters to the interests of men.

The Nun was written by a principal figure of the French Enlightenment; if it were not for the precedence claimed by the extraordinary thinkers Voltaire and Rousseau, he would take the lead. The founder and editor, initially with d'Alembert, of the famed *Encyclopedia*, Diderot was a materialist and atheist who protested, as had Voltaire, the repressions of the Catholic Church, and advocated freedom of sexual expression, in several works drawing on contemporary depictions of illicit sexuality circulating in the literary underground. He conveys his radical critique of traditional society in his many essays, treatises, plays, and novels, of which, among the latter, *Rameau's Nephew*, depicting an aimless and decadent member of Parisian society, is perhaps the best known. But *The Nun*, the only novel he allowed to be published in his lifetime, is arguably more daring still.

Diderot died in 1784, five years before the outbreak of the French Revolution. Of the authors previously introduced in this volume, only Herder lived into the revolutionary period, and his major works all predate it. But the last two authors to be considered here, Wollstonecraft and Gouges, both witnessed the French Revolution unfold, and squarely addressed the issues it raised in terms of women's lives.

A focal point was the *Declaration of the Rights of Man and the Citizen*, a brief document proclaimed in August 1789 by the National Assembly, which had been formed by representatives from the Third Estate to the former Estates-General, summoned by King Louis XVI. Its principles underlay subsequent legislation during the Revolution, and are still today inscribed in the French constitution. When originally published, it aroused much debate. The English statesman Edmund Burke responded to its claims, and to the whole revolutionary venture, in his *Reflections on the Revolution in France* (1790; see Chapter Twelve), and the American pamphleteer Thomas Paine celebrated the *Declaration* and ensuing revolution in his *Rights of Man* (1791/1792; see Chapter Eleven). Wollstonecraft had by then responded to Burke in her *Vindication of the Rights of Men* (1790), which preceded her most famous work, its complementary feminist manifesto, the *Vindication of the Rights of Woman* (1792). Gouges, meanwhile, had published her own *Declaration of the Rights of Woman as Citizen* in 1791, just as the Legislative Assembly was about to convene in France and undertake the task of drafting a constitution for the newly created republic.

Mary Wollstonecraft, the daughter of a violent father who was the head of her downwardly mobile middle-class family, was vividly aware of the predicament faced by women in a society governed by men for their financial and sexual advantage. She early became an advocate of women's education, which she believed was the path to women's advancement, working as a governess in private employ and as the head of a school for girls. Later, she moved to London and flourished in its literary circles, writing essays, treatises, and novels. Engaged notoriously in two affairs, and giving birth to an illegitimate child, at the late age of thirty-eight, Wollstonecraft eventually married the English political thinker William Godwin, by whom she was pregnant. Months later, she died in giving birth to their daughter, the future Mary Shelley, author of *Frankenstein*. Wollstonecraft's unconventional marital and sexual life was itself a comment on the traditional system of marriage.

With the outbreak of the French Revolution, Wollstonecraft moved to Paris to observe events firsthand, producing there her *Vindication of the Rights of Woman*, in which the political liberalism that she espoused in her *Rights of Men* expands into a broad and assertive feminism. Reiterating many of the themes Astell had raised, Wollstonecraft assails a marriage system that confined and infantilized women, raised to value only beauty and trinkets, and to trade a brief moment of glory during their youth, as they experienced courtship and marriage, for later decades of tedium, constraint, and subordination.

An illegitimate daughter reared in a modest family, Gouges was freed by the death of her husband after only a year of a loveless marriage and soon set off for Paris to pursue a literary career. She had already published a series of plays and pamphlets on feminist and abolitionist themes (Diderot and Wollstonecraft, as well, opposed slavery) when the Revolution broke out, and the *Declaration of the Rights of Man* was promulgated. Troubled that this foundational document did not address the concerns of women, she wrote her *Declaration of the Rights of Woman* in 1791.

In this document, which mimics the form and substance of the first *Declaration*, Gouges urges the extension to women of the rights guaranteed to men, and some others besides. Where the original *Declaration*, for instance, reads "Man is born and remains free," Gouges writes, "Woman is born and remains free"; and where the original version speaks of "the natural and imprescriptible rights of Man," Gouges writes of "the natural and imprescriptible rights of Woman and Man." She departs somewhat from the model, however, to address issues peculiar to women. In Article 7, for instance, where in the original men are constrained to obey the law, Gouges emphasizes that women as well as men—and this was not at the time the custom—"must accept the rigors of the Law." And in Article 10, where the original states the right of men not to be "disturbed" for their opinions, Gouges ventures quite a bit further: not only is no one to be disturbed for expressions of belief, but "Woman has the right to mount the scaffold"—that is, to be executed for a crime—"and equally the right to mount the rostrum"—that is, to speak in public.

Gouges appended to her *Declaration*, moreover, after a rallying "postamble," the draft of a "social contract," alluding to Rousseau's paradigm, and those of his predecessors, none of which dealt with relations between the sexes. It aims to govern the relations between men and women entering upon a partnership—one that she does not call "marriage"—to ensure women's freedom and the financial rights of even illegitimate children. Gouges' vision of marriage transforms women's role in the family and society, expanding the revolutionary outflow of Enlightenment thought to include both women and the children they bear.

The tone of Gouges' *Declaration*, as of her other works, is uncompromising. Understandably, it threatened male revolutionary leadership. And they responded. The irony of Gouges' Article 10 defending woman's "right to mount the scaffold" was unintentional, but now famous: for on November

3, 1793, aged forty-five, condemned as an enemy of the Revolution, Gouges herself mounted the scaffold and died by the guillotine.

No higher design than to get her a husband

Mary Astell, *Reflections on Marriage* (1700)

In a brief work that is indeed an assemblage of "reflections" rather than a formal treatise, Astell hammers out a few main themes. Marriage—characterized by this Anglican stalwart as "Christian"—is an inherently worthy and desirable institution, for it promises both happiness for the married couple and an environment for the rearing of children. But it has been corrupted by social and especially economic forces. Women are eager to marry, but men reap most of the benefits. They marry for money, as the financial arrangements in Astell's social milieu could establish the male partner for life; or they marry for beauty, or as we would say, sexual attraction. Astell deprecates both motives as deriving from "irregular appetites," or passions. A few men may marry for "wit"—attracted, that is, by the woman's clever verbal skills displayed in polite society; but that attribute, as well, Astell disparages as trivial.

Furthermore, the woman who accepts a man's offer of marriage if it has been prompted by any of these lures can expect to be treated, at best, as a glorified housekeeper, an "upper servant," expected to give birth to his children, entertain her husband when he is home, and comfort him when he is troubled. Why do women accept this condition of "entire subjection"? And why do they think that marriage is their "only preferment, the sum total of [their] endeavors"? Sarcastically, Astell explains, it is because men are great: "Have not all the great actions that have been performed in the world been done by them? Have not they founded empires and overturned them? . . . What is it they cannot do?" And so a woman is taught to have no "higher design than to get her a husband."

REFLECTIONS ON MARRIAGE

The Christian institution of marriage provides the best that may be for domestic quiet and contentment, and for the education of children; so that if we were not under the tie of religion, even the good of society and civil duty would oblige us to what that requires at our hands. . . .

. . .

But if marriage be such a blessed state, how comes it . . . that there are so few happy marriages? Now in answer to this, it is not to be wondered that so few [marriages] succeed; we should rather be surprised to find so many [that] do, considering how imprudently men undertake it, the motives they act by, and the very strange conduct they observe throughout.

For pray, what do men propose to themselves in marriage? What qualifications do they look after in a spouse? What will she bring is the first enquiry? How many acres? Or how much ready coin? Not that this is altogether an unnecessary question, for marriage without a competency, that is, not only a bare subsistence, but even a handsome and plentiful provision, according to the quality and circumstances of the parties, is no very comfortable condition. . . .

. . .

But suppose a man does not marry for money, though for one that does not, perhaps there are thousands that do; let him marry for love, a heroic action, which makes a mighty noise in the world, partly because of its rarity, and partly in regard of its extravagance, and what does his marrying for love amount to? There's no great difference between his marrying for the love of money, or for the love of beauty, as the man does not act according to reason in either case; but is governed by irregular appetites. But he loves her wit, perhaps, and this you will say is more spiritual, more refined; not at all if you examine it to the bottom. For what is that which nowadays passes under the name of wit? A bitter and ill-natured raillery, a pert repartee, or a confident talking about everything and in such a multitude of words, it would be strange if something or other does not pass that is surprising, though everything that is surprising does not please. . . .

. . .

Thus, whether it be wit or beauty that a man's in love with, there's no great hopes of a lasting happiness; beauty [even] with all the helps of art does not last long, [rather] the more it is helped the sooner it decays, and he who only or chiefly chose for beauty, will in a little time find the same reason for [making] another choice. Nor is that sort of wit which he prefers of a more sure tenure, or even if it lasts, it will not always please. . . .

But do the women never choose badly? Are the men only in fault? That is not pretended; for he who will be just, must be forced to acknowledge, that neither sex is always in the right. A woman, however, can't properly be said to choose; all that is allowed her is to refuse or accept what is offered. . . .

. . .

And if a woman runs such a risk when she marries prudently—according to the opinion of the world, that is—when she permits herself to be disposed of to a man equal to her in birth, education and fortune . . . at the very best her lot is hard. . . . A lover who comes upon what is called equal terms makes no very advantageous proposal to the lady he courts. . . . He wants one to manage his family, a housekeeper, an upper servant, one whose interest it will be not to wrong him, and in whom, therefore, he can put greater confidence than in any he can hire for money. One who may breed his children, taking all the care and trouble of their education, to preserve his name and family. One whose beauty, wit, or good humor and agreeable conversation will entertain him at home when he has been contradicted and disappointed abroad; who will do him that justice the ill-natured world denies him, that is, . . . sooth his pride and flatter his vanity, by having always enough good sense as to be on his side, to assure him that he is in the right, when others are so ignorant or so rude as to deny it. Who will not be blind to his merit nor contradict his will and pleasure, . . . whose softness and gentle compliance will calm his passions, to whom he may safely disclose his troublesome thoughts . . . ; whose duty, submission, and observance will heal those wounds other people's opposition or neglect have given him. In a word, one whom he can entirely govern . . . , who must be his for life, and therefore cannot quit his service, let him treat her how he will.

. . .

It is even so in the case before us: a woman who has been taught to think marriage her only preferment, the sum total of her endeavors . . . ; she who has seen a lover dying at her feet, and can't therefore imagine that he who professes to receive all his happiness from her can have any other design or desire than to please her; whose eyes have been dazzled with all the glitter and pomp of a wedding, and who hears of nothing but joy and congratulation; who is transported with the pleasure of being out of dependency and mistress not only of herself but of a family too; she who is either so simple, or so vain, as to take her lover at his word either as to the praises he gave her, or the promises he made for himself; in sum, she whose expectation has been raised by courtship . . . will find a terrible disappointment when the hurry is over, and when she comes calmly to consider her condition, and views it no more under a false appearance, but as it truly is. . . .

But how can a woman scruple entire subjection, how can she forbear to admire the worth and excellence of the superior sex, if she at all considers it? Have not all the great actions that have been performed in the world been done by them? Have not they founded empires and overturned them? Do not they make laws and continually repeal and amend them? Their vast minds lay kingdoms waste, no bounds or measures can be assigned to their desires. War and peace depend on them, they form cabals and have the wisdom and courage to get over all these obstacles which may lie in the way of their desired grandeur. What is it they cannot do? They make worlds and ruin them, form systems of universal nature and dispute eternally about them; their pen gives worth to the most trifling controversy. . . . All that the wise man pronounces is an oracle, and every word the witty [man] speaks [is] a jest. It is a woman's happiness to hear, admire and praise them. . . .

. . .

But, alas! What poor woman is ever taught that she should have a higher design than to get her a husband?

The days of my bondage begin

Anna Stanisławska, *Orphan Girl* (1685)

Stanisławska's extraordinary account, both painful and witty, of her marriage to the repulsive Aesop, is preceded by her last unsuccessful attempt to persuade her father to spare her that fate. Her father seems to want the best for his daughter, but that outcome, in his mind, is assured by the wealth and privilege that the marriage will confer upon her. The daughter hopes her father will rescue her from a lifelong captivity.

ORPHAN GIRL

Threnody 5 (Stanzas 25–32)

The wedding is fast approaching,
    The articles are being written.
Melancholy and great sadness
    Have me feeling weak and feverish.
My head is filled with thoughts of death,
    With thoughts of escaping this fate.
Many think that I should be pleased
    To be planning my wedding feast.

My father is far from cheery
    When he pens me in a corner

The wedding day was announced, and from melancholy I fell into a feverish state.

And speaks words of great passion:
     "You, my only daughter, my own
Flesh and blood, are trying very hard
     To shatter my sorely-tried heart.
Rid yourself of girlish regret
     And submit to the plans I've made!"

My perturbed father speaks with me.

I am not spared a verbal lashing
     From the mistress, with her saying
That nothing can be done at this stage,
     And that I'll grow to love my leash.
"It's no use you crying these tears,
     And whining will get you nowhere.
You'll not find in your father's eye
     A hint of concern for his child."

My stepmother pleads with me, threatening the displeasure of my father.

And so, I pluck up the courage
     To speak to Father of my plight,
Hoping against hope that he may
     Just feel some pity for his prey.
I fall to my knees, so saying:
     "I'm ready to do your bidding.
Just think well here on what you have,
     Or you'll be seeing me in the grave."

I mustered the courage to speak to my father.

Clearly moved by my spoken fears,
     My father's eyes now fill with tears.
And he says in a gentle voice:
     "I'd sooner kill the animals
Of the forest than act against
     My beloved daughter's interest.
I've spoken true, so hear me now:
     You'll do what your father tells you!

My father speaks to me with sorrow.

If tyranny's the stock and trade
     Of your father-in-law, you'll not
Have to live under the man's roof.
     You can always come here to live.
Just think of the lands and forests
     That'll be yours. All the trees and beasts.
And where things seem unbearable,
     Riches will make up the shortfall.

You'll have all sorts of independence,
    And as Lady you'll have servants.
Once again, I say, not a hair
    Of yours will be touched. Have no fear.
Bring your new husband to our hearth—
    Before all ye'll both play your part.
I shall embrace him like a son—
    This man I'll take under my wing."

There's no hope for a solution.
    So snared by wily Fortune,
My future is anyone's guess.
    So, Father, I'll submit to this,
Your will. Though I know that one day   *I give him my answer.*
    A father's heart will break to see
His child, a prisoner in bonds,
    Shackled to a monstrous husband.

Threnody 6 (Stanzas 35–39, 41, 43)

Three days pass and guests from both sides
    Converge and exchange niceties.   *The Castellan's son sends a mes-*
From the wrong side is a go-between,   *senger to bring me to the church.*
    Who is blind from what I discern,   *My father does not agree.*
Sent ahead by Aesop to march
    Me up to the door of the church.
But my father is just livid:
    "The groom must come and fetch his bride!"

When Aesop enters the courtyard,
    My family rushes out to bid
Him welcome. He looks like a gander
    Peering out the carriage window.
He barely bows to my father;
    With the rest he doesn't bother.
They're pulling me by my dress
    And pushing me towards . . . This!

O heart, what it was like back then
    As we struggle to recall the pain?
Had you thought our youth would ever
    Be sold down that sorry river?

O Death, you should have struck me down
    When you first pondered the notion   *My sorrow.*
Of slitting my neck with your scythe.
    How is it that this wretch still lives?

Here now at the altar I stand,
    And why, I'm asking, have you bound
My temple with a golden wreath?
    Let all and sundry here behold
The blushing groom and red-faced bride.
    What a coupling for Nature's pride!—
He with his overgrown moustache,
    She with a crane's neck that looks stretched.

The Bishop binds our hands with his stole.
    Oh, how my heart jolts and recoils   *The wedding.*
At the sight of my companion:
    The ugliest man it's ever seen!
He hardly knows what's going on here,
    For the oath's being whispered in his ear
By someone who has been ordered
    To whisper each and every word.

               . . .

The days of my bondage begin;
    A bondage I have not chosen.
My sad silence is all that's left.
    Indeed, there's little to be said.
And now shrill music fills the air,
    Greeting my fall through the trap door.
The wedding guests now take their seats
    And brace themselves for the speeches.

A dying victim dragged to the altar
Denis Diderot, *The Nun* (1760/1780)

The third of three sisters, whose legitimacy her father doubted, Marie-Suzanne Simonin narrates, in the words supplied by the author Diderot, the story of her coerced conventualization, of which the opening pages are excerpted here. Economic considerations and untold emotional vectors lead to the preferment of the elder two sisters, the youngest to be disposed of cheaply and conveniently in a nearby cloister. Brought there unwittingly, she is compelled to take the habit—to become, that is, a novice, preparatory to making a permanent commitment—and is pressured, in due course, to make a final profession of vows. Determined to resist, in full view of those gathered to witness her profession, she refuses to give her assent.

Italicized subheads are supplied by the editor to clarify the narrative sequence.

THE NUN

My father was a lawyer. He had married my mother at a rather advanced age, and had three daughters by her. He had more than enough wealth to settle them all comfortably, but to do so his affection for them would have needed to be at least equally shared—and I cannot come close to making that estimation. I clearly exceeded my sisters in qualities of mind and body, character and talents, something that seemed to irritate my parents. . . .

Some things my father blurted out when he was angry, as he often was, and certain incidents at different times, comments made by neighbors, remarks dropped by the servants, caused me to suspect the reason that might explain his words. Perhaps my father felt some uncertainty about my birth; perhaps I reminded my mother of some deed she had done, and the ingratitude of a man she had trusted too much; I do not know. . . .

As we had come into the world each soon after the other, all three of us grew up together, and suitors came to call. A charming young man pursued my eldest sister, but soon I realized that it was me he sought out, and that she was only the pretext for his frequent advances. I recognized the heap of troubles that his preference could mean for me, and so alerted my mother. That is perhaps the only thing I had ever done in my life that pleased her, and here is how I was repaid. Four days later, or in any case just a few days, I was told that a place had been arranged for me in a convent; and there I was brought the very next day. My life at home was so unpleasant that I was not at all displeased, and I set off for Sainte-Marie, my first convent, with a light heart. . . .

Once my two sisters were married and settled, I thought I would be remembered, and that I would soon leave the convent. I was then sixteen and a half years old. My sisters had been given ample dowries; I assumed I would be given the same, and my head was full of enticing possibilities when I was called to the parlor. It was Father Seraphin, my mother's confessor, who had also been mine, so he did not hesitate to explain to me the reason for his visit: to persuade me to take the veil. I was astonished at this strange proposal, and declared firmly that I had no taste for the religious life. "What a pity," he said, "since your parents have been ruined by your sisters' settlements, and I cannot see what they will be able to do for you in the poverty to which they are reduced. Think it over, Mademoiselle. You must either enter this convent forever, or be sent to one in the countryside which will take you for a modest fee, and which you will not leave until your parents are both dead, which may not be for some time . . . ."

The Mother Superior of the convent pressures her to take the veil, or at least to stay for two years more.

She delivered these invidious proposals with so many endearments, so many protestations of friendship, so many tender falsehoods . . . , and I allowed myself to be persuaded. Then she wrote to my father—what a good letter it was! Oh, for its purpose, it could not have been better done! It would have tricked a shrewder girl than I was, I assure you. She did not omit my pain, my sorrow, my protests; but then she closed by conveying my consent. How quickly everything was done! The day was set, my habit ordered, the time for the ceremony arrived, such that today I cannot recall the slightest interval between these events. . . .

She enters upon her novitiate at Sainte-Marie, a period of preparation for an eventual lifelong commitment.

I will not relate the full details of my novitiate. If all its austerities were observed, it could not be endured, but in fact it is the easiest period of the monastic life. The supervisor of the novices is the most indulgent nun who could be found. Her task is to disguise from you all the harshness of that estate, pursuing a course of seduction both subtle and deliberate in the extreme. It is she who darkens the shadows that surround you, who lulls you, who soothes you, who envelops you, who mesmerizes you. Ours was especially intent on me. . . .

By these beguilements, young women are lured into a life of despair—or madness. Our novice, however, is determined not to be won over.

Now had arrived the moment when I had to show if I knew how to keep my word. One morning after devotions the Superior approached me, holding a letter. On her face were written sadness and despair; her arms sagged, her hand seemed not to have the strength to lift the letter. . . .

The letter is handed over, and read. It contains another dismal account of the affairs of her family.

"And so, my child, how shall we respond to this?"

"Madame, you know how."

"But no, I do not. This is a difficult time, your family has suffered losses, your sisters' affairs are in disorder, and both are burdened by several children; your parents drained their funds in marrying them, and now ruin themselves to assist them. They cannot offer you a sure settlement; you have taken the habit; funds have been committed toward that end, one toward which you have nurtured expectations; the rumor that you will soon make profession of your vows has spread far and wide. . . . Will you make your vows?"

"No, Madame."

"You have no appetite for the religious life?"

"No, Madame."

"You will not obey your parents?"

"No, Madame."

"What then do you wish to be?"

"Anything but a nun. I do not want to be one, and I will not."

"Very well! You will not be one. So now, let us see how to answer your mother."

Another letter is written, and again surrogates are sent to dissuade her.

I resisted them all. Meanwhile the day was set for my profession of vows. Everything was done that could be to obtain my consent, but when they saw it was useless to press any further, they gave up the attempt.

From this moment, I was shut up in my cell, with silence imposed on me, separated from the world, abandoned to myself; and I saw clearly that they were determined to dispose of me despite myself.

When the day of her profession arrives, she plans to make a public statement of refusal during that ceremony.

All arrangements had been set the day before. The bells rang out to tell the world that a woman was about to be destroyed. My heart pounded constantly. They came to adorn me; this is a day for grand display. . . . They led me to the church, where Mass was celebrated, and the good vicar, who believed I had resigned myself as in fact I had not, preached a long sermon of which not one word was true. . . . When it was time to enter the place where I was to pronounce my final vows, my legs failed me. Two of my attendants held me up by my arms, on one of which lay my head, and they pulled me along. I don't know what passed through the minds of those in attendance, but what they saw was a young dying victim being dragged to the altar. From all sides came the sound of sighs and sobs, amid which I am certain there were none to be heard from my father and mother. Everyone stood up, and some young people climbed on chairs or hung from the bars of the grille [separating the altar from the congregants in the nave]. A profound silence fell when the cleric who presided at my profession said to me: "Marie-Suzanne Simonin, do you promise to tell the truth?"

"I do promise."

"Are you here of your full accord and your own free will?"

I answered "no"; but my assistants responded for me, "yes."

"Marie-Suzanne Simonin, do you promise God chastity, poverty, and obedience?"

I hesitated a moment; the priest waited; and I answered, "No, Monsieur."

He repeated: "Marie-Suzanne Simonin, do you promise God chastity, poverty, and obedience?"

I answered him in a louder voice: "No, monsieur, no."

He stopped and said to me: "My child, collect yourself and listen to me."

"Monsieur," I told him, "you ask me if I promise God chastity, poverty, and obedience; I have heard you clearly, and my answer is no . . . "

Turning toward my assistants, among whom there had arisen a great murmuring, I gave a sign that I wanted to speak. The murmuring ceased and I said:

"Messieurs, and especially you, my father and my mother, I ask you all to witness . . . "

At these words one of the nuns lowered the gate of the grille, and I saw that it was useless to continue. The nuns surrounded me, overwhelming me with reproaches. I listened without saying a word. I was conducted to my cell, and kept there under lock and key.

Created to be the toy of man

Mary Wollstonecraft, *Vindication of the Rights of Woman* (1792)

The excerpts presented here are taken from chapter 2 of the *Vindication*, entitled "The Prevailing Opinion of a Sexual Character Discussed"—a discussion, that is, of the commonly held assumptions about the nature of women. Among the observations raised are these. Women's domination by men has been ascribed to the different capacities of either sex, with men attaining to a standard of excellence of mind and character not achieved by women. To the extent that is true, Wollstonecraft argues, it is because women have been kept in ignorance, and taught "from their infancy," and by their mothers, that if they are only beautiful, "everything else is needless for, at least, twenty years of their lives." Docile and obedient, they entertain their husbands: "created to be the toy of man, his rattle, [she] must jingle in his ears whenever, dismissing reason, he chooses to be amused."

The "arbitrary" and "illegitimate power" over men that beauty gives to women, allowing them "to exercise a short-lived tyranny" while they are young is, however, obtained by self-degradation; and it is a power which, if they sought true equality with men, they would need to surrender. Rather than cling to the illegitimate power afforded by beauty, women should seek to better themselves: "the grand end of their exertions should be to unfold their own faculties and acquire the dignity of conscious virtue," which, as for men, is the only acquisition that "can satisfy an immortal soul," such as Wollstonecraft believed the human being possesses. Moreover, by improving herself and committing herself to the management of her family rather than simply to "adorn[ing] her person," she will "become the friend, and not the humble dependent of her husband." She will gain her liberty, and with it, her self-worth; for "liberty is the mother of virtue," enabling both men and women to "become more wise and virtuous."

VINDICATION OF THE RIGHTS OF WOMAN, CHAPTER 2

To account for, and excuse the tyranny of man, many ingenious arguments have been brought forward to prove, that the two sexes, in the acquirement of virtue, ought to aim at attaining a very different character: or, to speak explicitly, women are not allowed to have sufficient strength of mind to acquire what really deserves the name of virtue. Yet it should seem, allowing them to have souls, that there is but one way appointed by Providence to lead *mankind* to either virtue or happiness.

If then women are not a swarm of ephemeral triflers, why should they be kept in ignorance under the specious name of innocence? Men complain, and with reason, of the follies and caprices of our sex, when they do not keenly satirize our headstrong passions and groveling vices. Behold, I should answer, the natural effect of ignorance! . . . Women are told from their infancy, and taught by the example of their mothers, that a little knowledge of human weakness, justly termed cunning, softness of temper, *outward* obedience, and a scrupulous attention to a puerile kind of propriety, will obtain for them the protection of man; and should they be beautiful, everything else is needless for, at least, twenty years of their lives.

. . .

Still the regal homage which [women] receive is so intoxicating, that till the manners of the times are changed, and formed on more reasonable principles, it may be impossible to convince them that the illegitimate power which they

obtain, by degrading themselves, is a curse, and that they must return to nature and equality, if they wish to secure the placid satisfaction that unsophis-
ticated affections impart. But for this epoch we must wait—wait, perhaps, till
kings and nobles, enlightened by reason, and, preferring the real dignity of
man to childish state, throw off their gaudy hereditary trappings: and if then
women do not resign the arbitrary power of beauty—they will prove that
they have *less* mind than man. . . .

Connected with man as daughters, wives, and mothers, their moral character may be estimated by their manner of fulfilling those simple duties; but
the end, the grand end of their exertions should be to unfold their own faculties and acquire the dignity of conscious virtue. They may try to render their
road pleasant; but ought never to forget, in common with man, that life
yields not the felicity which can satisfy an immortal soul. . . .

. . .

The woman who has only been taught to please will soon find that her
charms are oblique sunbeams, and that they cannot have much effect on her
husband's heart when they are seen every day, when the summer is passed
and gone. Will she then have sufficient native energy to look into herself for
comfort, and cultivate her dormant faculties? Or, is it not more rational to
expect that she will try to please other men; and, in the emotions raised by the
expectation of new conquests, endeavor to forget the mortification her love or
pride has received? When the husband ceases to be a lover—and the time will
inevitably come, her desire of pleasing will then grow languid, or become a
spring of bitterness; and love, perhaps, the most evanescent of all passions,
gives place to jealousy or vanity.

. . .

In a seraglio [harem], I grant, that all these arts [of seduction] are necessary; . . . but have women so little ambition as to be satisfied with such
a condition? Can they supinely dream life away in the lap of pleasure, or
the languor of weariness, rather than assert their claim to pursue reasonable pleasures and render themselves conspicuous by practicing the virtues
which dignify mankind? Surely she has not an immortal soul who can
loiter life away merely employed to adorn her person, that she may amuse
the languid hours, and soften the cares of a fellow-creature who is willing
to be enlivened by her smiles and tricks, when the serious business of life
is over.

Besides, the woman who strengthens her body and exercises her mind
will, by managing her family and practicing various virtues, become the
friend, and not the humble dependent of her husband, and if she deserves his
regard by possessing such substantial qualities, she will not find it necessary to

conceal her affection, nor to pretend to an unnatural coldness of constitution to excite her husband's passions. In fact, if we revert to history, we shall find that the women who have distinguished themselves have neither been the most beautiful nor the most gentle of their sex.

. . .

How women are to exist in that state where there is to be neither marrying nor giving in marriage, we are not told.—For though moralists have agreed that the tenor of life seems to prove that *man* is prepared by various circumstances for a future state, they constantly concur in advising *woman* only to provide for the present. Gentleness, docility, and a spaniel-like affection are, on this ground, consistently recommended as the cardinal virtues of the sex; and, disregarding the arbitrary economy of nature, one writer has declared that it is masculine for a woman to be melancholy. She was created to be the toy of man, his rattle, and it must jingle in his ears whenever, dismissing reason, he chooses to be amused.

. . .

It appears to me necessary to dwell on these obvious truths, because females have been insulated, as it were; and, while they have been stripped of the virtues that should clothe humanity, they have been decked with artificial graces that enable them to exercise a short-lived tyranny. Love, in their bosoms, taking place of every nobler passion, their sole ambition is to be fair, to raise emotion instead of inspiring respect; and this ignoble desire, like the servility in absolute monarchies, destroys all strength of character. Liberty is the mother of virtue, and if women are, by their very constitution, slaves, and not allowed to breathe the sharp invigorating air of freedom, they must ever languish like exotics, and be reckoned beautiful flaws in nature.

. . .

I shall not pursue this argument any further than to establish an obvious inference, that as sound politics diffuse liberty, mankind, including woman, will become more wise and virtuous.

Man, are you capable of being just?

Olympe de Gouges, *Declaration of the Rights of Woman as Citizen* (1791)

"Man, are you capable of being just?" With this challenge Olympe de Gouges opens her *Declaration* which champions female equality in both the public and domestic arenas. Systematic where Wollstonecraft offers rambling "reflections," Gouges seconds her English contemporary in linking the liberty that is the hoped-for result of political change to the improved character of both men and women—but especially permitting women, at last, to earn the honor due their character and real achievements. Written on the model, almost to the point of parody, of the French *Declaration of the Rights of Man and the Citizen* of 1789, it moves from preface to preamble to a series of seventeen articles (of which thirteen appear here); then on to a *postamble*, or epilogue, calling for female action; and finally to a new proposed "social contract" to be established between "man and woman," founded on the equality of the two sexes—for marriage, as it then existed, she wrote, was "the tomb of trust and love."

DECLARATION OF THE RIGHTS OF WOMAN

Preface

Man, are you capable of being just? It is a woman who asks you this question; you will at least not strip her of this right. What have you to say? Who gave you sovereign authority to oppress my sex? Your strength? Your talents? Consider the wisdom of God: look everywhere at nature in its grandeur, . . . and give me, if you dare, one example of this tyrannical empire.

Man alone has cobbled together this notion. Blind, bizarre, bloated with petty knowledge, and in this age of wisdom and enlightenment lapsed into crass ignorance, he wants to lord it over a sex that possesses full intellectual capacity. Yet he pretends to rejoice in the Revolution, claiming his right to equality, but not anyone else's.

Declaration of the rights of woman as citizen

To be decreed by the National Assembly[1] in its last sessions or in that of the next legislature.

---

1. Created by the representatives of the Third Estate, the revolutionary National Assembly (or National Constituent Assembly) existed from June 13, 1789 until replaced by the Legislative Assembly on September 30, 1791.

Preamble

Mothers, daughters, and sisters, as representatives of the nation, demand to be constituted as a National Assembly. Considering that the ignorance, neglect, or disparagement of the rights of Woman are the only causes of public misery and the corruption of governments, they have resolved to present in a solemn declaration the natural, inalienable, and sacred rights of Woman, so that this declaration, placed always before the eyes of all members of society, may remind them constantly of their rights and their duties. . . .

In consequence, that sex which is superior in beauty as it is in courage, manifested in the suffering of childbirth,[2] recognizes and declares, in the presence and under the auspices of the Supreme Being, the following rights of Woman as Citizen.

ARTICLE 1.

Woman is born and remains equal to man in rights. Social distinctions can be based only on the common utility.

ARTICLE 2.

The goal of every political association is the preservation of the natural and imprescriptible rights of Woman and Man. These rights are liberty, property, and security, and above all, the right to resist oppression.

ARTICLE 3.

The principle of all sovereignty resides essentially in the Nation, which is nothing other than the union of Man and Woman. No body, and no individual, can exercise authority that does not derive expressly from [the Nation].

ARTICLE 4.

Liberty and justice consist in restoring to all persons whatever they have a right to. Accordingly, the only limits on the exercise of the natural rights of Woman being the perpetual tyranny that Man has imposed, those limits must be reformed according to the laws of nature and of reason.

---

2. The comparison between male courage in battle with women's even greater courage in childbirth is a commonplace going back to ancient Greece; cf. Euripides, *Medea*, 250.

ARTICLE 5.

The laws of nature and of reason proscribe all acts harmful to society. Anything that is not forbidden by these wise and divine laws cannot be proscribed, and no one can be compelled to do what they do not command.

ARTICLE 6.

Law must be the expression of the general will. All male and female citizens must agree either personally, or through their representatives, to the formulation of the laws, which must be the same for all. . . .

ARTICLE 7.

No woman is an exception: she may be accused, arrested, and detained as each case is determined by Law. Women, like men, must accept the rigors of the Law.

. . .

ARTICLE 10.

No one may be disquieted for their deeply held opinions. Woman has the right to mount the scaffold [i.e., for execution], and equally the right to mount the rostrum [i.e., speak publicly], provided that those actions do not disturb the public order established by the Law.

ARTICLE 11.

The free communication of thoughts and opinions is one of the most precious rights of Woman, since this freedom establishes the recognition of children by their fathers. Thus any female Citizen can say freely, "I am the mother of a child who belongs to you," without being forced by a barbarous prejudice to conceal the truth.[3]

. . .

ARTICLE 13.

Woman and Man should make equal contributions for the support of the public force [i.e., the military and police] and for government expenditures. . . .

---

3. It was important for women who had been sexually exploited to be able to publicly identify the father of an illegitimate child so as to gain some financial redress.

ARTICLE 14.

Both male and female citizens have the right to establish, by themselves or through their representatives, what will be the burden of taxation. . . .

. . .

ARTICLE 16.

No society has a constitution at all if rights are not guaranteed nor the separation of powers established; and the constitution does not exist if the majority of the individuals who make up the Nation have not joined in creating it.

ARTICLE 17.

Either sex may possess property, whether they are single or married, as property is an inviolable and sacred right for each, and not one can be deprived of it, as it is nature's true patrimony. . . .

POSTAMBLE

Awake, woman! The trumpet call of reason sounds throughout the universe: know your rights! . . . The flame of truth has dispelled all the clouds of stupidity and usurpation. To break free of his chains, enslaved Man has reinforced his strength, and has set his sights on yours. Now that he is free, he had turned on his companion. O women, women, when will you cease to be blind? What benefits have you received from the Revolution? A more conspicuous scorn, a more outspoken disdain. . . .

If they persist [in their prejudice], . . . boldly wield the force of reason against their empty pretensions of superiority. . . . It is in your power to free yourselves; you have only to want to do so. . . .

Template for a Social Contract between Man and Woman[4]

We, _____ and _____, of our own free will, join with each other for the rest of our life, and for the duration of our mutual inclinations, on the following conditions: We wish and intend to hold our wealth in common, reserving to ourselves, however, the right to assign part of it to our children, . . . both

---

4. Gouges' proposed "social contract" posits mutuality between man and woman (for the union envisioned is distinctly heterosexual) that is expected to endure lifelong but can result in separation, while it notably protects the legal and financial interests of children both legitimate and illegitimate.

recognizing that our possessions belong directly to our children, whatever their parentage, who all without distinction have the right to bear the name of the fathers and mothers who have acknowledged them. . . . We bind ourselves equally, in the event of separation, to divide our wealth, setting aside first the portion that is to go to our children as the law directs. In addition, when the partnership comes to an end, the one who dies first will confer half of his possessions upon his children; and if one of us dies without children, the survivor will inherit any property, unless the one who died first conveyed one-half of the goods held in common to a person of his choice.

Here, roughly, is the formula I propose to be instituted as a marriage contract. When they read this strange prescription, . . . a mob will rise up against me of hypocrites, prudes, and priests and all their infernal followers . . . [but] what I offer here is an invincible means by which to elevate the soul of women.

Chapter Eleven

American Reverberations: 1771–1792

Introduction

When Benjamin Franklin set up his printshop in Philadelphia, the story with which this chapter opens, the English settlement of North America was one hundred years old. In another fifty, it would come to an end, transformed into a new political, social, and cultural entity, the United States of America. While many forces cooperated to bring about this result, prominent among them was that of Enlightenment thought, with which the founders of this new civilization, immigrants themselves and the children of European immigrants, were thoroughly familiar.

The four authors of the five works presented in this chapter reflect that European past variously. Franklin (1706–1790) was the son of an English immigrant and his native-born second wife, both Puritans. Largely self-taught, he became, as a printer, a disseminator of ideas and an intellectual leader. Thomas Paine (1737–1809), son of a Quaker father and Anglican mother, who had received only an elementary schooling in his native England, had only recently emigrated to America, arriving in 1774, on the cusp of the Revolution that he was to promote and celebrate. Thomas Jefferson (1743–1826) and James Madison (1751–1836) were both sons of Virginia planters, both reared as Anglicans, both slaveholders, both future presidents of the United States (the third and the fourth to hold that title), and both finely educated, respectively at the College of William and Mary (now part of the University of Virginia) and the College of New Jersey (now Princeton University). All four were powerful writers who employed Enlightenment thought to envision and forge a new national identity.

One of the most revered and consequential Founding Fathers of the United States of America, Franklin was the youngest son of a youngest son, whose immigrant father, a candlemaker, had fled religious persecution in England. Descended from artisans, Franklin's older brothers were artisans as well: skilled craftsmen and entrepreneurs. But his brother James was the master of a particular trade—printing—that had enormous importance in colonial America, as it had in Europe. The printshop produced the newspapers, pamphlets, and broadsides that an increasingly literate public devoured, and was the home of intellectual conversation for the learned, especially in the absence of large capital cities that hosted salons and academies. Franklin spent his youth in his brother's printshop in Boston, as described in the excerpt appearing here, and went on to found his own in Philadelphia. It was a fitting start for one of the first great intellectuals of an independent United States, a statesman and inventor, and the founder of Philadelphia's public library and fire department, models for those of the nation at large, and of the University of Pennsylvania.

That tale of the printshop is related in Franklin's *Autobiography*, finished in 1771, a late entry among his many works. He intended it as a private memoir for his son William, whose son William Temple Franklin, Benjamin's grandson and secretary, would eventually publish it (in 1818) from the manuscript in his possession. In the meantime, however, it would first be translated into French as *Mémoires de la vie privée de Benjamin Franklin* (*Memoirs of the Private Life of Benjamin Franklin*) and published in Paris in 1791; the French, then engaged in their own revolution, were great admirers of Franklin, who had been ambassador during the American Revolution and negotiated the Franco-American alliance of 1778 essential for its victory. The memoirs were then retranslated into English and published in London in 1793. The full text was only established in 1868, and a modern authoritative edition not until 1986. It is a rich document of the life of a man revered for his wisdom and prudence, who had served his country over many decades as statesman and ambassador.

When he published the pamphlet *Common Sense*, one of those rare works that directly stimulated public opinion and action, Paine was a recent immigrant from his native England, who signed himself as "Tom Paine, an Englishman." But it had not taken him long to identify fully with the American colonial insurgency against imperial Great Britain. *Common Sense* appeared—or, rather, exploded—into print in January 1776, the midpoint of the interlude between the Battles of Lexington and Concord in April 1775, the first hostilities of the American Revolution, and the ratification of the *Declaration of Independence* on July 4, 1776, officially announcing the formation of a new and independent nation. Paine's pamphlet, running to seventy-nine pages in its third edition (February 1776), not only presented a logical case for American independence, drawing on the wellsprings of Enlightenment thought supported by historical and biblical example, but couched it in stirring and scintillating language—it is virtually a prose poem. Among his arguments, of which a few are illustrated in the sections presented here, were the fundamental injustice of hereditary monarchy, such as existed in England; the need to create a new political entity where the law, and not an individual, was king; the commercial prospects of the American colonies once they were freed from the mercantilist regulations imposed by the British Parliament; the difficulty of communications across the Atlantic, which meant that petitions went unanswered and instructions delayed; and the role of America as a "refuge for mankind," a place of religious freedom and economic opportunity for emigrants from all over Europe.

Paine was prescient, foreseeing not only an independent United States but identifying many of its enduring ideals. His other works—notably the wartime pamphlet series, *The Crisis* (1776–1783), *The Rights of Man* (1791–1792), of which more later, and *The Age of Reason* (1794–1807)—similarly displayed his agile pen while trumpeting American values and disseminating Enlightenment political and religious ideas; but none equaled *Common Sense* in immediate and long-term impact.

A more serious thinker than Paine, the native Virginian Jefferson, third president of the United States from March 1801 to March 1809, and like Franklin, ambassador to France at a critical juncture, was author of *Notes on the State of Virginia* and the *Virginia Statute for Religious Freedom*, among other writings, and a vast correspondence. But the work for which he is most famous, though he was its inspired creator and not its sole author, is the American *Declaration of Independence*. In it he draws on the entire Enlightenment discussion of natural rights and the foundations of government and society, but Locke especially, to enunciate in a mere 1,700 words or so the basic principles that still underlie the American polity today. The second sentence alone warrants extended reflection: "We hold these truths to be self-evident, that all men are created equal, that they are endowed by their Creator with certain unalienable Rights, that among these are Life, Liberty and the pursuit of Happiness."

To unpack this statement: These truths are "self-evident," meaning they are directly apprehended and absolutely true, as are axioms in a geometric proof. "All men," using the terminology of the day to speak of all humankind, "are equal," indisputably so, a claim putting into question all social distinctions. They possess "unalienable rights," which are natural, innately implanted by the hand of a transcendent deity whose name and nature is carefully unspecified; and which cannot be erased or removed by the hand of any person or government. And "among" those rights, "life, liberty and the pursuit of happiness" are named as of first importance, a slight modification of Locke's triad of life, liberty, and the right to private property. This pronouncement of truths about the human condition is embedded in the statement that, the king of England having denied and abused them (a list of twenty-seven ways he has so offended is included), the American colonies would respond by constituting a new and separate nation.

Even while the revolutionary war that followed upon this *Declaration* was in progress, the Second Continental Congress, in 1777, sought approval for the text of the Articles of Confederation, which provided for a loose federation of the autonomous former colonies. By 1781, the Articles had been ratified by all thirteen states and became the first constitution of the new, still nascent nation. The limits placed by the Articles on the power of the central government, however, made it difficult for that government to act. The war having been ended in 1783 by the Treaty of Paris, with the convocation in Philadelphia of a Constitutional Convention in May 1787, the process began of constructing a new constitution for the United States. Madison, a native Virginian, who would serve from 1809 to 1817 as the fourth president of the United States, was one of the committee of five tasked to provide a final draft of the Constitution. Firmly grounded in Enlightenment political theory and especially Montesquieu's principle of the separation of powers, it was approved in that Convention in September 1787.

The process of ratification by the states then began. To promote the draft constitution, Madison and fellow congressional delegate Alexander Hamilton, with anonymous contributions from statesman John Jay, all advocates of the Federalist position in favor of a strong central government, wrote a series of eighty-five articles defending it clause by clause. Published separately in various New York newspapers, these articles were subsequently gathered into a body called *The Federalist,* or *The Federalist Papers.* Included here are excerpts from *Federalist No. 10,* authored by Madison.

Madison not only contributed to the creation and finalization of the Constitution, but was the originator, as well, of its first ten amendments. Drawing on concepts inscribed in the Virginia Declaration of Rights and the English Bill of Rights of 1689, those amendments would be ratified in 1791 and promulgated as the Bill of Rights.

The Revolution over, the Constitution adopted, what was Thomas Paine, the professional revolutionary, now going to do? A new revolution had begun in France in 1789, and in 1790, Paine arrived in that nation to observe it. The product was his massive *Rights of Man,* which bound together commentaries on the English Glorious Revolution of 1688, to which Locke had been witness, the American Revolution of 1776, and now the French, still underway. It consisted of thirty-one articles, plus prefaces, dedicatory letters (to George Washington and the Marquis de Lafayette, the French liberal who had fought for America in the Revolutionary War), and a complete transcription, in English, of the 1789 French *Declaration of the Rights of Man and the Citizen.* Paine conceived the work as a response to the 1790 *Reflections on the Revolution in France* by English statesman and thinker Edmund Burke. The first part, completed 1791, is explicitly labeled as a response to Burke, but the second part, completed 1792, also engages Burke by name at many points.

Burke had argued (as will be seen in Chapter 12) the primacy of traditional social norms, cultural continuity, and inherited custom in any move for political change. Paine sharply rejects these as favorable to monarchy and aristocracy, the forms of government he most reviled. Instead, echoing the assertion of inborn unalienable rights pronounced in the *Declaration of Independence*, and previously by Locke, its progenitor, Paine posits those rights as the only possible foundation for a just and effective government. In the excerpt given in this chapter, he advances that proposal, arguing that the natural rights of human beings are the sole basis of the civil rights they possess in society, and that every one of the latter derives from the former.

In his *Rights of Man*, Paine sums up the Enlightenment discussion of human rights, natural and civil, that Locke had initiated, that had been pursued by Voltaire and Rousseau, developed by Montesquieu, Beccaria, Ferguson, and Smith, and placed center stage by the Americans Jefferson and Madison. That discourse goes on; but only after the cataclysmic interruption of the French Revolution, the problem confronted, as the next chapter relates, by Burke and Condorcet.

I took upon me to assert my freedom

Benjamin Franklin, *Autobiography* (1771/1792)

These portions of Franklin's *Autobiography*, composed decades later on the eve of the American Revolution, follow him from 1715 to 1724. The narrative begins when Franklin, then ten years old, after less than two years of schooling, worked as an assistant in his father's candlemaking shop; proceeding to when, at age twelve, he was made an apprentice to his brother, a printer; and to when, at age twenty-one, he had become a successful printer in Philadelphia, soon to have a shop of his own.

Italicized subheads are added by the editor to clarify the narrative.

AUTOBIOGRAPHY

1715

My elder brothers were all put apprentices to different trades. I was put to the grammar school at eight years of age, my father intending to devote me . . . to the service of the church. My early readiness in learning to read (which must have been very early, as I do not remember when I could not read) encouraged him in this purpose of his. . . . I continued . . . at the grammar school not quite one year. . . . But my father, in the meantime, from a view of the expense of a college education, which, having so large a family, he could not well afford, . . . altered his first intention, took me from the grammar school and sent me to a school for writing and arithmetic. . . . At ten years old I was taken home to assist my father in his business, which was that of a tallow-chandler and soap-boiler. . . . Accordingly, I was employed in cutting wick for the candles, filing the dipping-mold and the molds for cast candles, attending the shop, going of errands, etc. . . .

I continue thus employed in my father's business for two years; that is, till I was twelve years old; and . . . there was all appearance that I was destined to supply his place and become a tallow-chandler. But my dislike to the trade continuing, my father was under apprehensions that if he did not find one for me more agreeable l should break away and get to sea. . . . He therefore some-times took me to walk with him, and see joiners, bricklayers, turners, braziers, etc., at their work, that he might observe my inclination, and endeavor to fix it on some trade or other on land. . . .

1717

From a child I was fond of reading, and all the little money that came into my hands was ever laid out in books. Pleased with *The Pilgrim's Progress* my first collection was of [its author] John Bunyan's works in separate little vol-umes. . . . Plutarch's *Lives* there was, in which I read abundantly, and I still think that time spent to great advantage. . . .

This bookish inclination at length determined my father to make me a printer, though he had already one son (James) of that profession. . . . I . . . signed the indentures when I was yet but twelve years old. I was to serve as an apprentice till I was twenty-one years of age. . . . In a little time I made great proficiency in the business, and became a useful hand to my brother. I now had access to better books. An acquaintance with the apprentices of booksellers enabled me sometimes to borrow a small one, which I was careful to return soon and clean. Often I sat up in my room reading the greatest part of the night, when the book was borrowed in the evening and to be returned early in the morning, lest it should be missed or wanted. . . .

1721

Franklin's brother is the printer of a newspaper, the New England Courant, *to which the young Franklin anonymously contributes some well-received pieces.*

Encouraged . . . by this, I wrote and conveyed in the same way to the press several more papers which were equally approved; . . . [*until finally I revealed it*], when I began to be considered a little more by my brother's [compan-ions], and in a manner that did not quite please him. . . . And perhaps this might be one occasion of the differences that we began to have about this time. . . . [M]y brother . . . had often beaten me, which I took extremely amiss; and, thinking my apprenticeship very tedious, I was continually wishing for some opportunity of shortening it, which at length offered in a manner unexpected.

One of the pieces in our newspaper on some political point, which I have now forgotten, gave offense to the Assembly [i.e., the Boston authorities]. [My brother] was taken up, censured, and imprisoned for a month. . . . During my brother's confinement, . . . I had the management of the paper. . . . My brother's discharge was accompanied with an order of the House (a very odd one) that "James Franklin should no longer print the paper called the *New England Courant.*"

There was a consultation held in our printing-house among his friends what he should do in this case. . . . [I]t was finally concluded on, . . . to let it be printed for the future under the name of Benjamin Franklin; and to avoid the censure of the Assembly, that might fall on him as still printing it by his apprentice, the contrivance was that my old indenture should be returned to me. . . .

A very flimsy scheme it was; however, it was immediately executed, and the paper went on accordingly, under my name, for several months. At length a fresh difference arising between my brother and me, I took upon me to assert my freedom. . . . I then thought of going to New York, as the nearest place where there was a printer. . . .

September 1723

Franklin ventures by sea to New York and then to Philadelphia.

I have been the more particular in this description of my journey, and shall be so of my first entry into that city, that you may in your mind compare such unlikely beginnings with the figure I have since made there. I was in my working-dress. . . . I was dirty from my journey, my pockets were stuffed out with shirts and stockings, and . . . I was fatigued with traveling, rowing, and want of rest; I was very hungry; and my whole stock of cash consisted of a Dutch dollar and about a shilling in copper. . . .

Then I walked up the street, gazing about till near the market-house I met a boy with bread. I . . . went immediately to the baker's he directed me to, in Second Street, and . . . [h]e gave me . . . three great puffy rolls. I was surprised at the quantity, but took it, and . . . walked off with a roll under each arm, and eating the other. Thus I went up Market Street as far as Fourth Street, passing by the door of Mr. Read, my future wife's father, when she, standing at the door, saw me and thought I made, as I certainly did, a most awkward, ridiculous appearance. . . .

[*The next day*], I made myself as tidy as I could and I went to Andrew Bradford, the printer's, . . . [who] told me he did not at present want a hand, . . . but there was another printer in town, lately set up, one Keimer, who, perhaps, might employ me; if not, I should be welcome to lodge at his house. . . .

[*Bradford's father introduced Franklin to Keimer, who*] . . . asked me a few questions, put a composing-stick in my hand to see how I worked, and then said he would employ me soon, though he had just then nothing for me to do. . . . [*After a time*], . . . he had got another pair of cases, and a pamphlet to reprint, on which he set me to work. . . .

[Keimer] did not like my lodging at Bradford's while I worked with him. He . . . could not lodge me; but he got me a lodging at Mr. Read's, before mentioned, who was the owner of his house; and, my chest and clothes being come by this time, I made rather a more respectable appearance in the eyes of Miss Read than I had done when she first happened to see me eating my roll in the street.

I began now to have some acquaintance among the young people of the town that were lovers of reading, with whom I spent my evenings very pleasantly; and gaining money by my industry and frugality, I lived very agreeably, forgetting Boston as much as I could. . . . [*Having received a letter from a kinsman urging Franklin's return there,*] I wrote an answer to his letter, thanked him for his advice, but stated my reasons for quitting Boston fully and in such a light as to convince him I was not so wrong as he had apprehended.

Sir William Keith, governor of the province, was then at Newcastle; [*and Franklin's kinsman, then in his company, just then receiving the young man's letter, showed it to Keith*]. . . . The governor read it, and seemed surprised when he was told my age. He said I appeared a young man of promising parts, and therefore should be encouraged; the printers at Philadelphia were wretched ones; . . . for his part, he would procure me the public business, and do me every other service in his power. . . . [*Then*], one day, Keimer and I being at work together near the window, we saw the governor and another gentleman . . . , finely dressed, come directly across the street to our house, and heard them at the door.

Keimer ran down immediately, thinking it a visit to him; but the governor inquired for me, came up, and . . . made me many compliments, desired to be acquainted with me, . . . and would have me away with him to the tavern. . . . I was not a little surprised, and Keimer stared like a pig poisoned. I went, however, with the governor . . . to a tavern at the corner of Third Street, and over the Madeira [a fortified wine] he proposed my setting up my business, laid before me the probabilities of success. . . . On my doubting whether my father would assist me in it, Sir William said he would give me a letter to him, . . . and he did not doubt of prevailing with him. So it was concluded I should return to Boston in the first vessel. . . .

April 1724

Franklin returns to Boston.

My unexpected appearance surprised the family. All were, however, very glad to see me, and made me welcome, except my brother. I went to see him at his printing-house. I was better dressed than ever while in his service, having a genteel new suit from head to foot, a watch, and my pockets lined with near five pounds sterling in silver. He received me not very frankly, looked me all over, and turned to his work again.

Freedom has been hunted round the globe

Thomas Paine, *Common Sense* (1776)

In these passages from part three of *Common Sense*, which opens with the author's famous claim that he offers only "simple facts, plain arguments, and common sense," Paine proposes that the tie between England and America be severed, and a new form of government created. He denies, as some believed, that the American colonies had flourished under English rule, arguing instead that they have been held back by selfish regulations, and will prosper more greatly if freed from the mother country. Far from having enjoyed England's protection, similarly, religious refugees from both England and the rest of Europe have fled to safety and freedom in America. England's entanglements with other European countries, moreover, with whom Americans would rather be at peace, have often drawn them into war. Another issue is the relative size of England and America: it "reverses the common order of nature" that England, a small island off the northwest corner of Europe, should pretend to rule the vast expanse of America: "there is something very absurd in supposing a continent to be perpetually governed by an island." Instead, America must form its own government: one in which the "Law is king," and not the flawed heir to some fortunate dynasty. This section closes with a rousing plea for action: "Every spot of the old world is overrun with oppression. Freedom has been hunted round the globe. . . . O! receive the fugitive, and prepare in time an asylum for mankind."
Italicized subheads are added by the editor to clarify the narrative.

COMMON SENSE

Thoughts on the Present State of American Affairs

In the following pages I offer nothing more than simple facts, plain arguments, and common sense: and have no other preliminaries to settle with the reader, than that he will divest himself of prejudice and prepossession, . . . and generously enlarge his views beyond the present day.

Volumes have been written on the subject of the struggle between England and America. Men of all ranks have embarked in the controversy . . . ; but all have been ineffectual, and the period of debate is closed. Arms as the last resource decide the contest; the appeal was the choice of the King, and the Continent [i.e., America] has accepted the challenge.

. . .

The sun never shined on a cause of greater worth. It is not the affair of a city, a county, a province, or a kingdom; but of a continent—of at least one-eighth part of the habitable globe. It is not the concern of a day, a year, or an age; posterity is virtually involved in the contest, and will be more or less affected even to the end of time, by the proceedings now. Now is the seed-time of Continental union, faith and honor. The least fracture now will be like a name engraved with the point of a pin on the tender rind of a young oak; the wound would enlarge with the tree, and posterity read in it full grown characters.

. . .

I have heard it asserted by some, that as America has flourished under her former connection with Great Britain, the same connection is necessary towards her future happiness. . . . Nothing can be more fallacious than this kind of argument. We may as well assert that because a child has thrived upon milk, that it is never to have meat. . . . But . . . I answer roundly that America would have flourished as much, and probably much more, had no European power taken any notice of her. The commerce by which she has enriched herself are the necessaries of life, and will always have a market while eating is the custom of Europe.

But she has protected us, say some. That she has engrossed us is true, and defended the Continent at our expense as well as her own, is admitted; and she would have defended Turkey from the same motive, that is—for the sake of trade and dominion.

. . .

But Britain is the parent country, say some. Then the more shame upon her conduct. Even brutes do not devour their young, nor savages make war upon their families. . . . Europe, and not England, is the parent country of America. This new world has been the asylum for the persecuted lovers of civil and religious liberty from every part of Europe. Hither have they fled, not from the tender embraces of the mother, but from the cruelty of the monster. . . .

. . .

I challenge the warmest advocate for reconciliation to show a single advantage that this continent can reap by being connected with Great Britain. . . . Our corn [i.e., grain] will fetch its price in any market in Europe, and our imported goods must be paid for buy them where we will.

But the injuries and disadvantages, which we sustain by that connection, are without number; and our duty to mankind at large, as well as to ourselves, instruct us to renounce the alliance: because any submission to or dependence on Great Britain tends directly to involve this Continent in European wars and quarrels, and sets us at variance with nations who would otherwise seek our friendship, and against whom we have neither anger nor complaint. . . .

Europe is too thickly planted with kingdoms to be long at peace, and whenever a war breaks out between England and any foreign power, the trade of America goes to ruin, because of her connection with Britain.

. . .

As to government matters, it is not in the power of Britain to do this continent justice: The business of it will soon be too weighty and intricate to be managed with any tolerable degree of convenience, by a power so distant from us, and so very ignorant of us; for if they cannot conquer us, they cannot govern us. To be always running three or four thousand miles with a tale or a petition, waiting four or five months for an answer, which when obtained requires five or six more to explain it in, will in a few years be looked upon as folly and childishness—There was a time when it was proper, and there is a proper time for it to cease.

Small islands not capable of protecting themselves are the proper objects for kingdoms to take under their care; but there is something very absurd in supposing a continent to be perpetually governed by an island. In no instance has nature made the satellite larger than its primary planet, and as England and America, with respect to each other, reverses the common order of nature, it is evident they belong to different systems: England to Europe, America to itself.

. . .

Paine expands on the matter of Britain's inability to rule the colonies, and sketches a plan for colonial self-government.

But where says some is the king of America? I'll tell you, friend, he [i.e., God] reigns above, and does not make havoc of mankind like the Royal Brute [i.e., king] of Britain. Yet that we may not appear to be defective even in earthly honors, let a day be solemnly set apart for proclaiming the charter [i.e., a constitution]; let it be brought forth [and] a crown be placed thereon, by which the world may know . . . that in America the Law is king. . . .

A government of our own is our natural right: And . . . it is infinitely wiser and safer, to form a constitution of our own in a cool deliberate manner, while we have it in our power, than to trust such an interesting event to time and chance. . . .

. . .

You that tell us of harmony and reconciliation, can you restore to us the time that is past? . . . Neither can you reconcile Britain and America. . . . There are injuries which nature cannot forgive. . . . The Almighty has implanted in us these inextinguishable feelings for good and wise purposes. . . . They distinguish us from the herd of common animals. The social compact would dissolve, and justice be extirpated from the earth, . . . did not the injuries which our tempers sustain provoke us into justice.

O you that love mankind! You that dare oppose, not only the tyranny, but the tyrant, stand forth! Every spot of the old world is overrun with oppression. Freedom has been hunted round the globe. Asia, and Africa, have long expelled her.—Europe regards her like a stranger, and England has given her warning to depart. O! receive the fugitive, and prepare in time an asylum for mankind.

Endowed by their Creator with certain unalienable Rights

Thomas Jefferson and Others, *Declaration of Independence* (1776)

Drafted by Thomas Jefferson and revised by other members of the Second Continental Congress, the *Declaration of Independence* concisely states the core principles of the new American republic. It opens with an explanation of purpose: as it is necessary for the American colonies to dissolve its relationship with England, "a decent respect to the opinions of mankind requires" that the causes for that dissolution be declared. That weighty statement is followed by a weightier one, the famous enunciation of the "self-evident" truths that will undergird the American polity: "that all men are created equal, that they are endowed by their Creator with certain unalienable Rights, that among these are Life, Liberty and the pursuit of Happiness." Governments are founded to protect these rights, and when they fail to do so, it is the people's prerogative to disband them. There follows an enumeration of twenty-seven ways in which the English government had failed in its trust, of which the first two are given here. Although attempts had been made to seek redress, no satisfactory resolution had been reached. Inevitably, therefore, the American colonies assert their independence: "these United Colonies are, and of Right ought to be Free and Independent States; that they are Absolved from all Allegiance to the British Crown, and that all political connection between them and the State of Great Britain, is and ought to be totally dissolved. . . ."

The transcription made available by the National Archives is given here abridged as indicated, but otherwise unaltered.

In Congress, July 4, 1776.

The unanimous Declaration of the thirteen united States of America, When in the Course of human events, it becomes necessary for one people to dissolve the political bands which have connected them with another, and to assume among the powers of the earth, the separate and equal station to which the Laws of Nature and of Nature's God entitle them, a decent respect to the opinions of mankind requires that they should declare the causes which impel them to the separation.

We hold these truths to be self-evident, that all men are created equal, that they are endowed by their Creator with certain unalienable Rights, that among these are Life, Liberty and the pursuit of Happiness.—That to secure these rights, Governments are instituted among Men, deriving their just powers from the consent of the governed, —That whenever any Form of Government becomes destructive of these ends, it is the Right of the People to alter or to abolish it, and to institute new Government, laying its foundation on such principles and organizing its powers in such form, as to them shall seem most likely to effect their Safety and Happiness. Prudence, indeed, will dictate that Governments long established should not be changed for light and transient causes; and accordingly all experience hath shewn, that mankind are more disposed to suffer, while evils are sufferable, than to right themselves by abolishing the forms to which they are accustomed. But when a long train of abuses and usurpations, pursuing invariably the same Object evinces a design to reduce them under absolute Despotism, it is their right, it is their duty, to throw off such Government, and to provide new Guards for their future security.—Such has been the patient sufferance of these Colonies; and such is now the necessity which constrains them to alter their former Systems of Government. The history of the present King of Great Britain is a history of repeated injuries and usurpations, all having in direct object the establishment of an absolute Tyranny over these States. To prove this, let Facts be submitted to a candid world.

He has refused his Assent to Laws, the most wholesome and necessary for the public good.

He has forbidden his Governors to pass Laws of immediate and pressing importance, unless suspended in their operation till his Assent should be obtained; and when so suspended, he has utterly neglected to attend to them.

Twenty-five further charges follow.

In every stage of these Oppressions We have Petitioned for Redress in the most humble terms: Our repeated Petitions have been answered only by repeated injury. A Prince, whose character is thus marked by every act which may define a Tyrant, is unfit to be the ruler of a free people.

Nor have We been wanting in attentions to our British brethren. We have warned them from time to time of attempts by their legislature to extend an unwarrantable jurisdiction over us. We have reminded them of the circumstances of our emigration and settlement here. We have appealed to their native justice and magnanimity, and we have conjured them by the ties of our common kindred to disavow these usurpations, which, would inevitably interrupt our connections and correspondence. They too have been deaf to the voice of justice and of consanguinity. We must, therefore, acquiesce in the necessity, which denounces our Separation, and hold them, as we hold the rest of mankind, Enemies in War, in Peace Friends.

We, therefore, the Representatives of the United States of America, in General Congress, Assembled, appealing to the Supreme Judge of the world for the rectitude of our intentions, do, in the Name, and by Authority of the good People of these Colonies, solemnly publish and declare, That these United Colonies are, and of Right ought to be Free and Independent States; that they are Absolved from all Allegiance to the British Crown, and that all political connection between them and the State of Great Britain, is and ought to be totally dissolved; and that as Free and Independent States, they have full Power to levy War, conclude Peace, contract Alliances, establish Commerce, and to do all other Acts and Things which Independent States may of right do. And for the support of this Declaration, with a firm reliance on the protection of divine Providence, we mutually pledge to each other our Lives, our Fortunes and our sacred Honor.

The signatures of fifty-six delegates follow.

A safeguard against faction and insurrection

James Madison, *Federalist No. 10* (1787)

Madison's densely argued and theoretically complex article addresses the inevitable tendency for human beings to form factions opposed to the established government, potentially leading to insurrection. He discards two of the possible preventive remedies: the first to limit freedom of expression and association; and the second to alter the nature of the human being. The first would be wrong and the second, impossible.

Madison then considers how the effects of factionalism might be controlled. If the adherents of a faction number less than the majority, then they are overruled by the majority, and the matter is contained. But if the adherents of a faction include a majority of the citizenry—if, that is, a majority of citizens have been lured into a stance contrary to the interests of the republic itself—then that majority "must be rendered . . . unable to concert and carry into effect schemes of oppression." A pure democracy, in which every citizen participates in government, is helpless in such a case: as has frequently happened in the past, the government will fall, for such democracies "have in general been as short in their lives as they have been violent in their deaths." A republic, however, in which government is in the hands of elected representatives of the whole citizenry, can withstand such a faction. The "chosen body of citizens" who hold power will in their wisdom "best discern the true interest of their country," and who possess the "patriotism and love of justice" that will make them unlikely "to sacrifice [their country] to temporary or partial considerations." It is just such a republican form of government that Madison and his colleagues advocate for the United States of America.

FEDERALIST NO. 10: FROM THE NEW YORK PACKET, FRIDAY, NOVEMBER 23, 1787

The Same Subject Continued: The Union as a Safeguard Against Domestic Faction and Insurrection

Among the numerous advantages promised by a well-constructed Union, none deserves to be more accurately developed than its tendency to break and control the violence of faction. The friend of popular governments never finds himself so much alarmed for their character and fate, as when he contemplates their propensity to this dangerous vice. He will not fail, therefore, to set a due value on any plan which, without violating the principles to which he is attached, provides a proper cure for it. . . .

By a faction, I understand a number of citizens, whether amounting to a majority or a minority of the whole, who are united and actuated by some common impulse of passion, or of interest, adversed [i.e., opposed] to the rights of other citizens, or to the permanent and aggregate interests of the community.

There are two methods of curing the mischiefs of faction: the one, by removing its causes; the other, by controlling its effects.

There are again two methods of removing the causes of faction: the one, by destroying the liberty which is essential to its existence; the other, by giving to every citizen the same opinions, the same passions, and the same interests.

It could never be more truly said than of the first remedy, that it was worse than the disease. Liberty is to faction what air is to fire, an aliment [nutriment] without which it instantly expires. But it could not be less folly to abolish liberty, which is essential to political life, because it nourishes faction, than it would be to wish the annihilation of air, which is essential to animal life, because it imparts to fire its destructive agency.

The second expedient is as impracticable as the first would be unwise. As long as the reason of man continues fallible, and he is at liberty to exercise it, different opinions will be formed. . . . The diversity in the faculties of men, from which the rights of property originate, is not less an insuperable obstacle to a uniformity of interests. . . .

The latent causes of faction are thus sown in the nature of man; and we see them everywhere brought into different degrees of activity, according to the different circumstances of civil society. A zeal for different opinions concerning religion, concerning government, and many other points, as well of speculation as of practice; an attachment to different leaders ambitiously contending for pre-eminence and power . . . , have, in turn, divided mankind into parties, inflamed them with mutual animosity, and rendered them much more disposed to vex and oppress each other than to co-operate for their common good. . . . The regulation of these various and interfering interests forms the principal task of modern legislation, and involves the spirit of party and faction in the necessary and ordinary operations of the government.

. . .

The inference to which we are brought is that the causes of faction cannot be removed, and that relief is only to be sought in the means of controlling its effects.

If a faction consists of less than a majority, relief is supplied by the republican principle, which enables the majority to defeat its sinister views by regular vote. It may clog the administration, it may convulse the society; but it will be unable to execute and mask its violence under the forms of the Constitution. When a majority is included in a faction, the form of popular government, on the other hand, enables it to sacrifice to its ruling passion or interest both the public good and the rights of other citizens. To secure the public good and private rights against the danger of such a faction, and at the same time to preserve the spirit and the form of popular government, is then the great object to which our inquiries are directed. . . .

By what means is this object attainable? Evidently by one of two only. Either the existence of the same passion or interest in a majority at the same time must be prevented, or the majority, having such coexistent passion or interest, must be rendered, by their number and local situation, unable to concert and carry into effect schemes of oppression. . . .

From this view of the subject it may be concluded that a pure democracy, can admit of no cure for the mischiefs of faction. A common passion or interest will . . . be felt by a majority of the whole; . . . and there is nothing to check the inducements to sacrifice the weaker party or an obnoxious individual. Hence it is that such democracies have ever been spectacles of turbulence and contention; have ever been found incompatible with personal security or the rights of property; and have in general been as short in their lives as they have been violent in their deaths. . . .

A republic, by which I mean a government in which the scheme of representation takes place, opens a different prospect, and promises the cure for which we are seeking. Let us examine the points in which it varies from pure democracy, and we shall comprehend both the nature of the cure and the efficacy which it must derive from the Union.

The two great points of difference between a democracy and a republic are: first, the delegation of the government, in the latter, to a small number of citizens elected by the rest; secondly, the greater number of citizens, and greater sphere of country, over which the latter may be extended.

The effect of the first difference is, on the one hand, to refine and enlarge the public views, by passing them through the medium of a chosen body of citizens, whose wisdom may best discern the true interest of their country, and whose patriotism and love of justice will be least likely to sacrifice it to temporary or partial considerations. . . .

. . .

The other point of difference is the greater number of citizens and extent of territory which may be brought within the compass of republican than of democratic government; and it is this circumstance principally which renders factious combinations less to be dreaded in the former than in the latter. . . .

Hence, it clearly appears, that the same advantage which a republic has over a democracy, in controlling the effects of faction, is enjoyed by a large over a small republic, [and] is enjoyed by the Union over the States composing it. . . .

In the extent and proper structure of the Union, therefore, we behold a republican remedy for the diseases most incident to republican government.

And according to the degree of pleasure and pride we feel in being republicans, ought to be our zeal in cherishing the spirit and supporting the character of Federalists.

An end to government by force and fraud

Thomas Paine, *The Rights of Man* (1791–1792)

Paine's *Rights of Man*, a miscellaneous commentary on history and politics in the light of the ongoing events of the French Revolution, has as its main purpose the refutation of Edmund Burke's counterrevolutionary argument. To Burke's valorization of custom, traditional institutions, and inherited values, Paine opposes the original and innate rights that human beings possess from the creation of the species, and with each individual birth. If justice is to be obtained, these rights must be concretized in social and political institutions.

In the passage that follows from part one of *The Rights of Man*, Paine offers a brief demonstration that "natural" rights precede "civil" rights, and that every civil right is grounded in natural right. Civil rights are not to be viewed, then, as the outcome of a long evolution, conditioned by experience, as Burke would have it, but are intrinsically and timelessly related to original natural rights. All governments not rooted in these rights have no other foundation than "force and fraud."

THE RIGHTS OF MAN, PART ONE

Hitherto we have spoken only . . . of the natural rights of man. We have now to consider the civil rights of man, and to show how the one originates from the other. Man did not enter into society to become worse than he was before, nor to have fewer rights than he had before, but to have those rights better secured. His natural rights are the foundation of all his civil rights. But in order to pursue this distinction with more precision, it will be necessary to mark the different qualities of natural and civil rights.

A few words will explain this. Natural rights are those which appertain to man in right of his existence. Of this kind are all the intellectual rights, or rights of the mind, and also all those rights of acting as an individual for his own comfort and happiness, which are not injurious to the natural rights of others. Civil rights are those which appertain to man in right of his being a member of society. Every civil right has for its foundation some natural right pre-existing in the individual, but to the enjoyment of which his individual power is not, in all cases, sufficiently competent. Of this kind are all those which relate to security and protection.

From this short review it will be easy to distinguish between that class of natural rights which man retains after entering into society and those which he throws into the common stock as a member of society.

The natural rights which he retains are all those in which the power to execute is as perfect in the individual as the right itself. Among this class . . . are all the intellectual rights, or rights of the mind; consequently religion is one of those rights. The natural rights which are not retained are all those in which, though the right is perfect in the individual, the power to execute them is defective. They answer not his purpose. A man, by natural right, has a right to judge in his own cause; and so far as the right of the mind is concerned, he never surrenders it. But what does it avail him to judge, if he has not power to redress? He therefore deposits this right in the common stock of society, and takes the arm of society, of which he is a part, in preference and in addition to his own. Society grants him nothing. Every man is a proprietor in society, and draws on the capital as a matter of right.

From these premises two or three certain conclusions will follow:

First, That every civil right grows out of a natural right; or, in other words, is a natural right exchanged.

Secondly, That civil power properly considered as such is made up of the aggregate of that class of the natural rights of man which becomes defective in the individual in point of power, and answers not his purpose, but when collected to a focus becomes competent to the purpose of every one.

Thirdly, That the power produced from the aggregate of natural rights, imperfect in power in the individual, cannot be applied to invade the natural rights which are retained in the individual, and in which the power to execute is as perfect as the right itself.

We have now, in a few words, traced man from a natural individual to a member of society, and shown, or endeavored to show, the quality of the natural rights retained, and of those which are exchanged for civil rights. Let us now apply these principles to governments.

In casting our eyes over the world, it is extremely easy to distinguish the governments which have arisen out of society, or out of the social compact, from those which have not; but to place this in a clearer light than what a single glance may afford, it will be proper to take a review of the several sources from which governments have arisen and on which they have been founded.

They may be all comprehended under three heads. First: Superstition. Secondly: Power. Thirdly: The common interest of society and the common rights of man.

The first was a government of priestcraft, the second of conquerors, and the third of reason.

When a set of artful men pretended, through the medium of oracles, to hold intercourse with the Deity, . . . the world was completely under the government of superstition. The oracles were consulted, and whatever they were made to say became the law; and this sort of government lasted as long as this sort of superstition lasted.

After these a race of conquerors arose, whose government, like that of William the Conqueror, was founded in power. . . . Governments thus established last as long as the power to support them lasts; but that they might avail themselves of every engine in their favor, they united fraud to force, and set up an idol which they called Divine Right. . . .

When I contemplate the natural dignity of man, when I feel (for nature has not been kind enough to me to blunt my feelings) for the honor and happiness of its character, I become irritated at the attempt to govern mankind by force and fraud, as if they were all knaves and fools. . . .

We have now to review the governments which arise out of society, in contradistinction to those which arose out of superstition and conquest.

It has been thought a considerable advance towards establishing the principles of freedom to say that government is a compact between those who govern and those who are governed; but this cannot be true, because it is putting the effect before the cause; for as man must have existed before governments existed, there necessarily was a time when governments did not exist, and consequently there could originally exist no governors to form such a compact with.

The fact therefore must be that the individuals themselves, each in his own personal and sovereign right, entered into a compact with each other to produce a government: and this is the only mode in which governments have a right to arise, and the only principle on which they have a right to exist.

Chapter Twelve

Enlightenment's End: 1790–1794

Introduction

Two last figures remain to be considered, both writing during the waning years of Enlightenment when its streams of thought intersected with the maelstrom of the French Revolution. They are the English statesman Edmund Burke (1729–1797) and the French aristocrat Condorcet (Marie Jean Antoine Nicolas de Caritat, marquis de Condorcet, 1743–1794). The first disturbances of 1789–1790 prompted Burke to assemble as a lengthy letter, phrased as a response to an inquiry, his *Reflections on the Revolution in France* (1790). Condorcet, a supporter of the Revolution in its early stages who had fled to safety during the Reign of Terror of 1793 to 1794, composed in his hideout his *Esquisse d'un tableau historique des progrès de l'esprit humain* (*A Sketch of a Historical Portrait of the Progress of the Human Mind*[1]), left unfinished at his death and published posthumously by his widow.

Burke was a paradox: a liberal, and yet a counterrevolutionary. He was a determined reformer, who had during more than thirty years in Parliament supported the independence of the American colonies in rebellion against the crown; pursued the corrupt East India Company, an effort culminating in the 1786 impeachment of Warren Hastings, former governor-general of Bengal; and defended the rights of Catholics (among them his wife, his sister, and his mother), who constituted the majority of the population of his native Ireland, but who suffered discrimination under English law. And yet this liberal statesman, in his sixtieth year, published in 1790 his counterrevolutionary best seller *Reflections on the Revolution in France*. Burke opposed that revolution not because it sought to champion the rights of the French people, but because it did so by discarding traditions, beliefs, and institutions that were knit into the nation's consciousness, to replace them with invented systems, he charged, that had no rootedness in the nation's past. When Burke left Parliament in 1796 to retire to his home in Beaconsfield, twenty-four miles from London, he established a school there for the refugee children of French aristocrats, deprived of their nation and their history.

---

1. As I have translated the title here, out of fidelity to Condorcet: for *esquisse*, "sketch" has been preferred to "outline," found elsewhere, which obscures his clear allusion to the visual arts; and for *tableau*, "portrait" has been preferred to "picture" or "view," as the picture that is drawn is of the human species, the human face writ large.

Condorcet, too, was a paradox: an aristocrat and yet a liberal. A wealthy nobleman educated by Jesuits, yet an admirer of Voltaire and protégé of Turgot's, he saw history as a trail of wrongdoing and detested the oppressions of the Catholic Church. In his early career, he wrote mostly about mathematics, contributing importantly to the theory of probability, and held from 1774 to 1791 the official position of master of the mint. In the meantime, Condorcet circulated in the salons where Enlightenment ideas flourished, and hosted one himself, led by his wife, twenty years his junior, who was herself a liberal intellectual and his perfect counterpart. He announced his abolitionist and feminist positions squarely, in two works of 1781 and 1790, respectively; and when the Revolution broke out, Condorcet was elected a representative to the Legislative Assembly in 1791, and helped write a draft of a future constitution, never adopted. Aligned with the more moderate Girondin party even as the radical Jacobins were rising, Condorcet in vain opposed the execution of King Louis XVI.

Condorcet's liberal associations and his aristocratic birth were both fatal detriments when the Jacobins came to power in the spring of 1793, his fiftieth year, and launched the Reign of Terror. Even as the death toll mounted daily, in the refuge to which he had fled, Condorcet wrote his *Sketch of a Historical Portrait*. A work brimming with optimism, it traced the evolution of humankind from its savage origins, echoing Rousseau, to its future perfection in a world without war, without poverty, without social distinctions, without ignorance, and without misery. This monumental project was not quite finished when, on March 27, 1794, having left his place of safety, Condorcet was recognized, arrested, and imprisoned for the crime of being who he was. On March 28, the eve of his scheduled execution, cheating the guillotine, he died in his cell: likely a suicide, or possibly murdered by a kindly hand.

The two signature works of these two paradoxical men also pose a clear contrast. Neither claims to be as massive a statement of principle as it is: Burke writes mere "reflections," Condorcet offers only a "sketch." But Burke's *Reflections* lays down the firm foundations of modern conservatism, and Condorcet's *Sketch* enunciates principles central for modern progressivism. Both map out a future: Burke, a future that is organically connected to the past; Condorcet, a future released from the past's dead hand.

For Burke, a political revolution that seeks to undo the past, to tear down institutions and replace them, to delegitimize beliefs and values that had sustained populations, to destroy and discard the inherited culture embodied in its books and monuments, can never be warranted because it tears at the sinews of the human embodiments of that past: the nation—understood as a community of those sharing a common birthplace and associated heritage—and the family. He does not deny that people and institutions can be corrupted and require correction; in his own life, Burke had fought relentlessly for such correction, embracing goals that today would be considered liberal. Yet he opposed the radical revolution that he saw in progress in France. The cannibalism of tradition can only result in tragedy, he believed, and a worse tyranny than presently exists.

In contrast to Burke, who embraces history, and the cultural evolution that it embodies, as the key to national identity and personal wholeness, Condorcet rejects it as the aggregate of past failure and cruelty. The notion of progress, inherently, involves the notion of past deficiency, a deficit that is to be overcome. Yet having jettisoned the past, the future that Condorcet envisions is captivating; and he is prescient. He foresees an end to colonialism (not an entirely satisfactory one by the standard of modern postcolonial theory) with the repudiation of its past brutality and exploitation, and an era of international peace with the establishment of systems of global cooperation. He anticipates a future when equality means not only the equitable application of the laws, but also an equitable distribution of goods to the extent possible given the differing innate capacities of individuals. He advocates universal education; the elevation of women, heretofore the victims of male power; the victory of medicine over illness and even, to some extent, death; and the attainment of perpetual peace among nations. Thus Condorcet's "sketch of a historical portrait" conveys as an epiphany his vision of the future of the human species.

Burke and Condorcet both respond to the challenge of the French Revolution with works that are about much more than politics—as the Enlightenment, in toto, was about much more than politics, as has been seen in this volume. But it was with politics that it comes to an end. The two revolutions and their aftermath created conditions unfavorable for a continuation of the Enlightenment conversation, daring in its explorations, but delicate in its formulations, and limited to arcane circles of generally well-born and certainly well-mannered intellectuals. The Enlightenment had offered a rational rebuke of traditional culture. It is superseded by the radical dismantling of political structures in France and America, preparing the ground for new sets of ideas, in the age to come, about politics and society, nature and art, and the mind, soul, and destiny of the human being.

A partnership of the living, the dead, and those unborn

Edmund Burke, *Reflections on the Revolution in France* (1790)

A work of close to three hundred pages, undifferentiated by chapter headings or other subdivisions, and, having originated as a letter to an acquaintance, informal in presentation, the *Reflections* is not an undisciplined work, but one whose essential argument is restated many times and amplified in different ways. The excerpts here state some of Burke's main points, of which a bare summary follows.

A nation consists of people, related by ties of association and blood, descended from ancestors and hopeful of offspring, who share a culture and history, and constitute a living organism. It is not possible to resurrect the human being in the "state of nature," as Locke and Rousseau and others of the era had tried to do, as human beings are always embedded in the experience of their nation or community. Their rights, similarly, which they surely possess, are not presumed "natural rights" abstracted from theoretical speculation, but those that have emerged from the national experience. Government, likewise, is an expression of the history of the people, and has evolved over time—imperfectly, but always in response to current circumstances. It cannot safely be destroyed and begun anew, as revolutionaries may imagine—"dissolv[ing] it into an unsocial, uncivil, unconnected chaos of elementary principles"—without incurring a more terrible tyranny than the one that has been resisted. It can and should be changed and reformed, but always within the boundaries of the cultural organism that engendered it. Political society, therefore, is not formed by a theoretical "social contract," as Burke's contemporaries had speculated, but is a lived contract, a "partnership not only between those who are living, but between those who are living, those who are dead, and those who are to be born."

No alterations have been made to Burke's archaic but eloquent prose in these extracts.

REFLECTIONS ON THE REVOLUTION IN FRANCE

You will observe, that, from Magna Charta to the Declaration of Right, it has been the uniform policy of our Constitution to claim and assert our liberties as an *entailed inheritance* derived to us from our forefathers, and to be transmitted to our posterity,—as an estate specially belonging to the people of this kingdom, without any reference whatever to any other more general or prior right. . . . We have an inheritable crown, an inheritable peerage, and a House of Commons and a people inheriting privileges, franchises, and liberties from a long line of ancestors.[2]

---

2. Magna Carta (1215) and the English Declaration of Rights (1689), both limiting the power of the monarchy, are two of the most important documents of English history. They also form part of the English "constitution," which is an assemblage of precedents and laws and not a composed document. An inheritance is "entailed" when it is limited so that the property remains over generations within a biologically related family. The House of Commons is one of the two houses of the English Parliament.

This policy appears to me to be the result of profound reflection,—or rather the happy effect of following Nature, which is wisdom without reflection, and above it. A spirit of innovation is generally the result of a selfish temper and confined views. People will not look forward to posterity, who never look backward to their ancestors. Besides, the people of England well know that the idea of inheritance furnishes a sure principle of conservation, and a sure principle of transmission, without at all excluding a principle of improvement. . . . By a constitutional policy working after the pattern of Nature, we receive, we hold, we transmit our government and our privileges, in the same manner in which we enjoy and transmit our property and our lives. . . . Our political system is placed in a just correspondence and symmetry with the order of the world . . . wherein, by the disposition of a stupendous wisdom, . . . the whole, at one time, is never old or middle-aged or young, but, in a condition of unchangeable constancy, moves on through the varied tenor of perpetual decay, fall, renovation, and progression. . . . By adhering in this manner and on those principles to our forefathers, we are guided, not by the superstition of antiquarians, but by the spirit of philosophic analogy. In this choice of inheritance we have given to our frame of polity the image of a relation in blood: binding up the Constitution of our country with our dearest domestic ties; adopting our fundamental laws into the bosom of our family affections; keeping inseparable, and cherishing with the warmth of all their combined and mutually reflected charities, our state, our hearths, our sepulchers, and our altars.

Through the same plan of a conformity to Nature in our artificial institutions, . . . we have derived several other, and those no small benefits, from considering our liberties in the light of an inheritance. Always acting as if in the presence of canonized forefathers, the spirit of freedom, leading in itself to misrule and excess, is tempered with an awful gravity. . . . By this means our liberty becomes a noble freedom. It carries an imposing and majestic aspect. . . . All your sophisters [i.e., purveyors of abstract theories] cannot produce anything better adapted to preserve a rational and manly freedom than the course that we have pursued, who have chosen our nature rather than our speculations, our breasts rather than our inventions, for the great conservatories and magazines of our rights and privileges.

. . .

Far am I from denying in theory, full as far is my heart from withholding in practice, . . . the *real* rights of men. In denying their false claims of right, I do not mean to injure those which are real, and are such as their pretended rights would totally destroy. If civil society be made for the advantage of man, all the advantages for which it is made become his right. . . . Men have a right to live by that rule; they have a right to justice, as between their fellows, whether their fellows are in politic function or in ordinary occupation. They have a right to the fruits of their industry, and to the means of making their industry fruitful. They have a right to the acquisitions of their parents, to the nourishment and improvement of their offspring, to instruction in life and to consolation in death. Whatever each man can separately do, without trespassing upon others, he has a right to do for himself; and he has a right to a fair portion of all which society, with all its combinations of skill and force, can do in his favor.

In this partnership all men have equal rights; but not to equal things. He that has but five shillings in the partnership has as good a right to it as he that has five hundred pounds has to his larger proportion; but he has not a right to an equal dividend in the product of the joint stock. And as to the share of power, authority, and direction which each individual ought to have in the management of the state, that I must deny to be amongst the direct original rights of man in civil society; for I have in my contemplation the civil social man, and no other. It is a thing to be settled by convention. . . .

Government is not made in virtue of natural rights, which may and do exist in total independence of it,—and exist in much greater clearness, and in a much greater degree of abstract perfection: but their abstract perfection is their practical defect. By having a right to everything they want everything. Government is a contrivance of human wisdom to provide for human *wants*. Men have a right that these wants should be provided for by this wisdom. Among these wants is to be reckoned the want, out of civil society, of a sufficient restraint upon their passions. Society requires not only that the passions of individuals should be subjected, but that even in the mass and body, as well as in the individuals, the inclinations of men should frequently be thwarted, their will controlled, and their passions brought into subjection. . . .

The moment you abate anything from the full rights of men each to govern himself, and suffer any artificial, positive limitation upon those rights, from that moment the whole organization of government becomes a consideration of convenience. This it is which makes the constitution of a state, and the due distribution of its powers, a matter of the most delicate and complicated skill. It requires a deep knowledge of human nature and human necessities, and of the things which facilitate or obstruct the various ends which are to be pursued by the mechanism of civil institutions. . . . What is the use of discussing a man's abstract right to food or medicine? The question is upon the method of procuring and administering them. In that deliberation I shall always advise to call in the aid of the farmer and the physician, rather than the professor of metaphysics.

The science of constructing a commonwealth, or renovating it, or reforming it, is, like every other experimental science, not to be taught *a priori* [i.e., from theoretical deduction rather than from experience]. . . . In states there are often some obscure and almost latent causes, things which appear at first view of little moment, on which a very great part of its prosperity or adversity may most essentially depend. The science of government being, therefore, so practical in itself, and intended for such practical purposes, a matter which requires experience, . . . it is with infinite caution that any man ought to venture upon pulling down an edifice which has answered in any tolerable degree for ages the common purposes of society, or on building it up again without having models and patterns of approved utility before his eyes.

. . .

To avoid, therefore, the evils of inconstancy and versatility, ten thousand times worse than those of obstinacy and the blindest prejudice, we have consecrated the state, that no man should approach to look into its defects or corruptions but with due caution; that he should never dream of beginning its reformation by its subversion; that he should approach to the faults of the state as to the wounds of a father, with pious awe and trembling solicitude. . . .

Society is, indeed, a contract. Subordinate contracts for objects of mere occasional interest may be dissolved at pleasure; but the state ought not to be considered as nothing better than a partnership agreement in a trade of pepper and coffee, calico or tobacco, . . . to be taken up for a little temporary interest, and to be dissolved by the fancy of the parties. It is to be looked on with other reverence; because it is not a partnership in things subservient only to the gross animal existence of a temporary and perishable nature. It is a partnership in all science, a partnership in all art, a partnership in every virtue and in all perfection.

As the ends of such a partnership cannot be obtained in many generations, it becomes a partnership not only between those who are living, but between those who are living, those who are dead, and those who are to be born. Each contract of each particular state is but a clause in the great primeval contract of eternal society, linking the lower with the higher natures, connecting the visible and invisible world, according to a fixed compact sanctioned by the inviolable oath which holds all physical and all moral natures each in their appointed place. This law is not subject to the will of those who, by an obligation above them, and infinitely superior, are bound to submit their will to that law. The municipal corporations of that universal kingdom are not morally at liberty, at their pleasure, and on their speculations of a contingent improvement, wholly to separate and tear asunder the bands of their subordinate community, and to dissolve it into an unsocial, uncivil, unconnected chaos of elementary principles.

The future destiny of the human species

Nicolas de Condorcet, *A Sketch of a Historical Portrait of the Progress of the Human Mind* (1793–1794)

Just as Rousseau, in the *Discourse on the Origins of Social Inequality* (see Chapter Nine), had looked back to the first era of human existence on earth, so Condorcet begins to paint his portrait of the advancement of the human condition in that distant time—but then proceeds to portray eight further stages of human existence before arriving at a tenth and final epoch when the full promise of the human species will be realized. The passages given here from that tenth epoch explore that destiny that awaits when "the sun in its orbit will illumine only free peoples, who recognize no other master than their reason"; when all forms of social and economic inequality will disappear, and with it poverty and ignorance; when women will no longer be denigrated but become equal partners and citizens; when perpetual peace will reign between nations; when new technologies will permit rapid intellectual progress, and a universal language will enable communication across cultures; and when improvements in health and medical practice will extend life expectancy perhaps indefinitely. Condorcet writes in the style of an aristocrat, lavish in words and not too burdened with detail, but his prose glows with his warm faith in the future betterment of humankind.

Italicized subheads have been supplied by the editor to clarify the order of argument.

A Sketch of a Historical Portrait

Tenth Epoch: The future progress of the human spirit

If human beings can predict with near certainty those phenomena whose laws they know; and if, given past experience of even those whose laws they know not, they can with fair probability predict the future; why should we regard as fanciful the attempt to sketch with some exactitude the future destiny of the human species, given our knowledge of its history? . . .

Our hopes for the future of the human species come down to these three important points: first, the elimination of inequality between nations; second, the progress toward equality among the people of each single nation; and finally, the fulfillment of the promise of the human condition. . . .

The difference in extent of knowledge, of skills, or of wealth prevailing heretofore among the different groups of people composing each civilized nation—does this inequality . . . inhere in the civilization itself, or does it result from identifiable social imperfections? Must it not be continually eroded, to be replaced by a real equality, which, softening the effects even of a natural difference in capacities, leaves in place only an inequality that is useful to all, that will encourage the progress of the civilization, of education, and of industry, without promoting dependency, humiliation, and impoverishment? . . .

And so, will it not be the case that the human condition will be advanced, whether by new discoveries in the arts and sciences and, accordingly, in the means of personal well-being and communal prosperity; or by progress in norms of ethical conduct and practical morality; or, finally, by the actual expansion of our intellectual, moral, and physical capacities . . . ?

In addressing these three questions we shall find, in our consideration of the past, in the observation of our progress in the sciences that our civilization has made to this point, and in the analysis of the journey of the human mind and the enhancement of its faculties, evidence that compels us to believe that Nature has set no limits to our aspirations. . . .

. . .

Equality among nations:

Can one doubt that prudence, or perhaps the mindless competition between the European nations, along with the slow but steady progress of their colonies, will not soon achieve the independence of the New World [i.e., the Americas]? And that thereafter, will not the rapid expansion of European peoples into this immense territory civilize and absorb, without conquest, the savage nations that still occupy these vast spaces?

Consider the history of our undertakings and settlements in Africa or Asia: you will see that our commercial appropriations, our betrayals, our murderous contempt for peoples of another color or another faith; that the insolence of our usurpations, the outrageous proselytism and scheming of our priests; that all these have destroyed the feelings of respect and good will that our cultural and commercial superiority had at first aroused.

But the moment surely approaches when, ceasing to present ourselves to them only as cheats and tyrants, we shall become their useful helpers, or bountiful liberators. . . .

. . .

Then that moment will arrive when the sun in its orbit will illumine only free peoples, who recognize no other master than their reason. . . . Then it will be our only concern to exercise . . . a keen vigilance so as to recognize and crush under the weight of reason the first seedlings of superstition and tyranny, should they ever dare to grow again!

Social and economic equality:

In reviewing the history of societies, we can observe that often a great distance intervenes between the rights that the law grants to citizens and the rights that they actually enjoy, [as] between the equality that is established by political institutions and that which actually exists among individuals. . . .

These differences have three principal causes: first, the inequality of wealth; second, the inequality of status between one who enjoys an assured subsistence that [has been transferred to him by his family and] will be transmitted in turn to his, and one whose subsistence [is earned and so] lasts only so long as he lives, or rather so long as he is capable of work; and finally, the inequality of education.

We must show that these three kinds of inequality will continually diminish, although they cannot be eliminated entirely. . . .

It is readily seen that fortunes tend naturally toward equality, and that their excessive disproportion either could not exist, or would promptly cease, if the civil laws had not been designed deliberately to perpetuate and increase them, and if by the introduction of free commerce and industry, the many prohibitory laws and fiscal privileges that protect the wealthy were removed. . . .

. . .

Universal education:

The equality of education that we hope to attain ... is one that excludes any kind of dependency, whether coerced or voluntary. Within the limits of the current state of human knowledge, we shall be able easily to arrive at this goal, even for those who can give to studies only a few of their early years, and for the rest of their lives, only scattered hours of leisure. We shall explain how by a prudent choice of the subjects of study and of the methods of instruction, we can teach the entire population all that each person must know for the management of a household, for the administration of his financial affairs, for the free development of his skills and mental faculties; to know, defend, and exercise his rights; . . . and to be no stranger to any of the elevated and refined sentiments that are the glory of humankind. . . .

. . .

The fulfillment of the promise of the human condition:

The advantages that must result from this anticipated progress . . . can only culminate in the perfect fulfillment of the promise of the human species, since the more that each kind of equality comes to be realized—supplying a subsistence that far exceeds our needs, a broader universal education, a more complete liberty—the more robust it will be, and the more it will come to truly encompass everything that pertains to human welfare. . . .

. . .

Equity for women:

One of the advances of the human mind essential for the general welfare is the eradication of the prejudice that has led to an inequality of rights between men and women, damaging even to those that it favors. The reasons that might be supplied to justify it are baseless, such as some deficiency in women's physical capacity, intellectual strength, or moral awareness. This inequality has had no other origin than the abuse of [the male's greater] strength, and the attempt ever since to excuse it with sophistries has been futile.

We shall show how greatly the destruction of the customs authorized by this anti-woman prejudice, and the laws it has dictated, can further the well-being of families. It will nourish domestic virtues, the wellspring of all the others; and enhance progress in education, above all by making it truly universal, both because instruction will be provided more equitably to both sexes, and because it could not become universal, even for males, without the support of mothers. . . .

Perpetual peace:

As people become more enlightened, reclaiming their right to dispose as they please of their blood and their treasure, they will come step-by-step to view war as the most terrible scourge, and most horrible crime. . . .

Nations will understand that they cannot become conquerors without losing their liberty; that permanent confederations are the only means of maintaining their independence; and that they must seek security and not power. . . . As they come to agreement at last on common principles of politics and morals, . . . all the causes that arouse, envenom, and perpetuate hatred between nations will gradually disappear, and no longer supply fuel or pretext for war fever. . . .

. . .

New technologies and a universal language:

Two tools of a general nature that will aid both in education and scientific research remain to be discussed: first, the more intensive and sophisticated use of what may be called technical methods; and second, the introduction of a universal language.

By "technical methods," I mean the art of presenting systematically a great quantity of data, so that at a glance, one can see connections, quickly discern combinations, and more easily form new [hypotheses]. . . .

A universal language is one that communicates by signs either actual objects, or delimited collections of simple and general ideas that are recognized or can easily be made recognizable to all people. . . . Accordingly, those who know these signs, the method of their combinations, and the laws of their formation will understand what is written in this language, and will be able to convey it with equal facility in the common language of their country. . . .

· · ·

Improvement in health, medicine, and life expectancy:

The organic perfectibility or degeneration of vegetable and animal species can be seen as one of the general laws of nature.

This law extends to the human species, and no one can have any doubt that progress in the practice of medicine, the availability of more wholesome food and housing, a lifestyle that develops strength through exercise and does not destroy it by excess, and lastly, the removal of the principal causes of physical deterioration, poverty and inordinate wealth, will necessarily prolong the normal life expectancy of people, assuring them better health over time and a more robust constitution. It seems that improvements in preventive medicine . . . will in time put an end to infectious or contagious illnesses, and to those ordinary illnesses caused by climate, diet, and the stresses of labor. . . . Certainly the human being will not become immortal; but the distance between the moment when he first draws breath and the moment, experienced by all, when naturally, troubled by neither illness nor accident, he finds it difficult to continue to exist—can it not be extended indefinitely? . . .

· · ·

Conclusion:

These are the issues whose examination will bring to a close this tenth [and final] epoch [of this work]. And how greatly this portrait of the human species, freed from all its chains, rescued from the empire of chance as from that of the enemies of his advancement, marching onwards with firm and sure step on the road to truth, virtue, and happiness, presents to the philosopher a spectacle that consoles him for the errors, the crimes, and the injustices with which the earth has been defiled, and by which he has been long oppressed! It is in contemplating this portrait that he receives the reward for the effort he has expended for the advancement of reason, and the defense of liberty. . . .

TEXTS AND STUDIES

General Introduction

Classic studies and interpretations of the Enlightenment in English include (in chronological order of publication) Carl L. Becker, *The Heavenly City of the Eighteenth-Century Philosophers* (New Haven, CT: Yale University Press, 1932); Ernst Cassirer, *The Philosophy of the Enlightenment*, translated by Fritz C. A. Koelln and James P. Pettegrove (Princeton, NJ: Princeton University Press, 1951; orig. German ed. 1932); Paul Hazard, *The European Mind,* translated by J. Lewis May (New Haven, CT: Yale University Press, 1953); Peter Gay, *The Enlightenment: An Interpretation,* 2 vols. (New York: Knopf, 1966–1969); Ira O. Wade, *The Intellectual Origins of the French Enlightenment* (Princeton, NJ: Princeton University Press, 1971). To these may be added the valuable collection of essays edited by Roy S. Porter and Mikuláš Teich, *The Enlightenment in National Context* (Cambridge: Cambridge University Press, 1981), following up on which, addressing the somewhat neglected story of the Enlightenment in Germany, is Martin Muslow's *Enlightenment Underground: Radical Germany, 1680–1720,* translated by H. C. Erik Midelfort (Charlottesville: University of Virginia Press, 2015). For overviews of individual figures and problems, see valuable entries in the online *Stanford Encyclopedia of Philosophy* at https://plato.stanford.edu/, and the annotated bibliographies in the Philosophy, Renaissance and Reformation, and Atlantic Studies modules of Oxford Bibliographies, online at http://www.oxfordbibliographies.com/.

Since around 1980, scholars have tended to focus on particular themes or dimensions of the Enlightenment. The radical dimensions of the Enlightenment, and its swerve into countercultural movements, is discussed by Margaret C. Jacob in *Living the Enlightenment: Freemasonry and Politics in Eighteenth-Century Europe* (Oxford: Oxford University Press, 1991), and, among many works on the intellectual history of the Enlightenment by Jonathan Israel, his three-part account, published by Oxford University Press over a period of ten years: *Radical Enlightenment: Philosophy and the Making of Modernity, 1650–1750* (2001); *Enlightenment Contested: Philosophy, Modernity, and the Emancipation of Man, 1670–1752* (2006); and *Democratic Enlightenment: Philosophy, Revolution, and Human Rights, 1750–1790* (2011). The most recent of several works by Robert Darnton on the history of publishing in the Enlightenment, especially of forbidden books, is his *Censors at Work: How States Shaped Literature* (New York: W. W. Norton, 2014). Dena Goodman's study *The Republic of Letters: A Cultural History of the French Enlightenment* (Ithaca, NY: Cornell University Press, 1994) considers the cultural institutions that were the foundation for intellectual discourse, especially that of the salon, in which women's role was prominent, while Meghan K. Roberts explores the family relationships of Enlightenment thinkers in *Sentimental Savants: Philosophical Families in Enlightenment France* (Chicago: University of Chicago Press, 2016). Dorinda Outram's brief *The Enlightenment* (Cambridge: Cambridge University Press, 1995) considers several social and cultural structures that engendered that movement, such as consumerism, gender, and awareness of exotic places, and Sankar Muthu looks specifically at the Enlightenment resistance to contemporary European imperialist ventures in *Enlightenment against Empire* (Princeton, NJ: Princeton University Press, 2003). On a different note, David J. Sorkin explores the religious dimensions of the Enlightenment in *The Religious Enlightenment: Protestants, Jews, and Catholics from London to Vienna* (Princeton, NJ: Princeton University Press, 2008). Among recent overviews of the Enlightenment as an intellectual movement, finally, that of Louis K. Dupré, *The Enlightenment and the Intellectual Foundations of Modern Culture* (New Haven, CT: Yale University Press, 2004), is especially compelling.

Chapter One

Francis Bacon. The translation is based on the Latin text of the *Novum organum* (part 2 of the *Instauratio magna*), book one, aphorisms 1–2, 6, 11–12, 19, 31, 36, and 38–44, online at the Latin Library: http://www.thelatinlibrary.com/bacon.html. The classic edition and translation of *The Works of Francis Bacon* by James Spedding, Robert Leslie Ellis, and Douglas Denon Heath, has also been consulted, specifically vol. 8 (Boston: Houghton Mifflin, 1900), the *New Organon*, constituting part 2 of the *Great Instauration*, 59–350; orig. London: Longman's, 1857–1874. An authoritative study of Bacon's life and work is provided by Perez Zagorin, *Francis Bacon* (Princeton, NJ: Princeton University Press, 1998). For the controversies about Bacon's career and character, see also (in chronological order of publication) Nieves Mathews, *Francis Bacon: The History of a Character Assassination* (New Haven, CT: Yale University Press, 1996); and Lisa Jardine and Alan Stewart, *Hostage to Fortune: The Troubled Life of Francis Bacon* (New York: Hill and Wang, 1999). See also the essays edited by Markku Peltonen in *The Cambridge Companion to Bacon* (Cambridge: Cambridge University Press, 1996).

René Descartes. The translation is based on the French text available online at UQAC (Université de Québec à Chicoutimi): René Descartes, *Discours sur la méthode* (1637), part 4, extracts; online at http://classiques.uqac.ca/classiques/Descartes/discours_methode/discours_methode.html. Also consulted: the translations of Laurence J. Lafleur, René Descartes, *Discourse on Method* and *Meditations* (Indianapolis, IN: Liberal Arts Press, 1960), at 24–30; and of Donald A. Cress (3rd ed.; Indianapolis, IN: Hackett, 1998), at 18–22. Useful guides to Descartes' philosophy are provided by Stephen Gaukroger, *Descartes' System of Natural Philosophy* (Cambridge: Cambridge University Press, 2002); and, more briefly, Justin Skirry, *Descartes: A Guide for the Perplexed* (London: Continuum, 2008). See also the biographies by Desmond M. Clarke, *Descartes: A Biography* (Cambridge: Cambridge University Press, 2006); and Steven Nadler, *The Philosopher, the Priest, and the Painter: A Portrait of Descartes* (Princeton, NJ: Princeton University Press, 2013). Also valuable are the essays edited by Janet Broughton and John Carriero, *A Companion to Descartes* (West Sussex, UK: Wiley-Blackwell, 2011).

Baruch Spinoza. The translation is by Samuel Shirley: Baruch Spinoza, *Ethics: Treatise on the Emendation of the Intellect: and Selected Letters*, 2nd ed., translated by Samuel Shirley, edited and introduced by Seymour Feldman (Indianapolis, IN: Hackett, 1992); excerpts from part one: Concerning God; definitions 1–8; axioms 1–7; propositions 1–3, 5–8, 11, 13–15, 17, 19–20, 25–27, 29, 33–35, at pages 31–34, 37, 39–40, 44, 49–51, 54, and 56, abridged. Useful introductions to Spinoza's thought are provided by Michael della Rocca in his *Spinoza* (New York: Routledge, 2008) and Steven Nadler in *Spinoza's "Ethics": An Introduction* (Cambridge: Cambridge University Press, 2006); see also Nadler's authoritative biography, *Spinoza: A Life* (Cambridge: Cambridge University Press, 1999). For Spinoza's impact on the Enlightenment, see especially the first (of three) volumes of Jonathan Israel's exploration of its radical currents: *Radical Enlightenment: Philosophy and the Making of Modernity, 1650–1750* (Oxford: Oxford University Press, 2001).

Isaac Newton. The translation is based on the 1871 reprint by William Thomson and Hugh Blackburn (Glasgow: James MacLehose) of the third edition of Newton's *Philosophiae naturalis principia mathematica* (London: Guil. & Joh. Innys, 1726), available online through Google Books. Excerpts are from axioms 1–3; book 3 preface; rules 1–4; propositions 2–7, 10, 11, at pages 13–14, 386–89, 395–96, 399–400, 403, 406, and 408; abridged. Both major English translations of the *Principia* are also based on the 1726 edition. The first is the 1729 translation by Andrew Motte, 2 vols. (London: Benjamin Motte), reprinted often in parts or as a whole and available online, including (in a modernized "American" version of 1846, ed. N. W. Chittenden) at Wikisource: https://en.wikisource.org/wiki/The_Mathematical_Principles_of_Natural_Philosophy_(1846). The second is the 1999 translation of I. Bernard Cohen and Anne Whitman, with Julia Budenz, *The Principia: Mathematical Principles of Natural Philosophy* (Berkeley: University of California Press). The latter volume also contains Cohen's helpful prefatory guide to the *Principia*. See the biographies by Richard S. Westfall, *Never at Rest: A Biography of Isaac Newton* (Cambridge: Cambridge University Press, 1980); Mordechai Feingold, *The Newtonian Moment: Isaac Newton and the Making of Modern Culture* (Oxford: Oxford University Press, 2004); and Rob Iliffe, *Newton: A Very Short Introduction* (Oxford: Oxford University Press, 2007), as well as Iliffe's more expansive *Priest of Nature: The Religious Worlds of Isaac Newton* (Oxford: Oxford University Press, 2017). See also the studies edited by I. Bernard Cohen and George E. Smith, *The Cambridge Companion to Newton* (Cambridge: Cambridge University Press, 2002).

Pierre Bayle. The translation is based on the authoritative fifth edition of the *Dictionnaire historique et critique*, 4 vols. (Amsterdam: P. Brunel et al., 1740), online at Google Books and at the ARTFL Project: https://artfl-project.uchicago.edu/content/dictionnaire-de-bayle; excerpts from entries on Pyrrho (3:731–35); Machiavelli (3:244–46, 248–49); Luther (3:222–25, 231); Loyola (3:138–39, 141–46); Spinoza (4:253, 255, 257, 265, 267); abridged and ordered chronologically. Also consulted: the complete English translation of *The Dictionary Historical and Critical of Mr. Peter Bayle*, 2nd ed., 5 vols. (London: Printed for J. J. and P. Knapton [etc.], 1734–1738), widely available in research libraries, with vols. 2–5 only available online at HathiTrust: https://catalog.hathitrust.org/Record/001598333. A selection of biographies of philosophical entries (including Pyrrho and Spinoza) was edited by Richard H. Popkin in 1965: *Pierre Bayle: Historical and Critical Dictionary: Selections*; republished in 1991 (Indianapolis, IN: Hackett), with critical introduction at viii–xxix. A selection of articles related to Bayle's political thought (including Machiavelli and Loyola) was edited by Sally L. Jenkinson in 2000, *Bayle: Political Writings* (Cambridge: Cambridge University Press), with critical introduction at xviii–xli. Bayle's important work on toleration, of related interest, is available in the edition and translation of Amie Godman Tannenbaum, *Pierre Bayle's Philosophical Commentary: A Modern Translation and Critical Interpretation* (New York: Peter Lang, 1987). The major biography of Pierre Bayle, in French, is by Elisabeth Labrousse, *Pierre Bayle*, 2 vols. (The Hague: Martinus Nijhoff, 1963–64); a 2nd ed. of vol. 1 appeared in 1985, and of vol. 2 in 1996 (Paris: Albin Michel). It is available in the English translation of Denys Potts, *Bayle* (Oxford: Oxford University Press, 1983). See also the more recent biography of Hubert Bost, *Pierre Bayle* (Paris: Fayard, 2006). Continuing Popkin's exploration of the history of skepticism in early modern Europe, finally, in which Bayle plays a central role, is Anton M. Matytsin's *The Specter of Skepticism in the Age of Enlightenment* (Baltimore: Johns Hopkins University Press, 2016).

Chapter Two

For women's role in the Enlightenment generally, see (in chronological order of publication) Carolyn Lougee, *Le paradis des femmes: Women, Salons, and Social Stratification in Seventeenth-Century France* (Princeton, NJ: Princeton University Press, 1976); Erica Harth, *Cartesian Women: Versions and Subversions of Rational Discourse in the Old Regime* (Ithaca, NY: Cornell University Press, 1992); Dena Goodman, *The Republic of Letters: A Cultural History of the*

French Enlightenment (Ithaca, NY: Cornell University Press, 1994); Dena Goodman, *Becoming a Woman in the Age of Letters* (Ithaca, NY: Cornell University Press, 2009); and Carol Pal, *Republic of Women: Rethinking the Republic of Letters in the Seventeenth Century* (Cambridge, Cambridge University Press, 2012).

Anna Maria van Schurman. The translation is based on the 1648 edition of her works: *Opuscula hebræa, græca, latina, gallica: Prosaica et metrica*, edited by J. van Beverwijck (Leiden: Elsevier, 1648), with *Cum foeminae christianae convenit studium litterarum* at 28–56, excerpts from 28, 30–31, 33–36, 38, 40–42, 44–45, 56; available online from Google Books and at Science Direct: https://doi.org/10.1016/B978-1-4933-0397-7.50004-2. Also consulted: the 1998 edition and translation of Joyce L. Irwin, *Whether a Christian Woman Should Be Educated and Other Writings from Her Intellectual Circle* (Chicago: University of Chicago Press, 1998); and the 1659 version: *The Learned Maid: or, Whether a Maid May Be a Scholar?* (London: John Redmayne, 1659). In addition to Irwin's critical introduction at 1–21, see also among recent studies in English those of Anne R. Larsen, *Anna Maria van Schrman, "The Star of Utecht": The Educational Vision and Reception of a Savante* (Oxford: Routledge, 2016); Bo Karen Lee, *Sacrifice and Delight in the Mystical Theologies of Anna Maria van Schurman and Madame Jeanne Guyon* (Notre Dame, IN: University of Notre Dame Press, 2014); and the chapters on van Schurman in Desmond M. Clarke, *The Equality of the Sexes: Three Feminist Texts of the Seventeenth Century* (Oxford: Oxford University Press, 2013), 79–93; and in Carol Pal, *Republic of Women: Rethinking the Republic of Letters in the Seventeenth Century* (Cambridge: Cambridge University Press, 2012), 52–77.

Margaret Cavendish. The text is Margaret Cavendish, *The Description of a New World, Called the Blazing-World*, 2nd ed. (London: A. Maxwell, 1668; orig. 1666), digitized and unpaginated at http://digital.library.upenn.edu/women/newcastle/blazing/blazing.html and https://ebooks.adelaide.edu.au/c/cavendish/margaret/blazing_world/chapter1.html; the original text is reproduced, preceded by the companion work *Observations upon Experimental Philosophy*, at Internet Archive: https://archive.org/details/bub_gb_e_dmAAAAcAAJ, where selected passages are found at 13, 15–16, 19–20, 25–28, 56–59, and 159–60. See also the edition by Kate Lilley, *The Blazing World and Other Writings* (London: Penguin, 1992); and more recently by Sara H. Mendelson, *The Description of a New World, Called the Blazing World* (Petersborough, Ontario: Broadview, 2016). Recent biographies and studies include David Cunning, *Cavendish* (London: Routledge, 2016); Lisa Walters, *Margaret Cavendish: Gender, Science and Politics* (Cambridge: Cambridge University Press, 2014); Katie Whitaker, *Mad Madge: The Extraordinary Life of Margaret Cavendish, Duchess of Newcastle* (New York: Basic Books, 2002); and the essays collected in Brandie R. Siegfried and Lisa T. Sarasohn, eds., *God and Nature in the Thought of Margaret Cavendish* (Burlington, VT: Ashgate, 2014).

Bathsua Makin. The text is based on the original edition, *An Essay to Revive the Antient Education of Gentlewomen in Religion, Manners, Arts and Tongues* (London: Printed by J. D. to be sold by Tho. Parkhurst, 1673), online at http://digital.library.upenn.edu/women/makin/education/education.html (unpaginated). See also the recent edition by Frances Teague and Margaret J. M. Ezell, assoc. ed. Jessica Walker, of Bathsua Makin and Mary More, *Educating English Daughters: Late Seventeenth-Century Debates* (Toronto: Iter Press; Tempe, AZ: Arizona Center for Medieval and Renaissance Studies, 2016), 51–96 (cf. 75–96 *passim* with excerpts given here from the 1673 edition), with critical introduction at 27–49. The 2016 edition is based on Teague's earlier study and edition: *Bathsua Makin: Woman of Learning* (Lewisburg, PA: Bucknell University Press, 1998). See also the studies by J. R. Brink, "Bathsua Reginald Makin: 'Most Learned Matron,'" *Huntington Library Quarterly* 54 (1991): 313–27; Patricia Hamilton, "Bathsua Makin's Essay and Daniel Defoe's 'An Academy for Women,'"

Seventeenth-Century News 59 (2001): 146–53; and Pieta van Beek, "'One Tongue Is Enough for a Woman': The Correspondence in Greek between Anna Maria van Schurman and Bathsua Makin," *Dutch Crossing* 19 (1995): 24–48.

Madame de Maintenon. The texts are based on Mme. de Maintenon, *Lettres sur l'éducation des filles*, edited by Théophile Lavallée (Paris: Charpentier, 1854), letter dated August 1, 1686, at 21–27; and Mme. de Maintenon, *Conseils et instructions aux demoiselles pour leur conduite dans le monde*, vol. 1, edited by Théophile Lavallée (Paris: Charpentier, 1857), instruction dated 1707, at 87–91; both titles online at Google Books. Also consulted: the 2004 edition and translation by John J. Conley, SJ, of Maintenon's *Dialogues and Addresses* (Chicago: University of Chicago Press), with the address *Of the World* at 114–17, and critical introduction at 1–26; and *The Correspondence of Madame, Princess Palatine, Mother of the Regent; of Marie-Adelaide de Savoie, Duchesse de Bourgogne; and of Madame de Maintenon, in Relation to Saint-Cyr*, edited and translated by Katharine Prescott Wormely (Boston: Hardy, Pratt, 1899), letter at 239–42. Biographies include the English classic by Charlotte Haldane, *Madame de Maintenon: Uncrowned Queen of France* (Indianapolis, IN: Bobbs-Merrill, 1970); and more recently, in French, that of André Castelot: *Madame de Maintenon: La reine secrète* (Paris: Perrin, 1996).

Emilie du Châtelet. The text is based on *Institutions de physique* (Paris: Chez Prault fils, 1740), preface and sections 1–6, pages 1–10 (abridged), online at the Bibliothèque nationale de France: http://catalogue.bnf.fr/ark:/12148/cb30363544v. Also consulted: the extensive selection from the *Institutions*, translated by Judith P. Zinsser and Isabelle Bour, in Zinsser's edition of Du Châtelet's *Selected Philosophical and Scientific Writings* (Chicago: University of Chicago Press, 2009). Zinsser has done the most important recent work on du Châtelet; see her critical introduction at 1–24 of *Selected Philosophical and Scientific Writings*, and her biography, *La Dame d'Esprit: A Biography of the Marquise Du Châtelet* (New York: Viking, 2006).

Chapter Three: John Locke

See the biography by Roger Woolhouse, *Locke: A Biography* (Cambridge: Cambridge University Press, 2007), and, among recent studies, Peter Anstey, *John Locke and Natural Philosophy* (Oxford: Oxford University Press, 2011); Galen Strawson, *Locke on Personal Identity* (Princeton, NJ: Princeton University Press, 2011); and Gideon Yaffe, *Liberty Worth the Name: Locke on Free Agency* (Princeton, NJ: Princeton University Press, 2000).

Letter on Toleration. The text is based on the *Epistola de tolerantia* printed in John Locke, *Letters Concerning Toleration* (London: Printed for A. Millar, 1765), 3–28, with excerpts taken from 3–6 and 10. This Latin edition follows but corrects the original 1689 version (Gouda, Netherlands: Apud Justum ab Hoeve). The Latin text also appears in the bilingual edition of Mario Montuori: *A Letter Concerning Toleration* (The Hague: M. Nijhoff, 1963), based on the original 1689 version, and accompanied by the English translation of William Popple (London: Printed for Awnsham Churchill, 1689); and in the bilingual edition edited by Raymond Klibansky, translated by John W. Gough, *Epistola de tolerantia: A Letter on Toleration* (Oxford: Clarendon Press, 1968). The latter edition, published in part to make a contemporary statement about toleration, was translated into French, Italian, Greek, Spanish, Polish, Magyar, and Japanese, and widely distributed.

Second Treatise on Civil Government. The text is based on the sixth reprinting, in 1764, of the 1689 text: *Two Treatises of Civil Government*, edited by Thomas Hollis (London: published for A. Millar et al.), 193–416, available at the Online Library of Liberty in multiple formats, with the facsimile pdf of the original at http://lf-oll.s3.amazonaws.com/titles/222/0057_Bk.pdf;

excerpts given here from chapter 2, nos. 4 and 6; chapter 3, nos. 16, 21; chapter 4, no. 22; chapter 5, nos. 27, 32; chapter 8, nos. 95, 97; chapter 9, nos. 123, 131; chapter 13, no. 149; chapter 18, nos. 199, 202; chapter 19, no. 243, at pages 195–97, 206–7, 211–13, 215–17, 220–21, 279–81, 305–6, 309–10, 328, 373–74, 376, 384, 415–16. The work is also available in various formats at several other online sites. A complete pdf with legible modernized text by Jonathan Bennett (2005, rev. 2008) is available at Early Modern Texts: http://www.earlymoderntexts.com/assets/pdfs/locke1689a.pdf. See also the authoritative critical edition by Peter Laslett, *Two Treatises on Civil Government*, 2nd ed. (Cambridge: Cambridge University Press, 1967).

Essay Concerning Human Understanding. The text is based on the twelfth edition of the original 1689 version: *The Works of John Locke, in Nine Volumes* (London: C. and J. Rivington et al., 1824), vols. 1 and 2, available online in multiple formats at the Online Library of Liberty, with facsimile pdf at http://lf-oll.s3.amazonaws.com/titles/761/0128-01_Bk.pdf. Excerpts given here are from vol. 1, book 2, chapter 1, sections 1–5, at pages 77–79. It is also available in various formats at several other online sites. A pdf of book 2 with legible modernized text by Jonathan Bennett (2004, rev. 2007) is available at Early Modern Texts: http://www.earlymoderntexts.com/assets/pdfs/locke1690book2.pdf.

Some Thoughts Concerning Education. The text is based on the twelfth edition of the original 1693 version: *The Works of John Locke, in Nine Volumes* (London: C. and J. Rivington et al., 1824), vol. 8, available online in multiple formats at the Online Library of Liberty, with facsimile pdf at http://lf-oll.s3.amazonaws.com/titles/1444/0128-08_Bk.pdf. Excerpts given here are from vol. 8, sections 32–33, 47–48, 50–52, 64–66, 147–49, and 195, at pages 27, 37–38, 45–46, 142–44, and 187. It is also available in the Harvard Classics series no. 37, part one of three (New York: P. F. Collier and Son, 1909–1914) online at Bartleby.com: http://www.bartleby.com/37/1/.

The Reasonableness of Christianity. The text is based on the twelfth edition of the original 1695 version: *The Works of John Locke, in Nine Volumes* (London: C. and J. Rivington et al., 1824), 6:1–158, available online in multiple formats at the Online Library of Liberty; facsimile pdf of original at ttp://lf-oll.s3.amazonaws.com/titles/1438/0128-06_Bk.pdf, with excerpts at 4–5, 7, 9–11, and 15–20. See also the recent edition by John C. Higgins-Biddle, *The Reasonableness of Christianity, as Delivered in the Scriptures* (Oxford: Clarendon Press, 1999); and more generally, that by Victor Nuovo, *John Locke: Writings on Religion* (Oxford: Clarendon Press, 2002).

Chapter Four

Giambattista Vico. The translation is based on the critical edition of Paolo Cristofolini and Manuela Sanna (Rome: Edizioni di storia e letteratura, 2013), 279–81, 283–84, 339, and 343–45, online in the electronic text edition *La scienza nuova 1744* (Laboratorio dell'ISPF, XII, 2015), which is collated with the *editio princeps* of 1744 and a unique manuscript witness at DOI: 10.12862/ispf15L101. The 1744 edition is also available in Paolo Rossi's edition of Vico's works: Vico, *Opere* (Milan: Rizzoli, 1959); online at Biblioteca della Letteratura Italiana: www.letteraturaitaliana.net/pdf/Volume_7/t204.pdf. It is translated, also from the 1744 edition, as *The New Science of Giambattista Vico*, by Thomas Goddard Bergin and Max Harold Fisch (Ithaca, NY: Cornell University Press, 1948) in an edition based on the standard text of Fausto Nicolini (Bari: Laterza, 1928), utilizing Nicolini's system of numbered paragraphs. See also the recent edition of the first, 1725, version: *Scienza nuova (1725): The First New Science*, edited and translated by Leon Pompa (Cambridge: Cambridge University Press, 2002).

For Vico, see the classic by Isaiah Berlin, *Vico and Herder: Two Studies in the History of Ideas* (New York: Viking, 1976), at 1–142; and also by Berlin, the more recent and posthumous compilation of three essays in *Three Critics of the Enlightenment: Vico, Hamann, Herder*, edited by Henry Hardy (Princeton, NJ: Princeton University Press, 2000). Recent studies include Giuseppe Mazzotta, *The New Map of the World: The Poetic Philosophy of Giambattista Vico* (Princeton, NJ: Princeton University Press, 1999; reissued 2014); Barbara A. Naddeo, *Vico and Naples: The Urban Origins of Modern Social Theory* (Ithaca, NY: Cornell University Press, 2011); and Donald Phillip Verene, *Vico's "New Science": A Philosophical Commentary* (Ithaca, NY: Cornell University Press, 2015). See also the historiographical overview of Joseph Mali, *The Legacy of Vico in Modern Cultural History: From Jules Michelet to Isaiah Berlin* (Cambridge: Cambridge University Press, 2012).

Carolus Linnaeus (Carl von Linné). The translation is based on the thirteenth revised and enlarged edition by Johann Friedrich Gmelin, *Systema naturae, per regna tria naturae*, 3 vols. (Lyon, Fr.: Apud J. B. Delamolliere, 1789–1796), 1:3–7. The tenth edition, in 2 vols. (Stockholm: Impensis Direct. Laurentii Salvii, 1758–1759) is also often cited. The first (Apud Theodorum Haak, Ex typographia Joannis Wilhelmi de Groot, 1735), often reprinted, runs a mere ten pages consisting mostly of taxonomical charts. Also consulted: the English version of 1802–1806, in 7 vols., edited and translated by William Turton (London: Lackington, Allen, and Co.), at 1:1–3—a translation that departs significantly from the original, omitting much material and minimizing Linnaeus' religious vision. The 1971 biography by William Blunt, available now in a revised edition, is still useful: *Linnaeus: The Compleat Naturalist*, 2nd ed. (Princeton, NJ: Princeton University Press, 2001), as is *Linnaeus: The Man and His Work*, edited by Tore Frängsmyr, with contributions by Sten Lindroth and Gunnar Broberg, rev. ed. (Canton, MA: Science History Publications, 1994; orig. Berkeley: University of California Press, 1983). The valuable overview by Helene Schmitz, Nils Uddenberg, and Pia Östensson, *A Passion for Systems: Linnaeus and the Dream of Order in Nature* (Stockholm: Natur & Kultur, 2007), is not widely available. Lisbet Koerner's *Linnaeus: Nature and Nation* (Cambridge, MA: Harvard University Press, 1999) focuses on the economic and political vision of the botanist, depicted as a "cameralist."

Anne-Robert-Jacques Turgot. The translation is based on *Sur les progrès successifs de l'esprit humain* (December 11, 1750), online in a new edition at the Institut Coppet: http:// www.institutcoppet.org/2016/06/25/turgot-discours-sur-les-progres-successifs-de-lesprit-humain-1750. Also consulted: the translation by W. Walker Stephens, *The Life and Writings of Turgot* (London: Longmans, Green and Co., 1895), 159–73; and that by Ronald L. Meek in his *Turgot on Progress, Sociology and Economics* (Cambridge: Cambridge University Press, 1973; reprinted 2010), 41–59, reprinted in *The Turgot Collection: Writings, Speeches, and Letters of Anne Robert Jacques Turgot, Baron de Laune*, edited by David Gordon, introduction by Murray N. Rothbard (Auburn, AL: Ludwig von Mises Institute, 2011), 321–43, online at https://mises.org/library/turgot-collection. For Turgot see also the essays in Mark Blaug, *Richard Cantillon (1680–1734) and Jacques Turgot (1727–1781)* (Aldershot, UK: Ashgate, 1991); and Peter D. Groenewegen, *Eighteenth-Century Economics: Turgot, Beccaria and Smith and Their Contemporaries* (London: Routledge, 2002). Condorcet (see Chapter Twelve) wrote a brief biography of the somewhat younger Turgot: *Vie de Monsieur Turgot* (Paris: Association pour la diffusion de l'économie politique, 1997), online at the Institut Coppet: http://www.institutcoppet.org/2011/12/19/condorcet-vie-de-monsieur-turgot-1786.

Jean le Rond d'Alembert. The translation is based on the *Discours préliminaire* as it appeared in the first edition of Denis Diderot and d'Alembert of the *Encyclopédie, ou Dictionnaire raisonné des sciences, des arts et des métiers* (Paris, 1751), 1:i–xlv; online at Wikisource/France: https://

fr.wikisource.org/wiki/L'Encyclopédie/1re_édition/Discours_préliminaire. Also consulted: the translation of Richard N. Schwab with the collaboration of Walter E. Rex (Chicago: University of Chicago Press, 1995), 3–140, available at *Encyclopedia of Diderot & d'Alembert: Collaborative Translation Project*: http://hdl.handle.net/2027/spo.did2222.0001.083. Biographies include Ronald Grimsley, *Jean d'Alembert (1717–1783)* (Oxford: Clarendon Press, 1963), and Thomas L. Hankins, *Jean d'Alembert: Science and the Enlightenment* (Oxford: Clarendon Press, 1970); also more recently, in French, Veronique Le Ru, *Jean Le Rond d'Alembert, philosophe* (Paris: J. Vrin, 1994); and Guy Chaussinand-Nogaret, *D'Alembert: Une vie d'intellectuel au siècle des lumières* (Paris: Fayard, 2007).

Immanuel Kant. The translation is based on Kant's *Was ist Aufklärung?* (1784), online at http://gutenberg.spiegel.de/buch/-3505/1. Several English translations, many unattributed, are available online. Particularly useful has been that by James Schmidt, ed., *What Is Enlightenment? Eighteenth-Century Answers and Twentieth-Century Questions* (Berkeley, CA: University of California Press, 1996), 58–64. Schmidt compiles sixteen eighteenth-century statements in German by Kant's contemporaries and Kant himself on the theme of Enlightenment; Kant was not alone. Recent biographies and studies include (in chronological order of publication): Manfred Kuehn, *Kant: A Biography* (Cambridge: Cambridge University Press, 2001); Allen W. Wood, *Kant* (Malden, MA: Wiley-Blackwell, 2004); and Jennifer K. Uleman, *An Introduction to Kant's Moral Philosophy* (Cambridge: Cambridge University Press, 2010). See also the essays in Paul Guyer, ed., *The Cambridge Companion to Kant and Modern Philosophy* (Cambridge: Cambridge University Press, 2006).

Chapter Five

David Hume. The text is taken from Hume, *An Abstract of a Book Lately Published, Entituled [sic] A Treatise of Human Nature* (London: Printed for C. Borbet [sic; C. Corbett]. . . . , 1740), available at Eighteenth Century Collections Online: http://name.umdl.umich.edu/004773773.0001.000; available also in the modern edition by Eric Steinberg, *An Enquiry Concerning Human Understanding: With Hume's Abstract of A Treatise of Human Nature and A Letter from a Gentleman to His Friend in Edinburgh*, 2nd ed. (Indianapolis, IN: Hackett, 1993), 125–38. Recent biographies include (in chronological order of publication) Nicholas Phillipson, *David Hume: The Philosopher as Historian* (New Haven, CT: Yale University Press, 2012), and James A. Harris, *Hume: An Intellectual Biography* (Cambridge: Cambridge University Press, 2015). See also the essays in David Fate Norton and Jacqueline Taylor, eds., *The Cambridge Companion to Hume* (Cambridge: Cambridge University Press, 2009); and Mark G. Spencer, ed., *David Hume: Historical Thinker, Historical Writer* (University Park: Penn State University Press, 2013).

Julien Offray de La Mettrie. The translation excerpted here is that in the bilingual edition, now more than a century old, of *Homme Machine: Man a Machine*, translated and edited by Gertrude Carman Bussey (Chicago: Open Court, 1912), 83–149, a somewhat abridged version, frequently reprinted, which faithfully captures La Mettrie's distinctive prose style; excerpts from 89, 98, 103–4, 113–14, 116–17, 128, 145–46, and 148–49. Also available are the more recent translations of Richard A. Watson and Maya Rybalka in *Man a Machine and Man a Plant* (Indianapolis, IN: Hackett, 1994), 18–76, with critical introduction and notes by Justin Leiber; and of Ann Thomson in her edition and translation *Machine Man and Other Writings* (Cambridge: Cambridge University Press, 1996), 1–40. Studies include Aram Vartanian's introductory monograph to his edition *La Mettrie's L'Homme Machine: A Study in the Origins of an Idea* (Princeton, NJ: Princeton University Press, 1960); and Kathleen Wellman,

La Mettrie: Medicine, Philosophy, and Enlightenment (Durham, NC: Duke University Press, 1992). A recent study, in French, considers all three of the French materialists included in Chapter Five: Sophie Audidière, *Matérialistes français du XVIIIe siècle: La Mettrie, Helvétius, d'Holbach* (Paris: Presses universitaires de France, 2006).

Claude-Adrien Helvétius. The text is based on Helvétius, *De l'esprit* (Paris: Durand, 1758), digitized at UQAC (Université de Québec à Chicoutimi): http://classiques.uqac.ca/classiques/helvetius_claude_adrien/de_l_esprit/de_l_esprit.html, 22–27 and 29–30. After it appeared in France in 1758, the work was immediately translated into English with the title *De l'esprit, or, Essays on the Mind, and Its Several Faculties,* and published in London in 1759 ("Printed for the translator, and sold by Mr. Dodsley and Co." et al.), and again in 1807 (London: M. Jones) in the identical translation, with biographical preface and critical introduction by William Mudford; the latter edition was reprinted, unaltered, several times from the early nineteenth into the late twentieth centuries. Studies of Helvétius are few; see, however, in French, Jean-Louis Longué, *Le système d'Helvétius* (Paris: Honoré Champion, 2008). Also in French is the recent study considering all three of the French materialists included in Chapter Five: Sophie Audidière, *Matérialistes français du XVIIIe siècle: La Mettrie, Helvétius, d'Holbach* (Paris: Presses universitaires de France, 2006). See also the complete edition of Helvétius' correspondence: *Correspondance générale d'Helvétius,* edited by Peter Allan, J. A. Dainard, Jean Orsoni, Marie-Thérèse Inguenaud, and David Smith, 5 vols. (Toronto: University of Toronto Press; Oxford: Voltaire Foundation, 1981–2004).

Paul-Henri Thiry, baron d'Holbach. The text is based on d'Holbach, *Bon sens, ou Idées naturelles opposées aux idées surnaturelles,* edition of [Paris?: s.n.], 1789, 5–9, 11, 17–18, and 240. The first edition, published anonymously in Amsterdam in 1772, is an abridgement of the author's 1770 magnum opus *Système de la nature* (*The System of Nature*), also published anonymously. Also consulted: the English version of *Bon sens* by an American translator (possibly "T. N.") and edited by "N. T.," which attributes the work incorrectly to the cleric Jean Meslier (1664–1729), known to Voltaire: *Good Sense: or Natural Ideas Opposed to Ideas That Are Supernatural* (London: R. Carlile, 1826). The 1826 version includes a table of contents omitted in the 1772 edition but included in the 1822 French edition. At least two other English translations (by Anna Knoop, from 1878, and H. D. Robinson, from 1836), not seen, have been frequently reprinted, as are other unattributed translations that may be identical to these. The title may be translated as *Good Sense* or, as done here, as *Common Sense.* D'Holbach is included in passing in recent studies of Enlightenment atheism or materialism, but has not received close study recently in an English-language monograph. See the classic study of Alan Charles Kors, *D'Holbach's Coterie: An Enlightenment in Paris* (Princeton, NJ: Princeton University Press, 1976); and in French, the recent study considering all three of the French materialists included in Chapter Five: Sophie Audidière, *Matérialistes français du XVIIIe siècle: La Mettrie, Helvétius, d'Holbach* (Paris: Presses universitaires de France, 2006).

Gotthold Ephraim Lessing. The translation is based on Lessing, *Nathan der Weise,* edited by George O. Curme (New York: Macmillan, 1898), Act III Scene 7, at pages 111–17; online at HathiTrust: https://babel.hathitrust.org/cgi/pt?id=uva.x002014289;view=1up;seq=7. Digitized versions of the original German edition (Berlin: Christian Friedrich Voss & Sohn, 1779), also consulted, are available at Spiegel Online: http://gutenberg.spiegel.de/buch/nathan-der-weise-1179/3; and Bookrix: https://www.bookrix.de/book.html?bookID=bx. lessing_1211883016.8127009869#0,558,98298. Also consulted: the English verse translation of William Taylor in *Nathan the Wise: A Dramatic Poem in Five Acts,* edited by Henry Morley (London: Cassell & Co., 1893), online at Gutenberg.org: https://www.gutenberg.org/files/3820/3820-h/3820-h.htm. Several modern translations exist, some performed in recent revivals of the play, reflecting renewed interest in Lessing. See also the explorations of Lessing's views on religious toleration in Christopher Adamo, "One True Ring or Many?: Religious Pluralism in Lessing's 'Nathan the Wise,'" *Philosophy and Literature*, 33, no. 1 (2009): 139–49; and in Ned Curthoys, "A Diasporic Reading of Nathan the Wise," *Comparative Literature Studies*, 47, no. 1 (2010): 70–95. Of recent studies on Lessing, see especially the authoritative biography by Hugh Barr Nisbet, *Gotthold Ephraim Lessing: His Life, Works and Thought* (Oxford: Oxford University Press, 2013); and the essays collected in Ritchie Robertson, ed., *Lessing and the German Enlightenment* (Oxford: Voltaire Foundation, 2013).

Chapter Six

Recent English-language biographies include (in chronological order of publication) Roger Pearson, *Voltaire Almighty: A Life in Pursuit of Freedom* (New York: Bloomsbury, 2005); Alexander J. Nemeth, *Voltaire's Tormented Soul: A Psychobiographic Inquiry* (Bethlehem, PA: Lehigh University Press, 2008); and Ian Davidson, *Voltaire: A Life* (New York: Pegasus, 2010). See also the important studies in Nicholas Cronk's edition of *The Cambridge Companion to Voltaire* (Cambridge: Cambridge University Press, 2009). The Voltaire Foundation, based at the University of Oxford, is in process of publishing complete, updated editions of all the works of Voltaire, as well as the series of essay collections "Oxford University Studies in the Enlightenment"; see http://www.voltaire.ox.ac.uk/. The works appearing in this chapter are available in multiple French editions and English translations in print and online.

Lettres philosophiques. The translation given here is that of Prudence L. Steiner, in *Philosophical Letters, Or, Letters Regarding the English Nation*, edited by John Leigh (Indianapolis, IN: Hackett, 2007), the first, fifth, sixth, and seventh letters, at pages 1–4 and 15–22. The *Lettres philosophiques* are also available online in French at Wikisource/France: https://fr.wikisource.org/wiki/Lettres_philosophiques.

Essai sur les moeurs et l'esprit des nations. The text is based on the 1829 edition (Paris: Werdet et Lequien fils) in 4 vols., at 4:473–90, abridged, available online at Gallica: http://gallica.bnf.fr/ark:/12148/bpt6k37526b. Also useful is the 1877 edition of the *Œuvres complètes de Voltaire* by Louis Moland (Paris: Garnier), vols. 11–13, at 13:2122–2136 in the digitized version available at Wikisource/France: https://fr.wikisource.org/wiki/Essai_sur_les_moeurs.

Candide. The translation given here is that of David Wootton: Voltaire, *Candide and Related Texts*, ed. and trans. David Wootton (Indianapolis, IN: Hackett, 2000), chapter 5, at 10–12. Multiple editions of *Candide* both in French and in English translation are available in print and online. Also consulted: the French version available online at http://www.blackmask.com.

Traité sur la tolérance. The text is based on the original edition *Traité sur la tolérance* (s.l., s.n. [Geneva: Cramer], 1763), online at http://athena.unige.ch/athena/voltaire/voltaire_traite_tolerance.html#c1, chapters 1 and 22 (unpaginated), abridged. Also consulted: the English version available at the Online Library of Liberty, entitled *Treatise on Tolerance on the Occasion of the Death of Jean Calas*, in *Toleration and Other Essays by Voltaire*, edited and translated by Joseph McCabe (New York: G. P. Putnam's Sons, 1912), 1–87, at http://oll.libertyfund.org/titles/voltaire-toleration-and-other-essays. An alternate version, the *Treatise on Tolerance*, its source unspecified, that includes the twenty-third chapter omitted from the OLL version, is available at Constitution Society: http://www.constitution.org/volt/tolerance.htm. See also the recent version edited by Simon Harvey, translated by Brian Masters, *Treatise on Tolerance and Other Writings* (Cambridge: Cambridge University Press, 2000), 1–106. For the surge of interest in Voltaire's *Treatise on Tolerance* following the Hebdo massacre, see the article in the *Guardian* by John Dugdale, "Voltaire's 'Treatise on Tolerance' Becomes Bestseller Following Paris Attacks" (January 16, 2015) at https://www.theguardian.com/books/2015/jan/16/voltaire-treatise-tolerance-besteller-paris-attack; and the transcript of the NPR (National Public Radio) program "After Paris Attacks, Voltaire's 'Tolerance' Is Back in Vogue" (February 15, 2015), at http://www.npr.org/sections/parallels/2015/02/15/385422239/after-paris-attacks-voltaires-tolerance-is-back-in-vogue.

Dictionnaire philosophique. The text is based on the edition of Louis Moland, *Œuvres complètes de Voltaire*, vols. 17–20 (Paris: Garnier, 1878–1879), online at Wikisource/France: https://fr.wikisource.org/wiki/Dictionnaire_philosophique/Garnier_(1878); entries on *Égalité* and *Esclaves* from vol. 18, and *Femme, Homme,* and *Liberté d'imprimer* from vol. 19.

Chapter Seven

Charles de Secondat, baron de Montesquieu. The translation given here is that of Melvin Richter, ed. and trans., Montesquieu, *Selected Political Writings* (Indianapolis, IN: Hackett, 1990), book 11, selections from chapters 4 and 6, at 181–90. Studies include, in English, Judith Shklar, *Montesquieu* (Oxford: Oxford University Press, 1987), a now classic biography; more recently, Paul A. Rahe, *Montesquieu and the Logic of Liberty: War, Religion, Commerce, Climate, Terrain, Technology, Uneasiness of Mind, the Spirit of Political Vigilance, and the Foundations of the Modern Republic* (New Haven, CT: Yale University Press, 2009); and, in French, the close study of the *Spirit of the Laws* by Bertrand Binoche, *Introduction à "De l'esprit des lois" de Montesquieu* (Paris: Publications de la Sorbonne, 2015); and the biography by Catherine Volpilhac-Auger, *Montesquieu* (Paris: Gallimard, 2017), forthcoming at this writing. See also the collection of essays, in English, edited by David W. Carrithers, Michael A. Mosher, and Paul A. Rahe, *Montesquieu's Science of Politics: Essays on "The Spirit of Laws"* (Lanham, MD: Rowman & Littlefield, 2000); and Annelien de Dun's study of Montesquieu's "aristocratic liberalism" and its afterlife in *French Political Thought from Montesquieu to Tocqueville: Liberty in a Levelled Society?* (Cambridge: Cambridge University Press, 2008).

François Quesnay. The text is based on Quesnay's *Maximes générales du gouvernement économique d'un royaume agricole*, 329–37, nos. 1, 3–5, 10–15, 17–20, 25–27, in Quesnay, *Oeuvres économiques et philosophiques*, edited by Auguste Oncken (Frankfurt: Joseph Baer; Paris: Jules Peelman, 1888). Also related is Quenay's *Despotisme de la Chine* (1767; *The Despotism of China*), most easily available in the English translation of Lewis A. Maverick, *China, A Model for Europe* (San Antonio, TX: Paul Anderson, 1946); see also the French text online at Institut Coppet: http://www.institutcoppet.org/2016/10/15/despotisme-de-chine-francois-quesnay-1767. For Quesnay, see Gianni Vaggi, *The Economics of François Quesnay* (Durham, NC: Duke University Press, 1987). See also the collection by Mark Blaug of twenty-eight articles in English published from 1895 to 1988, offering a general overview of the physiocrat's reception, in *François Quesnay (1694–1774)*, 2 vols. (Aldershot, UK: E. Elgar, 1991).

Cesare Beccaria. The translation is that of David Young, ed. and trans., Cesare Beccaria, *On Crimes and Punishments* (Indianapolis, IN: Hackett, 1986), 14–17, 29, 31, 48, 51, consisting of excerpts from chapters 6, 7, 16, and 17. An alternate translation is available in Cesare Beccaria, *On Crimes and Punishments and Other Writings*, edited by Aaron Thomas, translated by Aaron Thomas and Jeremy Parzen (Toronto: University of Toronto Press, 2008), 1–86. The Italian text is available online, in the edition of Renato Fabietti (Milan: Mursia, 1973), at Wikisource/Italy: https://it.wikisource.org/wiki/Dei_delitti_e_delle_pene. For Beccaria, see Renzo Zorzi, *Cesare Beccaria: Il dramma della giustizia* (Milan: Mondadori, 1996).

Adam Ferguson. The text is taken from Adam Ferguson, *An Essay on the History of Civil Society*, 5th ed. (London: T. Cadell, 1782), part 3, section 6, 260–64, 272–73, 278–79. The complete 1782 edition is available at the Online Library of Liberty: http://oll.liberty-fund.org/title/1428. See also the recent print edition by Fania Oz-Salzberger, *An Essay on the History of Civil Society* (Cambridge: Cambridge University Press, 1995). Recent studies include David Kettler, *Adam Ferguson: His Social and Political Thought*, rev. ed. (New Brunswick, NJ: Transaction Publishers, 2005); and Iain McDaniel, *Adam Ferguson in the Scottish Enlightenment: The Roman Past and Europe's Future* (Cambridge, MA: Harvard University Press, 2013). See also the essays edited by Eugene Heath and Vincenzo Merolle, *Adam Ferguson: Philosophy, Politics, and Society* (London: Pickering & Chatto, 2009). See also for the Scottish Enlightenment, of which Adam Ferguson and Adam Smith are representatives, Thomas Ahnert, *The Moral Culture of the Scottish Enlightenment, 1690–1805* (New Haven, CT: Yale University Press, 2014); Richard B. Sher, *The Enlightenment and the Book: Scottish Authors and Their Publishers in Eighteenth-Century Britain, Ireland, and America* (Chicago: University of Chicago Press, 2006); and the essays edited by Alexander Broadie, *The Cambridge Companion to the Scottish Enlightenment* (Cambridge: Cambridge University Press, 2003).

Adam Smith. The text is taken from Adam Smith, *An Inquiry into the Nature and Causes of the Wealth of Nations* (1776), introduction, book 1, chapters 1 and 2, and book 4, chapter 2, edited by Edwin Cannan (London: Methuen, 1904), online at http://www.econlib.org/library/Smith/smWNCover.html. The Cannan edition is a compilation of Smith's fifth edition (1789), the final edition in Smith's lifetime. Several modern editions are available in print and online. Recent studies include the biography by Ian Simpson Ross, *The Life of Adam Smith*, 2nd ed. (Oxford: Oxford University Press, 2010); the study by Iain McLean, *Adam Smith, Radical and Egalitarian: An Interpretation for the Twenty-First Century* (Edinburgh: Edinburgh University Press, 2006); and the essays edited by Ryan Patrick Hanley, *Adam Smith: His Life, Thought, and Legacy* (Princeton, NJ: Princeton University Press, 2016). See also for Smith and the Scottish Enlightenment, John Alfred Dwyer, *The Age of the Passions: An Interpretation of Adam Smith and Scottish Enlightenment Culture* (East Linton, Scotland: Tuckwell Press, 1998), and titles given above under Adam Ferguson.

Chapter Eight

Aphra Behn. The text is taken from Aphra Behn, *Oroonoko: or, the Royal Slave* (London: William Canning, 1688), digitized (unpaginated) and available online at https://ebooks.adelaide.edu.au/b/behn/aphra/b42o/index.html (spelling modernized); also at http://fiction.eserver.org/novels/oroonoko/ and at Wikisource: https://en.wikisource.org/wiki/Oroonoko_(Behn), as well as through several electronic databases accessible with subscription, and in multiple reprints and modern printed editions. Behn is a much-studied author, and *Oroonoko* possibly her most-studied work. Recent studies include (in chronological order of publication) Daniel Cooper Alarcon and Stephanie Athey, *"Oroonoko's" Gendered Economies of Honor/Horror: Reframing Colonial Discourse Studies in the Americas* (Durham, NC: Duke University Press, 1995); S. J. Wiseman, *Aphra Behn* (Plymouth, UK: Northcote House Publishers, 1996); Janet Todd, *The Secret Life of Aphra Behn* (New Brunswick, NJ: Rutgers University Press, 1997); and Margaret W. Ferguson, *Juggling the Categories of Race, Class and Gender: Aphra Behn's "Oroonoko"* (New York: St. Martin's Press, 1999). See also the fourteen essays edited by Derek

Hughes and Janet Todd in *The Cambridge Companion to Aphra Behn* (Cambridge: Cambridge University Press, 2004).

Mary Wortley Montagu. The text is taken from Mary Wortley Montagu's "embassy letters" (1716–1718) in *The Letters and Works of Lady Mary Wortley Montagu*, edited by James Archibald Stuart-Wortley Wharncliffe, 3 vols. (London: R. Bentley, 1837), 1:283–87, 296–300, 307–9, online at Internet Archive: https://archive.org/details/lettersworksofla01inmont. See the biography by Isobel Grundy, *Lady Mary Wortley Montagu: Comet of the Enlightenment* (Oxford: Oxford University Press, 1999). For her letter-writing particularly, see Cynthia J. Lowenthal, *Lady Mary Wortley Montagu and the Eighteenth-Century Familiar Letter* (Athens, GA: University of Georgia Press, 1994); and the recent separate edition of the *Embassy Letters* by Malcolm Jack, *Lady Mary Wortley Montagu: Turkish Embassy Letters* (Athens, GA: University of Georgia Press, 1993).

Guillaume-Thomas Raynal. The translation is based on Guillaume-Thomas Raynal, *Histoire philosophique et politique des établissemens et du commerce des Européens dans les deux Indes* (1770), 3rd ed., 10 vols. (Geneva: Chez J.-L. Pellet, 1781), online at Gallica: http://gallica.bnf.fr/ark:/12148/bpt6k5405912t?rk=21459;2. Also consulted: the English translation of John Obadiah Justamond, *Philosophical and Political History of the Settlements and Trade of the Europeans in the East and West Indies*, 6 vols. (Edinburgh: Mundell & Sons, 1804). Multiple editions and reprints are available online of both original and translation published from 1770 into the nineteenth century. Especially useful is the digital version of the French text available at the ARTFL Project: https://artflsrv03.uchicago.edu/philologic4/raynal/. For Raynal, see the twenty essays edited by Cecil P. Courtney and Jenny Mander, *Raynal's "Histoire des deux Indes": Colonialism, Networks and Global Exchange* (Oxford: Voltaire Foundation, 2015). For Raynal's network of collaborators, see the essays edited by Gilles Bancarel, *Raynal et ses réseaux* (Paris: Honoré Champion, 2011). For a recent translation of selected texts, see Raynal, *A History of the Two Indies: A Translated Selection of Writings from Raynal's "Histoire philosophique et politique des établissements des Européens dans les deux Indes"* edited and translated by Peter Jimack (Aldershot, UK: Ashgate, 2006).

James Cook. The text is taken from *A Voyage Towards the South Pole, and Round the World, Performed in His Majesty's Ships the Resolution and Adventure, in the Years 1772, 1773, 1774, and 1775* (1777), 2 vols. (London: Printed for W. Strahan; and T. Cadell in the Strand, 1777), 1:181–85, 187–88, from book 1, chapter 14; online at Google Books. The plain-spoken and capable Cook has recently become controversial, subject to the criticism of postcolonial scholars, while other authors continue to view him more favorably. Among recent studies, see the contrasting presentations by Frank McLynn, *Captain Cook: Master of the Seas* (New Haven, CT: Yale University Press, 2011); and Glyn Williams, *The Death of Captain Cook: A Hero Made and Unmade* (Cambridge, MA: Harvard University Press, 2008). For the controversy over the ability of Europeans to assess native cultures, see Marshall Sahlins, *How "Natives" Think: about Captain Cook, for Example* (Chicago: University of Chicago Press, 1995), responding to Gananath Obeyesekere, *The Apotheosis of Captain Cook: European Mythmaking in the Pacific* (Princeton, NJ: Princeton University Press; Honolulu, Hawaii: Bishop Museum Press, 1992). Other assessments (in chronological order of publication) include those of Richard Hough, *Captain James Cook* (New York: Norton, 1995); Anne Salmond, *The Trial of the Cannibal Dog: The Remarkable Story of Captain Cook's Encounters in the South Seas* (New Haven, CT: Yale University Press, 2003); Nicholas Thomas, *Cook: The Extraordinary Voyages of Captain James Cook* (New York: Walker, 2003); John Gascoigne, *Captain Cook: Voyager Between Worlds* (New York: Hambledon Continuum, 2007); and Dan O'Sullivan, *In Search of Captain Cook: Exploring the Man through His Own Words* (London: I. B. Tauris, 2008). Penguin Classics offers in a single volume an abridged edition of Cook's accounts of all three of his voyages: *The Journals of Captain Cook*, edited by Philip Edwards (New York: Penguin, 1999). A brief biography, extracts from Cook's journals, and information on his ships and crew are available at the Captain Cook Society website: http://www.captaincooksociety.com/.

Johann Gottfried von Herder. The translation is based on *Ideen zur Philosophie der Geschichte der Menschheit* (1784–1791), edited by Michael Holzinger (Berliner Ausgabe, 2013), online at Zeno.org: http://www.zeno.org/nid/20005051479. The selections are from books 7 and 8 (appearing in the second part, published 1785), at 183–84, 186–87, 189–91, 193–94, 196–200, 215, 218–19, 221–23. English translations available include those of Thomas Churchill, *Outlines of the Philosophy of a History of Man* (London: J. Johnson, 1800; reprint, New York: Bergman Publishers, 1966), available online at Google Books and elsewhere; and of Frank E. Manuel, *Reflections on the Philosophy of the History of Mankind* (Chicago: University of Chicago Press, 1968). For Herder, see especially Michael N. Forster's concise biography, "Johann Gottfried von Herder," *The Stanford Encyclopedia of Philosophy* (Aug. 25, 2017), edited by Edward N. Zalta, at https://plato.stanford.edu/archives/fall2017/entries/herder/. Forster's major study *Herder's Philosophy* is forthcoming from Oxford University Press. See also Frederick M. Barnard, *Herder on Nationality, Humanity, and History* (Montreal: McGill-Queen's University Press, 2003); Sonia Sikka, *Herder on Humanity and Cultural Difference: Enlightened Relativism* (Cambridge: Cambridge University Press, 2011); and the essays collected by Hans Adler and Wulf Koepke in *A Companion to the Works of Johann Gottfried Herder* (Rochester, NY: Camden House, 2009).

Chapter Nine

Recent English-language works on Rousseau include the biography by Leo Damrosch, *Jean-Jacques Rousseau: Restless Genius* (New York: Houghton Mifflin, 2005); and the studies (in chronological order of publication) of Nicholas Dent, *Rousseau* (London: Routledge, 2005); David Gauthier, *Rousseau: The Sentiment of Existence* (Cambridge: Cambridge University Press, 2006); and Jason Neidleman, *Rousseau's Ethics of Truth: A Sublime Science of Simple Souls* (London: Routledge, 2017). See also the collected essays by Robert Wokler, *Rousseau, the Age of Enlightenment, and Their Legacies*, edited by Bryan Garsten (Princeton, NJ: Princeton University Press, 2012); and, for the Genevan context, Helena Rosenblatt, *Rousseau and Geneva: From the "First Discourse" to the "Social Contract," 1749–1762* (Cambridge: Cambridge University Press, 1997).

Discours sur l'origine et les fondements de l'inégalité parmis les hommes. Composed in 1754, first published in 1755 (Amsterdam: M. M. Rey). The translation is based on the 2002 electronic edition by Jean-Marie Tremblay, based on the 1985 edition of Gaston Meyer (Paris: Bordas) at UQAC (Université de Québec à Chicoutimi), *Les classiques des sciences sociales*: http://classiques.uqac.ca/classiques/Rousseau_jj/discours_origine_inegalite/discours_inegalite.pdf, 18–19, 34–37, 41, 43–45. Also consulted: the translations of Donald A. Cress in Jean-Jacques Rousseau, *The Basic Political Writings*, 2nd ed., edited by David Wootton (Indianapolis, IN: Hackett, 2011); and of G. D. H. Cole (London–Toronto: J. M. Dent, 1923), available at the Online Library of Liberty: http://oll.libertyfund.org/titles/rousseau-the-social-contract-and-discourses. For a close philosophical study of Rousseau's concept of inequality, see also Frederick Neuhouser, *Rousseau's Critique of Inequality* (Cambridge: Cambridge University Press, 2014).

Du contrat social. The translation is based on the edition of Rousseau's *Du contrat social, ou principes du droit politique* (1762), in *Collection complète des œuvres* (Geneva: Aux Deux-Ponts,

Chez Sanson, 1780–1789), 1:189, 191, 202–8, 214, 220, online on Rousseau Online: http://www.rousseauonline.ch/Text/du-contrat-social-ou-principes-du-droit-politique.php. Many editions and translations are available in print and online. Pertinent recent studies include (in chronological order of publication) Christopher Bertram, *Rousseau and The Social Contract* (London: Routledge, 2003); Joshua Cohen, *Rousseau: A Free Community of Equals* (Oxford: Oxford University Press, 2010); and David Lay Williams, *Rousseau's Social Contract* (Cambridge: Cambridge University Press, 2014).

Julie. The translation is based on Rousseau's *Julie, ou la Nouvelle Héloïse* (1761; edition of Paris: A. Houssiaux, 1852–1853), available online at Wikisource/France: https://fr.wikisource.org/wiki/Julie_ou_la_Nouvelle_Héloïse, part one, letters I and IV, and part six, letter XII. Also consulted: the translations of William Kenrick, *Eloisa, or a Series of Original Letters Collected and Published by Mr. J.-J. Rousseau, Citizen of Geneva*, new ed., 4 vols. (London: H. Baldwin, 1784), available at Internet Archive: https://archive.org/details/eloisaoraseries00gardgoog; and of Philip Stewart and Jean Vaché, *Julie, or the New Heloise* (Hanover, NH: Dartmouth College Press, published by the University Press of New England, 1997).

Émile. The translation is based on Rousseau's *Émile, ou de l'éducation* (1762), edited by François Richard and Pierre Richard (Paris: Garnier frères, 1961), 6, 8–9, 12–17, 80–81, online at UQAC (Université de Québec à Chicoutimi), *Les classiques des sciences sociales*: http://classiques.uqac.ca/classiques/Rousseau_jj/emile/emile.html. Also consulted: the translations of Barbara Foxley, *Emile, or Education* (London: J. M. Dent; New York: E. P. Dutton, 1911; reprint, 1921), available at the Online Library of Liberty: http://oll.libertyfund.org/titles/rousseau-emile-or-education; and of Allan Bloom, *Emile, or On Education* (New York: Basic Books, 1979).

Les confessions. The translation is based on *Les confessions de Jean-Jacques Rousseau* (1770) (new ed.; Paris: Charpentier, 1841), online at Internet Archive: https://archive.org/details/lesconfessionsde00rous/. Also consulted: the translation of W. Conyngham Mallory (New York: Albert and Charles Boni, 1928), online at HathiTrust: https://babel.hathitrust.org/cgi/pt?id=mdp.39015001832792;view=1up;seq=1;size=75.

Chapter Ten

Mary Astell. The text is taken from *Some Reflections upon Marriage* (London: John Nutt, 1700), 11–13, 19, 22–23, 35–37, 56–58, 66; available online at http://digital.library.upenn.edu/women/astell/marriage/marriage.html. See also the modern editions by Bridget Hill, *The First English Feminist: "Reflections Upon Marriage" and Other Writings by Mary Astell* (New York: St. Martin's, 1986); and Sharon L. Jansen, *Some Reflections upon Marriage* (Steilacoom, WA: Saltar's Point Press, 2014), the latter reproducing the 1700 edition with modernized capitalization, punctuation, and spelling. For Astell, see the classic biography of Ruth Perry, *The Celebrated Mary Astell: An Early English Feminist* (Chicago: University of Chicago Press, 1986); the more recent study of her thought by Patricia Springborg, *Mary Astell: Theorist of Freedom from Domination* (Cambridge: Cambridge University Press, 2005); and the collection of essays edited by William Kolbrener and Michal Michelson, *Mary Astell: Reason, Gender, Faith* (Aldershot, UK: Ashgate, 2007).

Anna Stanisławska. The translation is that of Barry Keane, *Anna Stanisławska, Orphan Girl: A Transaction, or an Account of the Entire Life of an Orphan Girl by Way of Plaintful Threnodies in the Year 1685: The Aesop Episode*, verse translation, introduction, and commentary by Barry Keane (Toronto: Iter Academic Press; Tempe, Arizona: Arizona Center for Medieval and

Renaissance Studies, 2016), Threnody 5, Stanzas 25–32; Threnody 6, Stanzas 36–39, and 43, at pages 28–29, 31–33. For Stanisławska, see Keane's introduction (1–16) and commentary (107–20).

Denis Diderot. The translation is based on Diderot's *La religieuse* (1780; edition of Paris: A. Lemerre, 1925), 16–20, 22, 25–26, 29–33, 37–40, online at La Bibliothèque électronique du Québec: https://beq.ebooksgratuits.com/vents/Diderot-religieuse.pdf. For Diderot, see P. N. Furbank, *Diderot: A Critical Biography* (London: Seeker and Warburg, 1992); also the essays edited by James Fowler, *New Essays on Diderot* (Cambridge: Cambridge University Press, 2011); and the many essays published since 1949 in the irregularly appearing volumes of *Diderot Studies* (Droz), most recently its vol. 35 (2015). For *La religieuse*, see Christine Clarke-Evans, *Diderot's "La religieuse": A Philosophical Novel* (Montreal: CERES, 1995); and the introductions by Leonard Tancock to the edition of 1974 (London: Penguin) and by Heather Lloyd to that of 2000 (London: Bristol Classical Press). Catherine Cusset's *No Tomorrow: The Ethics of Pleasure in the French Enlightenment* (Charlottesville: University Press of Virginia, 1999) includes a discussion of *La religieuse* at 116–42.

Mary Wollstonecraft. The text is taken from *A Vindication of the Rights of Woman with Strictures on Political and Moral Subjects* (London: J. Johnson, 1792), online at http://lf-oll.s3.amazonaws.com/titles/126/Wollstonecraft_0730_EBk_v6.0.pdf, at pages 20, 22, 25–28, 31, 33–34. Several modern editions of this work are available, among them those by Janet Todd, included in her collection *Mary Wollstonecraft: Political Writings* (Oxford: Oxford University Press, 1994), 63–284; and Sylvana Tomaselli, *A Vindication of the Rights of Men and A Vindication of the Rights of Woman* (Cambridge: Cambridge University Press, 1995), 65–294. Recent biographies of Wollstonecraft include (in chronological order of publication) Janet Todd, *Mary Wollstonecraft: A Revolutionary Life* (London: Weidenfeld & Nicholson, 2000); Dianne Jacobs, *Her Own Woman: The Life of Mary Wollstonecraft* (New York: Simon & Schuster, 2001); and Lyndall Gordon, *Mary Wollstonecraft: A New Genus* (London: Little, Brown, 2005). The studies of her works and feminist outlook are innumerable.

Olympe de Gouges. The translation is based on the *Déclaration des droits de la femme et de la citoyenne* (1791), online at Wikisource/France based on the document in the Bibliothèque nationale de France (BnF): https://fr.wikisource.org/wiki/Déclaration_des_droits_de_la_femme_et_de_la_citoyenne. A website at the BnF posts 210 documents by or relating to Olympe de Gouges: http://data.bnf.fr/11905505/olympe_de_gouges/. For Gouges, see the recent biography by Sophie Mousset: *Women's Rights and the French Revolution: A Biography of Olympe de Gouges* (New Brunswick, NJ: Transaction Publishers, 2007), and the close study of her *Declaration* (with English translation) and related texts by John R. Cole, *Between the Queen and the Cabby: Olympe de Gouges's "Rights of Woman"* (Montreal: McGill-Queen's University Press, 2011). See also the Olympe de Gouges website, with English translations of many works, at http://www.olympedegouges.eu/index.php.

Chapter Eleven

For recent studies of the Enlightenment in America, see especially (in chronological order of publication) Robert A. Ferguson, *The American Enlightenment, 1750–1820* (Cambridge, MA: Harvard University Press, 1997); Gertrude Himmelfarb, *The Roads to Modernity: The British, French and American Enlightenments* (New York: Knopf, 2004); and Darren Staloff, *Hamilton, Adams, Jefferson: The Politics of Enlightenment and the American Founding* (New

York: Hill and Wang, 2005). Intersecting with these is Jonathan Israel's monumental study of the intellectual history of the American Revolution: *The Expanding Blaze: How the American Revolution Ignited the World, 1775–1848* (Princeton, NJ: Princeton University Press, 2017).

Benjamin Franklin. The text is taken from *The Autobiography of Benjamin Franklin* (1771–1790; published posthumously 1791), online at *The Electric Ben Franklin*: http://www.ushistory.org/franklin/autobiography/, part one, at 3, 5, 8, 9, 11–14. Many editions exist in print and online. Recent biographies of Franklin include (in chronological order of publication) Edmund S. Morgan, *Benjamin Franklin* (New Haven, CT: Yale University Press, 2002); Gordon Wood, *The Americanization of Benjamin Franklin* (New York: Penguin, 2004); and J. A. Leo Lemay, *The Life of Benjamin Franklin* (Philadelphia: University of Pennsylvania Press): Vol. 1: *Journalist, 1706–1730* (2006); Vol. 2: *Printer and Publisher, 1730–1747* (2006); Vol. 3: *Soldier, Scientist, and Politician, 1748–1757* (2008).

Thomas Paine: *Common Sense*. The text is taken from Robert Bell's authoritative third edition, *Common Sense* (Philadelphia: Bell, 1776), reprinted in *The Writings of Thomas Paine*, edited by Moncure Daniel Conway, 4 vols. (New York: G. P. Putnam's Sons, 1894), 1:67–120, excerpts at 1:84–89, 92–101; and online at http://www.ushistory.org/paine/commonsense/sense1.htm, unpaginated. Many editions exist in print and online. Recent biographies of Paine include (in chronological order of publication) John Keane, *Tom Paine: A Political Life* (Boston: Little, Brown, 1995); and Edward Larkin, *Thomas Paine and the Literature of Revolution* (Cambridge: Cambridge University Press, 2005).

Thomas Jefferson. The text is the transcription provided online by the National Archives: https://www.archives.gov/founding-docs/declaration-transcript, unpaginated. Many other online and printed versions are available. Recent biographies of Jefferson include (in chronological order of publication) Richard. B. Bernstein, *Thomas Jefferson* (Oxford: Oxford University Press, 2005); Peter S. Onuf, *The Mind of Thomas Jefferson* (Charlottesville: University of Virginia Press, 2007); and Kevin J. Hayes, *The Road to Monticello: The Life and Mind of Thomas Jefferson* (Oxford: Oxford University Press, 2008).

James Madison. The text is Madison's *Federalist No. 10: The Same Subject Continued: The Union as a Safeguard Against Domestic Faction and Insurrection* (1787), available online at Congress.gov: https://www.congress.gov/resources/display/content/The+Federalist+Papers#TheFederalistPapers-10. The *Federalist Papers* are available in multiple print and online versions. Recent biographies of Madison include (in chronological order of publication) Richard Brookhiser, *James Madison* (New York: Basic Books, 2011); Jeff Broadwater, *James Madison: A Son of Virginia and a Founder of a Nation* (Chapel Hill: University of North Carolina Press, 2012); and Kevin R. C. Gutzman, *James Madison and the Making of America* (New York: St. Martin's Press, 2012).

Thomas Paine: *The Rights of Man*. The text is taken from part one of Paine's *Rights of Man: Being an Answer to Mr. Burke's Attack on the French Revolution*, 2nd ed. (London: J. S. Jordan, 1791), available at the Online Library of Liberty: http://oll.libertyfund.org/titles/paine-the-rights-of-man-part-i-1791-ed, 51–56. See also *The Rights of Man* (1791–1792), in *The Writings of Thomas Paine*, edited by Moncure Daniel Conway, 4 vols. (New York: G. P. Putnam's Sons, 1894), online at the Online Library of Liberty: http://oll.libertyfund.org/titles/paine-the-writings-of-thomas-paine-vol-ii-1779-1792, 193–97. Other editions exist in print and online. For Paine's interface with Burke, see especially Yuval Levin, *The Great Debate: Edmund Burke, Thomas Paine, and the Birth of Right and Left* (New York: Basic Books, 2014).

Chapter Twelve

Edmund Burke. The text is taken from Burke's *Reflections on the Revolution in France*, edited by F. G. Selby (London: Macmillan, 1890), 36–38, 64–67, 107–8; online at Google Books. Many editions exist in print and online. See the authoritative recent biography by F. P. Locke, *Edmund Burke*, 2 vols. (Oxford: Clarendon Press, 1998, 2006); and the studies (in chronological order of publication) by Elizabeth R. Lambert, *Edmund Burke of Beaconsfield* (Newark: University of Delaware Press, 2003); Jesse Norman, *Edmund Burke: The First Conservative* (New York: Basic Books, 2013); Yuval Levin, *The Great Debate: Edmund Burke, Thomas Paine, and the Birth of Right and Left* (New York: Basic Books, 2014); and David Bromwich, *The Intellectual Life of Edmund Burke: From the Sublime and Beautiful to American Independence* (Cambridge, MA: Harvard University Press/Belknap Press, 2014). See also the essays edited by Ian Crowe, *An Imaginative Whig: Reassessing the Life and Thought of Edmund Burke* (Columbia: University of Missouri Press, 2005); and for the Irish connection, Luke Gibbons, *Edmund Burke and Ireland: Aesthetics, Politics, and the Colonial Sublime* (Cambridge: Cambridge University Press, 2003); and the essays in Séan Patrick Donlan, ed., *Edmund Burke's Irish Identities* (Dublin: Irish Academic Press, 2007).

Nicolas de Condorcet (Marie Jean Antoine Nicolas de Caritat, marquis de Condorcet). The translation is based on Condorcet's *Esquisse d'un tableau historique des progrès de l'esprit humain* (1793–1794), edited by O. H. Prior, new edition by Yvon Belaval (Paris: J. Vrin, 1970), 193–96, 198–99, 201, 203, 211–12, 214–19, online at UQAC (Université de Québec à Chicoutimi): http://classiques.uqac.ca/classiques/condorcet/esquisse_tableau_progres_hum/esquisse.html. See the recent study of David Williams, *Condorcet and Modernity* (Cambridge: Cambridge University Press, 2004); and, more broadly, Emma Rothschild, *Economic Sentiments: Adam Smith, Condorcet, and the Enlightenment* (2001); and, in French, the biography by Elisabeth Badinter and Robert Badinter, *Condorcet, 1743–1794: Un intellectuel en politique*, 2nd rev. ed. (Paris: Fayard, 2001).

INDEX

abolition (of slavery), xiii, 155, 201, 242

agriculture, xxi, 86, 118, 120, 134, 140–42, 182, 184

American Revolution, xv, xxiii, 221–25, 241

Anglicanism, 44, 49, 114, 116, 202, 221

antitrinitarianism, 49, 114, 111, 117

Arians. *See* antitrinitarianism

aristocracy, 23, 25, 36, 38, 41, 72, 74, 75, 111, 133, 137, 156, 162, 181, 199, 224, 241, 242, 248

Aristotle, Aristotelian, xviii, 1, 4, 6n3, 11, 27n2, 47, 48, 59n4, 67, 133

artisans, 82, 181, 221, 226

arts (humanistic studies), 24, 28, 29, 31, 34–36, 70, 80, 81, 84, 98, 99, 118–20, 130, 146, 249

Astell, Mary, xiii, xxiii, 198–199, 201–5, 267

astronomy, 3, 14–18, 30–32, 76–77, 82, 86, 156

atheism, xix, 2, 20, 22, 36, 48, 49, 63, 93, 94, 104–6, 130, 199

autobiography, xv, xxii, xxiii, xxv, 177, 180, 195–97, 199, 222, 225–29

axiom, axiomatic, 2, 6, 7, 11, 12, 14–16, 223

Bacon, Francis, xii, xix, 1–8, 11, 15, 18, 30, 32, 44, 46–48, 71, 80–83, 85n11, 91, 95, 254

Bayle, Pierre, xiii, xix, 3, 4, 18–22, 44, 45, 113, 114, 255

Beccaria, Cesare, xv, xxi, 132, 134, 143–46, 225, 263–64

Behn, Aphra, xiii, xxii, 154–56, 158–62, 264–65

Bentham, Jeremy, 93, 132, 134, 136

Bible, 1, 2, 11, 35, 48, 50, 63–67, 115, 126, 129, 130, 222

biology, xviii, xx, xxi, 67, 91, 172

blank slate, 46, 47, 58, 59

breast-feeding, 180, 193–94

Burke, Edmund, xvi, xxiv, 132n2, 200, 224–25, 238, 241–47, 270

Calas, Jean, 113, 123–27

Calvin, John, 116, 117, 125n19, 131

Calvinism, xxii, 26, 45, 111, 116, 125, 179, 181. *See also* Huguenots, Protestantism

capital (for investment), 149, 152–53

capital punishment. *See* punishment: capital

Catholicism, xix, xxi–xxiii, 3, 18, 19, 21, 25, 38, 45, 46, 49, 94, 111, 115, 116, 118, 119, 123–25, 131, 181, 199, 241, 242

Cavendish, Margaret, duchess of Newcastle, xii, xix, 23–26, 30–34, 256

Charles I, king of England, xii, 24, 25, 37

chemistry, xviii, 83, 84, 86

children, childhood, 36, 38, 39, 41, 47, 48, 60–63, 71, 75, 88, 99, 100, 105, 107, 110, 123, 126, 129, 130, 141, 159, 165, 168, 172, 175, 177, 179–83, 191–96, 198–202, 204, 206, 207, 209–12, 217–20, 226, 230, 241, 246. *See also* daughters, education, illegitimacy

Christ. *See* Jesus Christ

Christianity, xviii, xix, xxi, 3, 26–29, 44, 45, 48–50, 63–66, 91, 94, 95, 106–10, 112, 114–16, 123, 126, 131, 154, 162, 163, 167, 177, 202

citizen, xvi, xxii, 46, 49, 52, 89, 132, 135, 137–38, 140–49, 157, 181, 197, 216–20, 235–37, 248, 250

civil goods. *See* civil rights

civil government, xiii, xx, 44–46, 49, 52–58, 177, 178. *See also* civil society, constitution

civil rights, 46, 51, 52, 148, 201, 212, 216–20, 223–25, 230, 232–34, 236, 238–40, 244–46, 250

civil society, xv, xxii, 54, 55, 132, 135, 146–49, 183, 185, 187–88, 223, 236, 239, 245–46

climate, xxi, 128, 130, 133, 135, 149, 150, 155, 157, 167, 172–75, 252

colonialism. *See* imperialism

Comenius, Johann Amos, 25, 44, 46

commerce, xv, 7, 44, 81, 82, 115, 120, 132, 134, 135, 140–42, 147, 149–53, 165–68, 222, 230–31, 234, 239, 247, 249, 250

Table of Contents

Author Paul Pluta

Introduction

Thank you for reading my book about Collecting Louis Vuitton. I am very passionate about collecting Louis Vuitton and this book is the result of years of collecting. I have been a Louis Vuitton fan since I was 15 years old. My interest in Louis Vuitton started when I was reading the English classic car magazine – *Classic and Sports Cars*. Louis Vuitton at the time was sponsoring some classic car events and subsequently had an advertising campaign in some up market classic car magazines. I have always had a soft spot for high quality print advertisements.

I can recall how beautiful the Louis Vuitton advertisements were at the time. Louis Vuitton has always had very attractive print media advertisements. These advertisements are probably what planted the seeds for what was to become my love for all things Louis Vuitton.

A short time later a Louis Vuitton store opened up in my home town. My first trip to that store was an experience that I can remember to this day. The store was like no other store I had been in before. It seemed to me to be a combination of an art gallery, up-market shop and museum all rolled into one. Everything was so beautifully presented. The products were like pieces of art. It was almost like going to a beautiful European private museum. Everything was perfect – from the beautifully dressed staff who resembled international airline hostesses to the placement of the merchandise.

I can remember from that visit that the store had the most beautiful old Louis Vuitton trunks and suitcases on display. These were not for sale as such but gave the store the most wonderful ambiance. These beautiful antiques really started my thirst for all things Louis Vuitton.

Over the years I slowly learned about Louis Vuitton. Unfortunately many pieces from that first visit were very expensive. Louis Vuitton is a French-made luxury goods maker that has come to represent the best of the best. As can be expected, the items are not for those short of funds.

Although the prices are quite high, this needs to be put into perspective. The workmanship of most things Louis Vuitton is absolutely amazing.

The thing about buying a Louis Vuitton piece is that it will last you a lifetime provided you take good care of the item. You can easily buy far cheaper pieces of a lesser quality that do not last anywhere near as long. Are you really saving by buying an inferior item? Or are you paying the same once you have replaced it a few times?

Many Louis Vuitton pieces are therefore like future heirlooms to hand down to your family line. What could possibly be nicer than inheriting a lovely Louis Vuitton suitcase that is packed full of memories and experiences?

I was originally attracted to the Louis Vuitton hard case line – especially the hard-sided briefcases and the beautifully made hard-sided luggage.

Fast track a couple of years and I got a work bonus. I bought my first new Louis Vuitton piece A Louis Vuitton Keepall. I then added a few more purchases from the classifieds in the newspaper.

In 2002 I took a job working in Asia (Thailand, Singapore and Hong Kong) for a luxury watch dealer. I was amazed to find stores selling genuine used Louis Vuitton – there were also large numbers of shops selling fakes as well!

Slowly, as the eBay crazy took hold, I bought and sold hundreds of genuine pieces. Asia has a huge appetite for Louis Vuitton with over 30% of sales happening in Japan alone (Wikinvest); therefore it is only natural that the Asian market would cast off used pieces as readily.

The Asian market has a very different viewpoint on Louis Vuitton to Westerners. Many Asians see European brands as a status symbol to be replaced when the next session's range is released. Personally I feel this is missing the point as I believe quality products are timeless and are therefore design icons which have no use-by date.

If you take a look at the back of a printed Louis Vuitton catalogue you can see how strong the Asian presence is. Japan has the most Louis Vuitton stores per capita than anywhere in the entire world.

I have always had a soft spot for briefcases and travel goods. These items are a touch harder to find on the secondary market as Louis Vuitton has such a large female following.

As Louis Vuitton is so popular it is possible to buy and sell Louis Vuitton pieces. A few rules need to be understood. Mainly there is only one source for genuine Louis Vuitton. That is the Louis Vuitton store. Louis Vuitton jealously protects its distribution network. There is no such thing as wholesale Louis Vuitton or pieces direct from the manufacturer. All genuine pieces come only from the genuine Louis Vuitton store – period. Many false claims have been made on the internet about wholesale Louis Vuitton and these are from the peddlers of fakes.

You can buy genuine used Louis Vuitton on the internet; however, all these pieces would have originally come from a genuine Louis Vuitton store.

My interest in selling used genuine Louis Vuitton has ceased as I decided to remain a collector and not a dealer. A collector keeps pieces that he/she enjoys most. A dealer sells pieces that bring the best return. Some of my best buys on the used market are pieces I do not ever want to sell.

Today, the only time I sell a piece is to occasionally help finance another purchase. I prefer to remain a Louis Vuitton collector instead of a dealer doing things solely for the profit motive.

Although I am no longer dealing in used Louis Vuitton, it did give me a lot of experience in telling the genuine item from the fake. It also gave me a great insight into the brand and showed me the true craftsmanship that goes into Louis Vuitton pieces.

The thing about Louis Vuitton is that you don't need to use it continually to enjoy it. You can come home after a hard day and just open a Louis Vuitton item up and feel the lovely material. Just to absorb the smell and feel the texture of a genuine Louis Vuitton item. That is the love of collecting Louis Vuitton.

Some of my collection

Louis Vuitton as art & Monogram set

Hard-sided Louis Vuitton Suitcases and Briefcases

Books, Catalogues and Literature

Part of being a Louis Vuitton collector is that you want to get as much information as possible on the hobby that you have. With Louis Vuitton there are numerous sources of literature.

You firstly have the Louis Vuitton store itself. When a new line or item is released, the store also releases a catalogue or booklet. when the Damier Graphite line came out for example, a special Damier Graphite booklet was released which showed some of the pieces available in that new shade of Damier.

These special booklets and catalogues are only available for a limited time. Once that product line has been released and all the catalogues have been given out that is the end of them. Some of these mini booklets do appear on eBay from time to time.

eBay is a great source for superseded catalogues and booklets.

Another way to get Louis Vuitton literature is to hunt for the Louis Vuitton advertisements in magazines. Some of these older advertisements are even sold on eBay. Obviously it is much cheaper to find them yourself. eBay can be an easy way of getting this piece of print media history. Some of the advertisements I remember when I just started an interest in the subject are available via eBay this way. It is a trip down memory lane – to see items you lusted for when you were a teenager! Sort of like the boy with the Ferrari poster on his wall.

Louis Vuitton advertisements are generally works of art. They are well designed, beautifully photographed and have beautiful layout. They are put together by some of the leading advertising people in the world.

I have bought these old advertisements from eBay for about $10 each plus shipping. It certainly is not cheap but a lot quicker than going through a pile of old magazines. Another alternative is to buy a collection of old magazines from a jumble sale for a low price.

The advertisements I have bought have often been for products/items that I collect and which encompass the topic so well, therefore I don't mind outlaying $10 for them.

An excellent source of information is the Louis Vuitton yearly catalogue. Louis Vuitton has had a catalogue out for about 100 years! Some of the really old catalogues are very collectable and quite valuable. Catalogues from the 1970s and 1980s are getting very collectable and expensive. I have seen some early 1980s catalogues go for over $100 on eBay. Others I have seen for $100-$150. That price reflects the fact that they are becoming very scarce.

Older Louis Vuitton catalogues are a great source of information. I have bought a few older catalogues myself.

The terrible thing is that in my early collecting days I gave away my older catalogues once I obtained a later version! Now those same catalogues sell for over $100! It is one of those things that you do not appreciate how valuable the catalogues are at the time.

Officially Louis Vuitton seems to be phasing out the printed catalogue. This is something that I believe is sad. I have often asked at a Louis Vuitton store for the latest catalogue only to be told they do not have any in stock. I have been told to check the web site. I do love the internet but I feel it is a great shame to do away with the printed catalogue. The beautiful thing about the printed catalogue is that it serves as a historical document and reference source. On-line profiles change with the seasons and fashion cycle. The printed catalogues are fantastic to look through and see how fashions and styles have changed.

Interestingly I have rung up the Louis Vuitton toll free number and requested the catalogue and received it in the mail a few days later. It seems the Louis Vuitton phone hotline may have a reserve of catalogues for phone order customers.

I suppose the problem is that the store has so many people constantly asking for a catalogue. That could be very annoying if that customer had no intention of buying from the store.

Personally I would be more than happy to pay for a catalogue.

Another source of information is books (like this one) written on the topic itself. Louis Vuitton has even acted as an agent for Louis Vuitton commissioned works. Louis Vuitton prices for these books are generally fair. I have even seen these books put onto eBay at much higher prices. Amazon and Barnes and Noble have an excellent search facility. The internet is making this so much easier.

An excellent book I obtained recently is *Vintage Luggage* by Helenka Gulshan. This book has been out of print for some time and I have seen copies of this book sell for over $300. Although not a Louis Vuitton book solely it does have a major bias to Louis Vuitton.

The final source that I will mention is the Japanese specialty magazine. As Louis Vuitton is so popular in Japan they have specialty magazines about the topic! Unfortunately these magazines are not in English however the picture and details are very helpful.

These magazines reflect the fact that Louis Vuitton is so popular in Japan. These magazines often cover the latest version as well as older versions and limited editions. They also cover the many different variants, different limited edition products as well as providing a timeline of release details.

These Japanese magazines are not generally available in the Western world however they do come up on eBay from time to time. I am lucky enough to have a friend who goes to Japan regularly for business. Some of these magazines cover luxury goods – so they are not exclusively Louis Vuitton; others are exclusively Louis Vuitton based.

Some examples of Louis Vuitton literature.

Japanese magazines

Special Edition Pieces

Louis Vuitton often releases special edition pieces when launching a new color or style. This occurred when Louis Vuitton released the Damier Graphite range for men. Louis Vuitton released a President Classeur briefcase in this new style. These pieces are often only available for a short time. If you are sufficiently well-heeled this is a collection that surely cannot be bad.

Louis Vuitton also releases special edition pieces for its flagship store – the Champs-Élysées store. My Taiga green Alzer was such an item that was placed in this store for a special customer to purchase. Hard-sided items are also available on the special order program. Prices for special order are significantly higher than standard prices.

When a new color or style is released, each store will get a few hard-seeded items in this new variant. These special release hard-sided items have become very desirable with the rich and jet set. Due to the uniqueness of having a beautiful famous Louis Vuitton model in a rare style.

Louis Vuitton is also at the cutting edge of design. The *Le Challenge* series was released in 1987 to coincide with Louis Vuitton's sponsorship of the America's cup yacht race. The *Le Challenge* series was designed with Australia in mind. The texture of the range is supposed to resemble Aboriginal traditional art.

The *Le Challenge* series has dated by today's standards. I personally tried for ten years to track down one of these hard-sided suitcases. The suitcase is certainly an acquired taste but a beautiful addition to a Louis Vuitton hard-sided suitcase collection.

Some special order combinations have become so popular that they have become permanent fixtures. The Damier Alma is such a bag that was made a catalogue item after proving popular in the Japanese market.

America's Cup Le Challenge Suitcase

18

Special Order Taiga Green Alzer

Holy Grail Pieces

Holy Grail pieces are those pieces which are so unobtainable and/or so expensive that you just want to have them. For me my fascination with Louis Vuitton started when I was 15 years old. Louis Vuitton had just released the Taiga leather line. Subsequently Louis Vuitton had released some stunning print advertisements.

Some Holy Grail pieces for me have been the hard-sided luggage including the Alzer, Bisten and other hard-sided objectsincluding the hard-sided briefcases made by Louis Vuitton.

The final class of items that have been Holy Grail pieces to me are the Louis Vuitton desk sets – the writing pad, paper tray and pencil holder.

Due to the Global Financial Crisis I have been able to get some of these pieces on the secondary market – mainly via eBay.

I try and obtain pieces with as few flaws as possible.

Some collectors of Vintage Louis Vuitton luggage prefer to get pieces which have stood the test of time. Personally I prefer newer, better condition pieces. More modern pieces allow me to use the piece and put my own history into it.

If you have bought a 1930s or 1940s piece you need to be very careful not to damage it. You really need to preserve the piece in the condition it is in. This means that you often cannot use the piece as you would a newer item.For example a 1990s version of the same piece can be used without the same caution. I find it appealing to add my own history to the piece.

I like to use all my Louis Vuitton items. This includes my hard-sided luggage collection. Naturally I am neither brave nor silly enough to use these items on a commercial flight. This means we limit the use of this luggage to road journeys.

Commercial realities being what they are means that baggage handlers are time-poor and simply throw the items onto the plane.

I highly recommend using all your Louis Vuitton items when possible. Sure it is nice to have them tucked away at home, however nothing beats adding your own history to the item.

One of the funny things about collecting is that once you have found a desired piece, another slightly better piece often turns up. This is where you need to be disciplined and decide whether you can afford two pieces instead of one. I have often then resold the lesser quality piece on eBay. Thence the reason it is good to be active in small-time dealing.

The hunt is often the most fun in collecting. To this end I am still to acquire some Louis Vuitton desk set items. I have been very fortunate in acquiring some excellent Holy Grail pieces so I am patient to wait for the right item to turn up at a fair price.

Some of my Holy Grail pieces

Luxury Luggage

"It is very distinctive, it is very stylish – it is very Louis Vuitton…
wherever you go in the world you will see people carrying the distinctive
Louis Vuitton brand…whether it is a little bag or a huge suitcase. It talks
of distinction and taste" – *Cherie Blair at the London Louis Vuitton New Bond
Street Maison Opening.*

"I think it is an amazing brand, I love that it has got such a heritage and it
has been around for such a long time. I particularly like their luggage and
all the trunks" - *Alexa Chung at the London Louis Vuitton New Bond Street
Maison Opening.*

"My favorite things are the old suitcases, the classic luggage" – *Gwyneth
Paltrow at the London Louis Vuitton New Bond Street Maison Opening.*

Nothing says class more than quality luxury luggage. Louis Vuitton
famously ran the advertising by-line "show me your luggage, and I'll tell
you who you are." In this modern age of mass production there are only
two brands which tick the box in my book. Those brands are Louis
Vuitton and Goyard. Both brands are French and were founded at
approximately the same time (1854 for Louis Vuitton and 1853 for
Goyard).

The best pieces to own are the hard-sided trunks and suitcases. These
items are made the old fashion way – by skilled artisans much the same
way as originally intended. Trunks are the large boxes used for sea voyages
and months away from home. Trunks today are mainly for ornamental
purposes. Hard-sided suitcases are the most useful items to have. They
can be used for ornamental purposes but still have a use for modern
travel. Famous fans of hard-sided suitcases include Joan Collins, Madonna
and Sir Elton John. Recently on eBay three of Sir Elton John's Louis
Vuitton hard case suitcases were offered for auction. It is fascinating that
these are the best quality suitcases in the world and they are obtainable
(yet still very expensive).

Quality luggage is an heirloom that will last a lifetime and will always bring
pleasure in its usage. Care should be taken on commercial flights as many

expensive suitcases have been deliberately damaged by jealous workers. Recently Louis Vuitton has offered there hard-sided suitcases with a strong black cover. This adds a layer of protection whilst also provided a degree of discretion.

Louis Vuitton is probably the most famous maker of beautiful luggage in the world. Classic suitcases from Louis Vuitton include the Alzer, Bisten, Cotteville and Braken. Louis Vuitton also has a range of other hard-sided items to go together with the suitcases including the President Classeur briefcase, Boite Pharmacie cosmetic case and Boite Bijoux Jewellery case. Louis Vuitton offers these products in a range of colors/patterns including Monogram, Damier, Epi and Taiga.

The Monogram range is probably the most recognizable line whilst Epi and Taiga lines provide a degree of discretion. I personally have a mix match of colors/patterns to match my mood.

Louis Vuitton Hard-Sided items

(from back) Le Challenge Suitcase 80, Taiga Alzer 70, Monogram Bisten 70, Monogram Bisten 65, Taiga President Classeur, Monogram President Classeur and Taiga Diplomate.

Telling Fakes from Genuine Items

In this chapter I hope to reveal some of the ways to differentiate fakes from the genuine article. I have collected, dealt and admired Louis Vuitton items for over 20 years. During that time I have seen a lot of real pieces and also a lot of fake pieces.

I have put together a five point plan to help you decide if the piece in question is genuine.

Point 1 – Check the item in a Louis Vuitton catalogue

The first thing to do in order to confirm whether the piece is real or not is to check a Louis Vuitton catalogue. This will help you work out whether the item is an actual genuine item. Often with fake items they are a mix match of a couple of Louis Vuitton styles and different products combined into one item. Therefore the piece does not actually exist.

Consulting a Louis Vuitton catalogue will help you in determining whether the item is correct. The design and structure should be the same as the same model in the catalogue. The Louis Vuitton catalogue will also give you approximate dimensions of the item.

Be aware that some Louis Vuitton items that you have may not be in the latest Louis Vuitton catalogue. This would be the case for a discontinued line. Personally I have a reference library going back a few decades. This is invaluable in determining if the item did ever exist.

It is always worth keeping in mind that you need to match the items age to the correct catalogue. A ten year old piece may not be in a 5 year old catalogue. Many pieces are design classics and remain in the catalogues for years. Some pieces are however fashion pieces and have a much shorter production run.

To determine the age of a Louis Vuitton catalogue see the last couple of pages for a copyright date.

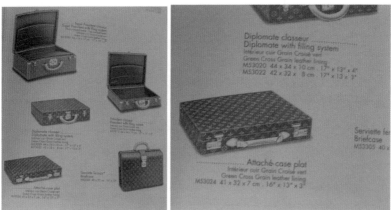

Some Louis Vuitton Catalogues

Point 2 – Brassware/Metal Work

Most Louis Vuitton items use brass for the metal work of a piece. Some newer items are now using a silver colored metal ware however most items continue to use brass.

The secret is to look at the brassware/metal work and compare it to other Louis Vuitton items that you know are genuine. Louis Vuitton uses standardized brassware on most pieces. Therefore the way a clip, lock or zip appears on one piece will be similar to another item in the range.

A lot of the fakes use a much lower quality of metal work. Often the metalwork is gold color plated in too bright a color. The attention to detail of the metal work is a major clue in determining whether an item is genuine or not.

I have seen fakes fitted with a genuine Louis Vuitton lock. The lock is a relatively inexpensive item to purchase from Louis Vuitton. Be aware of this mixing when purchasing any item outside of the Louis Vuitton store.

Point 3 – Stamping & Date Code

The next step in the authentication process is to check the stamped text on the item. Louis Vuitton pays exceptional attention to detail with all its stamping. The font is a very particular font. The stamp will be perfect and even. Fakes often have the incorrect font and or are not perfectly done.

All the stamping on a Louis Vuitton item should be in accordance with its price. A $2000 bag should have perfect stamping. Many of the fakes are poorly stamped with even spelling mistakes!

Even if an item has had considerable wear the stamping should still be in good condition.

The other clue to authenticating an item is to check the code inside the bag. This is often referred to as its serial number when in fact it is a batch code. This code is used by Louis Vuitton to work out the date of manufacture. Genuine Louis Vuitton items never mention the actual item code on the item. The item code will be like M51126, as seen in the yearly Louis Vuitton catalogue. I have seen fakes which did not have a batch code but instead had a model number code! This is a dead give away for a fake.

The batch code itself is not something that is easily interrupted. It is in an encoded format – see Batch Code Appendix at the rear of this book.

The stamping of these batch codes should also be perfect. Many fakes have misaligned stamping on these batch codes.

The presence of a batch code itself does not mean the item is genuine. Many fakes now have these batch codes inside them now as some people mistakenly believe these batch codes authenticate the piece. Some of these batch codes are difficult to find. I have even had the odd genuine piece that did not have a batch code!

Point 4 – Handle Some Genuine Louis Vuitton Pieces

One of the best ways to become familiar with genuine Louis Vuitton items is to handle some real pieces. Nothing beats a bit of experience when it comes to knowing the correct feel of a genuine item.

If possible go to a Louis Vuitton store and ask to look at a few pieces. I have always found the staff at Louis Vuitton to be very polite and knowledgeable.

When inspecting a genuine item take a close look at the stamping, the stitching and how the item is put together. 90% of fakes do not have the same feel as a genuine item.

All the little details are tell-tale signs that a piece is genuine or not.

Point 5 – The Stitching

The fifth and final point is to look at the stitches itself. Louis Vuitton uses a set number of stitches for each item. For example on an Alma handbag where the handles join the Monogram sides of the item. The number of stitches is a set number of stitches. Each handle side will have the same number of stitches. Comparing one part to the other three parts should reveal that they have the same number of stitches.

Often with fakes the stitching is of an inferior quality. This is because they are not taking the same care and attention that the Louis Vuitton workshop takes. Often fakes are being churned out as quickly as possible.

Even older pieces should have intact stitching

Brassware often reveals if an item is genuine or fake

Stamping should be perfect even on older pieces

Date Codes inside 2 President Briefcases

The Japanese Super Fake

One of the negative outcomes of the internet age is the distribution of high grade fakes. The eBay marketplace has been so affected by this item that the resale price of genuine items has fallen.

Traditionally Japanese eBay resellers have been one of the most honest resellers on eBay. This has all changed with the introduction of the Japanese mafia. The Japanese mafia has been very clever to release a range of high grade fakes which have been artificially aged and matched with genuine Louis Vuitton locks. The items affect have been the Keepall, Speedie and Noe.

The items I have seen are probably 8.5 out of 10. To the untrained buyer they seem to be correct. I suspect some Louis Vuitton staff would have trouble telling. Whilst I am able to differentiate the Japanese super fake today the worrying prospect is the improvement in the fake.

I call these high quality fakes "Japanese super fakes" as the items are manufactured in China and distributed by Japanese eBay resellers.

What to look for to avoid a Japanese Super Fake

1) Item appears too good for its age.
2) Brassware is often treated with chemicals to make it prematurely old – look for any greening of the brassware.
3) Leather is aged but is a lower grade than genuine Louis Vuitton leather trim.
4) Check the date code. Date codes used are usually early 1980s codes.
5) Stamping – often the stamping is in the wrong font.
6) Check previous seller auctions – check to see if the seller is selling the same item over and over again.

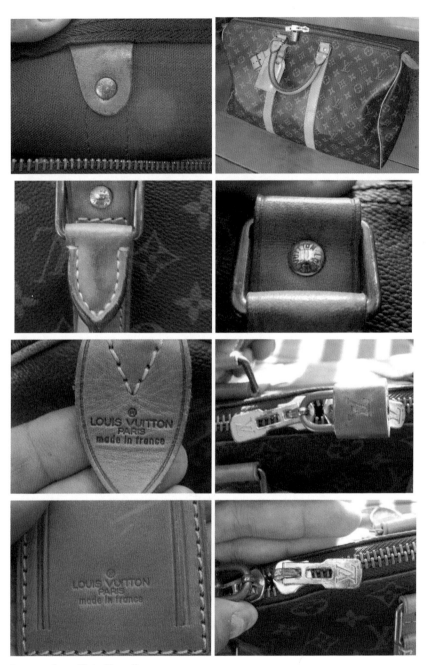

Japanese Super Fake Keepall

Buying Genuine Louis Vuitton from eBay

eBay is one of the best ways to purchase used goods at a fair price. eBay allows sellers to sell their items in a world market place instead of dealing with a traditional second hand dealer or consignment store.

Unfortunately it has also given many unscrupulous sellers the chance to make money from inexperienced buyers who are not able to determine if an item is genuine or fake.

Point 1 – Buy the seller before buying the item

Ensure you are buying from a reputable seller. Check how long that person has been in business. Confirm the amount of feedback a seller has – be careful of new and low feedback sellers. Check to see how many negative feedback comments have been left.

It can also be beneficial to see what type of items the feedback has been left for. Often with sellers of imitation goods the seller will sell the exact same model again and again. Louis Vuitton items can not be bought wholesale or new from any source other than the genuine Louis Vuitton store. All Louis Vuitton items that are genuine can only have come from the genuine Louis Vuitton store. Therefore any items that are being sold second hand are the result of somebody originally buying the item from a Louis Vuitton store and then disposing of the item on eBay or through a second hand dealer.

When buying an item on eBay be very suspicious of the item being sold as unused or being sold as an unwanted gift. How many people do you know that don't want a $2000 handbag or briefcase? In my life I have received very few expensive gifts like that.

Always buy from sellers you feel confident with. Check to ensure they have not been selling the same item over and over.

Point 2 – Check how long the seller has been in business

Check to see how long the seller has been on eBay for. Has the seller just started selling items? Or does the seller have a long history of buying and selling over years.

Check the feedback to see if the seller is mainly buying or mainly selling.

Not one of these things is necessarily a bad thing. Somebody who has just started selling on eBay is not necessarily a fraudulent seller. It does not necessarily mean the deal is a no go. It just means you need to take some caution.

Point 3 – Confirm the item is genuine

Use the steps in the previous chapter to determine if the item is genuine or not.

Examine the photos supplied very carefully to determine if the item is genuine. It is easy to save the photos by right mouse clicking on the photo and selecting "save as." This provides a copy of the photos to compare the item with the item that turns up in the post if you are successful in winning the auction.

Point 4 – Pay by PayPal

It is always advisable to pay via PayPal on eBay as it provides some security. eBay offers protection up to a certain level if you pay via PayPal. It is often best to use a credit card combined with PayPal to handle the transaction. If the item turns out to be fake you then have two forms of recourse. You can firstly make a claim through PayPal and secondly you have the protection of your credit card company. If you have simply used a bank account to transfer the money into PayPal you would only have the PayPal option.

Buying on eBay with PayPal is the best security a buyer can have.

PayPal offers a dispute resolution process. If the item does not turn up you can file a claim. If the item is fake – you can also file a claim.

PayPal can be frustrating to deal with at times however I believe they are fair to deal with. I have had many dealings with PayPal and some deals have turned bad. In my case PayPal always reimbursed my money.

Buying by a wire transfer service means you are limited to disputing the matter. Often the cost and effort to file charges in a foreign country are extremely high and time consuming.

The most important thing to remember with PayPal is that you have only a 45 day period to lodge a dispute.

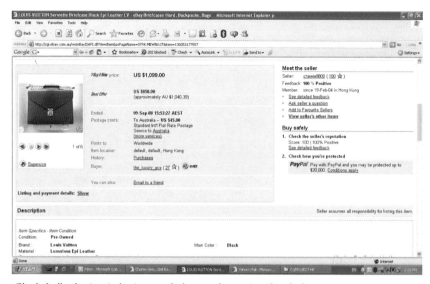

Check feedback, time in business and always ask question if in doubt.

Always check the product thoroughly before bidding.

Always ensure you trust the seller before bidding.

Buying new from the Louis Vuitton store

With the advent of the internet and eBay, many collectors have been showing frugality by never purchasing items from the store. There are many merits in buying secondhand, however one should not discount buying new from the store.

One of the great experiences for a Louis Vuitton collector is the experience of going into a Louis Vuitton store, seeing items in real life and selecting an item that you absolutely adore. As a collector and trader I would not make any money if I bought everything new, however it is enjoyable occasionally to buy something lovely from the store.

Savoring the moment is one of life's joys. I personally love all my items regardless of whether I bought them new or used. A bit of purchasing directly from the store can add a level of experience a bargain shopper could never experience.

On the following pages are the photos of a Damier Alma I purchased for my wife after receiving a small work bonus. Whilst the work assignment is long finished the experience of buying the Alma will never be forgotten.

Which pieces retain the most value if buying new pieces from the store?

Like most retail purchases, as soon as you leave the boutique you lose a percentage of the price the minute you walk out the door. This is to be expected in our free market economy, however there are some pieces which hold more value than others.

There are no 100% certainties with my predictions, however based on my years of experience I have found the best pieces to retain value are either Monogram or Damier. Monogram and Damier are usually cheaper than the full leather lines – like Epi or Taiga. In the secondary (used) market the canvas material has tended to resell for higher prices than the leather lines. This may also be due to the fact that the Epi line is continually changing the range of colors. Some colors are phased out and replaced. With Monogram and Damier they are permanent fixtures in the lineup.

I remember that Louis Vuitton released a two–tone range of Epi items in the 90s. Today these pieces are not achieving as high a price as Monogram pieces.

The next piece of advice is to go for the more classic icon type of pieces. Personally I would buy an Alma over a fashion release.

Summary –

1) Go for Monogram or Damier
2) Go for the classic icons in the range
3) Keep all the paperwork/boxes etc
4) If you really love the item – who cares about the resale vale
5) Pick the piece that sings most to you
6) Enjoy it!

Excitement of opening that new purchase at home

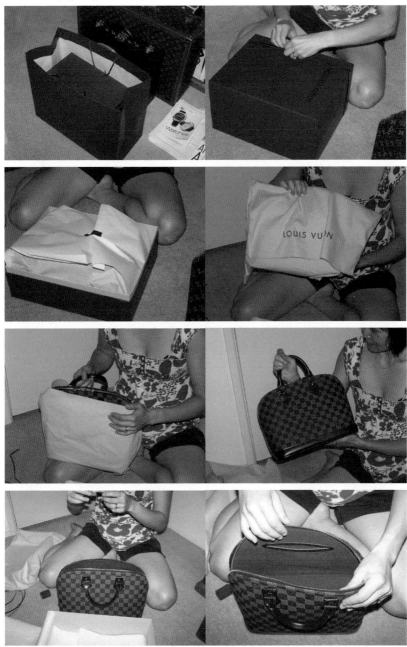

Louis Vuitton in the workplace

What are the rules for taking Louis Vuitton to work?
How do you stay stylish without making other people jealous or hurting your career?

When you enter a workplace you are entering an environment with its own culture, values and prejudices. It can be a very daunting process.

It is always advisable to enter a new environment on a neutral footing. This means that it is sometimes better not to enter that environment with "in your face" Louis Vuitton items.

I recently commenced a contract with a large American firm and my job involved IT support. It is a good job but it is certainly not at the top of the tree in salary or status. In my situation I have a variety of briefcases which would be suitable. I have chosen to use a more discrete soft sided black Epi piece instead of one of the larger imposing hard-sided Monogram pieces. The reason I chose that piece was because it was very non-confrontational whilst still being very stylish and French.

The black Epi piece only has one Louis Vuitton logo in the corner. It does not scream Louis Vuitton. If I had chosen my Monogram hard-sided President Classeur it is a much grander item. It is very expensive looking and proudly announces to the world that it is a President of briefcases.

The last thing you want to do in a workplace is make other people feel uncomfortable. In my opinion it is important to assess the workplace and decide what reaction the item will bring.

Your position and status within an organisation would also affect how other staff reacted. If you are the CEO or second in charge you could get away with a more prestigious item. If you are going into the environment as a contractor or casual worker it is much better to go in on a neutral footing. The last thing you want is to be the target of negative stereotypes.

It is a lot like turning up at work in a brand new convertible Mercedes. Whilst it may be fun, it may well make other people feel threatened. It could make other people jealous and make people question your motives and future in the firm.

If you turned up at work in a 5 year old Toyota Camry you would probably be invisible.

A simple guide is as follows:-

1. Assess the workplace.

2. What is your position in the company? A CEO could carry off an expensive LV Monogram item whilst it may cause nasty comments for an office junior to have the same item.

3. If in doubt, go for the discrete items - Epi, Taiga and perhaps the softer styles - i.e. if working as an admin person a soft leather Epi briefcase would be more suitable than a Monogram hard case President briefcase.

4. Just some food for thought... and remember to USE WHAT YOU LIKE IN YOUR OWN TIME!

Louis Vuitton and saving the environment

The best way to help the environment is to buy good quality items and keep them forever. Louis Vuitton items last the test of time - both aesthetically and practically. It is much better for the environment to buy items which last years instead of just one fashion season.

Buying expensive items makes one look after the piece to a higher degree. I am always more careful with an expensive item than a mass produced Chinese product. Naturally the more expensive item will still get damaged, scratched and marked. These however are character marks which give a piece history.

An example of this is buying a low cost, low quality suitcase and only getting a few uses out of it before you need to discard it and buy a replacement item. Buying a more expensive, better quality suitcase to start with has less of an effect on the environment.

The only exception to this rule is the fact that some people are jealous of Louis Vuitton items. I personally do not use my hard-sided suitcases on commercial flights. This is a sad reflection of society today.

In this disposable age in which we live it is often not worth repairing an item as the repair cost far exceeds the item's price. This is not the case with Louis Vuitton items.

Louis Vuitton is one of the few remaining firms to have a genuine repair service available. This means items can be professionally repaired and enjoyed for a long time.

Louis Vuitton will repair any hard case item irrespective of its age. I have had many repairs carried out by Louis Vuitton and the price for any hard-sided items has always been very reasonable.

Why buy a cheap briefcase that will only last one session? A Louis Vuitton item will last a lifetime and always be at the cutting edge of fashion.

Timeless elegance does not age.

Cleaning Louis Vuitton items

One of the most asked questions is how to best clean a Louis Vuitton item. Officially Louis Vuitton states items should only ever be cleaned with a damp cloth. This is obviously the result of Louis Vuitton protecting itself if things go wrong. With the right approach scruffy items can be brought up a level. The wrong approach can however have everlasting consequences.

Point 1 – Take your time

This is the most important rule to follow. If you are careful and take it slowly, the results will be outstanding. Don't be in a rush with solvents and cleaners. Take your time and you will be happier with the results.

Point 2 – Always start off with water and a damp cloth

Although the results will be slower it is always advisable to start off cleaning the piece with a damp cloth. Whenever using a damp cloth follow up with a wipe down with a dry cloth to remove any excessive water.

If the item is still dirty – follow up with wiping the item with a soapy cloth. The importance of wiping the item with a damp (no soap) cloth is that it stops you rubbing dirt into the material. This is the reason you should always rinse your car before washing it with soapy water – this stops you rubbing dirt into the paint.

Do not ever submerge the item in water.

I find it useful to work on one area at a time. This prevents you from being rushed.

Summary:-

1) Wipe item over with a damp cloth

2) Dry item with a dry cloth

3) Wipe item over with a damp soapy cloth

4) Dry item with a dry cloth

5) Rinse/remove any soapy residue by using a damp cloth (no soap)

6) Dry item with a dry cloth

Point 3 – Try to use as few chemicals as possible

Only use harsh chemicals and polishes if simple cleaning efforts have not worked. Always use chemicals as instructed and test it in an inconspicuous spot first.

Point 4 - Cleaning brassware

It is important to firstly understand the two different types of brassware.

Many Louis Vuitton handbags have a lacquer-coated brassware. Therefore using a brass cleaner on these items could damage the clear lacquer – which is not a good thing. Many of the hard-sided items (like an Alzer suitcase) have brassware which is not lacquered. This type of brassware can be cleaned with care.

On pieces which do not have lacquer-coated brassware I have used the brass cleaning chemical solution called "Brasso". Care should be taken to use this product sparingly – avoiding where possible getting the chemical on the canvas or leather.

I have often used a cotton bud dipped in Brasso to slowly clean the brassware. The importance of taking your time should be stressed again. This can be very frustrating, however the results will be much better. Always work on one piece of brass at a time. Always have a few dry cloths available to clean up any spills.

Point 5 – Removing marks

In determining if the removal of a mark is possible you need to firstly work out whether the mark is on top of the canvas/leather or has it cut into the material. Marks that have cut into the material are permanent – the only hope is to reduce the impact of that mark.

Marks that are on top of the canvas or leather can be removed carefully. Hopefully you can remove this type of mark fully or remove most of it.

Steps to remove marks that are on top of the canvas/leather

1) Wipe item over with a damp cloth
2) Dry item with a dry cloth
3) Wipe item over with a damp soapy cloth
4) Dry item with a dry cloth
5) Rinse/remove any soapy residue by using a damp cloth (no soap)
6) Dry item with a dry cloth
7) Use some automotive scratch remover (like Meguiars)
8) Wipe item over with a damp cloth
9) Dry item with a dry cloth
10) Wipe item over with a damp soapy cloth
11) Dry item with a dry cloth
12) Rinse/remove any soapy residue by using a damp cloth (no soap)
13) Dry item with a dry cloth

Always take your time when using Automotive scratch remover/chemicals. Use only the smallest amount of chemical possible. Work on the scratch little by little.

Removal of white marks with automotive scratch remover

Appendix A - Louis Vuitton Date/Batch codes

Since the early 1980s Louis Vuitton has been using a batch code on their product to determine the date and country of manufacture.

These codes are mainly for Louis Vuitton's own internal use. Vintage pieces made before 1980 therefore will not have a batch code.

The first batch codes used consisted of three or four letters. These would represent the month and year of manufacture. Therefore the code 842 would have a manufacture date of February 1984.

In the late 80s Louis Vuitton added 2 alphabetic letters to reveal which factory/country had produced the item.

Country codes:-

France: A0, A1, A2, AA, AN, AR, AS, BA, BJ, CT, DU, ET, FL, MB, MI, NO, RA, RI, SD, SL, SN, SP, SR, TH, VI

USA: FC, FH, LA, OS, SD

Spain: CA, LO, LB, LM, LW

Italy: CE, SA

Germany: LP

In the 90s the system further changed.

The 4 numbers are the manufacturing date, but now the date is staggered. The first and third numbers are the year, while the second and fourth numbers are the month.

Appendix B – Internet Resources

Forums

The Purse Forum

http://forum.purseblog.com/

The Bag Forum

http://www.thebagforum.com/

Effen Haute Forum

http://www.effenhaute.com/forum/

Quality On-Line Retailers

The Official Louis Vuitton Site

http://www.louisvuitton.com/

Fashionphile – Highly respected reseller of vintage Louis Vuitton items

http://www.fashionphile.com/

Websites of interest

My Poupette

http://www.mypoupette.com/

Collecting Louis Vuitton

http://www.collectinglouisvuitton.com/

Made in the USA
Lexington, KY
31 May 2014